Kunstsammlung
Nordrhein-Westfalen

PRESTEL
Munich • London • New York

AI WEIWEI

Edited by
Susanne Gaensheimer
Doris Krystof
Falk Wolf

PREFACE

Susanne Gaensheimer

Ai Weiwei's biography, from his earliest childhood to the present day, is shaped by the experience of political conflict and state repression. His father Ai Qing was one of the most prominent poets of Communist China and was sent into internal exile in China in 1958 for most of two decades—one year after Ai Weiwei's birth—because of criticism on the regime expressed within the context of the Hundred Flowers Campaign and was banned from writing until 1978. After spending his childhood and adolescence in banishment, Ai Weiwei seemed to take up his father's independent attitude from the very beginning and joined the Stars group in 1979, a group of artists that opposed the state's guidelines for artistic production. Soon thereafter, he went to New York until the early 1990s where he studied art and engaged intensively with various forms of European modernism and American post-war modernism. Marcel Duchamp's influence as a freethinker of the European avant-garde can be clearly seen in Ai Weiwei's early work from the 1980s. The works created at this time are inseparably linked to his political and social commitment in these years and testify to a critical engagement with the neoliberal values of American pop culture. To this day, the artist's formal language is clearly influenced by those system-critical currents of Western art history that, like Minimalism and Conceptual art, have attempted to counter the increasing commercialization of art and dominant social stereotypes.

It was only when Ai Weiwei returned to Beijing in 1993 due to his father's declining health that he began to concern himself with the artistic and cultural traditions of his own country. During this time, he took a keen interest in Chinese antiquities, which served as the starting point for an intensive investigation into the period before the Cultural Revolution. It was not in state academies and universities but rather in the antique markets of major Chinese cities that he was able to learn more about the rich treasures and traditions of past dynasties. From then on, a dense, multi-layered œuvre emerged which combined great sculptural mastery with a deeply rooted ethical commitment in each individual work.

When I invited the artist in the spring of 2012 to realize a work for the German Pavilion at the Fifty-Fifth Venice Biennale in 2013, it was precisely this unity of the aesthetic and the political that interested me. Our collaboration took place after Ai Weiwei's sudden and arbitrary detention by the Chinese government which had resulted in restrictions being placed on his movement and his being denied travel until the summer of 2015. His experiences during detainment, on which he reported in a differentiated and sober manner, influenced our conversations about the pavilion. In the work **Bang** (2013), which was ultimately created for the pavilion, as well as in various works from previous years, such as **Sunflower Seeds**—which Ai Weiwei developed for the Turbine Hall of Tate Modern in 2010 and which will be presented in the Düsseldorf exhibition for the first time again in full—the artist has succeeded in abstracting his personal experiences and speaking about human beings in general within the context of an overarching, dominant system. The critical content of his works is by no means bound solely to his own biography but to a fundamental preoccupation with human existence in connection with current crises. This interest also gave rise to a new set of works in which Ai Weiwei is concerned with refugee and migration movements of recent years. His one-hundred-forty-minute film **Human Flow**, which premiered in 2017 and became the starting point for a whole series of works on this subject, documents twenty-three refugee camps in different parts of the world and looks at the subject of flight

and migration within a global context. The focus is not on the concrete causes and consequences of the so-called "refugee crisis" but rather on the fundamental humanitarian aspects, and those aspects regarding "civilization" of this situation.

During a visit in the autumn of 2016 to the artist's studio in Berlin, where Ai Weiwei had resettled after his travel ban was lifted, an initial arrangement of the work **Laundromat** could be seen which was developed out of his stays in the refugee camp at Idomeni on the Greek-Macedonian border. The camp at Idomeni was evacuated by authorities in 2016 because of excessive overcrowding and inhumane conditions, thus becoming a symbol of the human misery arising from flight. Objects left behind, such as articles of clothing and shoes belonging to children, women, and men were collected by the artist. These were sent to his studio in Berlin, where each piece was mended, cleaned, documented, and finally arranged in his studio, to be seen in various configurations. At the time, I was still the director of the MMK Museum für Moderne Kunst in Frankfurt am Main and offered Ai Weiwei a platform at any time for presenting this important work. A little later, Ai Weiwei accepted the invitation, and together we have transferred the idea for an exhibition to Düsseldorf.

As part of the exhibition **Ai Weiwei** at the Kunstsammlung Nordrhein-Westfalen, the curatorial team—comprised of Doris Krystof, Falk Wolf, and me—aims to demonstrate the inseparable connection between artistic choices and political-ethical commitment in the works of Ai Weiwei. We want to use this exhibition—the artist's largest in Europe to date—to examine this connection more closely, to trace its roots in his early work, and to reveal its various manifestations. In addition to the early photo series from Ai Weiwei's time in New York, which already document his socio-critical and system-critical stances, and the key work **Straight** (2008–2012), in which the artist researched and exposed the local political connections to the destruction caused by the earthquake in the Chinese province of Sichuan, the exhibition also includes the unusual work **S.A.C.R.E.D.** (2011–2013), in which he reconstructed and visualized concrete situations of his eighty-one-days in secret detention. Also on view are the more recent works **Laundromat** (2016) and **Life Cycle** (2018) which revolve around the theme of flight and migration. Overall, the show, which extends through the two buildings K20 and K21 of the Kunstsammlung Nordrhein-Westfalen, is comprised of works from four decades in a wealth of different media. The differentiation and precision with which Ai Weiwei expresses his commitment and stance is conveyed, not least of all, through this diversity of his works.

I am deeply indebted to Ai Weiwei for preparing, developing, and realizing this important exhibition with us with such outstanding dedication and personal commitment. The fruitful exchange with him was a great inspiration for all of us and helped us experience new dimensions of collaboration. My special thanks also go to the curators Doris Krystof and Falk Wolf from the Kunstsammlung Nordrhein-Westfalen who developed the exhibition and the accompanying catalog together with Ai Weiwei and me, and who realized these with great professionalism and attentiveness. From Ai Weiwei's team, I would like to thank Jennifer Ng, Jennifer Schmachtenberg, and Darryl Leung in particular. I would also like to thank the gallery neugerriemschneider in Berlin with Tim Neuger and Felix von Lüttichau, as well as the Lisson Gallery in London with Nicholas Logsdail and Greg Hilty who helped us significantly with the realization of the exhibition and provided us with valuable advice. The team of the Kunstsammlung was challenged greatly by the dimensions of this exhibition; and I would like to thank our registrar Katharina Nettekoven, the exhibition management under the supervision of Stefanie Jansen, the conservator Nina Quabeck and her team, as well as the technical director Bernd Schliephake for their outstanding performance. My thanks also go to the authors for their contributions to the catalog and to L2M3, who designed both the catalog and the exhibition guide.

INTERVIEW

Hans Ulrich Obrist – Ai Weiwei

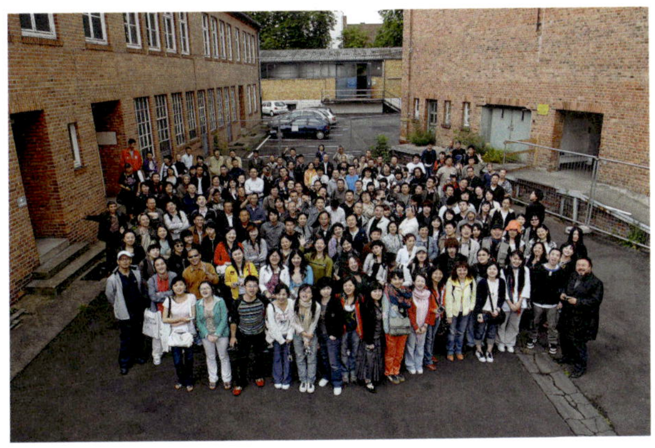

1
Fairytale, 2007,
Documenta 2007,
photograph of
the fourth group

Hans Ulrich Obrist: We met in 1996, twenty three years ago, and this is our twenty-first interview. Before we talk about the show in Düsseldorf, I wanted to ask you to speak a little bit about your relationship to Germany, because you have had a very long relationship with the country. And Germany has been very important in the reception of your work. It has also been very important in supporting your work. You are going to move to the U.S., but, at the moment, you are still in Berlin. Can you tell me a little bit about your relationship to Germany and what Germany means to you and your work?

Ai Weiwei: My relationship with Germany started when I first read the poetry of Heinrich Heine, the German poet. I think I was about ten years old. The book was **Germany, a Winter's Tale**. I like that poet. And as you might remember, he tells the story that he was once passing through customs, and the officials tried to search his luggage. When they came to search his books, he said, "You know, the most dangerous thing is in my brain." I really like that.
Later, Germany gave me my first opportunity to have an exhibition. It was not an art exhibition; it was on my architecture, together with a group of young Chinese architects, when I was still practicing architecture before the Olympic Stadium in Beijing. That was at Aedes Architekturforum in Berlin in 2001. They were the first who discovered me, but as an architect. Nobody knew I was also an artist.

Later, of course, there was the Kassel Documenta in 2007. And that provided big exposure to my work.

HUO: That's interesting because Kassel was a big social sculpture. You brought one thousand people from China to Kassel. And, of course, Kassel is also the city of Joseph Beuys's Documenta where he made many proclamations about not only the trees but also social sculpture. Can you talk a little bit about the Documenta piece and if there's a connection to Beuys and how you feel about him?

AWW: Maybe because of the history, maybe because I come from a communist society, my education, communist ideology or socialist ideas, when they asked me to take part in Documenta, my first thought was not to present a regular work. I wanted to invite people, an audience to visit this high-end Western art platform. I think it was very important to bring people from Communist China to Kassel in order for them to see "spiritually polluted Western art." This is what it has been called by the Chinese government. This was the first time I used social media. I collected those people from the Internet. I used the Internet to select them and to communicate with them. And finally, I brought them from virtual reality, through real travel, to Kassel. I am interested in the social movement which you can see from that piece. And you also see the power of the Internet. Today, you could not do the same work again because China has such a strong control over its Internet.
And the question about my relation to Beuys: It is a very casual relationship. I understand his work. But for me, as someone who lived in the United States for twelve years, his work remains a little mysterious. There is always his personal mysterious, almost religious, background. But, as far as social sculpture and social movement are concerned, I am totally in line with him.

HUO: And then, of course, talking about your relationship with Germany, one very important moment was the exhibition you did at the Haus der Kunst in Munich, where you worked on the scale of the Haus der Kunst and transformed the building not only from inside but also from outside. Certainly, besides Documenta,

this was your most public moment in Germany. It was also a very dramatic moment for you, biographically speaking.

AWW: I'm very fortunate that Chris Dercon invited me to the Haus der Kunst. It gave me the opportunity to really engage with the history of Germany. I had to deal with this museum, which was implemented by Hitler for the art he loved. So, I had to deal with both history and my current political involvement in relation to the Sichuan earthquake. Inside, I made a work called **Soft Ground**, which copies every piece of the stone floor of the museum. The work was a carpet that strongly resembled what was below it. I think, this is a very important work. Since then, it has even been shown at the Israel Museum in Jerusalem. This was completely shocking for me: They have a space that has exactly the same dimensions. And there, I presented this piece, which was extremely political.
Then, I also wanted to change the façade of the Haus der Kunst because it has such a difficult history. So, I used student backpacks to form one sentence: "She lived happily for seven years in this world." This sentence is from the mother of a victim of the Sichuan earthquake, Yang Xiaowan. She wrote me a letter saying this is all she wanted the world to remember. It is a very sad story, but I am glad that I could fulfill her wish.
But when I arrived in Munich, I had this tremendous headache caused by a police beating one month earlier when trying to testify in court in Tan Zuoren's case. The police raided my hotel in the middle of the night and beat me. This was the cause of my extreme headache. Chris told me, "You have to go to the hospital, now," because I had already lost my voice. So, I went to the hospital, and the doctor had to operate on me to release blood from my brain. If she had not done it, I would not be sitting in front of you now speaking with you. Our conversation would have been long finished.

HUO: Now is a very different moment because you are based in Berlin. I visited your studio several times, actually from the beginning. It's almost like an underground city. And there are not only your works but also the research you are doing with your team. I would like to ask you to tell me a little bit about what is happening in the studio right now and about your preparations for the show in Düsseldorf.

AWW: It is a different kind of show, but it's also a landmark show for my contribution, both to Germany and to Europe. So far, Düsseldorf will be the largest show I have made in Europe. And this is thanks to the ambitious plan of Susanne Gaensheimer. In 2013, she invited me to the German Pavilion at the Venice Biennale; I think she is very brave. Now she is director of K20/K21 and has given me the chance to show my work in its most complete form. Five major works will be shown together. It's almost impossible to find another location to do this. **Sunflower Seeds** (pp. 27–29) will be in its complete form for the first time since the exhibition at Tate Modern. There will also be **Straight**, the iron bars from the Sichuan earthquake, in its complete version. These two works have never been shown together in their complete versions. At the same time, there will be **S.A.C.R.E.D.** (pp. 164–173), the six metal boxes about my detention. And, I will show two other large works: **Laundromat** (pp. 98–99), the refugees' clothes from Idomeni, and **Life Cycle** (pp. 110–115), the refugee boat made from bamboo. To put these five major works together and many smaller works, works that relate to my struggle in China, but also the photographs from New York and Beijing—this is really a very ambitious show.

HUO: The exhibition at K20/K21 is not only a comprehensive retrospective but it also marks the first time ever that the complete version of **Straight** is shown in Europe. For this work, you used, or recycled, the rebar which was found in the rubble of collapsed school buildings in Sichuan in 2008. It's a very heavy piece. It weighs 164 tons. You used all these bars and over a period of three years re-straightened them. In a way, the memory of the earthquake is deeply inscribed in these bars. It is a piece about an apocalyptic disaster, but it's also a very optimistic piece because, in a way, the future can be invented based on these fragments of the past. Can you tell me a little bit about the genesis of **Straight** and how it all came together?

AWW: We always have to question why we have to make a show. A show is not just showing one aspect; it always needs

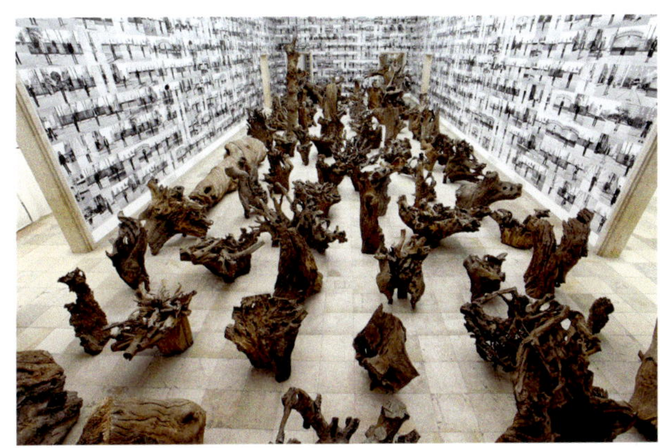

2

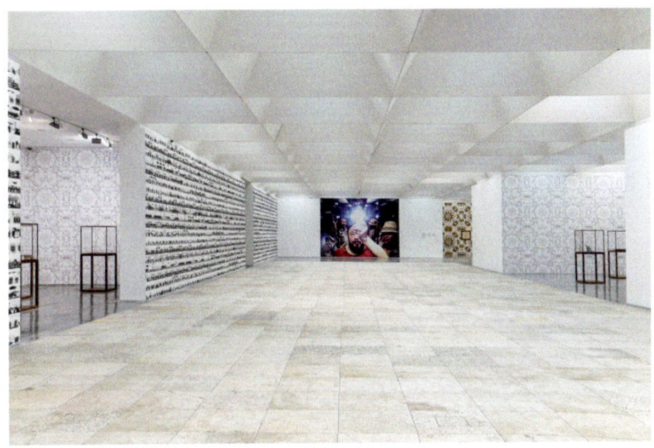

3

2
Soft Ground, 2009,
wool, 1061.5 × 3561.5 cm;
Rooted Upon, 2009,
100 tree trunk segments,
dimensions variable.
Installation view, Haus der
Kunst, Munich, 2009

3
Soft Ground, 2009,
wool, 1061.5 × 3561.5 cm.
Installation view, Israel
Museum, Jerusalem, 2017

13

to be a new statement. So, Germany is the place — and Düsseldorf is the place — that provides this opportunity for a more profound discussion. You know, they have this capacity to talk about meaning, which is quite rare today, to have a location where you can talk about meaning. And I think, Germany is one of the rare places where you can do that. Of course, we do not know what the outcome will be. But still, we make an effort to put up these extremely socio-political works. They talk about history, talk about crisis, talk about how art deals with the crisis, how humanity, personal humanity, or the state tries to cope with this kind of extreme situation. Such as the Sichuan earthquake, when five thousand students disappeared, seventy thousand people lost their lives, and the state tried to just cover it up, trying to make it sound like nothing really ever happened. When we are dealing with ruins, my simple idea was to collect the metal and straighten it back out, like it never ever happened, and to perform the manual work of hammering it out, to make it straight again, to come back to this unbearable stillness, this sadness about the history.
I myself have disappeared and have been under surveillance and in jail. I also have personal injuries that have had to be cured. But who is going to cure them? It can only be done by me. That's the way you have to do it, and nobody can really help. I put those things together, the refugee boat from bamboo, which is another very complicated work that took years to produce. I really draw a complete history of what happened in the past ten, fifteen years: my complete effort, all the major works. I think that will make the show very different.

HUO: And then, there is, of course, the return of a very rarely seen piece because it's very expensive and complicated to show: **Sunflower Seeds** from 2010. It will be the largest presentation of this piece since its beginnings at Tate Modern. There will be one hundred tons of sunflower seeds. They used to cover the Turbine Hall in 2010. And more than one thousand six hundred craftspeople from the ancient center of porcelain production, Jingdezhen in Jiangxi province, worked on that. **Sunflower Seeds** has to do with dissemination. Today there are many households in London where you can find some of those sunflower seeds. But I think, at some point, people began to take too many, and then, it needed to be fenced off. I was wondering, in this new version in Düsseldorf, how are you going to represent it? And also, because it is such an important piece, it would be great to hear what gave you the idea for **Sunflower Seeds**?

AWW: The idea was a struggle, actually. When Nicholas Serota asked me to do the show, I was quite excited. But, at the same time, I really thought it would be a very difficult task. I had been developing porcelain for years. And then there was this idea to create the smallest artwork in the largest space. Nobody would want to make a small work in the Turbine Hall. So, I said, "I will make the smallest work." Of course, one would like the work to be recognizable. It is not abstract; it is super realistic. Everybody can recognize it, but, at the same time, as you taste it, you understand it's fake. You know, people really put them in their mouths. But they had to see the dentist afterwards. The idea of the production was perfect because we could organize the whole city, thousands of people working for years, to make it happen. This process really fits with China as a labor market for the industries of the world in the age of globalization. And then, the sunflower seeds also relate to my childhood memories of the Cultural Revolution when we saw Chairman Mao as the sun; we all were the sunflowers facing the sun. All those things together make this work simple but also very political.

HUO: Besides revisiting these major works, there is also a new work in the exhibition which is very monumental: twelve **Zodiac** (pp. 34–45) Lego works, more than two-meter large. The zodiac heads originally started as a series of sculptures: **Circle of Animals** (pp. 186–187). You showed them here in London at Somerset House. But now the signs of the zodiac appear in a different form. They are two-dimensional and superimposed on landscapes or monuments from the **Study of Perspective** series (pp. 125–129). I wanted to ask you to speak about the **Zodiac** series and how you became interested in the zodiac animals, and of how you arrived from the sculptures to this idea of using Lego bricks. You have been doing quite a lot of these amazing Lego works. How was this idea born with Lego? Lego initially refused to work with you.

AWW: The **Zodiac** works deal with the Old Summer Palace in Beijing and its looting by French and British soldiers one hundred fifty years ago. Since then, China gradually became a powerful state over the past thirty years. This work deals with Chinese history, Chinese nationalism, the Chinese people, about how we look at things, as if it's a national treasure. The original sculptures were designed by an Italian priest and made by a French craftsman. But they were looted by British and French soldiers. It is complicated but really about modern Chinese history. Lego is very interesting. I found Lego to be the perfect tool to transform a two-dimensional image into a pixelated image, opening digital possibilities. I first used it for **Trace**, the images of 176 political prisoners in my exhibition at the former prison of Alcatraz. Amnesty International provided us with images in different formats. I noticed that many political prisoners do not have a "right image"—a so-called "right" image, you know, a sharp image, a clear image. Often, they only had an image you could download from the Internet, which could be blurred. So, I had to think about how to deal with that blurred image. I thought that pixelation could fix it because pixelated images can be made clear, equally sharp, with clear definition of colors and shapes.
And then came the idea that Lego would provide me with a really good possibility for making something look like a painting. It is two-dimensional, but it is not a painting because it is not free handed. It is digitally presented and designed, really precisely. It would be exactly the same if you made a million copies of the work because the color and form never change. All those qualities are so nice for me.
In the beginning, Lego refused to sell bricks to us. They said the company policy was not to support political works, which I think is ridiculous. I posted their response on Instagram, and it generated a large response from the public, including from artists and museums. So finally, Lego apologized and they changed their company's policy, and now they accept that anybody can use Legos.

HUO: Now it is an expanded notion of painting. It is still painting, but it is not painting with oil and canvas. Yet the exhibition also includes your beginnings which actually are paintings with oil and canvas. It is very rare that you show these early paintings. They are from the 1980s; there is a head from 1980; there is even a boat scene, **Untitled** (**Yantai, Shandong**) (p. 211), from 1977. Can you tell me a little bit about this earlier phase of you as a painter? In our interviews, we never really looked at those paintings which pre-date your arrival in New York City. Who were your influences? How do you see these works today?

AWW: Yes, I never showed these works before. Since this show is so important, and is more like a retrospective, I thought I should give a chance to those early works. These works are like the sketches of a student. Actually, the earliest work dating to 1977 is from the time before I became a student. It was then that I made this kind of bold image. So, that is very early. I made **Coke Painting** (p. 216) in New York when I was enrolled at the Art Students League. I feel somehow these early works convey my personal attitude about making art. I have been shifting and doing all kinds of works, not just through materials but also stylistically, and I have been influenced by a lot of different people and have been challenged by all kinds of possibilities. It gives people some notion of my beginning.

HUO: The paintings at the beginning are very figurative. They are connected to a more Chinese tradition of painting, if I think of the **Yantai, Shandong** boat scene. But when you were at Parsons School in the early '80s, there seems to be a Pop influence. **Coke Painting** for instance is very Warholian. What was the impact of Pop art on you?

AWW: In the 1980s there were two kinds of art in New York City: one was German Neo-Expressionism; the other was Pop art. And Pop art had a stronger impression or influence on me than any other art. It directly relates to American culture. And in the 1970s and 1980s this culture was very lively. It is about recognizing things, about loving things. Warhol said that Pop art is about loving things. Which is true, you are not, for instance, in the mode of

aesthetic judgment but rather in this sensitivity. You recognize that "things" can be very sensuous, or even lovable.

HUO: The exhibition also includes some rarely seen early sculptures such as **Safe Sex** (p. 223) from 1986. Of course, it was the moment of the AIDS crisis. Your first solo exhibition was called **Old Shoes - Safe Sex** and took place at Ethan Cohen's Art Waves Gallery in New York City. There is a very Duchampian element—we spoke about this in previous interviews—of readymades or combined readymades or altered readymades. As we spoke of your relationship to Beuys and to Warhol, it would be interesting to talk a little bit more about your relationship to Marcel Duchamp.

AWW: The relationship to Duchamp is truly a father-and-son relationship. I am deeply impressed by this Frenchman, his mindset, his attitude, the very graceful style and attitude towards art. He said, "If I were a fighter, I would fight with crossed arms." This guy is so special, unlike anybody else, so cool, so detached. And those things attracted me very much because he once again put art at the service of the mind rather than just trying to impress people with routine images. I love this kind of mental activity, this kind of state of mind. I think he is a one-man movement. He opened so many doors for other artists. I have to admit, I am totally influenced by his work. Basically, my show **Old Shoes - Safe Sex**, I dedicated to Marcel Duchamp. But that was not popular in the 1980s. Because the '80s were really about expressionist works, and I am not much of a fan of those works.

HUO: But what did you show in that exhibition?

AWW: I had a coat hanger: **Hanging Man**, that was a portrait of Duchamp made from a metal wire coat hanger. I also had this condom attached to a Chinese army raincoat. There were shoes and also a triptych of Chairman Mao's image, dripping, almost disappearing from the canvas.

HUO: The readymade idea continues to be relevant. Your later work has a lot to do with what I call "surveillance readymades." It has a lot to do with the police surveillance you were exposed to, if

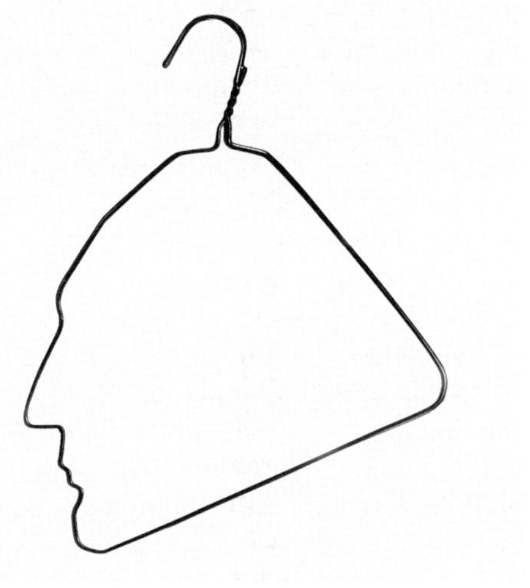

4

I think of the **Ashtray from Beijing's Solana Bookstore** (p. 182) from 2011 where two secret policemen observed you and you took their ashtray. It almost visualizes the time they had spent observing you. Or the camera with the plinth in marble, which is a translated readymade. You translated it into marble. Can we talk a little bit about these readymades of surveillance because they're also quite present in the show?

AWW: I think you point out a very important theme because Duchamp's readymades are really what he found in secondhand shops, you know, the **Bottle Rack**, the coat hanger, all those, or even these fixtures. But I think, my readymades are taking Chinese history or the Chinese political situation, or the world political condition, cultural conditions as a readymade. That's what I did with surveillance for years. The Chinese state has put me under heavy surveillance. The secret police were sitting on a deck, smoking cigarettes, and watching me walk in the park below. So, I took that small ashtray. And this work really smells. Extinguished cigarettes have this heavy smell. You know, we cannot just accuse an authoritarian society; we have to preserve some details. They have no interest in books but were very interested in watching this guy walking in the park below them. Later, I found out that they had planted these bugs in my living room and in my office behind the electrical sockets. And I took them. I think, those are such important and precious elements to show the details of this state. To show how they maintain the function of such a complicated political power. Those are the ends of the nerves that control each individual's mind and behavior.

HUO: These topics also enter your video works. Your videos are a much less visible, less well-known aspect of your work. But they are an important aspect, and you keep returning to video. As recently as 2018 you made **Calais** (pp. 120–121). This video addresses the migration crisis. But this is only one of many. Can you tell me a little bit about the importance of the videos? What do they mean in your practice?

AWW: I think we also have to use mass media as a readymade. We are so used to videos, to moving images, also on the

Internet. They are part of our daily lives, on Instagram, for instance. People automatically think, that is their own language. But these languages can be very polluted. Also, they can be very poisoning and very dangerous. They can carry the truth, but they can also carry fictions of all kinds. So, for me, as an artist, it is very hard to understand artists who do not directly draw on these moving images, because today, it's so easy to shoot a film. In the past few years of my art activity, video has been a constant. We always make films alongside our other artworks, or with our political efforts. So, we always record, and we always save the images. We don't even have enough time to edit the images. While working on **Human Flow**, we recorded over nine hundred hours of footage. So, we can easily develop more pieces from this material, and very often, these find a way into shows of my work. These videos are very attractive because people understand what is going on. And as an artist, you have to respect the audience. You have to talk the same language. To understand, the right communication needs to be set up. So that is why we always have the videos in our shows, because it works alongside the other works.

HUO: We are doing this interview for your Düsseldorf book, and I was curious about the role of books in your work because you are also exhibiting books. There is the **Fuck Off** exhibition catalog, there are the **Black** and the **White Cover Book** (pp. 236–238). What is the role of books?

AWW: Before I became an artist, I first recognized writing as a boy in the poetry of my father. Books are so important I am still writing books every day. I did a lot of writing. I wrote blogs, and I still have a lot of material to be published. And in my office, book writing and editing is always the most important thing we are doing. In the future, I will put more energy into writing because it is an action directly utilizing our intellect. It is so easy, it is so private, and there is so much freedom when you are writing.

HUO: And that, of course, leads us to another book you are doing: your autobiography. Can you tell me about that?

AWW: I started on my autobiography in 2014, almost five years now. And we finished the first round of editing; now, we are doing the second round of editing. But there will be another, third round. It is like a tree. When you plant a small tree, the next year you have a few more branches. Then the following year, you will see there are a few more branches. It can be endless; you could write the same book for the entirety of your life. And I think that is the beauty of a book.

HUO: As you know, I always ask about the unrealized projects. Because I'm curious about artists' unrealized projects. In 2019, there is this big exhibition at K20/K21, but when we see all your works together, it is interesting to know if there is anything you always wanted to but could not do. Projects that were too big or too small to be realized, maybe also censored projects.

AWW: The book is like a nightmare. Every day I am working on it, but still, it will take another two years to complete. And, if I am lucky enough, we will finish it. We are also working on a huge tree, cast from a mold of a tree, over thirty-meters high, we made in the Brazilian rain forest. Now it is being cast in China. It is a tremendous amount of work to put it back together. There are a hundred individual pieces to be cast. So that will take another year to accomplish. And also, we have a few more films, and that will also take some time. There's always something to do, you know.

HUO: One final question. Dan Graham says we can only understand an artist if we also understand what music he or she listens to. Or as your favorite poet Heinrich Heine said: "Where words leave off, music begins." In what kind of music are you interested? Have you ever made your own music? What are you listening to at the moment?

AWW: Perfect question. The answer is: I don't listen to any music. Not in my life, and maybe that tells you who I am. I have good equipment, but I never really turn it on. I once had the temptation to make music, a rock 'n' roll record. It is called **Dumbass** (p. 175); it is really terrible music, but somehow it carries a message.

CHAPTER I

Chapter I

In 2010, Ai Weiwei covered the floor of the Turbine Hall of Tate Modern in London with one hundred million sunflower seeds. They were, however, not genuine plant seeds but rather tiny, hand-painted sculptures made of porcelain. Ai Weiwei had them produced over the course of several years in small workshops in the Chinese "Porcelain Capital" Jingdezhen.

Porcelain is not just any ordinary material. In China, especially, it is associated with national pathos. Ceramics were already being produced in Jingdezhen during the Han dynasty (202 BC to AD 220). Around AD 1000, the city became an official production site for imperial porcelain. In the centuries to follow, however, demand for valuable porcelain not only came from the Chinese emperor. Via the Silk Road, porcelain also reached the West and was highly valued at European courts. From the seventeenth century onwards, Chinese workshops produced porcelain directly for the European market. Even after the European invention of porcelain production in Meissen at the beginning of the eighteenth century, Chinese porcelain remained a sought-after specialty.

When Ai Weiwei presented one hundred million porcelain sunflower seeds in London, hand-painted in the workshops which formerly produced imperial porcelain, he was thus also reflecting on the history and current status of "Made in China." Today, however, the focus is less on high-quality porcelain than on consumer and electronic goods, which, bearing the logos of Western brands, are often manufactured in China under dubious working conditions.

At the same time, with **Sunflower Seeds**, Ai Weiwei closely examines the relationship between the individual and the masses in a new way since each seed is unique among seemingly identical seeds. In this context, the sunflower seeds are also endowed with political symbolism. Communist propaganda depicted Mao Zedong as the sun and the Chinese people as sunflowers turning in his direction. Ai Weiwei alludes to this political symbolism especially in connection with his reflections on individual freedom.

The question of one's individuality within a totalitarian state has been one of the vital issues for Ai Weiwei since his earliest youth. His father Ai Qing (1910–1996) was one of the country's most outstanding poets. After studying art in Paris (1929–1932), he became a writer and, in 1941, joined the Communist Movement. In 1958, he fell out of favor during the Anti-Rightist Movement against the Hundred Flowers Campaign and was sent, along with his family, into internal exile in China, living under the most appalling conditions until his rehabilitation in 1976. This took place during the childhood of Ai Weiwei, who was born in 1957. In many of his works, Ai Weiwei raises the question as to the significance of the individual in such a society. In **Sunflower Seeds**, this question is formulated in a particularly drastic way by the sheer mass of seeds.

In the Klee Halle of K20 of the Kunstsammlung Nordrhein-Westfalen, Ai Weiwei combines **Sunflower Seeds**—which can be seen here in its entirety for the first time since 2010—with **I.O.U. Wallpaper** (2011–2013). He thus accentuates the connection between **Sunflower Seeds** and his own personal confrontation with the Chinese regime. After being arrested on April 3, 2011—during the exhibition of **Sunflower Seeds** in London—he was held for eighty-one days without charge in an unknown location. His company Beijing Fake Cultural Development Ltd. was subsequently accused of unspecified economic crimes. It was not until the end of 2011 that it was asked to pay back taxes amounting to 1.7 million euros. It was only possible to pay the fine on time with the help of private donations from China and abroad. This was essential in order to be able to lodge an official complaint against the proceedings. Ai Weiwei issued artistically designed promissory notes to the donors acknowledging each donation and guaranteeing repayment. The title of the work makes reference to the colloquial, phonetic abbreviation for such notes: I.O.U. for "I owe you." The promissory notes include the name of the respective donor, his or her address, and further details. The amount of the donation is recorded by means of fantastical stamps on which, among other things, the sunflower seed and the alpaca (or the "Grass Mud Horse") can

be recognized as symbols. On the walls of the Klee Halle, Ai Weiwei has arranged all of the roughly seventeen thousand promissory notes as wallpaper. The one hundred million sunflower seeds thus correspond to the many donors who supported Ai Weiwei's efforts for transparency and justice in China. In the meantime, all the donations have been repaid.

As a third layer, Ai Weiwei has included **Zodiac**, a new work from 2018, in the installation. Twelve large images made of interlocking Lego bricks depict the Chinese zodiac signs in front of sites and monuments of cultural and political power. With this work, he refers to the twelve fountain figures from the Old Summer Palace (Yuanming Yuan) in Beijing. The historical figures adorned a water clock in the "Western-style" palace (Xiyang Lou) designed by the Jesuit Giuseppe Castiglione beginning in 1747. After British and French troops destroyed the palace in 1860 during the Second Opium War, the figures were plundered. Some still remain lost while others achieved high auction prices and were later restituted. Although these are works by Western artists, they have nationally retained a status as Chinese cultural symbols—even within popular culture, as proven by Jackie Chan's 2012 action film **CZ12**. In **Circle of Animals**, Ai Weiwei translated the animal heads into monumental forms. With this, he alludes to the contradiction that works of art can be appropriated as national symbols. His point is that there can ultimately be only one human cultural heritage with all its facets. The animal heads are a particularly striking example of this since they emerged from a cooperation between Western artists and intellectuals at the Chinese imperial court. Ai Weiwei's **Circle of Animals** was first shown at the São Paulo Biennale in the autumn of 2010. The second venue of the exhibition tour took the work to New York, where it was unveiled at the entrance to Central Park, in a public space, while Ai Weiwei was still under arrest.

Ai Weiwei has now formed the heads using another material, namely Lego bricks. In K20, the mass produced toy bricks form a contrast to the individual elements of **Sunflower Seeds**. The heads also serve as a leitmotif

throughout the exhibition in Düsseldorf,
since they return in K21 both in the
refugee boat **Life Cycle** and in the apse
as scaled-down, golden versions of
the statues. The various backgrounds of
the Lego images are derived from the
series **Study of Perspective**, which is
also on view at K21.

Sunflower Seeds, 2010
Porcelain
100 tons, dimensions variable.
Installation view,
Tate Modern, London, 2010.
p. 28: Detail

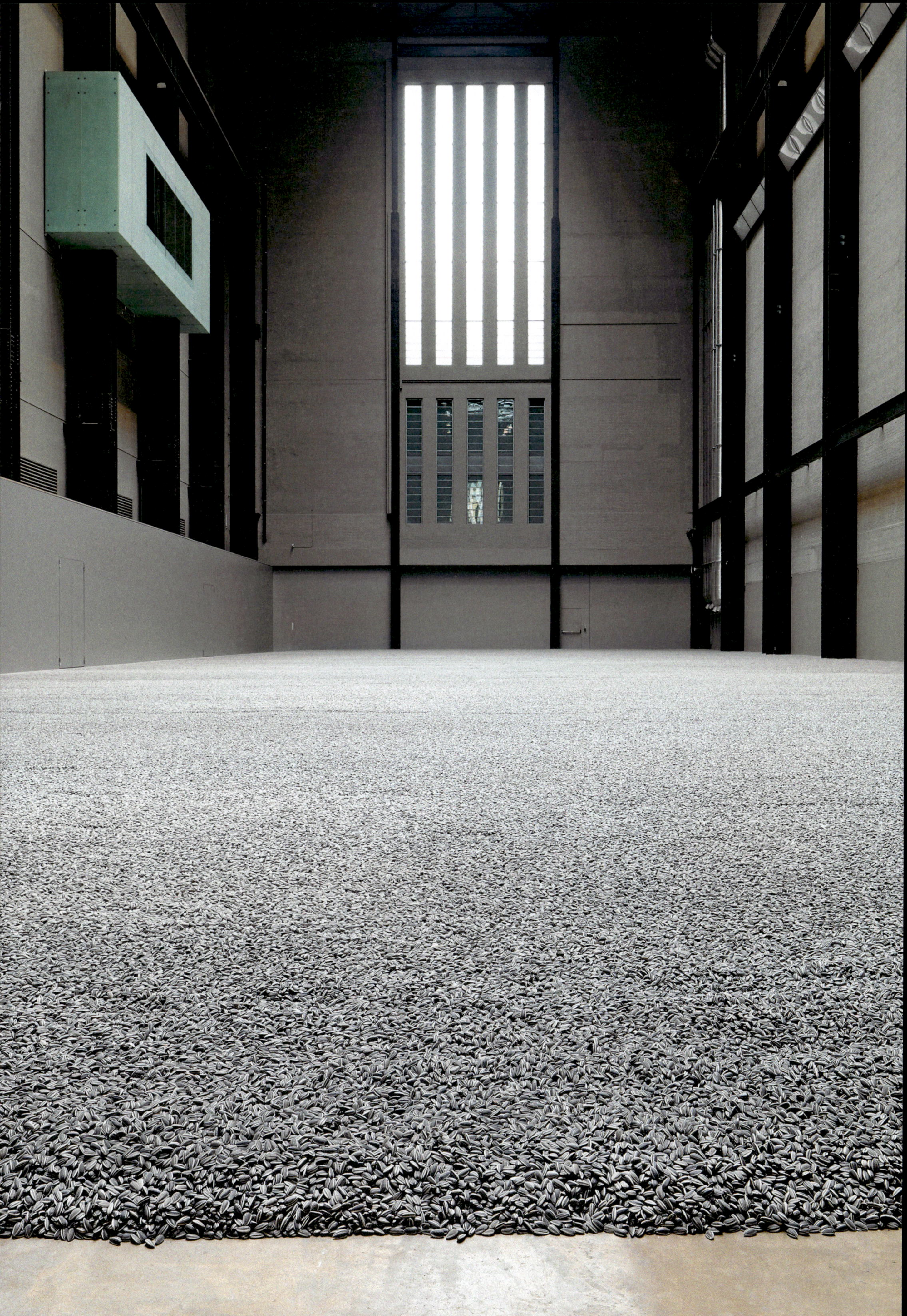

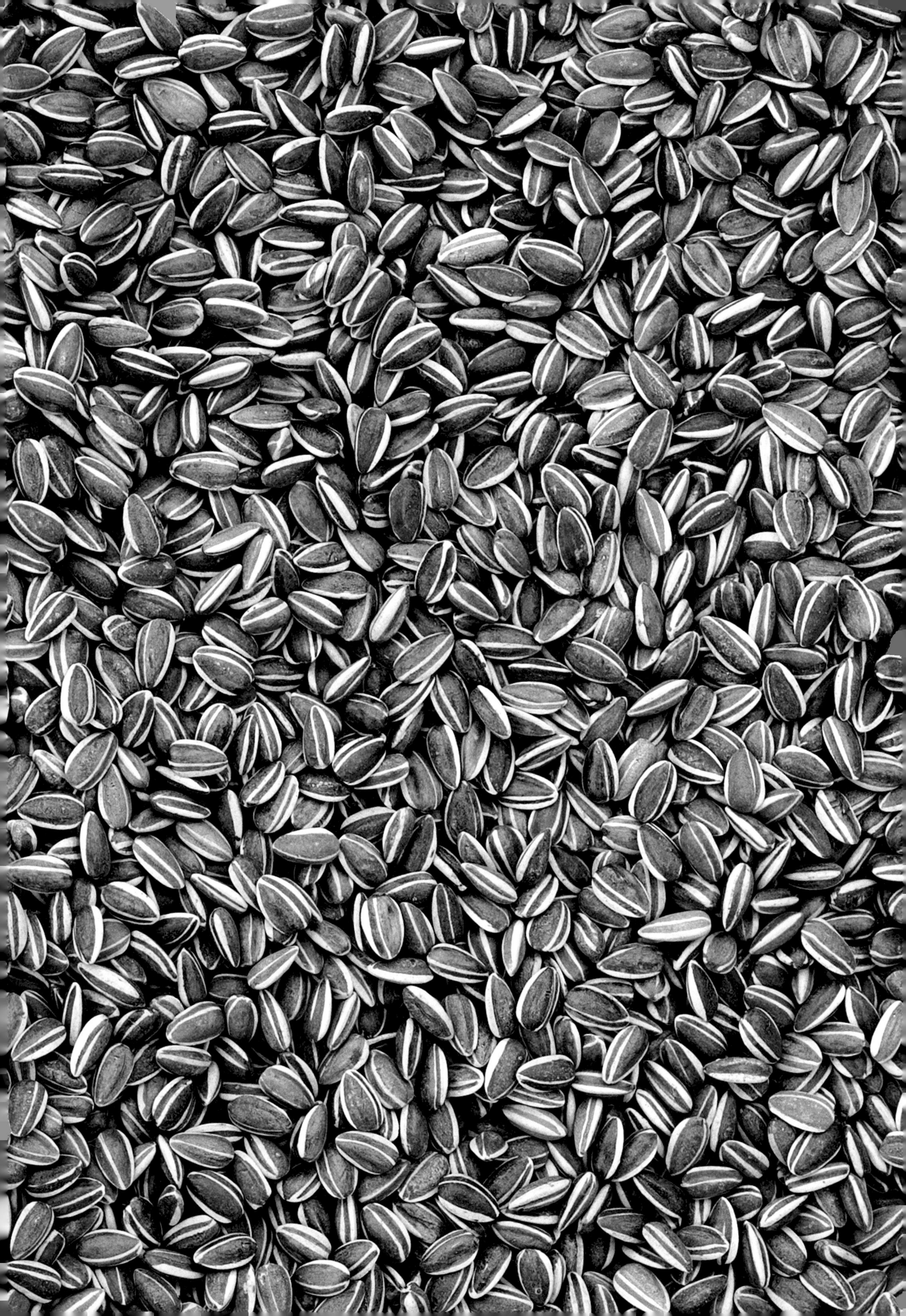

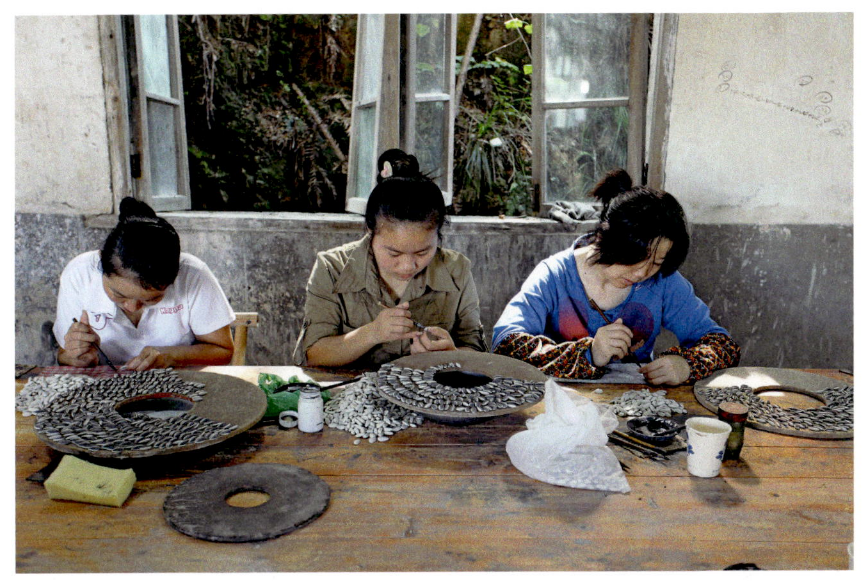

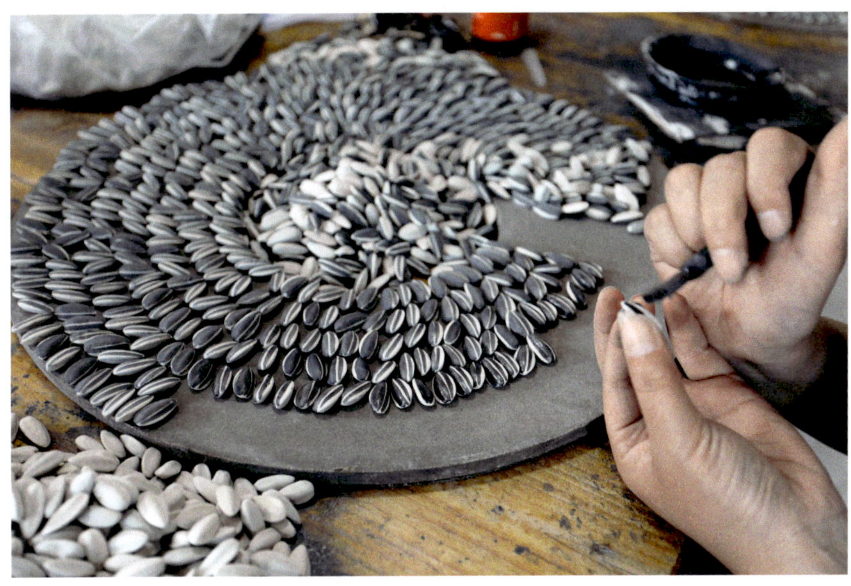

I.O.U. Wallpaper, 2011–2013
Wallpaper
Complete set of I.O.U.s
(13,719), each: 30.9 × 21.7cm.
Installation view,
Sakip Sabanci Museum,
Istanbul, 2017

Production of
Sunflower Seeds, 2010

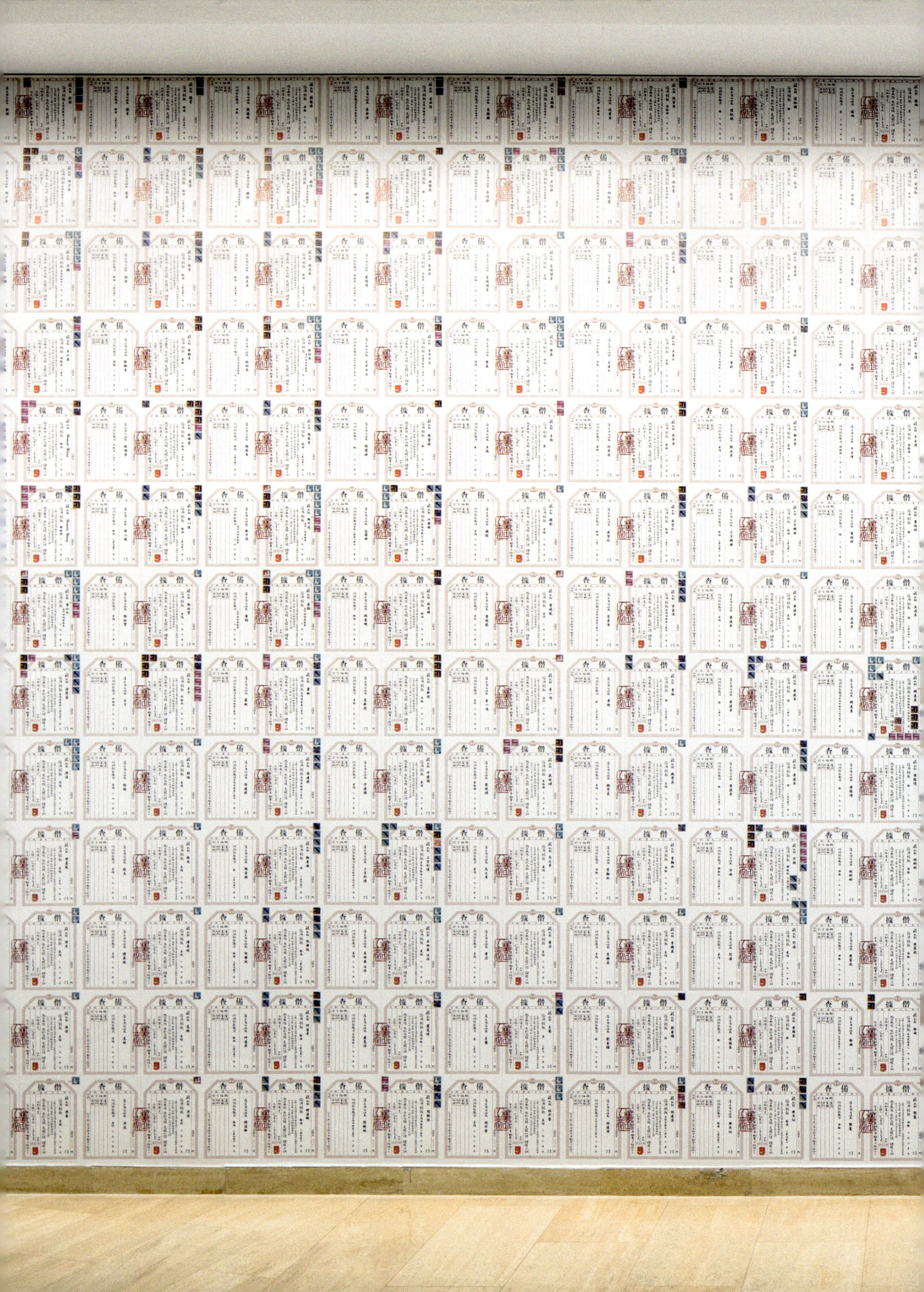

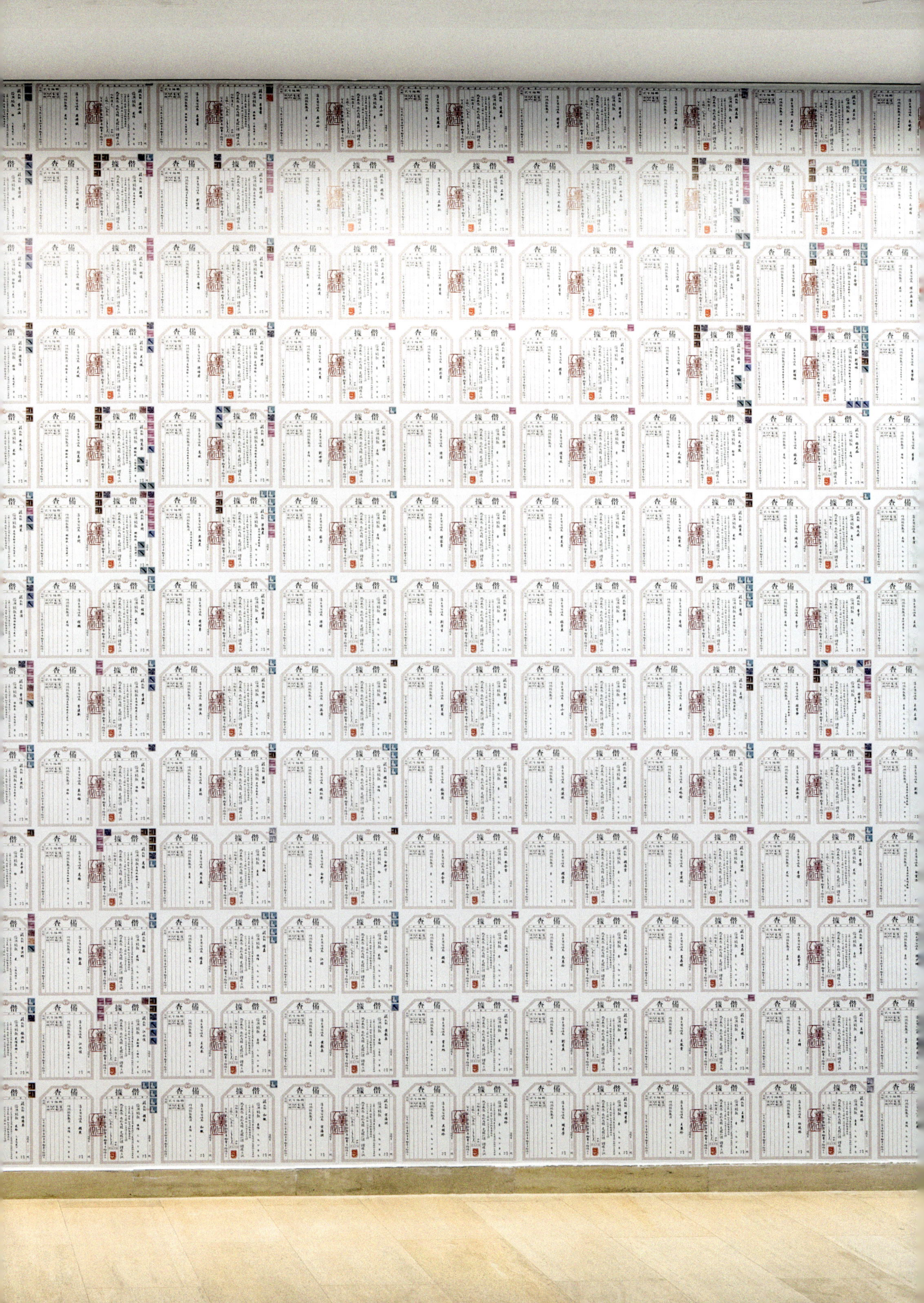

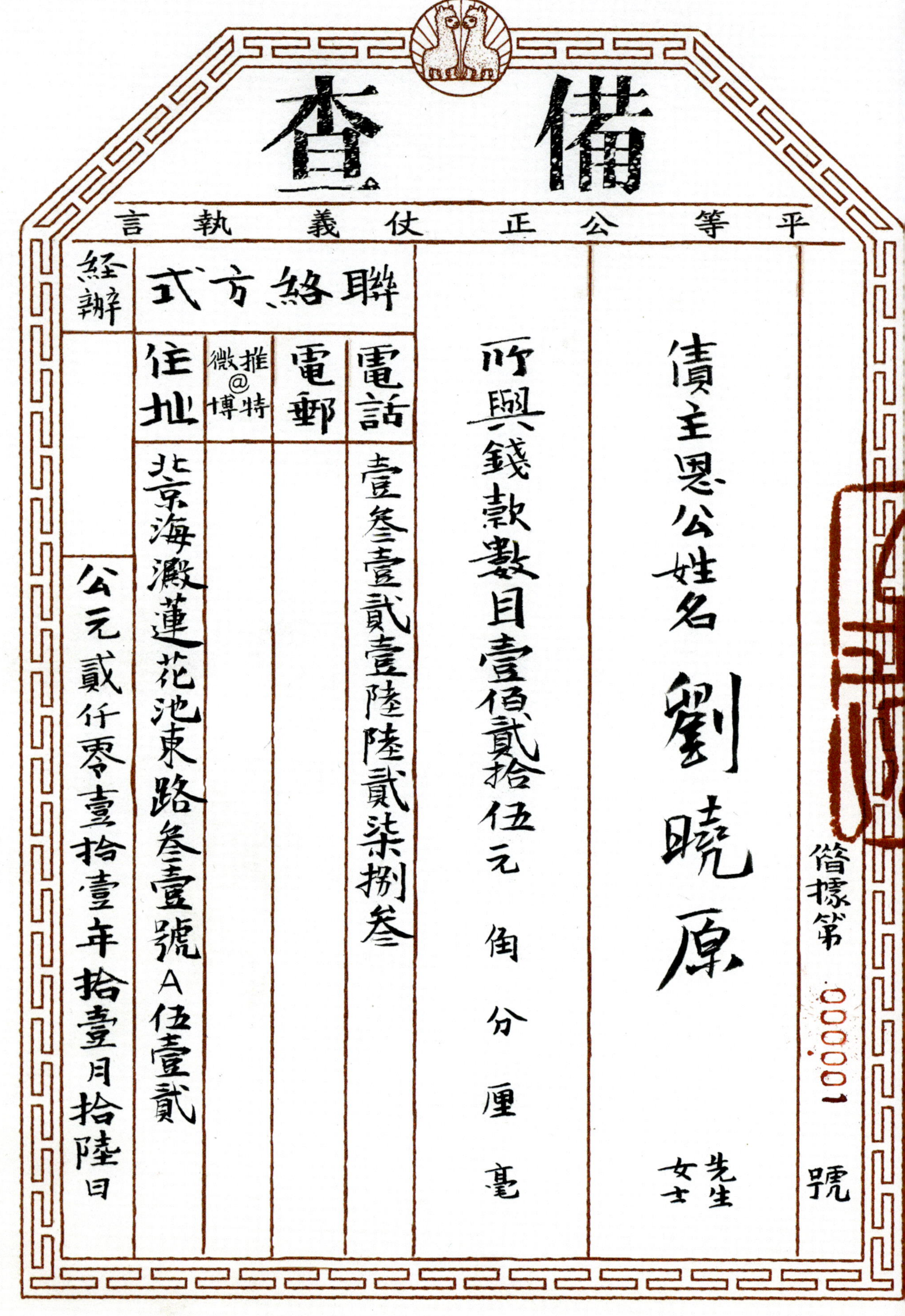

備查

平等　公正　仗義　執言

簽據第 000001 號

債主恩公姓名 劉曉原 先生 女士

所興錢款數目壹佰貳拾伍元 角 分 厘 毫

聯絡方式

電話 壹叁壹貳壹陸陸貳柒捌叁

電郵

推特@微博

住址 北京海澱蓮花池東路叁壹號A伍壹貳

經辦 公元貳仟零壹拾壹年拾壹月拾陸日

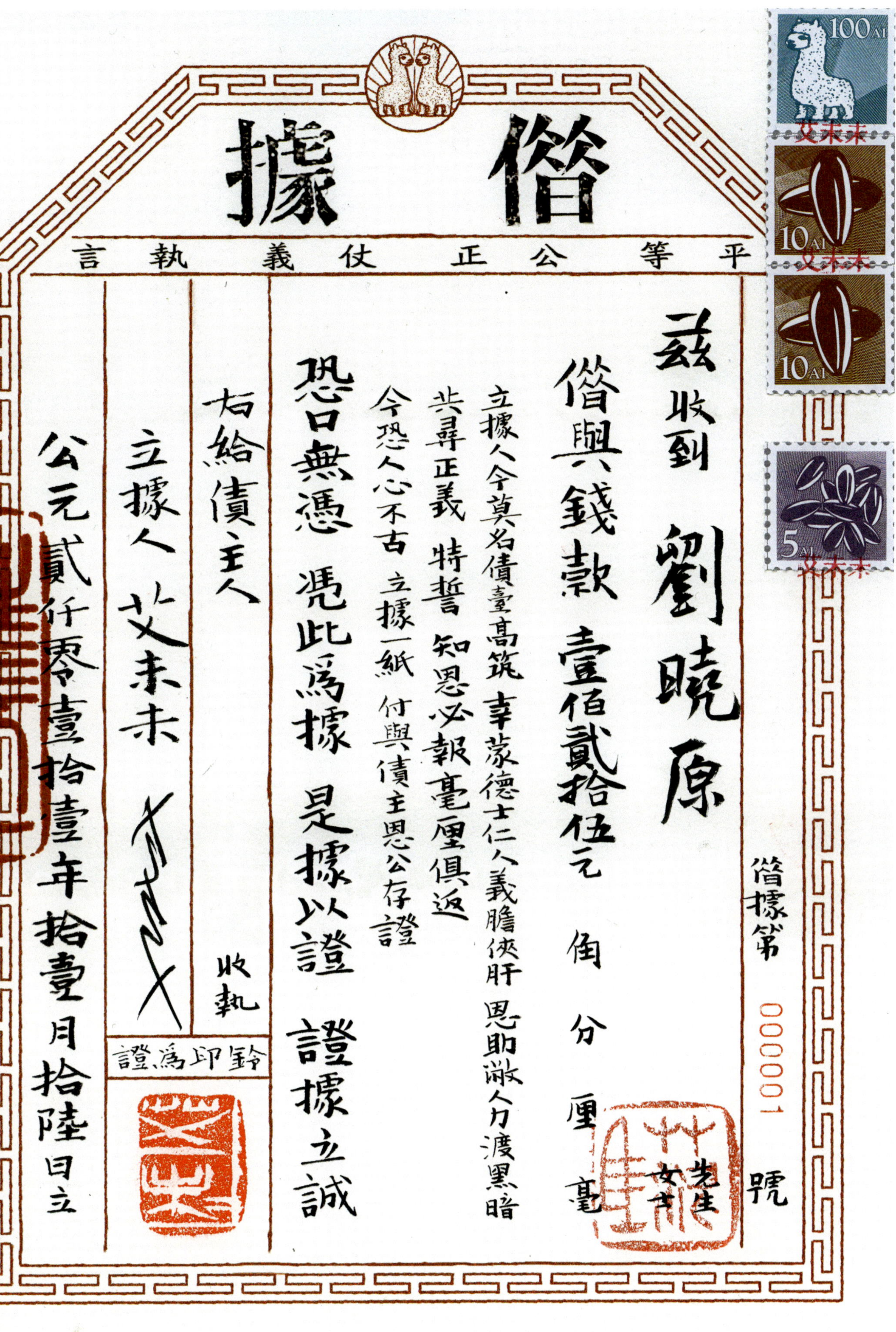

借據
平等公正仗義執言
茲收到 劉曉原
借與錢款 壹佰貳拾伍元 角 分 厘 毫
立據人今莫名債臺高築 幸蒙德士仁人義膽俠肝 恩助微力渡黑暗
共尋正義 特誓 知恩必報 毫厘俱返
今恐人心不古 立據一紙 付與債主恩公存證
恐口無憑 憑此為據 是據以證 證據立誠
右給債主人
立據人 艾未未 收執
證為卽鈴
公元貳仟零壹拾壹年拾壹月拾陸日立
借據第 000001 號
先生 女士

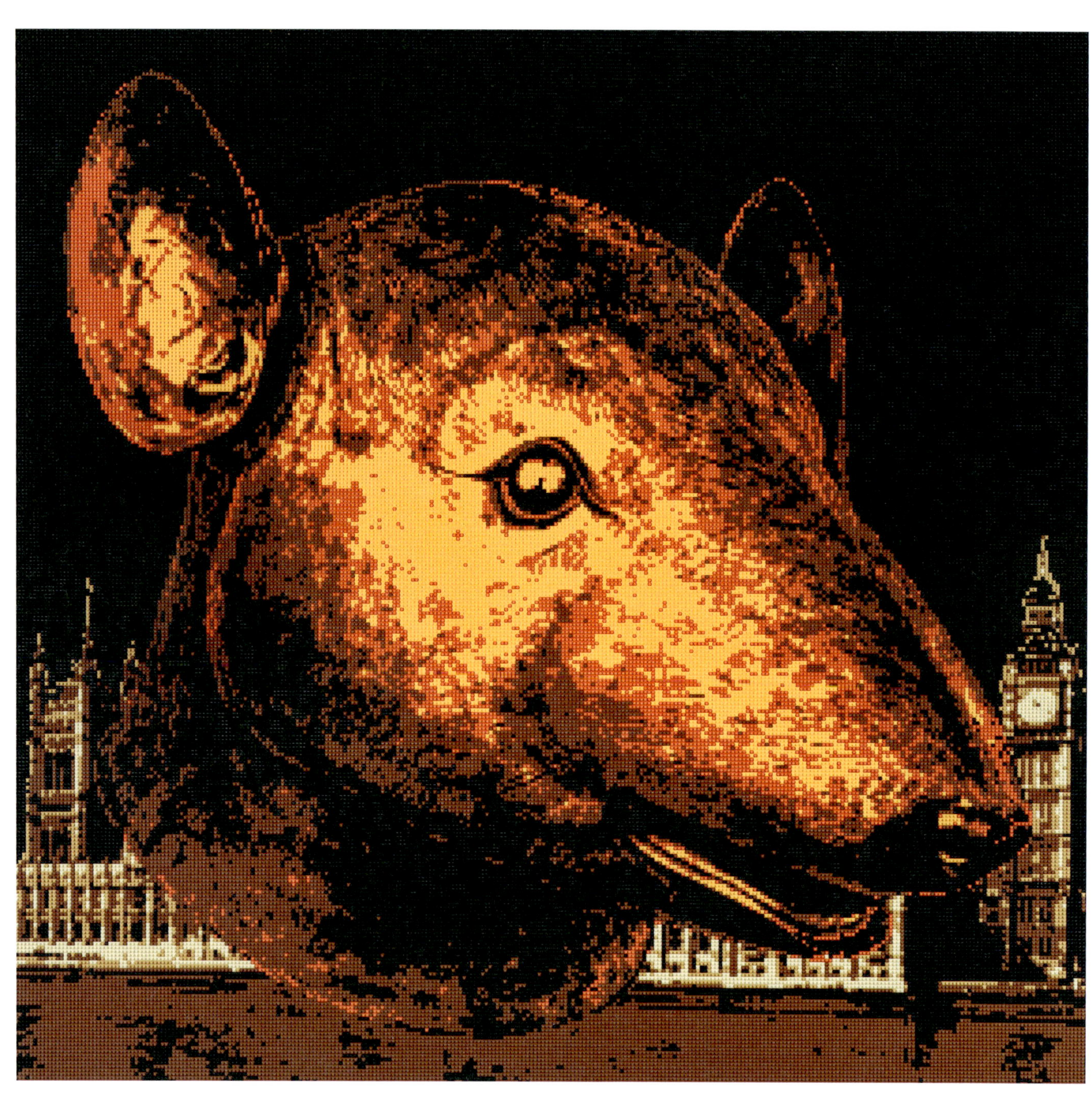

Zodiac, 2018
Lego bricks
Set of 12, each: 230 × 230 cm

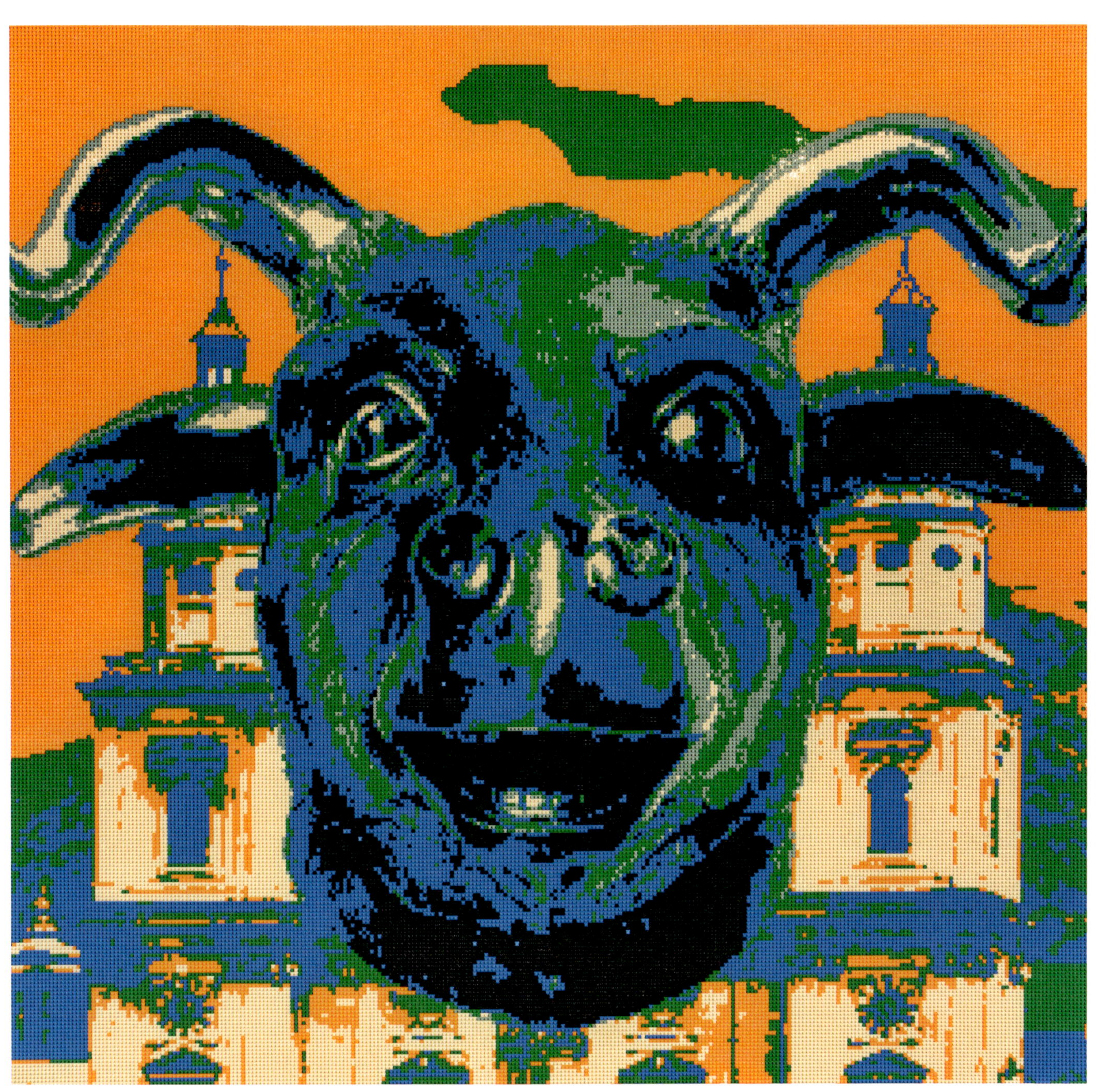

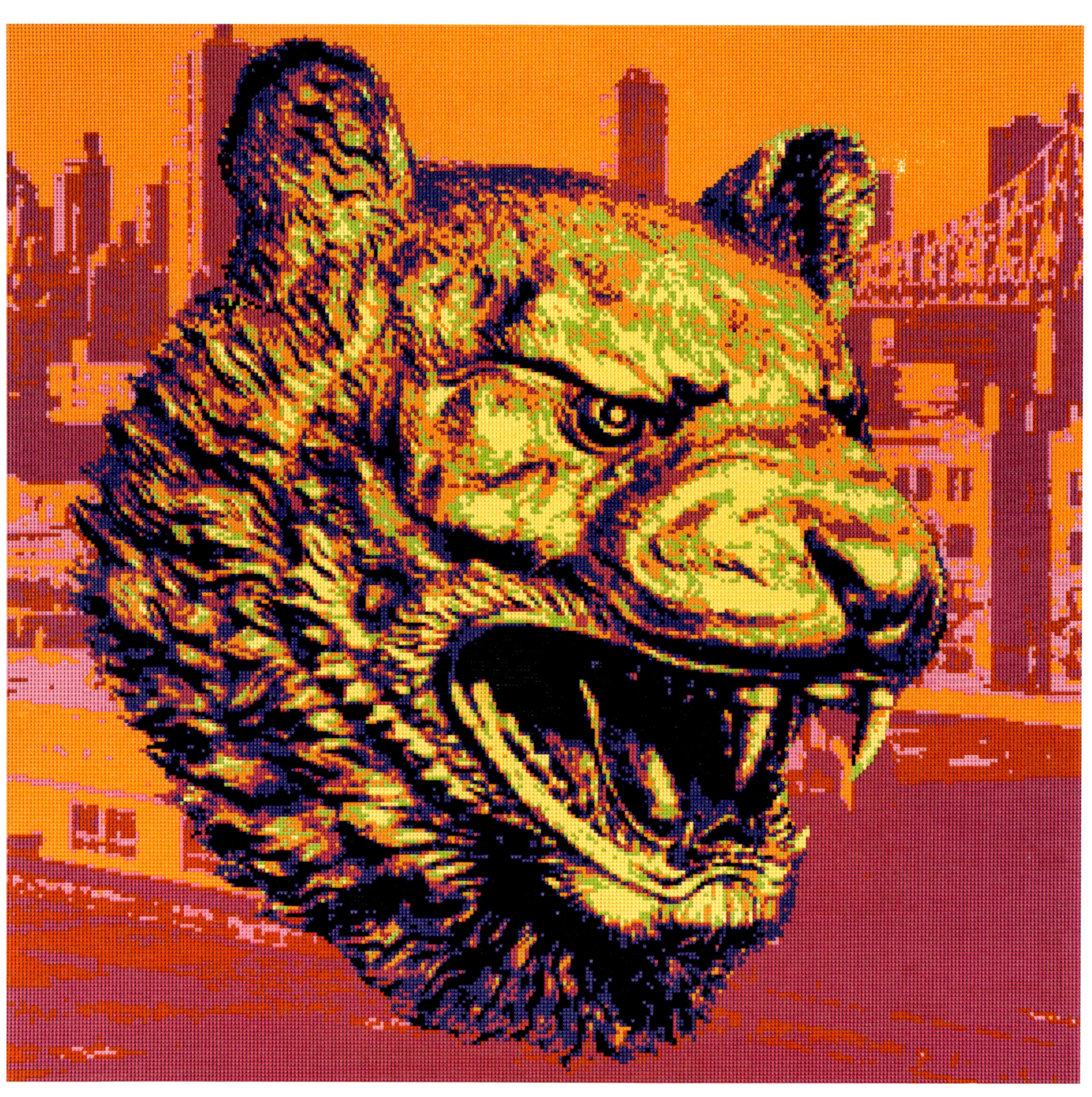

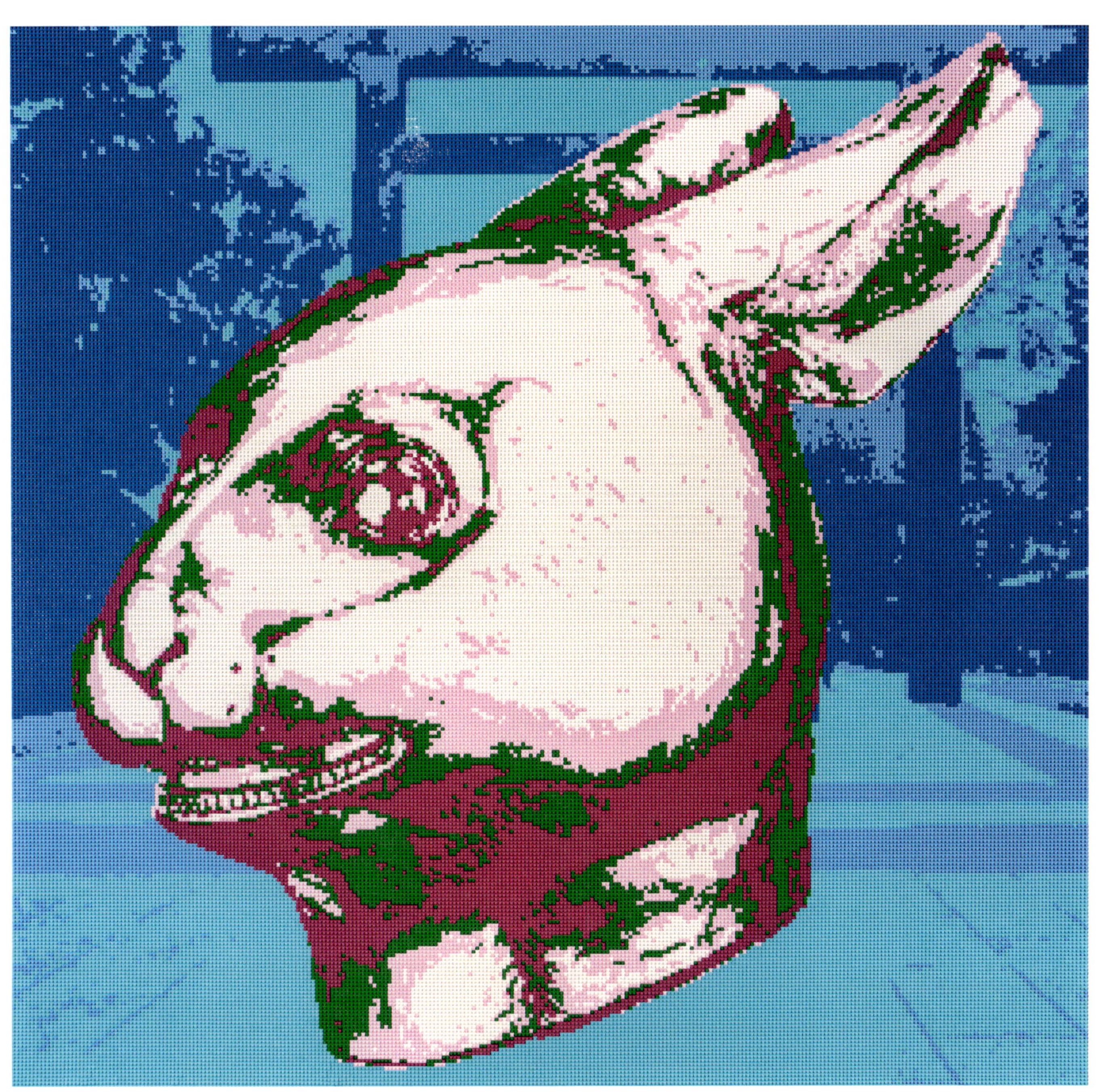

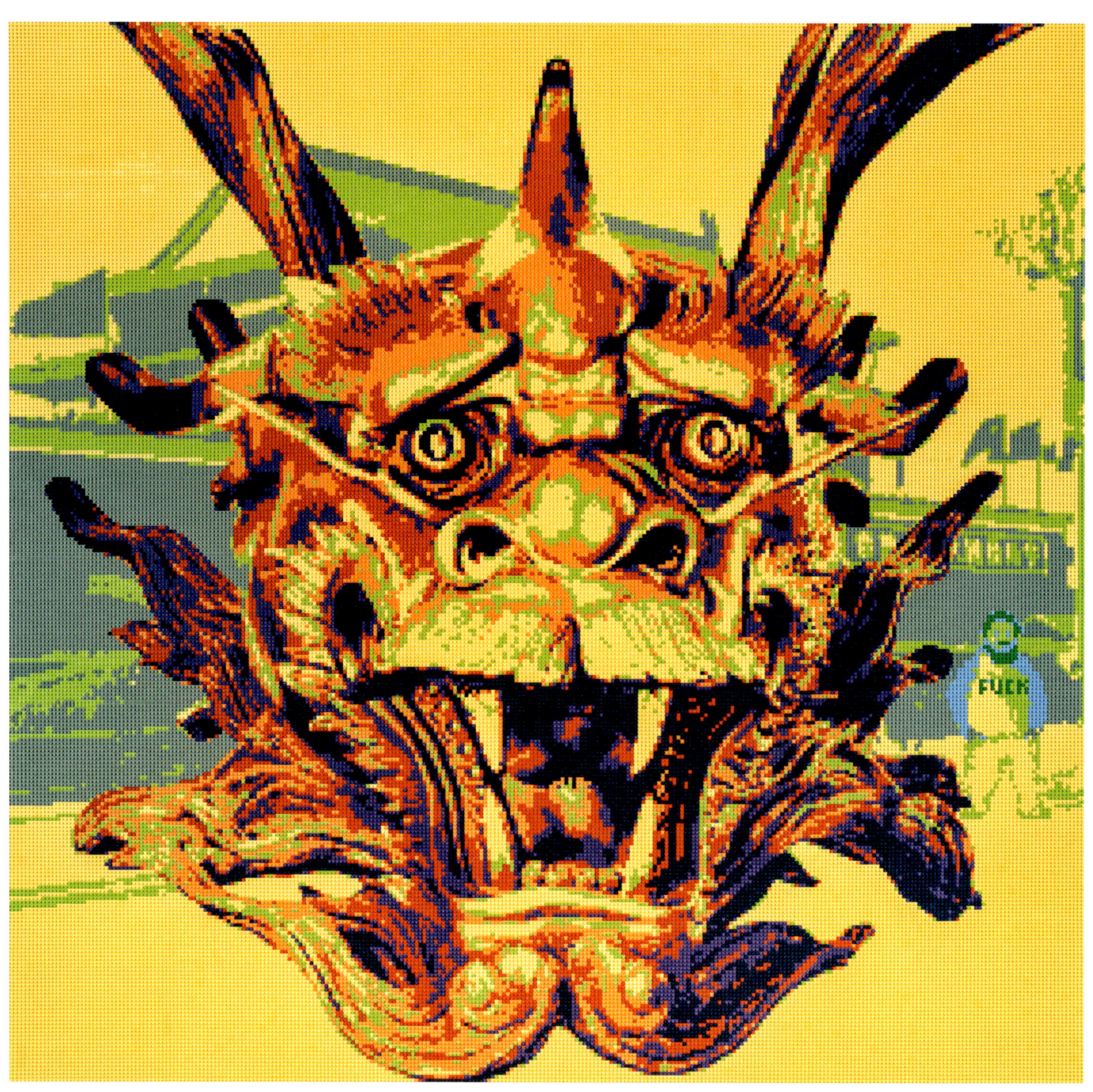
FUCK

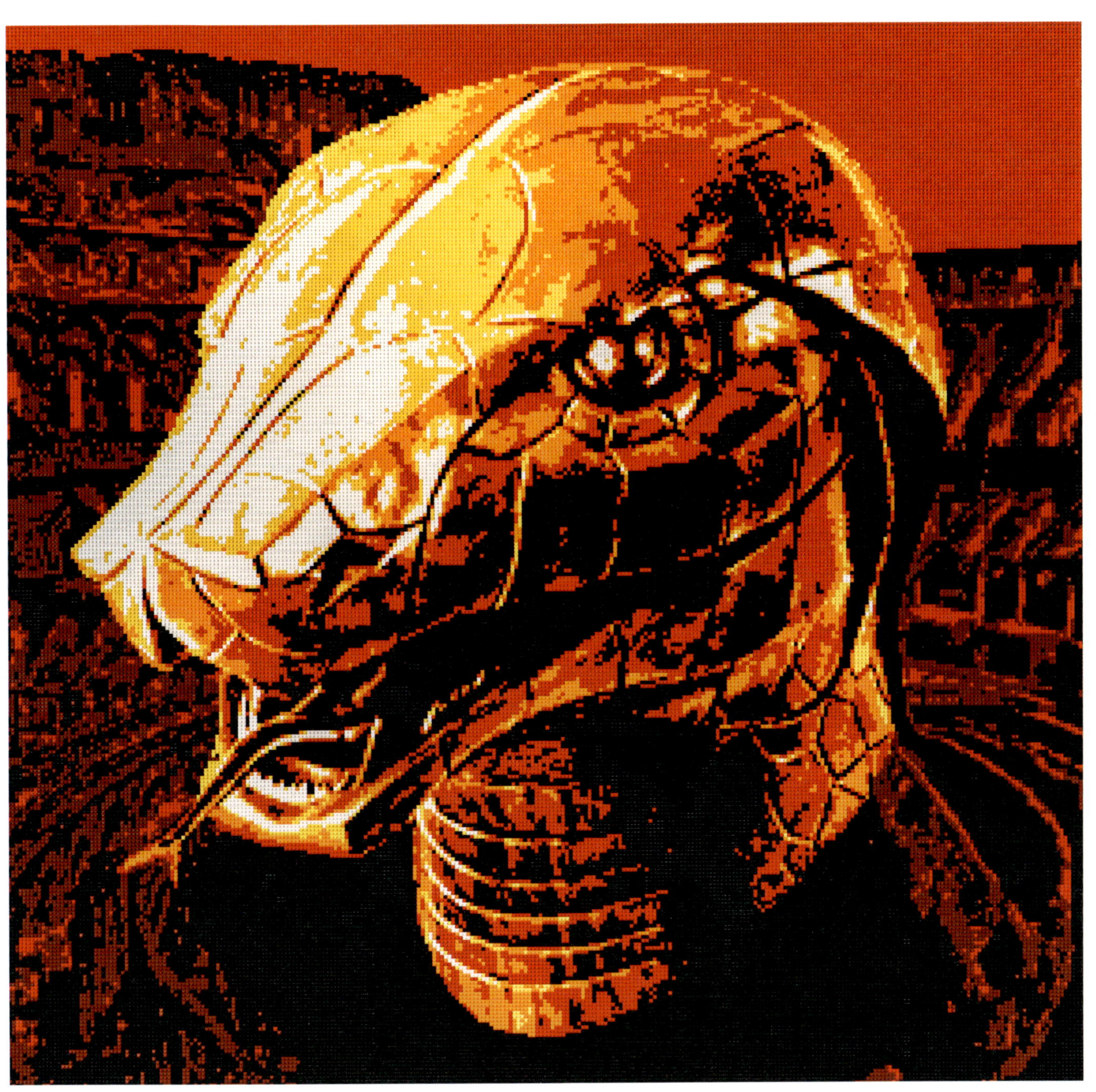

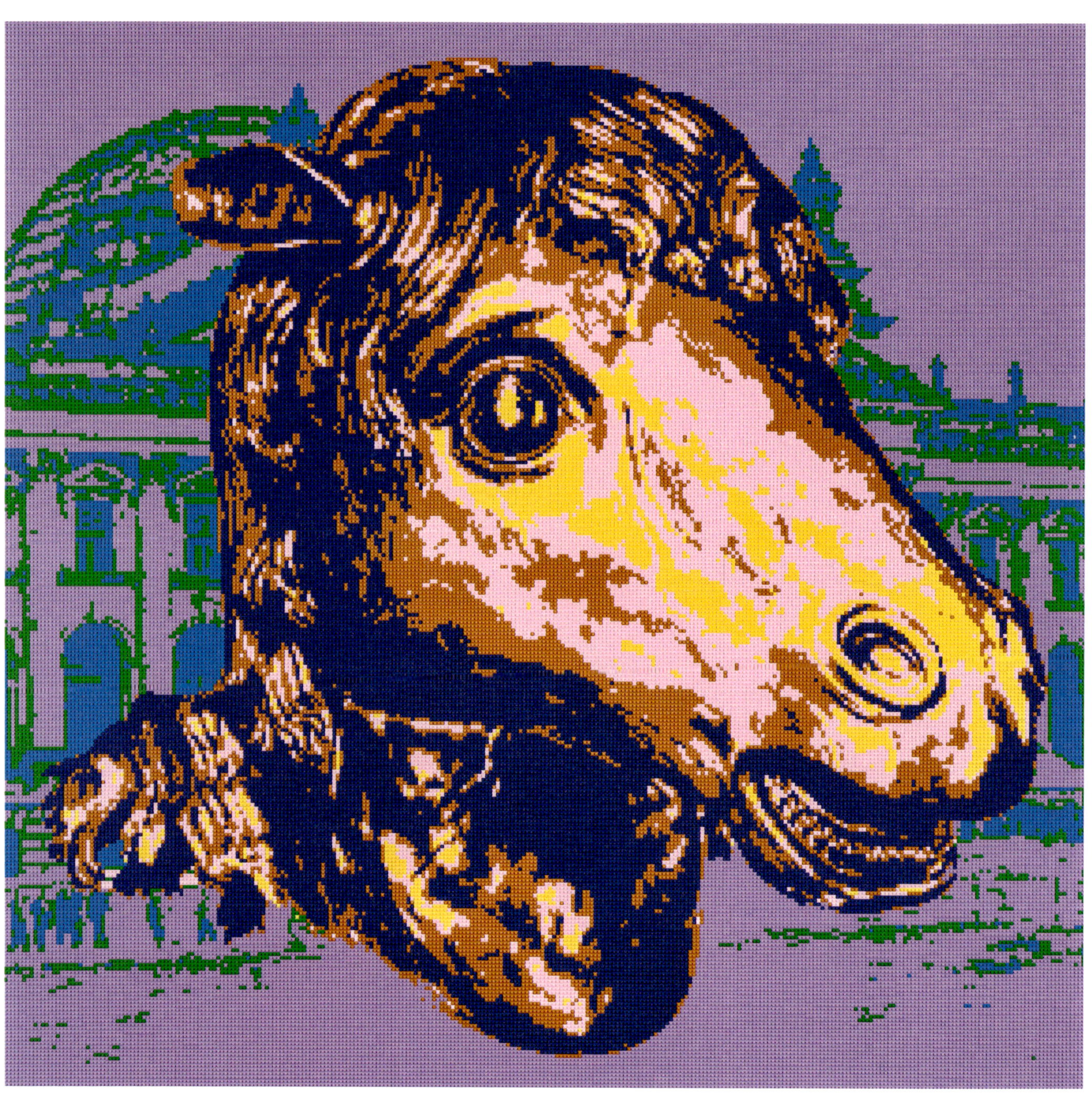

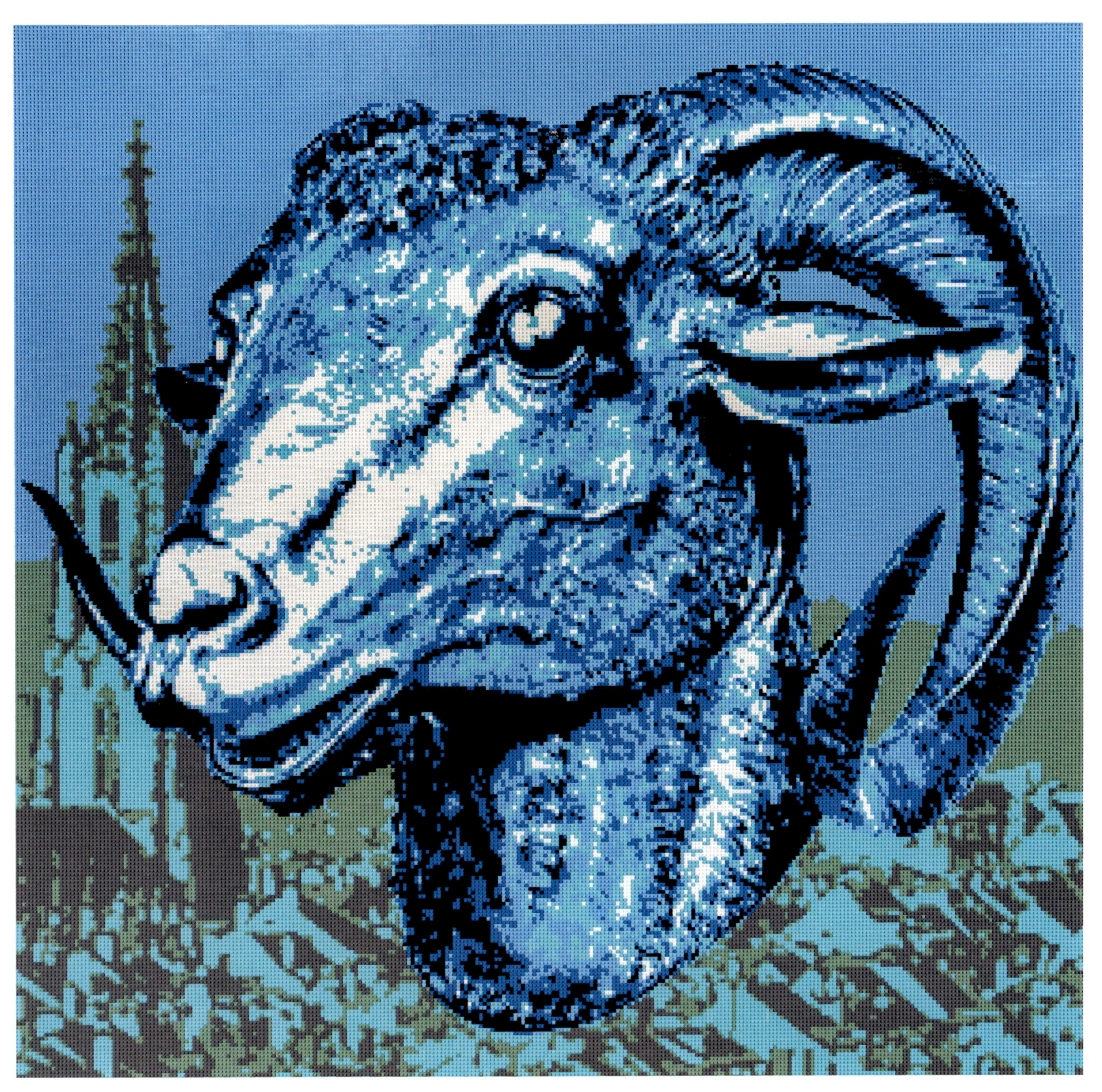

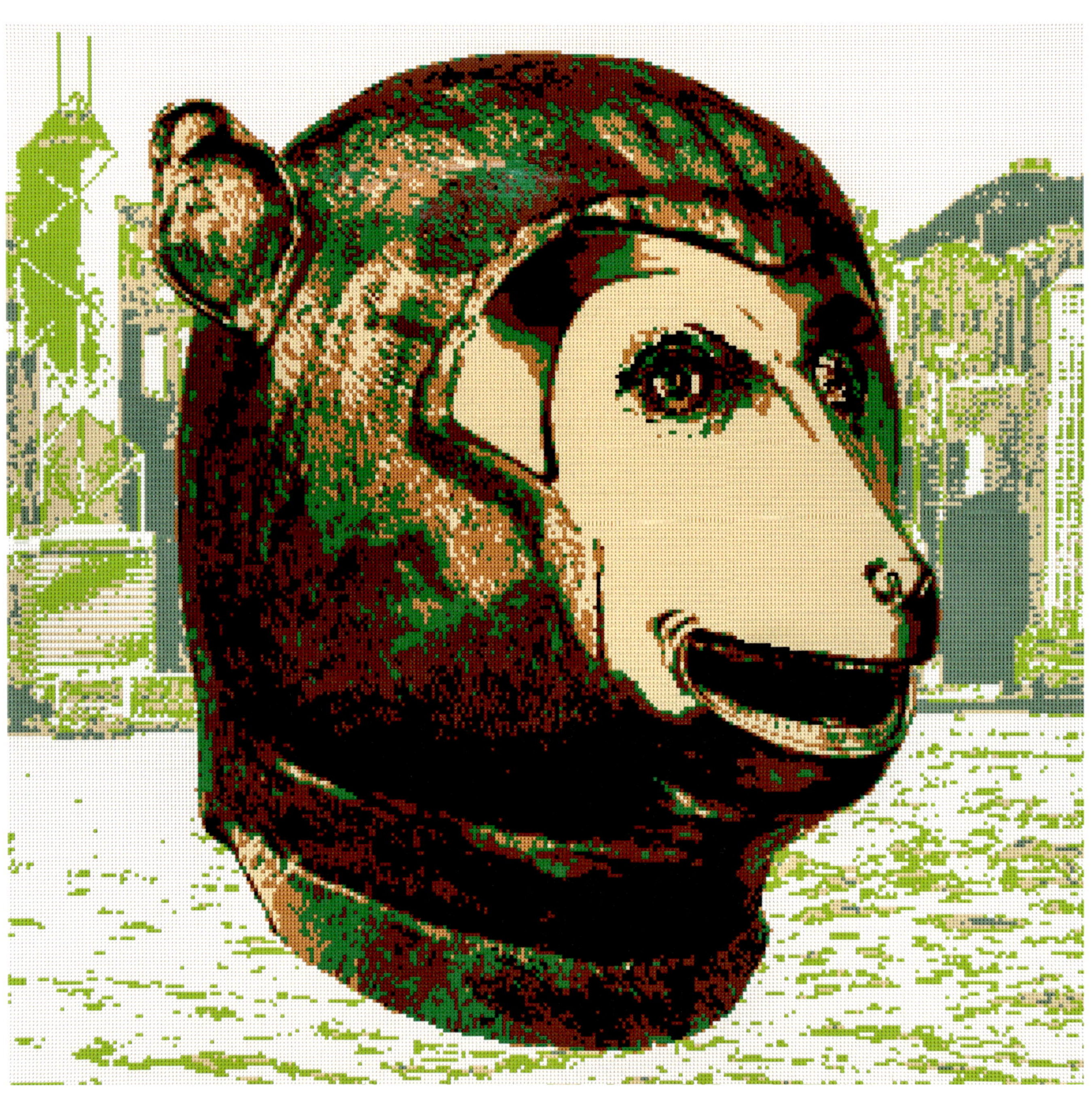

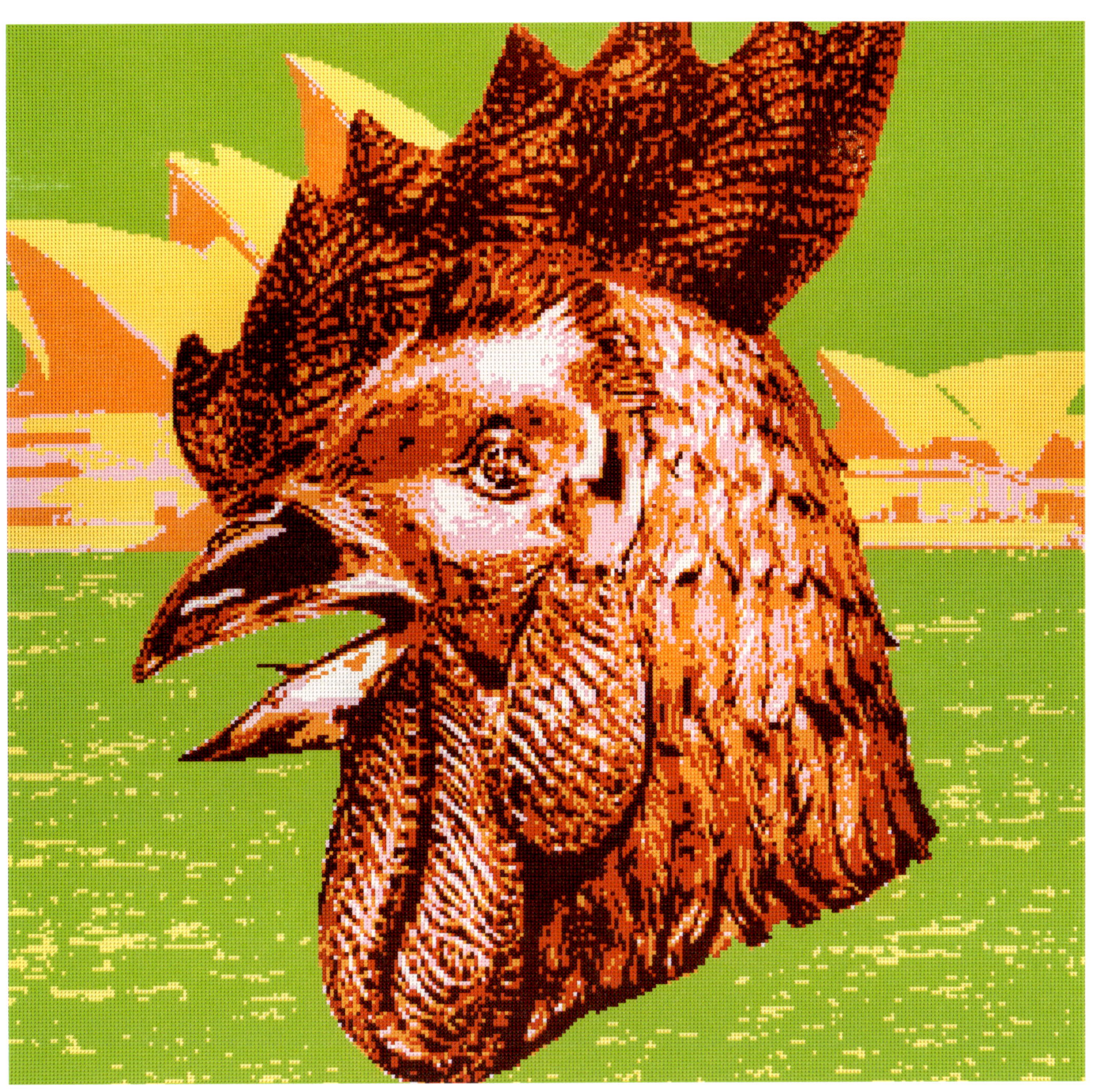

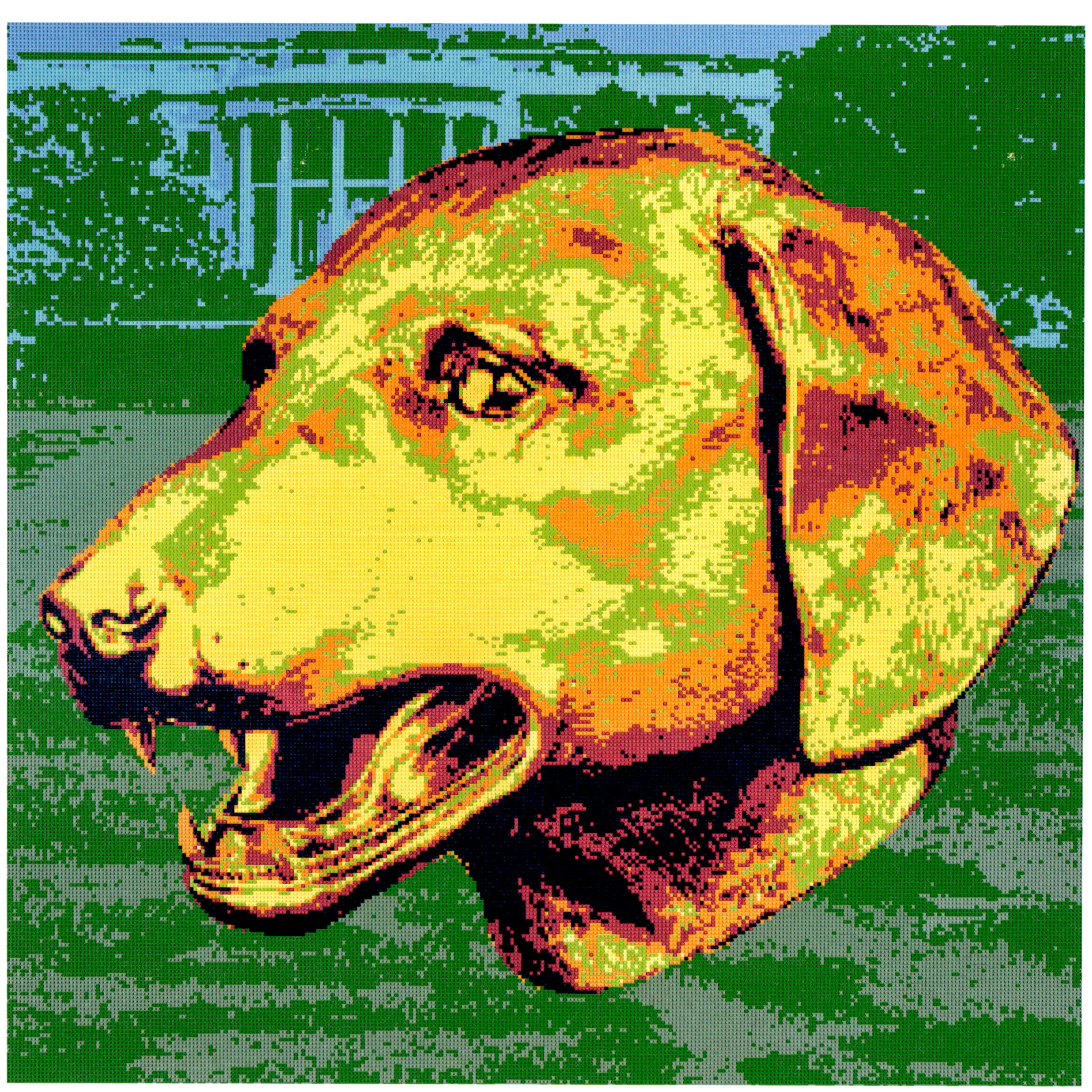

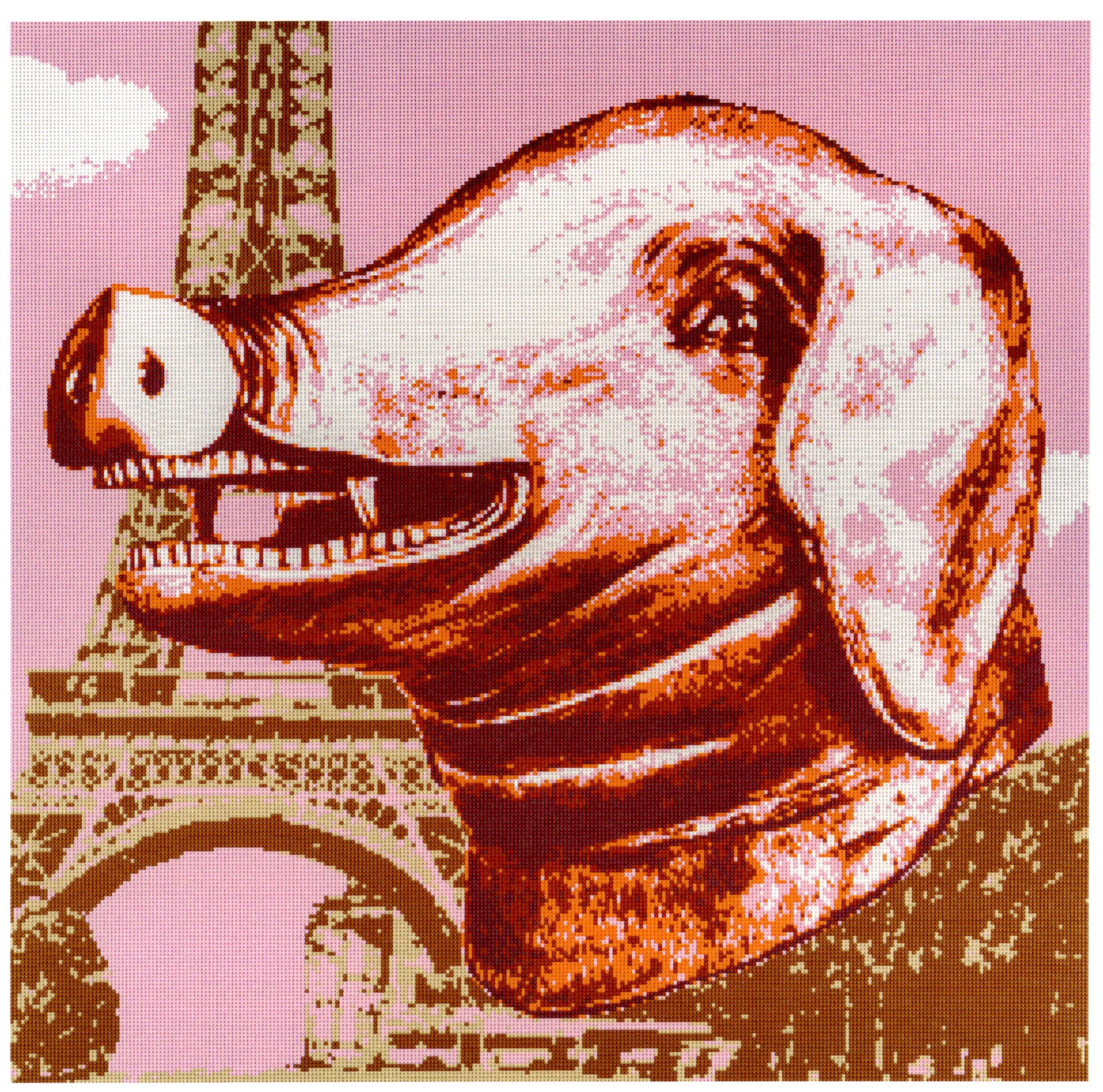

The Aesthetics of Quantity and the Inverted Readymade

Falk Wolf

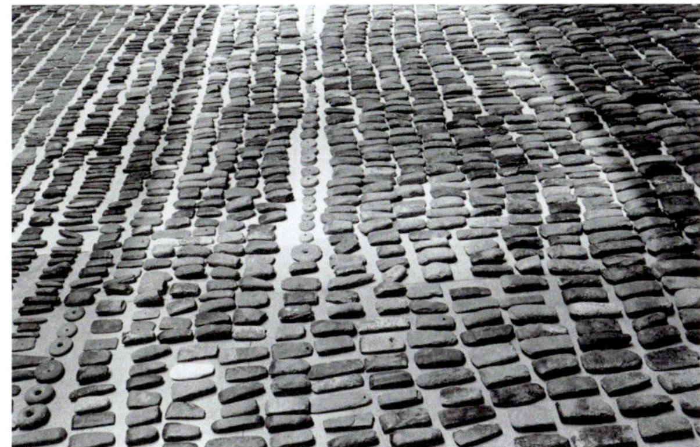

1

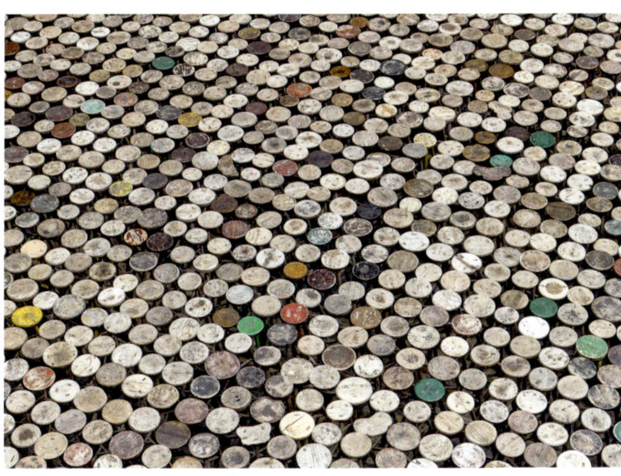

2

Still Life, 1993–2000,
stone tools dating from
the Stone Age to the Shang
dynasty (10000–1100 BC),
dimensions variable. Detail

Stools, 2013, wooden Qing
Dynasty stools, dimensions
variable. Detail

Several of Ai Weiwei's works consist of a multitude of more or less similar elements that are connected or arranged to form an installation. Where they do not merge to form a single sculpture, their composition produces an image while at the same time preserving the individuality and uniqueness of each element.

Examples: **Still Life**, roughly 10,000 ancient axes; **Stools**, 6,000 stools; **Straight**, 164 tons of steel rebar; **Laundromat**, 2,046 garments; **Sunflower Seeds**, 100,000,000 porcelain sunflower seeds.— That is a lot of material. We are used to emphasizing and appreciating quality rather than quantity, especially in matters of art. "Less is more" (a principle attributed to Ludwig Mies van der Rohe) is one of the catchphrases that has decisively determined aesthetic modernism since the 1920s. So how can an artistic strategy that points in a completely different direction be classified under these conditions?

Sunflower Seeds (pp. 27–28) initially operates with a change of material. A flower seed is slightly enlarged, formally somewhat idealized, and imitated in hand-painted porcelain. Through the precious material, patriotically charged within the Chinese context, and the complex manufacturing process, the everyday, inexpensive snack appreciates in value and, at the same time, traverses a level of reflection in the observation of nature.[1] In addition, the work refers to the communist propaganda, which depicted Mao Zedong as the sun and the Chinese people as sunflowers turning in his direction. The sunflower is thus a political plant. It has a political core.

In their multitude, the miniature sculptures, like any serial work, raise questions of originality. With one hundred million pieces, one may intuitively assume that this is an industrially manufactured mass product. But this is precisely not the case with **Sunflower Seeds**. In addition to the change in material and the political iconography of the sunflower seed, the deeper meaning lies in the fact that the work consists of an unimaginably large number of handcrafted and hand-painted sculptures—each unique, as unique as each natural sunflower seed. The production reality of a millennia-old craft tradition thus becomes evident in the hopeless competition with industrial mass products. It is, however, only the immeasurable number of individual seeds in the exhibition space that makes this evident — this means bringing it before one's eyes. The same applies to the allusion to Mao Zedong's political iconography. Here in particular, the work functions only as a mass of individual sculptures. It is this contradiction, and the making of this contradiction evident, that interests Ai Weiwei: "This is a society that's still not really paying attention to individuals, to who they are, and that's an essential question. [...] That's the kind of society I live in, that's the kind of reality I have to face and that's a debt I have to pay."[2]

The example of **Sunflower Seeds** thus demonstrates that only the multiplication of the individual elements reveals central levels of meaning. The work receives its specific artistic message through the quantitative accumulation of its individual components, the individuality of which is simultaneously maintained and made evident. With **Sunflower Seeds**, one cannot avoid acknowledging that the quantity makes a difference, which is understood as its own artistic quality. It is only through the quantity that the work acquires its specific quality. The transition from quantity to quality (and vice versa) is a central argument for the Logic of Being in Georg Wilhelm Friedrich Hegel's **Science of Logic** and forms the starting point for the transition to the Logic of Essence.[3] Karl Marx took up this argumentation and made the "transformation from quantity to quality," in addition to the "negation of negation," the focal point of his philosophy. Marx thus notes, in the transformation of surplus-value to capital, "that not every sum of money, or value, can be transformed into capital at will. In fact, it is a presupposition of this transformation that a certain minimum of money or of exchange-value is in the hands of the individual possessor of money or commodities."[4] It is only then, when so many workers can be employed that the factory owner not only lives from their extra work but can increase his wealth, that the surplus-value is transformed into capital — another quality that, according to Marx, leads to another social reality. When Ai Weiwei's installations undergo an aesthetic transformation from quantity to quality, it is not his intention to serve a topos of sublimity that puts us in a state of immobilized amazement — even if the sight of one hundred million sunflower seeds and the idea of their weight at one hundred tons initially leave us speechless, relying in their effect on the discursive history of the sublime from Joseph Addison, via Edmund Burke, to Immanuel Kant. They do, however, also draw our attention upon quantity to the social reality of living and the conditions of production: on the one hand, to the position of the individual in a totalitarian state and, on the other hand, to the work of the artisan against the backdrop of an unfettered global market. **Sunflower Seeds** brings this social reality before our eyes — for the seeds themselves and their number are not only symbols of this reality, they are products of this reality.

Marx was already concerned with the social consequences of this transformation when he theorized that surplus-value is transformed into capital. A comparable phenomenon is currently being discussed as a problem of scaling, especially in media studies. Marshall McLuhan had already described the social significance of media as a question of scaling in the first sentences of **Understanding Media**: The slogan, "the medium is the message," means "that the personal and social consequences of any medium [...] result from the new scale that is introduced into our affairs."[5] Thus, contrary to popular belief, in order to make a social difference, it is not the medium that must be new but, rather, the scale. Therefore, it is not the invention of the car or the telephone that makes the difference but their general distribution and availability. "Innovation," one may summarize, "is the result of scaling, not of technical invention."[6] Also from a media-historical perspective, quantity (as an index of scaling) thus makes a socially relevant difference.

As with telephones and cars, **Sunflower Seeds** is not about producing and exhibiting a single porcelain sunflower seed but rather about the question of how many there have to be in order for their socio-critical quality to become apparent. The question is reminiscent of the classic sorites paradox, to which Hegel had already referred in his transition from quantity to quality [7] and in which we must not let ourselves get caught up when answering the question. With Ludwig Wittgenstein, the question of how many grains of sand (or sunflower seeds) make up a heap can be exposed as a grammatical question since there is no meaningful opposite: no non-heap. [8] Instead, the result is the image of a threshold that spans the space between an above and a below. [9]

In order to uncover this threshold in the works of Ai Weiwei, we have to ask about the dispositif or apparatus of installation art. As an installation, the work has its historical location in the Turbine Hall of Tate Modern in 2010. It was conceived for this exhibition. Therefore, the number of seeds is mainly defined by the dimensions of that hall, which took on the appearance of a gigantic granary. In later exhibitions, the image of the generously poured material, on which, initially, visitors were even permitted to walk, gave way to a precisely defined surface area that was laid out like a carpet in the middle of the space. In Düsseldorf, the original quantity of seeds has been installed once again and for the first time in this way. Previously, the designated quanta have been specifically tailored to each respective spatial situation. The third arrangement was a poured pile of seeds. In each case, it is clear that the installed quantity was scaled to the space's architectural dimensions. The work was shown under the rhetorical idiom of "pars pro toto." The reduced number of seeds now metonymically stands for the whole, the incomparably larger total sum, and at the same time refers to the incomparably larger dimensions of the Turbine Hall. Thus, in addition to the visible quantity, the imaginary quantity that was not visible in each respective exhibition space was always added.

It is no coincidence that it is precisely the synecdoche, and here quite specifically "pars pro toto," that constitutes the core rhetorical principle of the museum as a model for the world: The objects in a collection metonymically represent the whole of the world, that reality outside the museum. [10] The sunflower seeds as a discrete, quantifiable, and yet unimaginably large quantity thus also stand

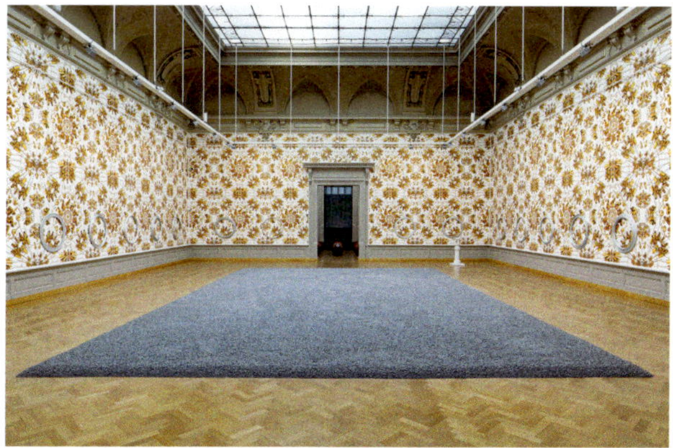

3

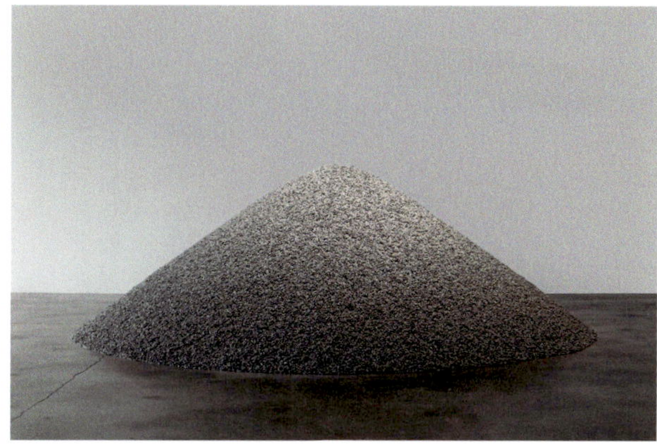

4

3
Sunflower Seeds, 2010;
The Animal That Looks Like a Llama but Is Really an Alpaca, 2015; **Untitled**, 2017;
Camera with Plinth, 2015.
Installation view, Musée cantonal des Beaux-Arts, Lausanne, 2017

4
Sunflower Seeds, 2010, porcelain, 5 tons.
Installation view, Magasin 3, Stockholm, 2012

49

for the overall social context not only with reference to China. They always receive this quality through their quantity tailored to the space. They are thus located on a threshold, at which—as with the heap and in contrast to Hegel and Marx—no exact point of transformation can be identified. Central to the effect of the work is the fact that it is scaled to the dimensions of the space. For **Sunflower Seeds**, therefore, there was never an absolute number of seeds but rather a quantum adapted to the effect within the particular spatial situation.

The installations **Still Life**, **Stools**, **Straight** (pp. 63–73), and **Laundromat** (pp. 98–99) also operate using this aesthetic of quantity: The multitude of elements determines their conception and effect to a decisive degree. Unlike **Sunflower Seeds**, however, their individual elements were not produced specifically for the installation but were rather found, collected, or purchased. They thus belong to those works by Ai Weiwei in which historical objects were utilized.

After his return to China in 1993, Ai Weiwei began to collect antiques: ceramics, porcelain, furniture, architectural elements, and entire buildings. Since then, many of his works have been created from these collected objects. Several were exhibited, in the form of readymades, in their found state. They thus transformed into works of contemporary art. Their temporal structure became fragile and precarious. Others were adapted in a conscious, iconoclastic act: painted, inscribed, completely immersed in paint, or destroyed, up to and including pulverization. However, do readymades still remain readymades when they are worked on further? Marcel Duchamp screwed his **Roue de bicyclette** (bicycle wheel) onto a stool and signed his **Fountain**. In several works by Ai Weiwei, found objects are not only altered, they are, above all, piled up. Unlike with Duchamp, they do not appear as one readymade lifted out of the crowd of its doubles, but rather, they appear as a crowd of many individualized readymades. Examples in this exhibition are **Straight** and **Laundromat**.

As with **Sunflower Seeds**, in **Straight**, the size of the installation has always

been adapted to the architectural conditions present. The work consists of 164 tons of steel rebar which Ai Weiwei recovered from the ruins of schools destroyed by the Sichuan earthquake of 2008 and subsequently re-straightened. Until 2018, only a portion of this work had been exhibited. Shortly after its first exhibition at the Venice Biennale in 2013, even Ai Weiwei was certain that he would never be able to present the work in its entirety. [11] Then, in 2018, on the occasion of the exhibition **Ai Weiwei Raiz** in São Paulo, the entire work was installed for the first time. The previous installations were, however, never considered deficient. The work had had different manifestations, which differed in the number of steel rods. Here as well, the installation was conceived as a transition between quantity and quality. It is the quantity of straightened steel bars and the idea of their weight that allow for the immensity of both Sichuan's natural and man-made catastrophe to be imagined.

In **Laundromat**, the number of garments is also determined by the quantity of clothes left behind in the refugee camp at Idomeni. The three previous exhibitions of the work included 2,046 garments. Here as well, the installation is scaled to the conditions of the space and the dramaturgy of the exhibition without thwarting the impression of an unimaginably large number of individual elements.

Historical stools, debris from an earthquake catastrophe, and clothes left behind in an abandoned refugee camp— each of the countless elements has the character of a readymade. Ai Weiwei himself has often enough emphasized his conceptual proximity to Marcel Duchamp and the concept of the readymade. It is worth noting, however, that in doing so, Ai Weiwei makes use of a very broad concept of the readymade. "Duchamp had the bicycle wheel, Warhol had the image of Mao. I have a totalitarian regime. It is my readymade." [12] This statement clearly demonstrates that Ai Weiwei understands the concept of the readymade in the broadest sense as a circumstance which has been found and which is to be dealt with artistically. This already implies the programmatic synthesis of art and life, art and politics, and the understanding of artistic work not so much as being dependent upon production but as an attitude. Both are aspects which he also derives from Duchamp. [13]

It is nevertheless appropriate to view Ai Weiwei's practice again in regard to several aspects of Duchamp's readymades. Duchamp declared an arbitrary product from the world of commodities to be a work of art and elevated it on a pedestal. Sebastian Egenhofer has pointed out that this gesture should not be narrowed down to an institutional critique. [14] In contrast to the surrealist objet trouvé, the readymade is not concerned with a mutual attraction, explained psychologically, between finder and object; rather, it concerns the act of purchasing an arbitrary object in the world of commodities which is carried out randomly, undirectedly, and indifferently. [15] Egenhofer thus emphasizes the aspect of the readymade which is critical of capitalism. It is precisely the arbitrariness in this movement that constitutes its essential aspect. Its individuality is not visible, but rather—as in Duchamp's **Bottle Rack**, for example— it consists only of the difference between those ultra-thin layers that arise, at most, from the unmeasurable wear of the casting molds. The object has no history whatsoever; because it is a mass product, it has its doubles in the world of commodities. As an object without history, its prehistory is characterized only by the accumulation of labor. Its individuality first reveals itself in its intended future use. [16] When an object is declared a readymade, it is stripped of its utility value. According to Egenhofer, it is pure exchange value elevated upon a pedestal, "the dazzling condensate of the abstracted hours of work" [17] that produced it. "That it is a serial product which is purchased, not 'found,' that it belongs to the paradigm of prostitution and not of love, of the replaceable not the singular object—these are reflexes of the relationship to the commodity form." [18]

If one considers these aspects and returns to Ai Weiwei's installations, his development of the Duchampian concept proves to be a reversal and inversion. Be it **Stools**, **Straight**, or **Laundromat**, these are not comprised of randomly purchased objects without any history. On the contrary, they are historically informed in a very specific, politically explosive way. Their origins from a particular historical context, collected at precisely this concrete time, constitute the political core of the works.

The material used in **Straight** is in fact that steel under which some of the five thousand children listed among the deceased were killed. The bars played a fatal, historically identifiable role. But Ai Weiwei was not satisfied with merely piling them up as a bundle of bent metal. Instead, he had the rods bent back into shape through years of work. Each individual piece of the 164 tons of rebar required roughly two hundred blows of a hammer. They thus regained their factory-new, original form. At first glance, they deny their origin and their involvement in the catastrophe. The individual rod seems to approach the Duchampian concept of the readymade and its anonymous commodity form. The pure exchange value is symbolically restored. The historical meaning remains invisibly enclosed within the material not within the form. What the form denies is contained in the material. Quite different from Marcel Duchamp's readymade, which must be understood as a replaceable, non-unique object.

Ai Weiwei was under enormous political pressure during the production of **Straight**, which lasted almost three years. His blog was shut down and completely deleted on May 28, 2009, precisely because of his advocacy for establishing the facts behind the earthquake catastrophe. In 2011, while still in production, he spent eighty-one days under secret detention. In the time that followed, he was placed under constant surveillance and was not permitted to leave the country. The decision to straighten the rods follows the impulse to straighten out something that went so fatally wrong. At the same time, however, the state's repression was undermined by straight metal bars. Once bent straight, no one could identify the origin of the material. It appeared—like with the Duchampian readymades—as a product of heavy industry without history. In a political climate, in which export permits for critical art are denied and unpopular artists are stifled, it could not be a disadvantage that, during transport, this highly political work only appeared

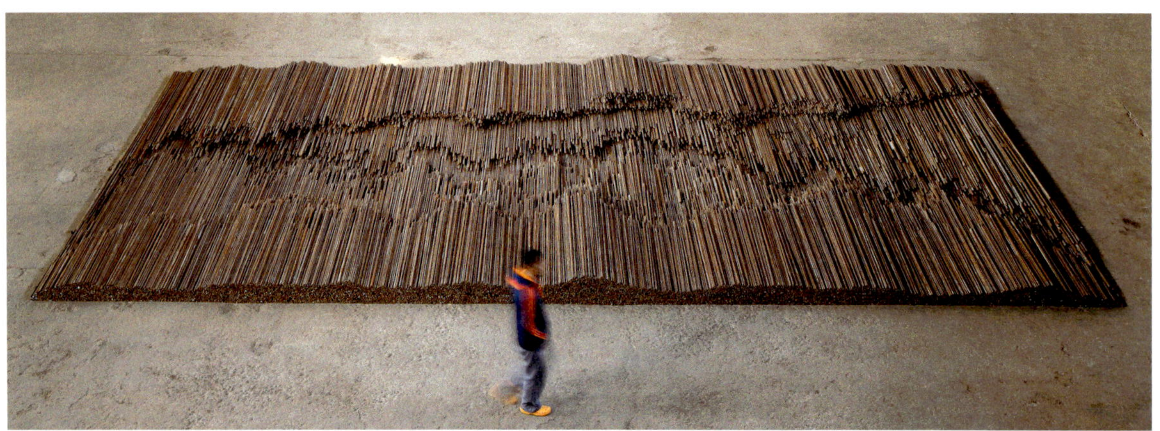

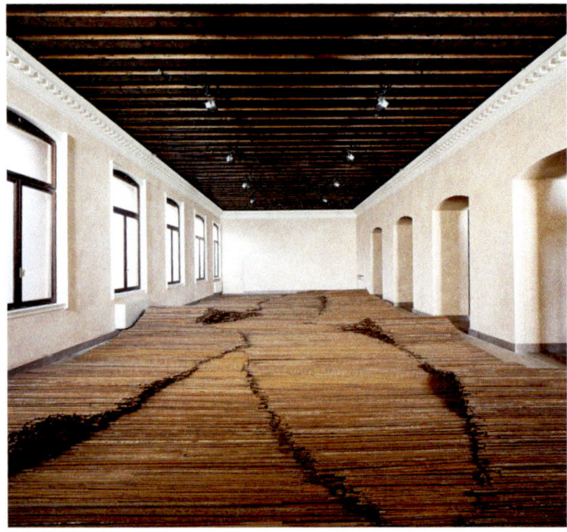

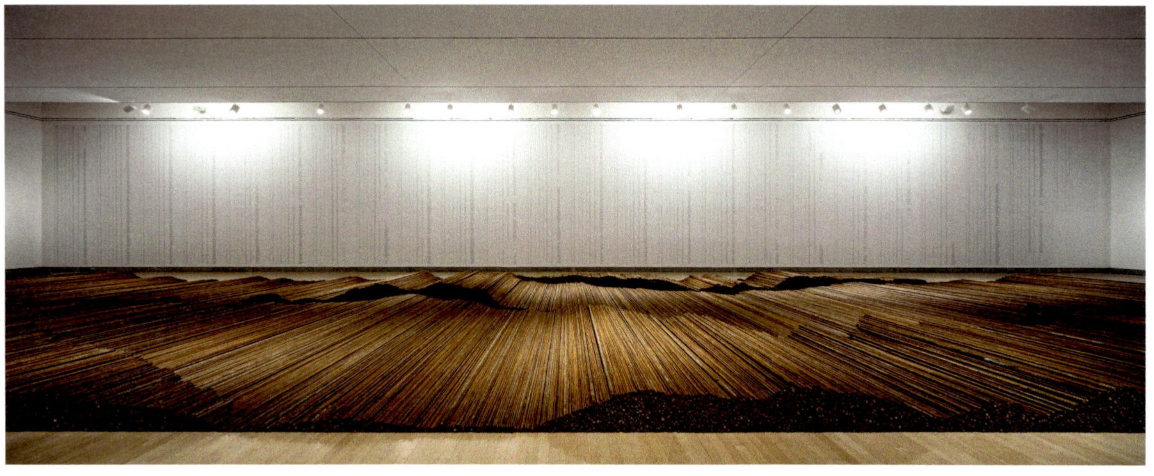

5
Straight, **2008–2012**,
steel rebar, 0.7 × 6 × 12 m
Installation view, Ai Weiwei's
Beijing studio

6
Straight, **2008–2012**,
steel rebar, 0.7 × 6.6 × 16.1 m
Installation view,
Zuecca Project Space,
Venice, 2013

7
Straight, **2008–2012**,
steel rebar, 0.7 × 6 × 25 m
Installation view, Brooklyn
Museum, New York, 2014

52

as a rather large container of rebar. Among the more than forty thousand tons of steel that China exports every year, it would certainly not arouse any suspicion. Just as many Asian martial arts use the principle of utilizing one's opponent's power for one's own ends, Ai Weiwei seems to have deflected the repressive power of the system into straightening the steel rods, so to speak.[19] It was only when the work was installed for the first time at the 2013 Venice Biennale that Ai Weiwei, who was still not authorized to leave the country at that time, had the work arranged as a rugged landscape shaken by seismic waves, reminiscent of the material's origin—as a quiet, heavy, oppressive monument for the over five thousand schoolchildren who lost their lives as a result of the tragic inter-play of natural forces and administrative failure.

Ai Weiwei used a similar strategy for **Laundromat**. Here, ostensibly brand-new clothes, clean and neatly sorted on clothes racks, are presented as in a de-partment store. They, too, are inverted readymades because the traces of their origin have been erased. After the closure of the refugee camp at Idomeni, Ai Weiwei washed and mended the clothes left be-hind by the residents, "like any parent would wash their own children's clothes."[20] It is precisely in this comparison that it becomes clear how much Ai Weiwei's inverted readymades belong to the paradigm of love and not prostitution. Ai Weiwei understood this as a "straight-ening out" of the ignoble living condi-tions of fugitives. On a porcelain plate in the exhibition, he is more explicit: Soldiers shoot tear gas at the refugees, but they hit the personification of Europe astride a bull (p. 133). The clothes in **Laundromat**, as well as the steel rods in **Straight**, become triple-inverted readymades. Firstly, they are in fact readymades, since they were found and not made. At the same time, however, they are not readymades, because they are historically informed. They are relics of historical events, not pure emanations of the world of com-modity. Secondly, they are not ready-made because Ai Weiwei has worked on them further. Conversely, however, it is precisely their reworking that makes them appear like Duchampian readymades,

brand-new and flawless. They are thus faked readymades, the historical emer-gence of which is captured in their material not in their form. Thirdly, Ai Weiwei reverses the relationship between the asserted readymades and their doubles by not emphasizing the individ-ual but rather by arranging the many. In doing so, he puts into effect an aesthetic of quantity, which is more than a mere gesture that overpowers the viewer, for it delves anew into the con-tradiction between individuality and mass and refers to the political and social circumstances of its origin. What is decisive here is that in the many dif-ferent arrangements by Ai Weiwei there is no hierarchical structure, just as there are hardly any vertical sculptures. No individual steel rod, no single piece of clothing, no lone stool, and certainly no sole sunflower seed claims a prominent position for itself. As readymades inverted several times, they are installed in non-hierarchical arrangements in which they neither align themselves with a sun nor generate super-forms. Instead, in their individuality, they are equally present in the space. This is the decidedly demo-cratic trait in Ai Weiwei's art, which never amalgamates the historical material into heroic forms but, rather, allows it to function, by virtue of its own presence, within its quantity.

1
See Jonathan Hay, **Sensuous Surfaces: The Decorative Object in Early Modern China** (Honolulu 2010).

2
"Rubble and Dinosaurs: Hans Ulrich Obrist in conversation with Ai Weiwei, 23 November 2013," in: Maurizio Bortolotti (ed.), **Ai Weiwei: Disposition**, exh. cat. Venice (London 2014), pp. 110–7, here p. 113.

3
Georg Wilhelm Friedrich Hegel, **The Science of Logic**, trans. George di Giovanni (Cambridge 2010), esp. pp. 298–301.

4
Karl Marx, "Chapter Eleven: The Rate and Mass of Surplus-Value," in: Karl Marx, **Capital: A Critique of Political Economy**, **Volume 1**, trans. Ben Fowkes (London 1990), p. 422.

5
Marshall McLuhan, **Understanding Media** (New York 1964), p. 7.

6
Carlos Spoerhase and Niklaus Wegmann, "Skalieren," in: Heiko Christians, Matthias Bickenbach, and Nikolaus Wegmann (eds.), **Historisches Wörterbuch des Mediengebrauchs**, vol. 2 (Cologne/Weimar/Vienna 2018), pp. 412–24, here p. 417 [translated].

7
Hegel 1999 (see note 3), esp. pp. 289–291.

8
Ludwig Wittgenstein, **Philosophical Investigations**, trans. G. E. M. Anscombe (Oxford 1986), § 251, p. 90. Wittgenstein calls those sentences grammatical that are correct but empty of content and without reference to the world.

9
Tania Eden, **Das Phänomen einer positiven Unbestimmtheit** (Paderborn 2017), p. 108.

10
Michael Fehr, "Das Würfelmuseum. Repräsentation einer Fiktion," in: Michael Fehr and Clemens Krümmel (eds.), **Aus dem Würfelmuseum.**

Zur Kritik der konstruktiven Kunst (Cologne 1990), pp. 9–11.

11
Obrist 2014 (see note 2), p. 112.

12
Ai Weiwei, in: Victor Maldonado "Harming the Art: Ai Weiwei's Wicked Sense of Humor," quoted in: Christian P. Sorace, "China's Lasts Communist: Ai Weiwei," in: **Critical Inquiry**, vol. 40, no. 2, 2014, pp. 396–419, here p. 396.

13
"[…] after Duchamp, I realized that being an artist is more about a lifestyle and attitude than producing some product. […] A way of looking at things." Ai Weiwei in conversation with Hans Ulrich Obrist, quoted in: Urs Stahel, "'After all, it's a mind game.': Interlacing and Communicating as an Art Form," in: Urs Stahel and Daniola Janser (eds.), **Ai Weiwei: Interlacing**, exh. cat. Fotomuseum Winthertur and Jeu de Paume, Paris (Göttingen 2011), pp. 62–9, here p. 65.

14
Sebastian Egenhofer, **Abstraktion – Kapitalismus – Subjektivität. Die Wahrheitsfunktion des Werks in der Moderne** (Munich 2008), p. 120. In particular, **Fountain**, the urinal declared as a work of art but not exhibited in 1917, was perceived as a criticism of the exhibition culture and the institutions of the art system.

15
Ibid., pp. 121–5.

16
Ibid., p. 135.

17
Ibid., p. 133 [translated].

18
Ibid., p. 137 [translated].

19
See also the concept of achieving victory "obliquely": François Jullien, "Ai Weiwei or the Art of Effective Variation," in: Susanne Gaensheimer (ed.), **Ai Weiwei, Romuald Karmakar, Santu Mofokeng, Dayanita Singh: German**

Pavilion 2013, **55th International Art Exhibition**, **La Biennale di Venezia**, exh. cat. Venice (Berlin 2013), pp. 66–73, esp. p. 70.

20
Ai Weiwei, quoted in: Jacoba Urist, "How Should Art Address Human Rights?" in: **The Atlantic**, April 4, 2017, https://www.theatlantic.com/entertainment/archive/2017/04/how-should-art-address-human-rights/521520. (last accessed on March 1, 2019).

CHAPTER II

Chapter II

On May 12, 2008, at 2:28 p.m. local time, the earth trembled in the Chinese province of Sichuan. With a magnitude of 7.9 on the Richter scale, it was one of the most devastating earthquakes ever in China. More than eighty-five thousand people lost their lives, including over five thousand schoolchildren.

Since October 2005, Ai Weiwei had published new posts on his Internet blog on an almost daily basis. The Internet had become one of his main forums. In the days after the catastrophe, no new posts were published. He then launched an initiative to find out how many schoolchildren had been killed in the earthquake. The authorities remained silent about the numbers. However, one striking fact was that an above-average number of schoolchildren were among the victims. There were two reasons for this: Firstly, the quake occurred in the early afternoon of a working day, during schooltime, and secondly, an above-average number of the buildings destroyed were schools. The suspicion that an inadequate quality in construction had led schools to collapse, while neighboring administrative buildings survived the earthquake, was subsequently confirmed.

After official inquiries failed to provide satisfactory answers, Ai Weiwei started a "Citizens' Investigation." He went to the earthquake region with a team of volunteers to speak with witnesses and affected parents to determine how many children were actually missing and to find out their names. He was, however, not the only person with this mission to come to the region of their own volition. Independently of Ai Weiwei, activists such as Tan Zuoren also tried to get at the reason behind the devastation. In their publications on the earthquake disaster, Christian P. Sorace and Bin Xu traced the various efforts of the activists to better understand the situation and the cover-up undertaken by authorities.[1] Today, there is no doubt that the defective construction of the schools is attributable to corruption at the level of local politics.

In April 2009, Ai Weiwei published the number determined by his team of schoolchildren killed. Shortly thereafter, on May 28, 2009, his blog was shut down and completely deleted. At the same time, Ai Weiwei developed several works in memory of the children killed, such as the monumental Chinese characters made up of children's backpacks hung on the façade of the Haus der Kunst in Munich in conjunction with his exhibition **So Sorry** which opened in October 2009: "She lived happily for seven years in this world." The sentence came from a mother whose young daughter lost her life in one of the school buildings. In an Internet-based, participatory project, Ai Weiwei had people from all over the world speak the names he had researched of the children killed; the recorded sound files were then sent to him. From these, he assembled an approximately seven-hour-long version of the names read aloud. He had employees of his studio shout the names and produced a video in which the names were reeled off like the never-ending closing credits of a feature film. His prime concern was that the names should never be forgotten, that the victims should be given names. At the same time, he strove to convey a sense of the enormous number of innocent children who had lost their lives. In this exhibition, the names are summarized as a tabular list on wallpaper in the Grabbe Halle of K20. Although written in small letters, the list takes up about seventy square meters of wall space.

The most monumental and, at the same time, most complex work by Ai Weiwei regarding the earthquake catastrophe is spread out on the floor of the Grabbe Halle in K20: **Straight** (2008–2012). It consists of 164 tons of rebar, which Ai Weiwei salvaged from destroyed school complexes and had transported to his studio in Beijing. The steel bars were bent and entangled with each other, still partly tainted with concrete residue. For **Straight**, Ai Weiwei had the rods straightened by metalworkers. Thus, their current form is also a reflection of social conditions in the globalized industrial world. **Sunflower Seeds** was produced by one thousand six hundred people over the course of several years; and **Straight** took three years to complete. In this way, both artworks are also manifestations of working time, of human effort. The bars seem to regain their factory-new form. Contrary to the state they were in when recovered, their present appearance no

longer recalls the violence of the earthquake; yet they played a tragic role in the story of corruption and the irresponsibility of authorities towards the schoolchildren who died under the rubble. The title **Straight** means both "in line" in the sense of "being put in line," but it also has the connotation of "putting something right." The idea of transparency also resonates in this: "to say something straight out." Now, for the first time in Europe and for only the second time ever, this work is being presented in its entirety.

In exhibition spaces, until now, the work has assumed the form of a floor sculpture, itself reminiscent of a rugged, shaken landscape. In this form, varying quantities of steel rods were arranged, each time depending on the size of the exhibition space and the bearing capacity of its floor. Therefore, the material form of this work in exhibition spaces is at times larger and at times smaller, sometimes higher and sometimes flatter. At the Hirshhorn Museum in Washington, D.C., it even bent along the characteristic curve of the building. In every case, however, in addition to the mere presence of the steel bars, with their inscribed history of murderous corruption and a fatal lack of building supervision, the shape of a landscape shaken by the earthquake was always inherent to the work.

For the first time, Ai Weiwei has done without this form for the exhibition in K20. Instead, with the greatest possible radicality, he refers back to the collected and straightened material. The steel bars are not laid out on the floor but are rather in the transport crates in which they already travelled before to Tokyo, Venice, Washington, D.C., Toronto, London, and São Paulo. Their placement is remotely reminiscent of the jagged lines of the floor sculpture at past stops.

The transport crates thus become part of the installation. The boxes tell of the previous exhibition venues, of the mobility of an enormous mass of rebar within the global art system. At the same time, however, they are also reminiscent of open coffins. In Düsseldorf, **Straight** is tougher, more brittle, more uncompromising, and more conceptual. Here, the rebar of the Sichuan schools appears even more out of place because it refuses the sculptural form that is commonly expected in an art museum. When this form is denied, the focus is once again on the material itself, on its mass, bent back into shape, packed, shipped, and exhibited: 164 tons of reinforcing steel entangled in the unnecessary death of thousands of children.

In their immensity, the steel bars are eternally linked to the list of names. In this exhibition, **Straight** is the second installation—after **Sunflower Seeds** in the Klee Halle—which addresses the question of the individual's place within society. The authorities refused to name the children. On the anniversary of the earthquake, Ai Weiwei wrote in one of his last blog posts: "Those children arrived, and were carelessly sent off, their limbs rashly buried by strangers. Even quicker than their passing was the speed with which some hoped they would be completely and utterly forgotten. The lives of those children were so short, it's as if they never existed."[2]

1
Christian P. Sorace, **Shaken Authority**: China's Communist Party and the 2008 Sichuan Earthquake (Ithaca, NY/London 2017); Bin Xu, **The Politics of Compassion: The Sichuan Earthquake and Civic Engagement in China** (Stanford 2017).

2
Ai Weiwei, "Memory Day: Posted on May 12, 2009," in: Ai Weiwei, **Ai Weiwei's Blogs: Writings, Interviews, and Digital Rants, 2006–2009**, ed. and trans. Lee Ambrozy (Cambridge, MA 2011), pp. 224f., here p. 224.

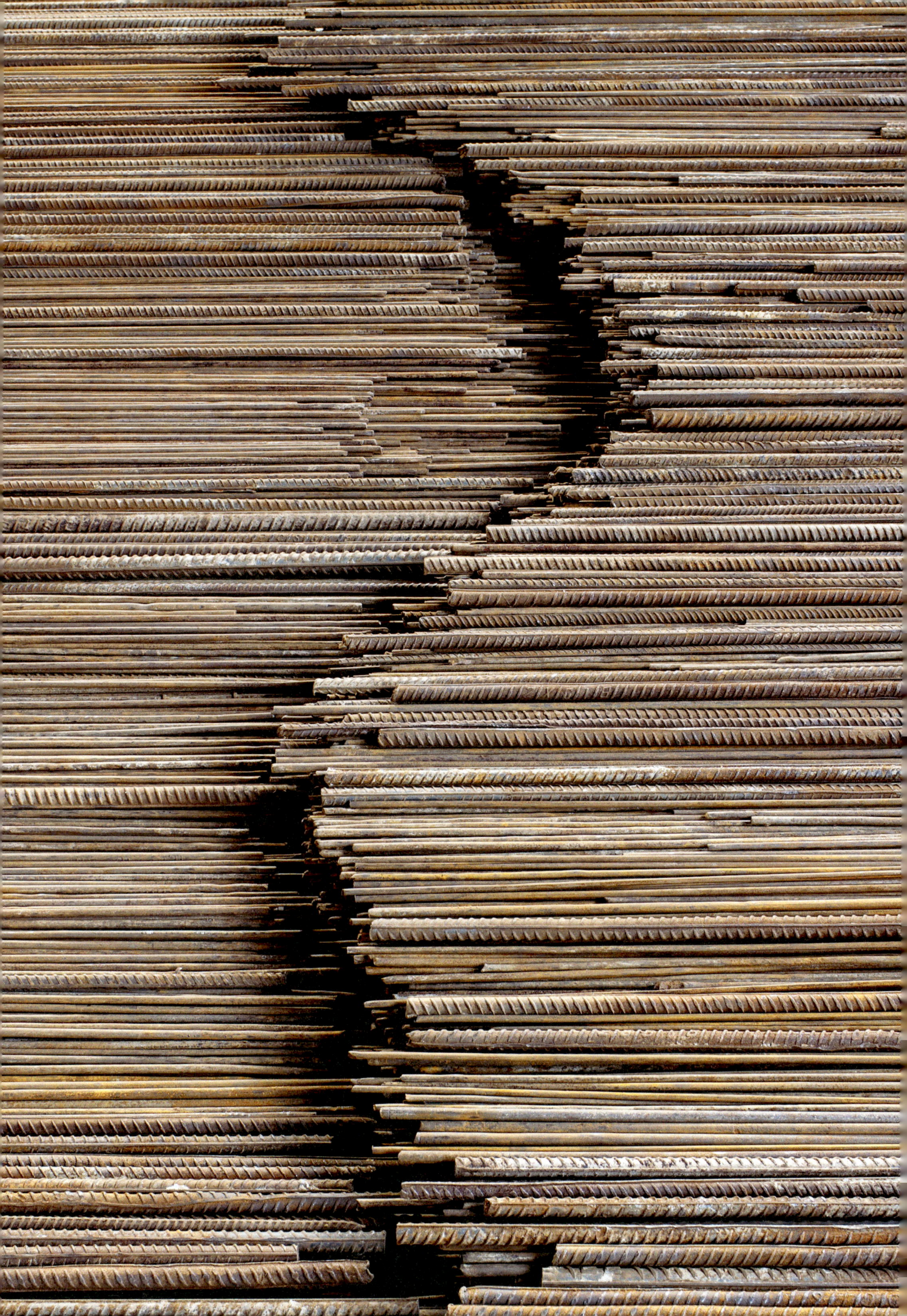

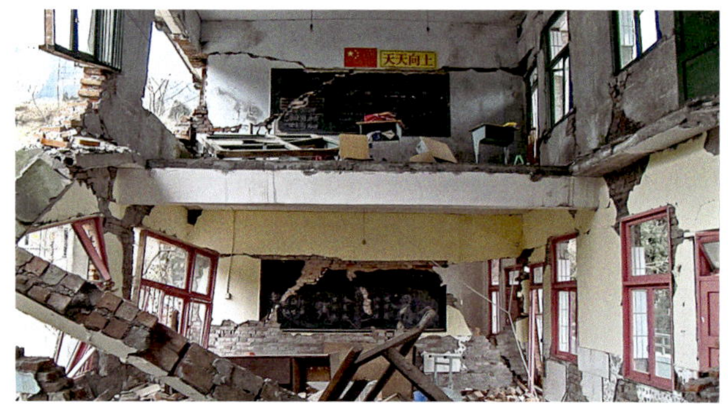 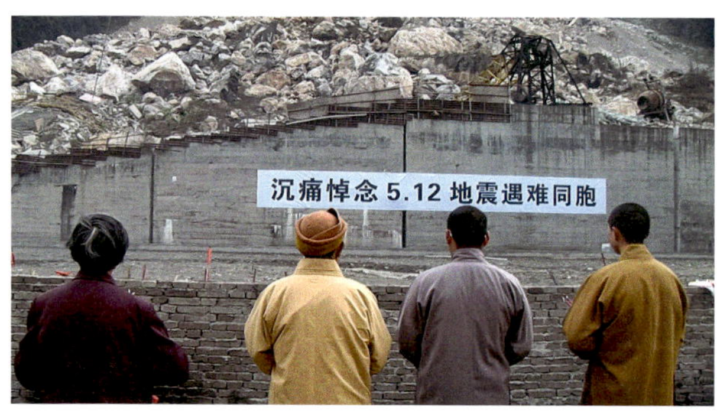

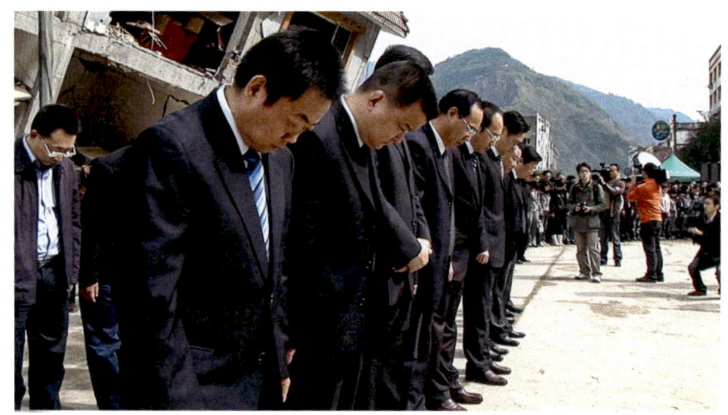 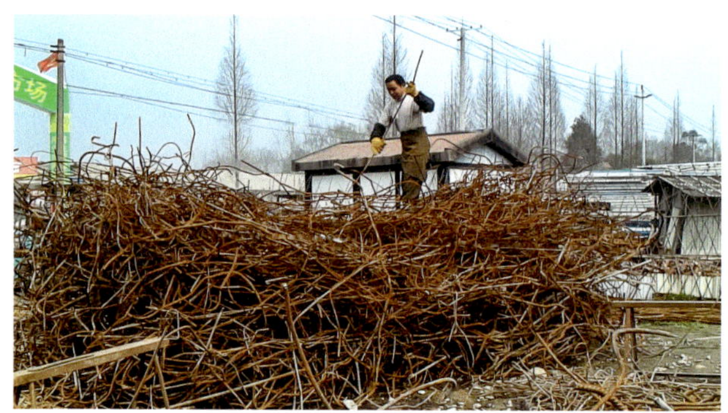

Straight, 2015
Video, color, sound, 15'4"

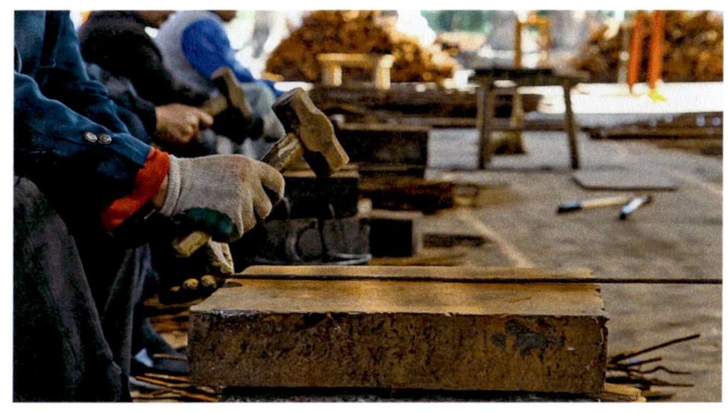

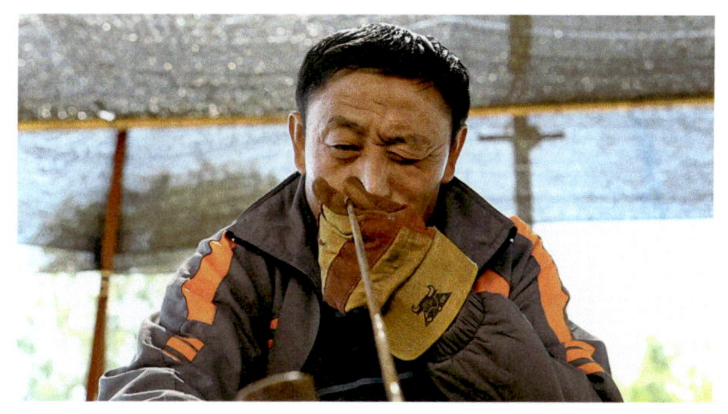

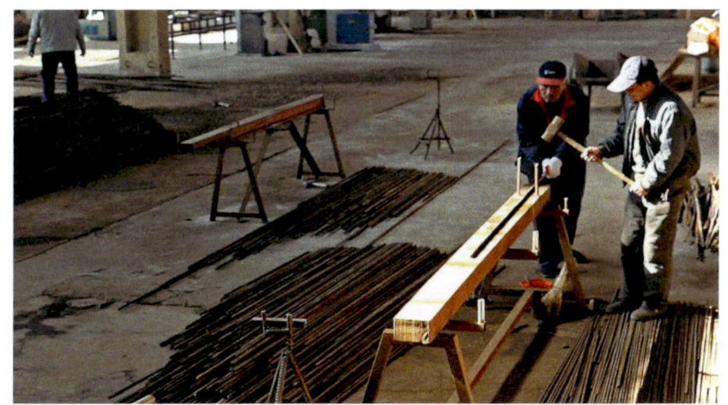

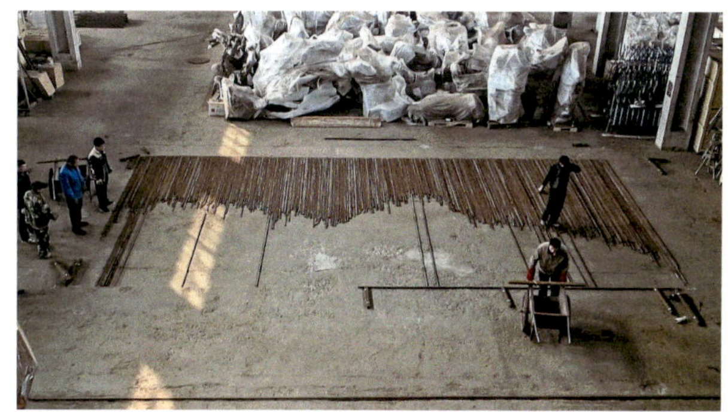

Straight, 2008–2012
Steel rebar,
164 tons of rebar,
Dimensions variable.
Installation view, Oca,
São Paulo, 2018

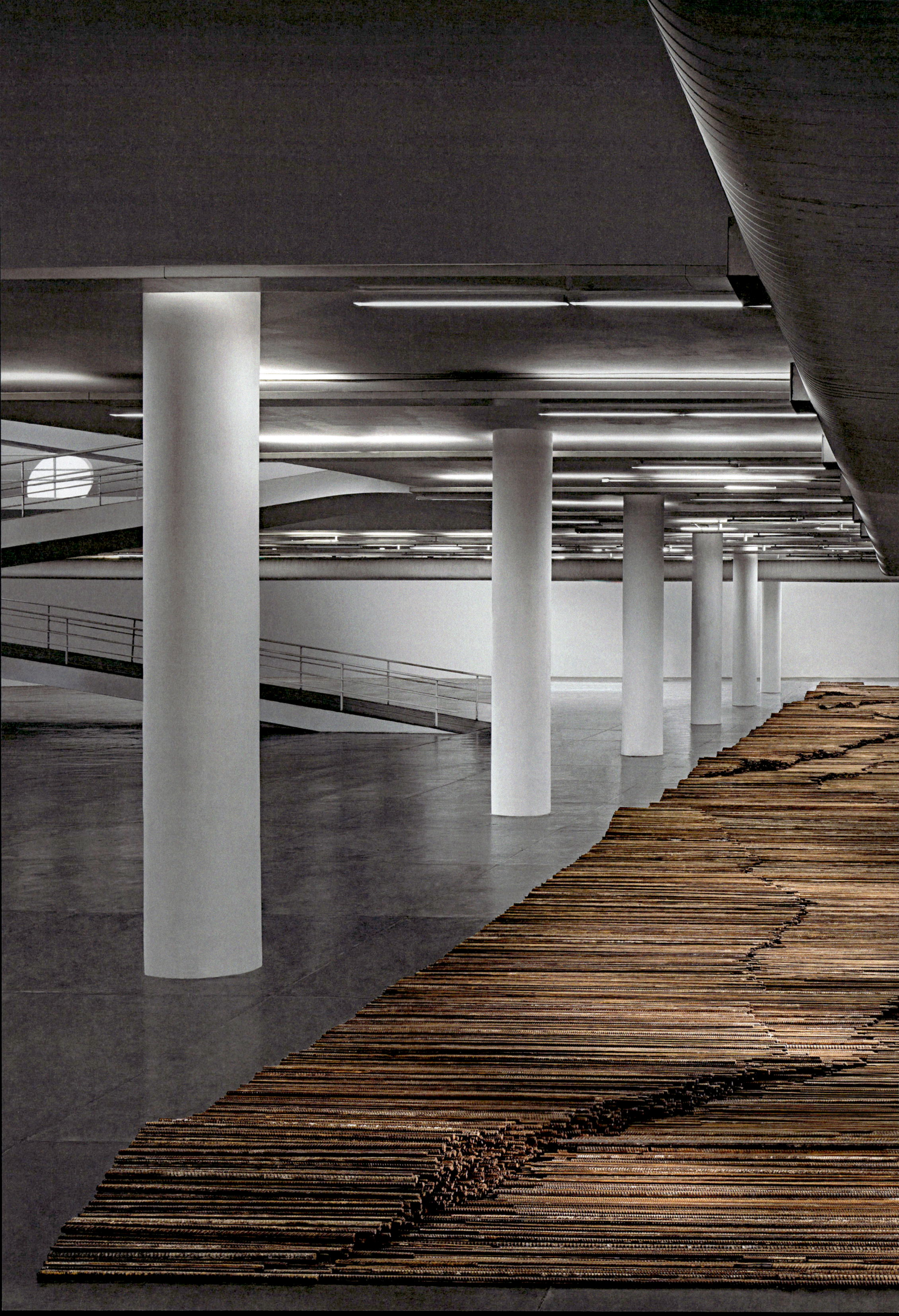

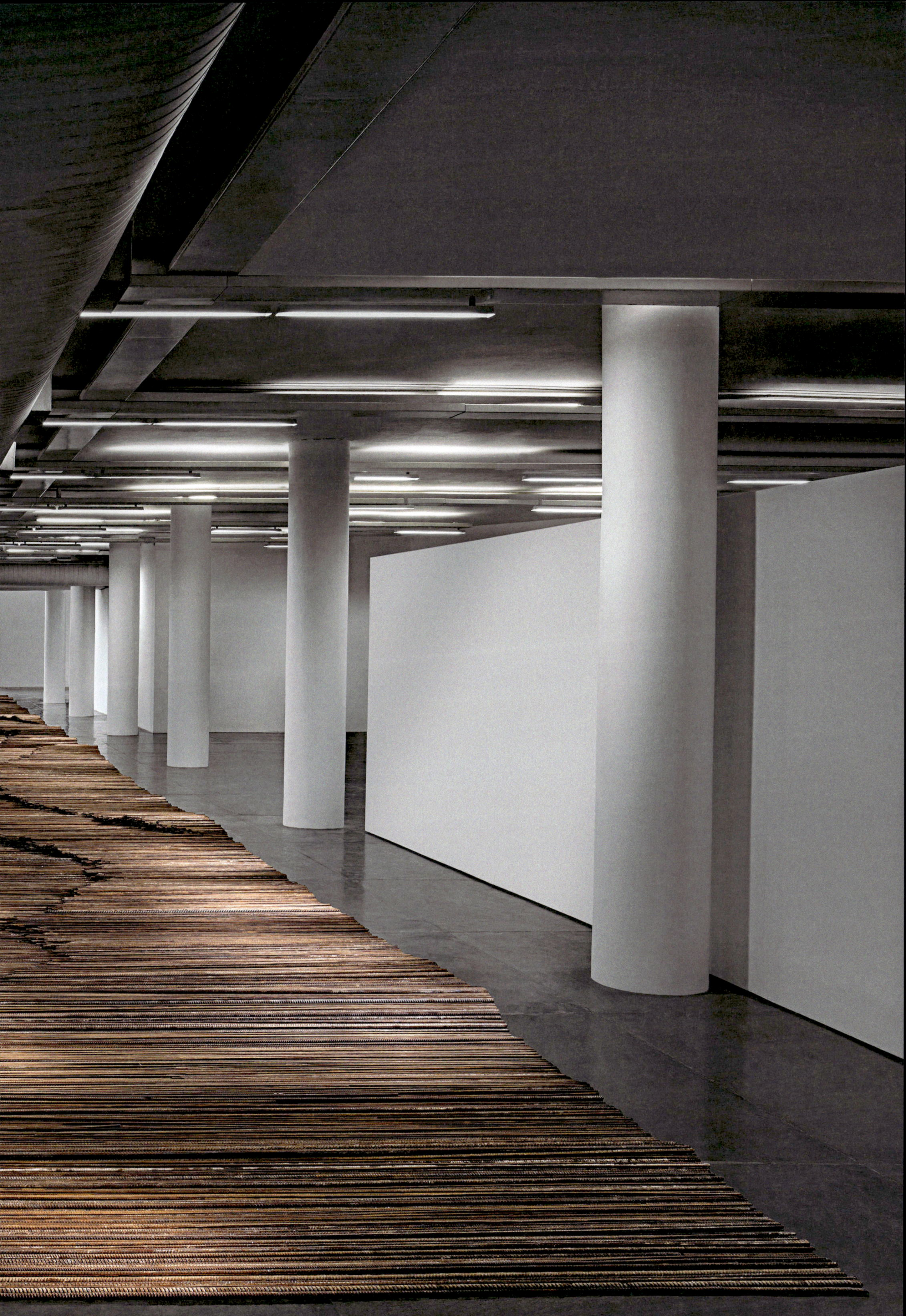

Straight, 2008–2012
Steel rebar, crates
164 tons of rebar, 142 crates
Dimensions variable.
Installation view K20,
Kunstsammlung
Nordrhein-Westfalen, 2019

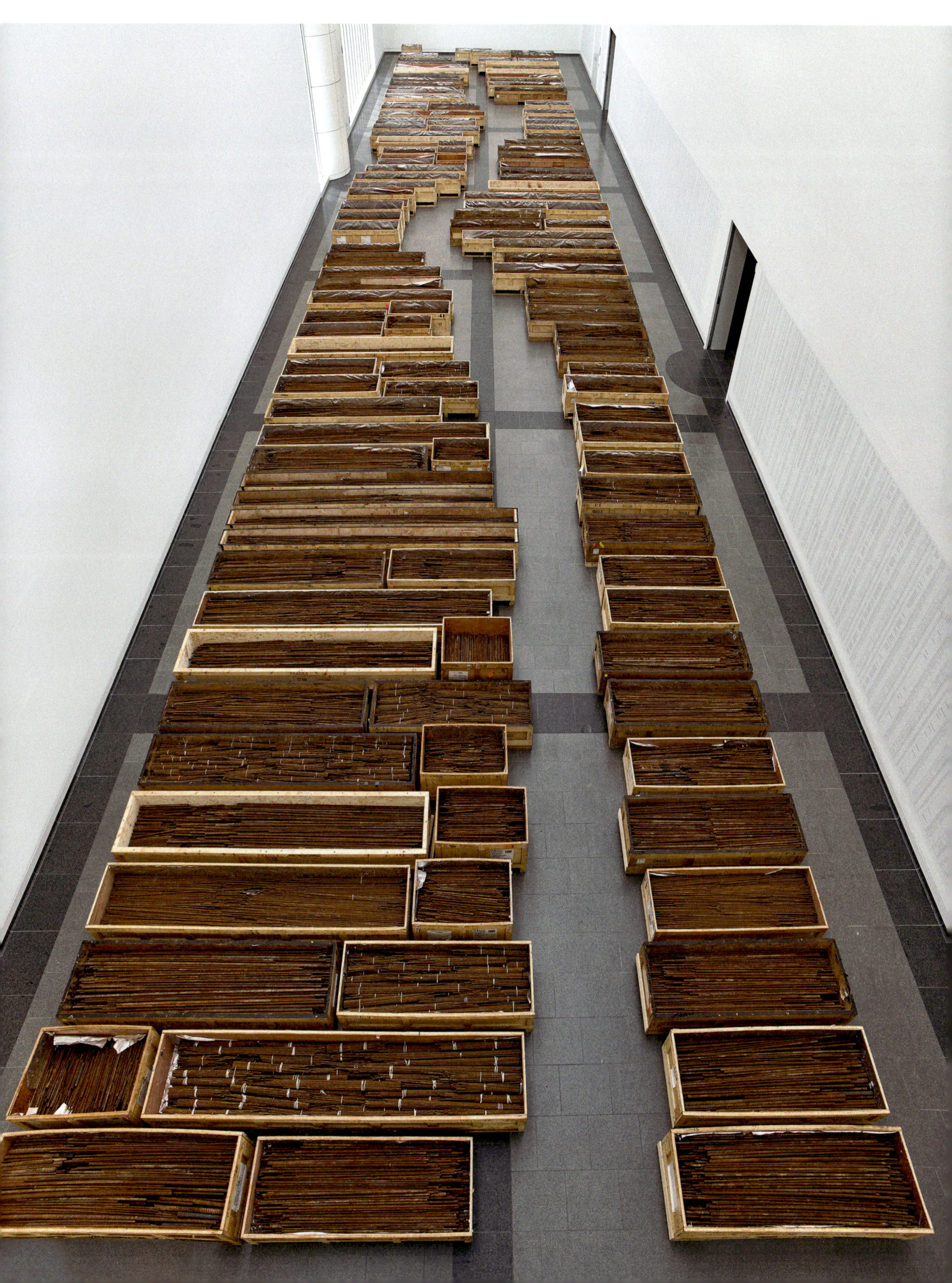

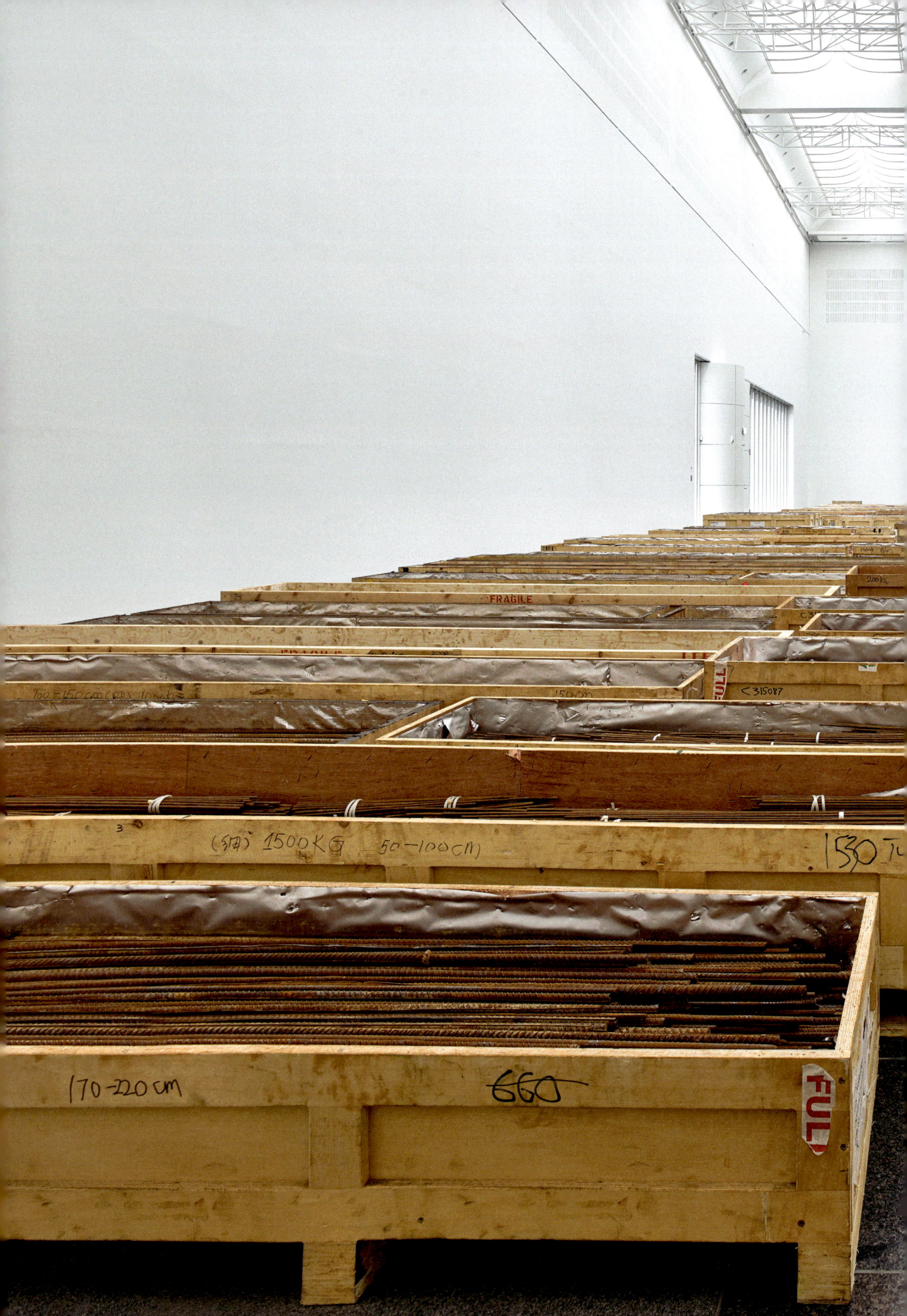

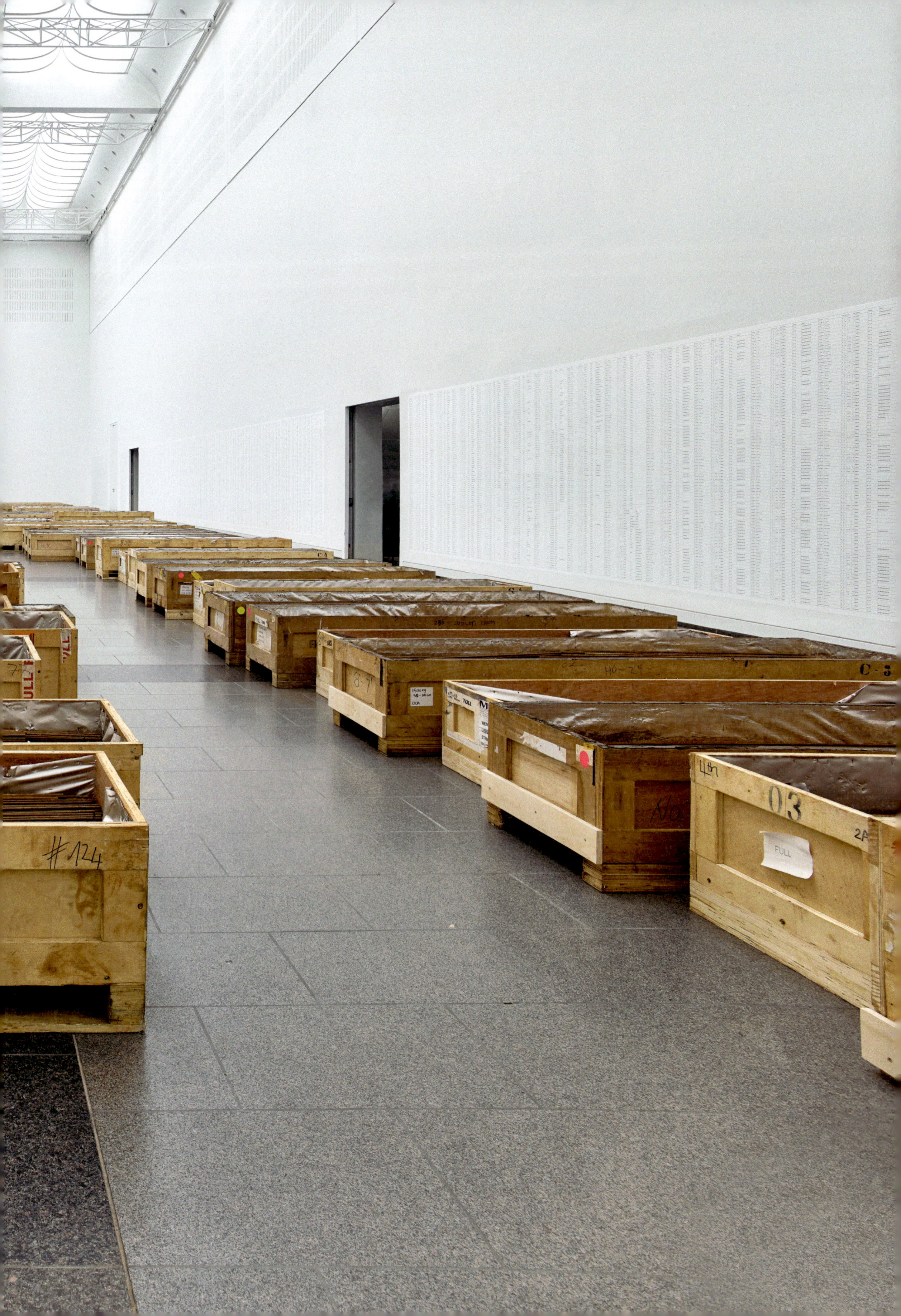

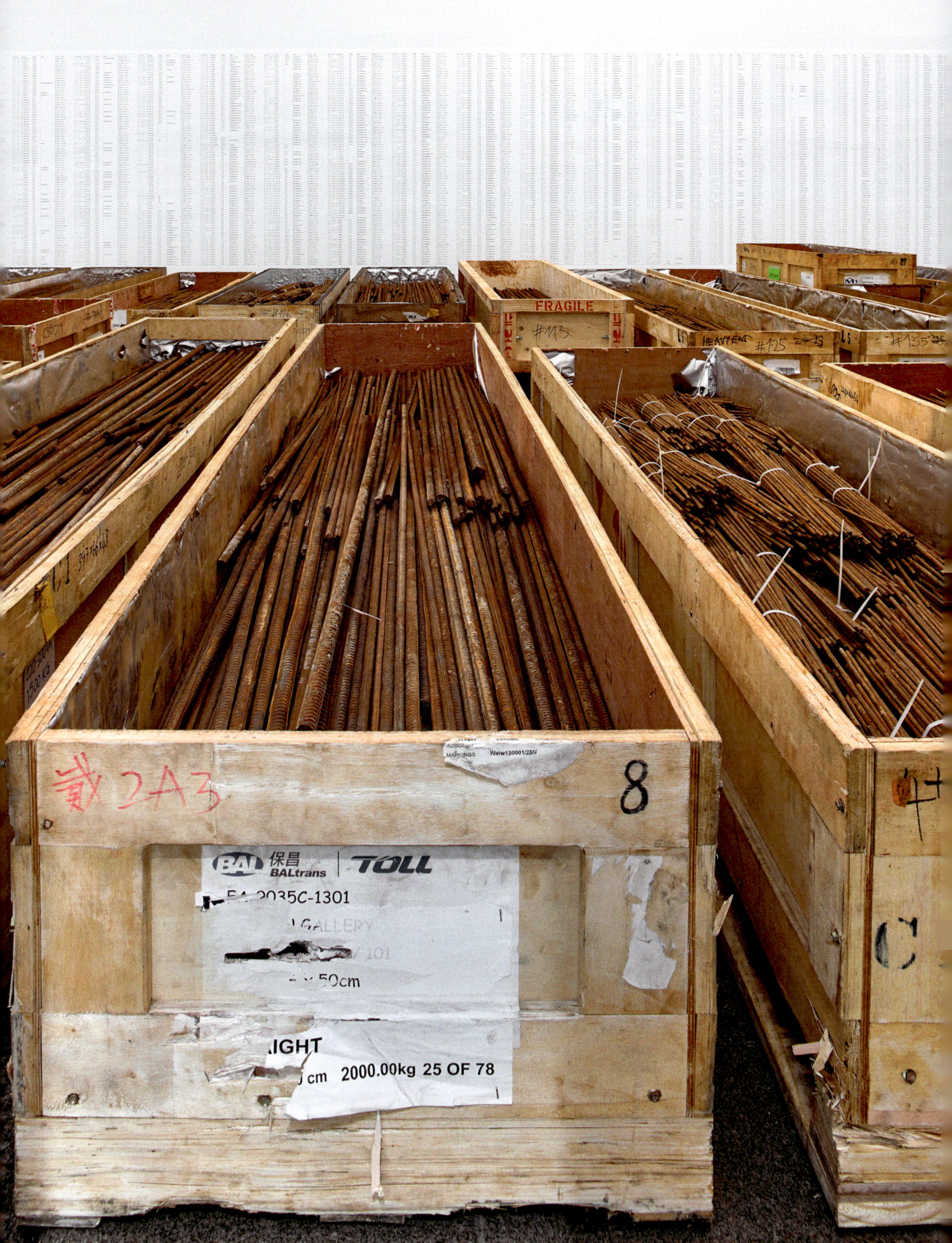
FRAGILE
#113.
HEAVY EM #125
#135
2A3
8
BAL 保昌 BALtrans TOLL
GALLERY
101
50cm
IGHT
2000.00kg 25 OF 78
C

序号	姓名	NAME	性别	SEX	生辰	年龄	所在学校	所在班级	家庭住址
1	何若冰	He Ruobing	女	F	8/23/01	7岁	八角镇中心小学	一年级	什邡市八角镇五马村七组
2	李国成	Li Guocheng	男	M	10/17/00	8岁	八角镇中心小学	一年级	什邡市八角镇天桥村八组
3	王少成	Wang Shaocheng	男	M	3/15/01	7岁	八角镇中心小学	一年级	什邡市八角镇杉木林村五组
4	易贞勇	Yi Zhenyong	男	M	4/28/01	7岁	八角镇中心小学	一年级	什邡市八角镇五马村六组
5	张鑫宇	Zhang Xinyu	女	F	9/15/01	7岁	八角镇中心小学	一年级	什邡市八角镇五马村六组
6	王美玲	Wang Meilin	女	F	4/27/98	10岁	八角镇中心小学	三年级	什邡市八角镇五马村十组
7	李竺宜	Li Zhuyi	男	M	8/29/96	12岁	八角镇中心小学	五年级	什邡市八角镇天桥村一组
8	董杰	Dong Jie	男	M	6/28/97	11岁	八一学校	四年级一班	江油市八一乡阳明村十一组
9	肖遥	Xiao Yao	男	M	-/-/96	12岁	坝底初中	初一二班	北川县坝底乡坝底村一社
10	秦英	Qin Ying	女	F	-/-/01	7岁	白方小学	幼儿班	
11	王兴怡	Wang Xingyi	女	F	8/23/04	4岁	白方小学	幼儿班	绵竹市汉旺镇武都村
12	张宇	Zhang Yu	男	M	-/-/04	4岁	白方小学	幼儿班	
13	陈思思	Chen Sisi	女	F	-/-/98	10岁	白方小学	三年级一班	
14	邓世竹	Deng Shizhu	女	F	8/25/98	10岁	白方小学	三年级一班	绵竹市武都镇八角村十二组
15	甘云竹	Gan Yunzhu	女	F	-/-/98	10岁	白方小学	三年级一班	
16	高瑞阳	Gao Ruiyang	男	M	-/-/99	9岁	白方小学	三年级一班	
17	何志秋	He Zhiqiu	女	F	-/-/99	9岁	白方小学	三年级一班	
18	胡文彬	Hu Wenlin	男	M	-/-/98	10岁	白方小学	三年级一班	
19	甯竹	Ning Zhu	女	F	-/-/99	9岁	白方小学	三年级一班	
20	彭世超	Peng Shichao	男	M	-/-/99	9岁	白方小学	三年级一班	
21	乔良	Qiao Liang	男	M	-/-/99	9岁	白方小学	三年级一班	
22	卿超	Qing Chao	男	M	-/-/99	9岁	白方小学	三年级一班	
23	唐杰林	Tang Jielin	女	F	-/-/99	9岁	白方小学	三年级一班	
24	万文	Wan Wen	女	F	-/-/99	9岁	白方小学	三年级一班	
25	席春银	Xi Chunyin	男	M	-/-/99	9岁	白方小学	三年级一班	
26	杨菊	Yang Ju	女	F	-/-/99	9岁	白方小学	三年级一班	
27	李双	Li Shuang	男	M	12/15/00	8岁	百花中心小学	二年级一班	
28	刘文杰	Liu Wenjie	男	M	-/-/99	9岁	百花中心小学	二年级一班	
29	胡伟	Hu Wei	男	M	11/12/99	9岁	百花中心小学	三年级一班	
30	唐文杰	Tang Wenjie	男	M	1/1/97	11岁	百花中心小学	三年级一班	
31	王家秀	Wang Jiaxiu	女	F	-/-/98	10岁	百花中心小学	三年级一班	
32	王婷婷	Wang Tingting	女	F	8/16/98	10岁	百花中心小学	三年级一班	

**Names of the Student
Earthquake Victims
Found by the Citizens'
Investigation**, 2008–2011
Wallpaper (5,219 names)
Dimensions variable

	姓名	拼音	性别	M/F	出生日期	年龄	学校	班级	家庭住址
33	杨浩	Yang Jie	男	M	-/-/97	11岁	百花中心小学	三年级一班	
34	杨康	Yang Tang	男	M	-/-/97	11岁	百花中心小学	三年级一班	
35	李艾玲	Li Ailin	女	F			板桥学校		绵竹市
36	李红	Li Hong	女	F	-/-/90	18岁	板桥中心学校		
37	蔡青春	Cai Qingchun	男	M	1/6/92	16岁	北川职中	2010级机2	北川县桃龙乡桃花村
38	蔡山林	Cai Shanlin	男	M	9/18/91	17岁	北川职中	2010级机2	北川县禹里乡白林村
39	柴发菊	Chai Faju	女	F	7/28/93	15岁	北川职中	2010级电信4	北川县马槽乡木坪村
40	陈昌达	Chen Changda	男	M	8/26/93	15岁	北川职中	2010级机3	北川县禹里乡沿河村八组
41	陈丹	Chen Dan	女	F	11/30/89	19岁	北川职中	2008级电工	北川县擂鼓镇银定村
42	陈定强	Chen Dingqiang	男	M	-/-/90	18岁	北川职中	2010级机2	北川县漩坪乡四松村
43	陈浩	Chen Jie	男	M	1/5/93	15岁	北川职中	2010级机2	北川县桂溪乡桂溪村
44	陈红	Chen Hong	女	F	11/24/92	16岁	北川职中	2010级机2	北川县桃龙乡铁龙村
45	陈晓君	Chen Xiaojun	女	F	9/18/92	15岁	北川职中	2010级电信4	北川县擂鼓镇茶坊村
46	陈永亮	Chen Yongliang	男	M	11/21/91	17岁	北川职中	2010级机2	北川县禹里乡紫阳村
47	杜贵林	Du Guilin	男	M	8/14/91	17岁	北川职中	2010级机2	北川县桃龙乡桃红村
48	范敏	Fan Min	男	M	9/25/92	16岁	北川职中	2010级机3	北川县禹里乡沿河村
49	付广虎	Fu Guanghu	男	M	7/18/92	16岁	北川职中	2010级机3	北川县陈家坝乡西河村
50	高德贵	Gao Degui	男	M	12/30/92	16岁	北川职中	2010级机3	北川县桃龙乡桃红村
51	苟勇	Gou Yong	男	M	4/18/92	16岁	北川职中	2010级机2	北川县禹里乡三坪村
52	何建勇	He Jianyong	男	M	-/-/93	15岁	北川职中	2010级机2	北川县擂鼓镇盖头村
53	侯光平	Hou Guangping	男	M	4/29/92	16岁	北川职中	2010级机2	北川县坝底乡清平村一社
54	侯国平	Hou Guoping	男	M			北川职中		
55	姜庆	Jiang Qing	女	F	7/3/92	16岁	北川职中	2010级电信4	北川县擂鼓镇郭牛村302号
56	姜焮淇	Jiang Xinqi	男	M	12/11/91	17岁	北川职中	2010级机3	北川县擂鼓镇柳林村
57	蒋仕林	Jiang Shilin	男	M	6/1/92	16岁	北川职中	2010级机2	北川县桂溪乡桂溪村
58	寇洁	Kou Jie	女	F	8/17/92	16岁	北川职中	2010级升学	北川县陈家坝乡双埝村
59	寇云星	Kou Yunxing	男	M	-/-/93	16岁	北川职中	2010级电信3	北川县陈家坝乡樱桃沟村
60	况兴建	Kuang Xingjian	男	M	12/27/91	17岁	北川职中	2010级机3	北川县桃龙乡铁龙村
61	兰菊华	Lan Juhua	女	F	-/-/94	14岁	北川职中	2010级电信4	北川县小坝乡大华村
62	李昌波	Li Changbo	男	M	-/-/93	15岁	北川职中	2010级机2	北川县擂鼓镇麻柳村
63	李长刚	Li Changgang	男	M	-/-/93	15岁	北川职中	2010级机2	北川县擂鼓镇麻柳村
64	李成述	Li Chengshu	男	M	-/-/92	16岁	北川职中	2010级机2	北川县贯岭乡岩林村
65	李刚	Li Gang	男	M	-/-/91	17岁	北川职中		

Calling for Reinforcement

Rembert Hüser

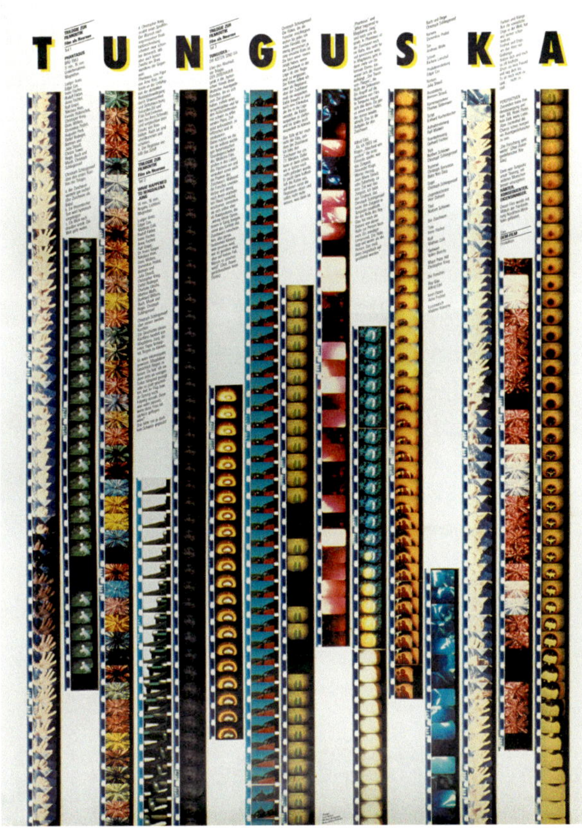

1
Poster for **Tunguska –
die Kisten sind da**, film by
Christoph Schlingensief,
1983/1984
Copyright: Filmgalerie 451

Something is being built. Only where exactly is not yet clear. The crates are here. And the first films are already running. Christoph Schlingensief's **Tunguska** from 1983/1984 comes to mind, for example, with its columns of film strips, as the letters announce on the poster, three avant-garde researchers take inventory. What's being held in store for us? What do the logistics of the whole undertaking look like?[1]

There is Ai Weiwei's complete stock of rebar, of which we have heard so much, which we have also seen in photos. And we had imagined what it might have looked like live as we stood in a space together with it, walking around it; but it is still—or has already, once again, been—crated. We came too early. Or too late. In any event, the crates are open. We can still venture a glance or two, reconstruct and project connections and context.

The boxed part of the unboxed exhibition makes everything even more difficult. And helps to explain the other part a little bit. With such dimensions, there is not much you can do on short notice. We have a lot of material which, to some degree, can be seen. Which, presented in this way, has changed its form, its figure, and has a different effect. What is otherwise never seen is suddenly invested with permanence. (But wasn't that always the case with **Straight**?)

Now, suddenly, we have such quantities of protection. The crates on the floor of the Grabbe Halle in K20 are tightly packed. 164 tons of rebar, from one wall to the other. With small paths, space to walk around them, to be able to inspect everything from different angles. Always along the wall. Protection front and back, on the side, 0.7 × 9.4 × 44.3 meters. 286 square meters. 1,000 kilos per meter. Protection without end. And now, on top of that, with protection around the protection. New walls between the old ones. The new wooden appearance of the rebar sculpture. And even more weight.

But the protection here, which—despite the hectic pace of all things provisional, seems to have all the time in the world, to be a haven of tranquility, almost frozen in movement—also hangs in the air, even though it lies there in crates. These metal rods are not inherently grounded. They do not function on their own, even when they come en masse. Or in loads, sorted by size. They first need assistance. As impressive as they are, something is still missing. The rods must first be put in a shuttering formwork, in a cavity, and there cast with concrete. Then, they can adapt themselves to their respective task. Change. And thus make a structure load-bearing. In the present form, bar on bar, crate next to crate, in this simulation of a building, it is still bare protection, purely an assertion, almost as if steel joists from a warehouse of building material had been delivered to the wrong location. And the workers, without whom nothing would be possible, are nowhere to be seen. But this rebar belongs here, in any event; it is quite clearly a form. They have a new purpose. The shuttering formwork in the Kunstsammlung Nord-rhein-Westfalen, on the property adjacent to the former Düsseldorf District Court, is communication in a very specific, concrete space and its echo over the years. The work resonates accordingly with this former site of justice. It is not just a piece of the People's Republic of China that's lying about, located here. As though it had just been flown in and stored temporarily. It doesn't appear to be jumbled. Or in any way fragile. These aren't packs of pick-up sticks. Nothing is trembling here. On the contrary, this compact, rust-brown material, which gazes out at us from its casing, radiates a peculiar security in its almost geological tranquility. Tenaciousness. Strength. Power. As well as gentleness.

The puzzling mass of protection pushed together in front of us, which we did not expect to find here in this public building, is exhibited as yet unprocessed protection in a state of transport. An offer. Rods with the potential to protect. A great deal of this. We have more than enough rebar. There's no shortage of it. You all can have some. Steel shouldn't be a problem. The heap of protection is ready for collection at any time. And anything but weary. Metal rods on the move. Which is why the protection is tense at the same time. It lurks. Is ready. Waiting only to make itself useful, to get going, to get down to work. Into the next con-crete situation that requires it. The next building project. The next performance

test. Protection that waits for us. People who know what to do with it. Reinforce-ment officers. People who can tackle the job. Who, first and foremost, can actually handle so much steel.

And as long as the material waits—and, at the same time, materializes this waiting as a potential of future, holds on to it, insists on it—it itself becomes an image and a landscape. An artificial, sedimented container landscape of building mate-rials, an area of demolition and develop-ment, the layout of a sunroom between unglazed walls with a roof above, a rust-brown sea of iron in pounds. Incorporated Land art. Steel sculpture. A small settle-ment, a reloading point. A world of rods with gaps and incisions in a display case. Density, abundance, and scarcity. In pieces, iron has once again become earth.

So this mass in front of us is both scrap and the separation of scrap. The protec-tion spread out on the floor—which is usually invisible, hidden from view, in-serted in stairs and ceilings and fulfilling its function there—has been extracted from heaps of rubble that have a name. The remains of the great earthquake of Wenchuan in Sichuan province on May 12, 2008, which claimed roughly eighty thousand lives. The impression of geo-logical time and its many layers, which is emphasized by the rods, some of which had peered out of the earth, is suddenly confronted with the time of the event. And becomes bitter in the process. Thus, every single one of these rods was already under way. Had its purpose. All this rebar, which has now been re-appropriated, in this re-enactment of the situation prior to their incorporation into the supporting elements of the Chinese schools, all this material in the crates spread out across the floor, the bones of the broken build-ings in rebar ossuaries, once looked quite different. Every single one of them. All of these rods are used. Have already been immersed in life. Were already used in a way that was fundamentally wrong.

And were later restored through arduous toil and sent into the world on a journey. They were not simply abandoned. Thus, the protection, which never was, has been given a second chance. Has been collec-ted in crates of various sizes and invited after the Fifty-Fifth Venice Biennale to

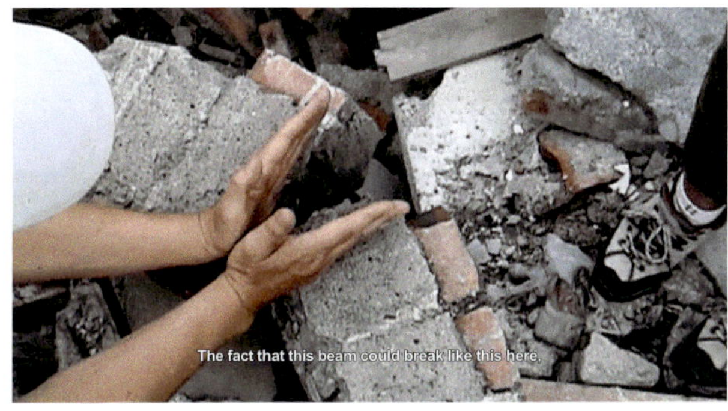

2

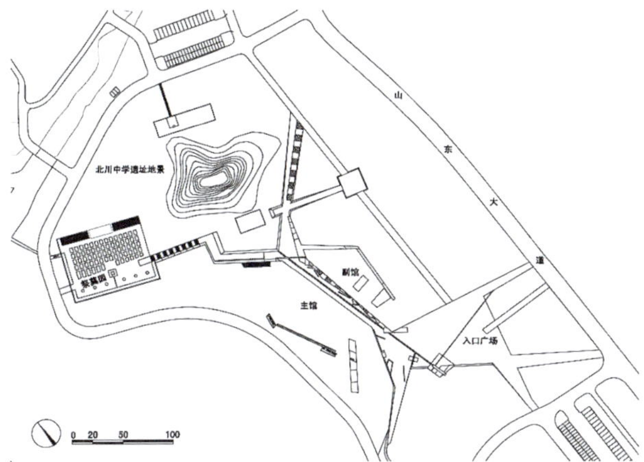

3

2
Wenchuan Rebar,
2008–2012, video, color,
sound, 18'30", film stills

3
Cai Yongjie: **Map of the
National Earthquake
Memorial**, 2013

Tokyo, to Washington, Toronto, London and, for the first time ever in its totality, to the Oca in São Paulo and then—in a different form—to the Kunstsammlung Nordrhein-Westfalen in order to, first and foremost, recount a story. To tell its story to the world. The silent congregation of protection comprised of standardized individual parts with its diagonally ribbed surface from the rolling mill, which is intended to guarantee greater adhesion when joining concrete and steel, has since resurfaced in various places and in various forms. It is moveable as a whole and can be scrutinized over and over again. This time, in 2019, protection will attend a hearing on accountability in K20, directly adjacent to the former court house. The rebar is no longer an isolated case. We are confronted with this problem, as it presents itself here, as a before and after. The rebar that teaches us something has once again become a school.

What went wrong? Why didn't the rebar resist when it was truly needed? When the going got tough? We've known, for a long time, what matters. Rebar was developed in the nineteenth century by a gardener who wanted to protect orange trees during transport because their wooden crates were constantly rotting and falling apart. [2] Now that the invention is in circulation, and there is a lot more at stake than just transporting orange trees, the rebar lies there as though dead, as though lying in state, with names written on the wall. [3] Unpacked. As if the names had cast shadows. Every single one of the small rebar bodies thus functions like an impossible echo. Outside on the wall, above on the floor, temporarily stored in crates, not buried within. This epitome of resilience, solidity, stability, and safety, on which we had built, which was supposed to protect the schoolchildren and guarantee a roof for learning over their heads, did not pass the test in Wenchuan. Its performance. The steel failed on all levels. Is it inferior? Is it the steel's fault? Obviously not. It has been brought back into shape. And acts quite innocent here. The schoolchildren are dead, while it is like new. Is something to be whitewashed here? In this recycled landscape of a botched job. What's the catch? How does a crooked thing become **Straight**? "Very straight." [4] A new beginning that provides encouragement. And leaves nothing behind. "When we came back we began thinking about using the rebars for a work that presents a kind of memory and a persistent questioning of the facts about what actually happened there." [5]

Let's quickly review the facts on paper. The way they present themselves at this moment. The ground plan of that world in the Chinese province which disappeared from the earth's surface in one fell swoop.

a) The Official Version

On the site where Beichuan Middle School stood in 2008, where more than one thousand schoolchildren and teachers died, the **National Earthquake Memorial** (2013) by Cai Yongjie now stands on fifteen hectares. A park with an enormous grassed area and an accompanying museum behind brown Corten steel walls, [6] with fissures and crevices in the landscape as access paths through which visitors can walk. "The new memorial landscape spans across the whole valley on a sloping level and is bordered on one side by a small road and on the other by a four-lane highway. Beyond the roads the landscape rises steeply and is covered with forest. Within the valley the road leads to the remains of old Beichuan Town; the ruins were kept as a memory for the people. [...] Although the administration ordered the removal of the ruins of the collapsed school buildings, the designers integrated the footprint of one building as well as the sport field into the concept. [...] As many experts afterwards agreed, more than 5000 students in the region were killed by collapsed schoolrooms due to corruption during construction that led to an unsafe use of building materials. For this reason, the local as well as the regional administration had no interest in keeping any memories about the failure of their own system. Covered under the name of land-art for the memorial, the traces still testify to the political failure." [7] The state's policy regarding memory, through which one can stroll so wonderfully—we should really go there one day—does not remind us of the circumstances at all. It transforms the incident into nature, earth, lets grass grow over it.

b) Ai Weiwei's **Straight**

Ai Weiwei's **Straight** is inconvenient. And puts considerable effort into getting a better view of the homemade, constructed part of the disaster. Which had an easy time of it, especially in those public buildings in which the rebar was not used correctly since the necessary money flowed into other pockets. And that is exactly what we're looking at in cases now. Fully concentrated. Without anything over it or added to it that could distract us. The problem in tens of thousands of variations: "Can these facts be altered? The hearts stopped beating, their limbs decayed, and their shouts disappeared with their breath, can these be returned? Wave upon wave of mighty propaganda from the national state apparatus cannot erase the persistent memories of the survivors. Crushed, the boneless and incompetent collapsed buildings belong to a generation of those unfortunate villagers, and the tofu-dregs engineering has been shielded, absolved by the clamor of desperate attempts at celebration. Those responsible for the offense are attempting to gloss over and distort in order to escape the condemnation." [8] And with the collection of the loose, lost rods, Ai Weiwei also collected the buried names of the pupils: **Names of the Student Earthquake Victims Found by the Citizens' Investigation**.

The material complex of **Straight** does not leave the heroism of the national monument intact, and this even before it has been built. The disruptions of geometry, the gaps, fault lines, puddle-shaped glimpses into deeper layers, there where the movements find their starting point, on interruptions that do not permit the traversal of individual lines, are still clearly visible from above, even in the crates. Ai Weiwei's turn to the remains of that which was previously constructed, the rebar, does not stop criticizing. What lies here before us, does not let go, is not simply abandoned, is the necessity of a fundamental complaint. Who begins in such a situation, and how? [9] One thing is certain: You can't start early enough.

Industrial Modernism, USA

The first image he resists is that of the earthquake ("Destruction Menaces"). There is nothing more to do. They had entirely different concerns. "Forget the silly tale" ("No One Believes Him"). Thus the official statements of the political elite. In the future, everything is sure to turn out fine. He really shouldn't set his mind on that. But he doesn't dream it. He still imagines the little boy extending his arms—then the building topples over. And he was already on his way. Clearing away the rubble ("Safe!"), going through numbers ("The Terrible Truth!"), considering, designing, and finally building something that clears the blockage ("A Strange Ship"). And with which the next in line can escape the vicious cycle of ignorance and catastrophe.

That's the beginning of **Superman**. One of the great myths of Western pop culture, the first time he appeared in the newspaper. Episode one by Jerry Siegel and Joe Shuster: **Superman Comes to Earth**. Six times a week, beginning on January 16, 1939. The birth of Superman from the spirit of the earthquake. The selfless Man of Steel, who can observe, who can keep accounts, who cannot be stopped and is there when you need him faster than any locomotive. The stars are lined up according to human possibilities. Parallel universes of perfectibility. "Krypton, a distant planet so far advanced in evolution that it bears a civilization of supermen—beings which represent the human race at its ultimate peak of perfect development." [10] The infant Superman, who is sent on his way to Earth in a spaceship by Superdad and Supermom while their old world bursts apart, is the symbol of help from outside. For passing on abilities. For one of us, who is clearly different from us, better in many ways, and who will help us out in case of emergency. His distinguishing feature, his identity, by which he can be recognized beyond doubt, is that he is capable of bending steel.

That which assisted the West at the time of the Second World War—when Hollywood films such as **An American Romance** (1944) were made about the national project as the triumph of the steel industry, about all that which people are

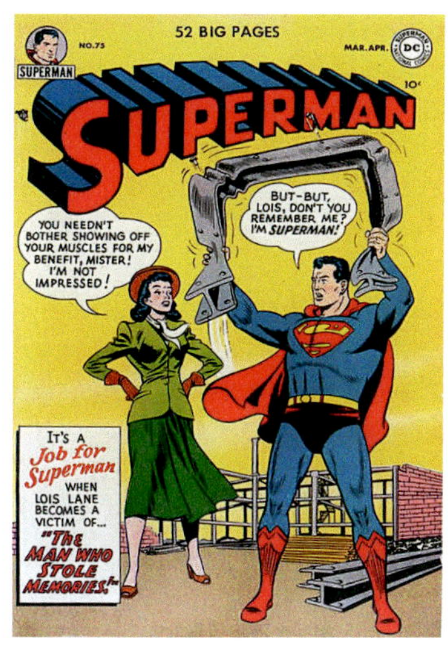

4

4
Cover of **Superman**, No. 75, 1939

capable of—is itself enormous and of a physical nature. The recognition of a need for help, to be sure, already bears the mark of the New Deal.

Postindustrial Areas, China

In 2008, the schoolchildren in Wenchuan did not receive any help from outside. The disaster was not averted at the last moment. The corrupt local decision-makers had already pulled the ground out from under their feet long before the earth trembled. Afterwards, when asked, they will say that everything was truly not at all to their liking. "What has never been clearly explained is: of more than one hundred schools scattered around the severe disaster area, only fourteen schools could claim a death toll in excess of one hundred due to collapse. Even though this was an earthquake of magnitude 8, the remaining ninety schools did not topple. Yet, among the fourteen schools that did, there was no unified pattern of destruction: rooms with larger widths collapsed, and while some of the classroom buildings were left unharmed, the dormitory buildings fell. Towers that had fallen into disrepair for many years remained standing, but newer buildings had collapsed. Identical teaching buildings came down, but not administrative buildings. Surrounding the areas where the most students were killed, at the Beichuan and Juyuan Middle Schools, many buildings were left standing. Thus, interpreting a magnitude 8 earthquake as a 'spicy hot pot' (where everything has a different flavor going in, but comes out tasting the same) is evidently a cruel explanation."[11] Against the numbing, insensitive nature of the language used by the authorities with regard to the far too harsh, "spicy" natural phenomenon, Ai Weiwei uses the familiar concept of the "tofu-dregs" for the irresponsible, unsafe construction methods, that is to say the human involvement, against which the schoolchildren never had a serious chance. That white-yellow mush that gets stuck in the sieve after the pureed soybeans have been filtered, which is highly susceptible to rot and is used as fertilizer or pig feed, or which immediately ends up in landfills as waste. If something had been incorrectly built here, it is rather likely to have been something along those lines. Ai Weiwei

thus remains within the rhetoric of the kitchen, proposed by politicians, but turns it against the cooks and suggests that one should primarily be interested in the ingredients. What went into the buildings? The signal is clear: More productive than the fatalism imposed by the state, for which only the nation can compensate, is first to deal locally with the infrastructure of "What's cooking?". The infrastructure of what's-happening-right-now? What exactly is going on? In the pot for all of us?

Ai Weiwei is thus fighting two myths.[12] The first image he fights against, like Superman before him, is that of the earthquake. Against official statements à la magnitude 8, past the eleventh hour—there's nothing more to be done, all cats look gray at night, and the district government of Sichuan now has entirely different worries. No, after an earthquake like the one of 2008, things cannot simply go on as usual. As if the quake was the most natural thing in the world. Simply put, too much has happened. Too many are dead. This image of the earthquake is anything but uniform. Not everything automatically falls like dominoes placed one behind the other. Some houses are still standing, others are not. And those that no longer stand are, first and foremost, places of education.

The second myth is that of national perfectibility and the optimization-mania that still went hand in hand with Superman in the 1930s and 1940s and is still even capable of benefiting from a catastrophe. That is to say, the image of a Superman State. That which is adopted from this model is a borrowing from the future. That which is constructed takes its wealth from the future (from its own possibilities). Borrows the growing energy of those who were still being educated. Who have been deprived of their future. One simply owes it to them to build something new together with them. To accomplish this, one does not need a super-artist who bends everything into shape for us, but rather collective work on infrastructure is needed.[13] It is the operations and practices that count. We have to take matters into our own hands. The process is recursive.

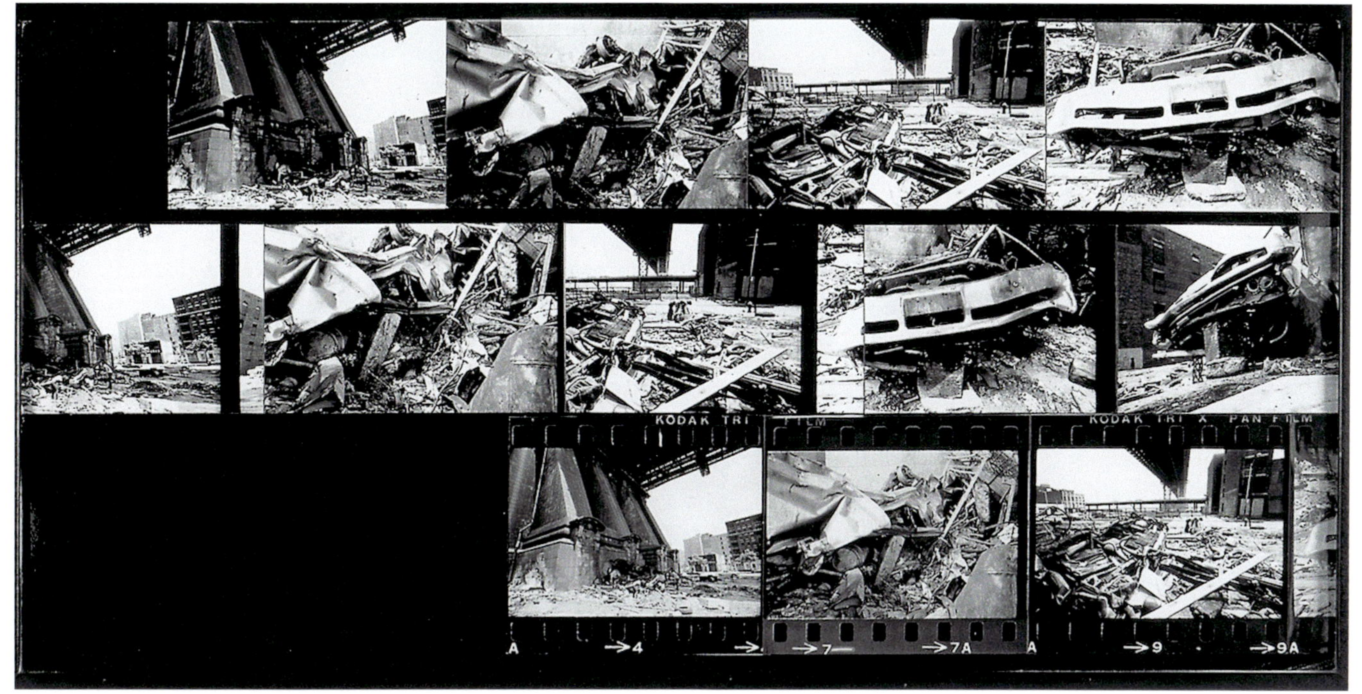

5

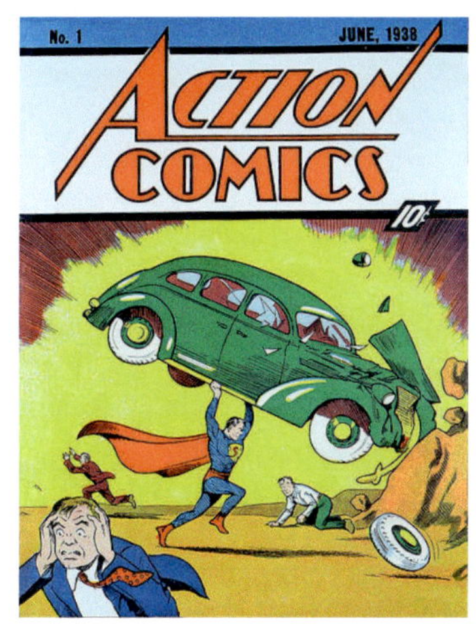

6

5
Gordon Matta-Clark: **Jacks**,
1971, photocollage, contact
prints, 51.0 × 99.0 cm,
Städel Museum, Frankfurt am
Main

6
Cover of **Action Comics**,
No. 1, 1938

Ai Weiwei had tracked the rebar of the collapsed school buildings to the scrap yards, purchased roughly two hundred tons, primarily from the Beichuan Middle School, in which one thousand five hundred school children perished, reloaded them and had them transported to his studio in Beijing. There, they were subjected to an extensive procedure, which was simultaneously a cleansing ritual. Each rod was given the greatest possible attention. In a first step, it was individualized. This was carried out in two variations. The first almost came from the lack of a better idea: "I didn't know what to do with them. It's such a strange thing to look at. I said, 'Maybe the first thing we can do is straighten them up.' We started hiring a lot of workers just to straighten them one by one, each rebar needing to be hammered a few hundred times to straighten it. Then I got arrested. The first thing I heard when I came out from my detention and walked toward my studio was the sound of the banging./Wachtel: The hammering./Ai: Hammering. I was so happy in that moment. I was just so happy. Then we got that work done. And I think it's a proper language: not too much, not too sentimental, not too dramatized. It just left us, like it just came out of a factory." [14] The restoration of a bit of sincerity, the haptic dimension of compassion, the moment of paying attention, and producing a signal, becoming loud, and then not simply stopping when confronted with resistance—all this triggers a sense of happiness. This rebar here, every rod of it, counts. Becomes perceptible. And keeps those buried under it further in our midst. [15] The transformation of rage into physical work, the gesture of not allowing something to go unchallenged, the solidarity with the families, and the humility in the face of suffering manifest themselves in the persistent, exhausting reworking of an everyday object, which has an effect on the body. The fact that each component of more than two hundred tons of steel has passed through many hands and has been purged at least two hundred times with a hammer, certainly also has a very concrete, symbolic meaning.

The second form of individualization is the copy. For another parallel work made of the same material, **Forge**—the title of which plays with the double meaning of "forge" in the sense of "shape/form" and of "counterfeit"—Ai Weiwei left a model series of found rebar not only in its respective shape, formed by the catastrophe, for later exhibition, but doubled and tripled it. By having new rebar bent into the exact form of that metal retrieved from the rubble, by deforming additional material so that it is indistinguishable from the wrongly used material, he demonstrates not only that something is not right, that the impossible has suddenly come true, but also that, in this situation, it is necessary to permanently monitor and to examine practice in detail. That one should be very precise and keep every constellation in mind. And at the same time, should always make comparisons. The individual case does not just disappear in the copy. The opening credits of **Wenchuan Rebar**, **2008–12**, which brings **Straight** and **Forge** together in a "making-of," comment ironically on this when the titles, like samples of handwriting, appear three times as signatures made of left-over rebar.

It is this constant repetition of the elementary, physical actions of the demoted worker within disintegrating or collapsing structures, with which Wang Bing, in the nine-hour documentary **West of the Tracks** (2003), had already filmed the decline of the Chinese steel industry using the example of the industrial complex Tie Xi Qu. In both post-industrial works, the presence of absence is tangible in every shot or perspective that is taken, and permits social processes in dealing with the remains, with whatever can be found, to be experienced, first and foremost. In Düsseldorf, **Straight** is exhibited alongside sculpture and writing, by means of the film **Straight**, **2015** on the monitor in the Grabbe Halle, explicitly as a network of different media. This work operates on all levels.

Could it perhaps be possible to build a bridge, a first small link between West and East, steel euphoria and depression, Ai Weiwei, artistic working methods, and the homeland of Superman? In 1971, at a time when the world's steel production was increasingly shifting from the USA and Europe to Asia, and massive job losses in these industries began in the West, the eighty-eighth anniversary of the Brooklyn Bridge, the world's first suspension bridge supported by steel cables, was celebrated in that mirror city to Clark Kent's Metropolis. Below the radar of the official celebrations, at the foot of the bridge, Alanna Heiss organized the exhibition **Under the Brooklyn Bridge**, also known as **The Brooklyn Bridge Event**, from May 22 to 24. Gordon Matta-Clark took the opportunity to inspect the scrap and debris under the pillars between which the homeless lived. He had a keen interest in the ingredients of food, the American dream of iron, and the lives it had obscured. The work he presented was titled **Jacks**. The common name used for the device that lifts your car. The DIY tool from the heroic Age of the Automobile. Which he then immediately lined up. Jack in the plural form — Jack on Jack on Jack, as in a card game, good luck, you need to have twenty-one — was a series of performances and their photographic documentation.[16] A chain of repetitions. The conversion and re-utilization of something that had long been abandoned. The turning out the sedimentary debris on the underside of the bridge. The mockery of the architecture and of the budgets that society provides to solve its self-made problems.

Jacks consisted of the serial production of makeshift shelters by propping up abandoned wrecked cars. Secured by car jacks, it immediately became possible to settle under the floor pans of the cars supported in the air. To move into a transitional home. Finally, to have a car over your head again. The gesture ironically quotes the promise of the Man of Steel.

At the end of his action, Matta-Clark roasted a pig for those who lived under the bridge. "Sometimes the chance audience happens upon mysterious 'traces' of past activities, which may or may not be decipherable at a later date."[17]

It now lies here in Düsseldorf — Ai Weiwei's rebar, the backbone of our products, like a pile of prostheses in the display window of shipping crates. Reinforcing steel is really pretty close to us.

1
See: Monika Dommann, "Handle With Special Care," in: Lucie Kolb, Christoph Lang, Wolfgang Ullrich, and Judith Welter (eds.), **Art Handling. Partituren der Logistik** (Zürich 2016), pp. 25–39; and Alexander Klose, **Das Container-Prinzip. Wie eine Box unser Denken verändert** (Hamburg 2009).

2
Rainer Schüler, "Handwerk wie zu Urgroßvaters Zeiten," in: **Märkische Allgemeine**, September 13, 2017, https://www.maz-online.de/Lokales/Potsdam/Handwerk-wie-zu-Urgrossvaters-Zeiten (last accessed on March 30, 2019).

3
"First, pull the dismembered children's limbs from the rubble, wipe them clean, find a quiet place, and bury them deep." See: Ai Weiwei, "Silent Holiday: Posted June 1, 2008," in: Ai Weiwei, **Ai Weiwei's Blogs: Writings, Interviews, and Digital Rants, 2006–2009**, ed. and trans. Lee Ambrozy (Cambridge, MA 2011), pp. 152f., here p. 152.

4
Ai Weiwei, **Straight**, 15'03", here 11:57; available online at: YouTube, May 8, 2018, https://www.youtube.com/watch?v=piWBzezxWOQ (last accessed on March 30, 2019).

5
Ibid., here 9:40.

6
Here, rebar becomes Corten steel. "Its acronym, Cor-Ten, was derived from the two properties that distinguish it from mild carbon steel and copper-bearing steel; namely, improved atmospheric corrosion resistance and higher yield and tensile strengths." See: P. Albrecht and A. H. Naeemi, **Performance of Weathering Steel in Bridges** (National Cooperative Highway Research Program Report 272), Washington, D.C., July 1984, p. 13; available online at: https://onlinepubs.trb.org/Onlinepubs/nchrp/nchrp_rpt_272.pdf (last accessed on March 30, 2019). Reinforcement

becomes rust resistance, rod tensile strength. In the manner in which it is often used for outdoor sculptures.

7
Eduard Koegel, "Earthquake Memorial in Sichuan," in: **world-architects**: **Profiles of Selected Architects**, December 13, 2015, https://www.world-architects.com/es/architecture-news/reviews/earthquake-memorial-in-sichuan-1 (last accessed on March 30, 2019).

8
Ai Weiwei, "Memorial Day: Posted on May 12, 2009," in: Ai Weiwei 2011 (see note 3), pp. 224f., here p. 224.

9
"How can we use the simplest, most direct form of expression to describe this kind of disaster, this kind of historic event?" Ai Weiwei, **Straight** (see note 4), here 6:48.

10
"The Superman is born!" in: **Superman**: **The Dailies**, **Vol. I**: **Strips 1–306, 1939–1940** (New York/Northampton, MA 1999), p. 13.

11
Ai Weiwei, "These Days I Can't Believe Anything You Say: Posted on May 7, 2009," in: Ai Weiwei 2011 (see note 3) pp. 219–21, here pp. 219f.

12
"In short, in the account given of our contemporary circumstances, I resented seeing Nature and History confused at every turn, and I wanted to track down, in the decorative display of 'what-goes-without-saying,' the ideological abuse which, in my view, is hidden there." Roland Barthes, **Mythologies**, trans. Annette Lavers (New York 1991), p. 10.

13
"The Citizens' Investigation for the Sichuan earthquake lasted for a year, covering the most severely affected earthquake zones in 14 counties, 74 towns, and over 300 schools. One hundred and sixty volunteers registered over the Internet, 38 of whom participated in field surveys in the disaster zones, and 34 participated in telephone surveys and data compilations. The Citizens' Investigation is China's largest investigation campaign launched by individual citizens for several decades." "Citizens' Investigation," in: Maurizio Bortolotti (ed.), **Ai Weiwei**: **Disposition**, exh. cat. Venice (London 2014), p. 52.

14
Wachtel, Eleanor, "An Interview with Ai Weiwei," in: **Brick**. **A Literary Journal**, no. 100 (Winter 2018), https://brickmag.com/an-interview-with-ai-weiwei (last accessed on March 31, 2019).

15
"[...] in the interval of his absence the roof of the hall where Scopas was giving the banquet fell in, crushing Scopas himself and his relations underneath the ruins and killing them; and when their friends wanted to bury them but were altogether unable to know them apart as they had been completely crushed, the story goes that Simonides was enabled by his recollection of the place in which each of them had been reclining at table to identify them for separate interment; and that this circumstance suggested to him the discovery of the truth that the best aid to clearness of memory consists in orderly arrangement. He inferred that persons desiring to train this faculty must select localities and form mental images of the facts they wish to remember and store those images in the localities, with the result that the arrangement of the localities will preserve the order of the facts, and the images of the facts will designate the facts themselves, and we shall employ the localities and images respectively as a wax writing tablet and the letters written on it." Cicero, **On the Orator**, **Books 1–2**, trans. E. W. Sutton and H. Rackham (London/Cambridge, MA, 1967), **De Oratore**, **II**, lxxxvi, 353–5, pp. 465–7.

16
"Photographs of **Jacks** appeared in Avalanche, an art magazine founded by Willoughby Sharp and Liza Bear, using the subtitle 'jacks: the autodemolition debris zone ripoff imitation neighbourhood group action cars abandoned raised propped dismantled and removed 24 hours service.'" Jeff Rian, "Rocking the Foundation: Gordon Matta-Clark," in: **Frieze**, June 5, 1993; available online at: https://frieze.com/article/rocking-foundation (last accessed on March 31, 2019).

17
Lucy R. Lippard, **Get the Message?**: **A Decade of Art for Social Change** (New York 1984), p. 59.

CHAPTER III

Chapter III

Following his release from secret detention in June 2011, Ai Weiwei was placed under probation, and his passport was confiscated, barring him from leaving the country. It was not until July 22, 2015, that his passport was returned to him and he was permitted to leave China. He settled in Berlin and accepted a guest professorship at the Berlin University of the Arts.

Parallel to Ai Weiwei's move to Berlin, the situation of refugees, mainly from Syria and the Arab world, on the external borders of the European Union, became more acute. Since then, in his works, Ai Weiwei has reflected and commented on the question of worldwide migration in a variety of ways. In 2017, his feature-length documentary **Human Flow** was premiered during the Venice Biennale, in competition. Ai Weiwei shot it, with various teams, at refugee camps in twenty-three different countries. The film is an eloquent testimony to Ai Weiwei's credo: "There is no refugee crisis, only a human crisis." **Human Flow** looks at local refugee movements from a global perspective and attempts to provide an overview of migration movements in different parts of the world. Ai Weiwei's focus is, therefore, not on the question of combating concrete causes of such flight in order to avoid migration but rather on the question of how humanity behaves towards those who are fleeing for whatever reason: "Human flow has always happened in human history. In many cases, it is part of our humanity and our civilization." He thus argues alongside current research in migration studies, which has proven the existence of the large-scale movement of people in every historical constellation of human history: "›Homo migrans‹ has existed ever since ›Homo sapiens‹ came into existence."[1]

The entrance of the exhibition at K21 offers a pointed summary of Ai Weiwei's view on this theme. In **Laundromat** (2016), reality breaks into the museum space as it does with **Straight** at K20. In March 2016, due to the increasingly restrictive attitude of many Balkan states towards refugees, the refugee camp at Idomeni on the Greek-Macedonian border grew to around fourteen thousand inhabitants. Ai Weiwei first visited the camp in March 2016, shortly after Macedonia closed its border with Greece. When the camp was evacuated by authorities in May 2016 and the refugees were resettled to other Greek camps, Ai Weiwei and his assistants collected the clothes and shoes left behind. He had the clothing sent back to his Berlin studio where each piece was cleaned and repaired. Hung on standard clothes racks and sorted as though in a department store, they now comprise the work **Laundromat**.

As with **Straight**, Ai Weiwei's goal here is to make the found materials look like brand-new goods. Yet, in fact, every single article of clothing tells a story of oppression, flight, persecution, and suffering. Ai Weiwei's art does not represent anything here. It does not depict anything but rather brings the almost unbearable reality of events at the EU's external borders directly into the "white cube." The human issue of flight is brought particularly close to us, for there is hardly anything closer to humans than clothing. These clothes are not exotic, not strange, when we see them with our own eyes. They are merely articles of clothing that could just as well be our own. This is what Ai Weiwei insists upon when understanding the refugee crisis as a human crisis, as a crisis in which it becomes clear that we all belong to one humanity.

Laundromat is surrounded by a plethora of photos taken by Ai Weiwei at Idomeni, as well as by **Newsfeed**, a floor covering that captures the exchange of information shared by Ai Weiwei's **Human Flow** film team via WhatsApp and other short message services. On the outside walls, a wallpaper with over seventeen thousand iPhone photos taken by Ai Weiwei, during the shooting of **Human Flow**, in the various refugee camps around the world connects the exhibition area of **Laundromat** with the adjacent installation **Life Cycle** (2018).

Unlike **Laundromat**, this seventeen-meter-long sculpture of a lifeboat made of bamboo and sisal, densely packed with 115 passengers, does not refer to a concrete historical situation but takes up the theme of crossing the sea as a timeless parable. Ai Weiwei not only included anonymous figures of fleeing men, women, children, and infants in the boat, but he also has personifications of each of the

twelve Chinese zodiac signs, as well as the Egyptian queen Nefertiti, travel with them. In addition, the signs of the zodiac always symbolize the cycle of becoming and passing. The title **Life Cycle** is a reminder of this. The boat made of bamboo and sisal was constructed using the traditional Chinese techniques of kite building. By reducing the figures to their contours, the impression is created of their complete transparency. They become translucent, ghostly. It is clear that this is a ship of the dead. The pharaoh's wife accentuates the connection with the realm of the dead. On the pedestal of the sculpture, quotations from a wide range of authors can be read which make reference to the dangerous journey while, at the same time, demand the acceptance of fleeing refugees. The boat, thus, becomes a symbol of dangerous passage, from the **Odyssey** to today's bands of refugees.

Nevertheless, the iconography of an overcrowded lifeboat is linked to the concrete voyage of many refugees across the Mediterranean. It is therefore also a memorial to the ubiquitous indifference shown towards the death of thousands of refugees in the Mediterranean. According to the International Organization for Migration, more than seventeen thousand people lost their lives fleeing across the Mediterranean between January 2014 and the end of February 2019.[2] The estimated number of unreported cases is well above this figure.

In addition to the seventeen thousand iPhone photos relating to fugitives, the black wallpaper **Odyssey** (2016) can be seen on the back wall of the space. Escape and migration are depicted in multiple scenes as though on a frieze. Ai Weiwei draws on traditional narrative pictorial formulas, such as Trajan's Column, and combines realistic depictions of flight in the twenty-first century with historical and mythological subject matter. The wallpaper thus corresponds to the timeless symbolic nature of **Life Cycle**; while, in addition, the elements within its frieze repeat themselves to form a never-ending repetitive epic. The individual themes of the wallpaper return in two series of works in porcelain: plates and vases in the tradition of blue-and-white ware. What at first appears to be valuable porcelain with appealing but ostensibly harmless decorations reveals itself, on closer inspection, to be an uncompromising inventory of the misery of human migration.

Ai Weiwei has hung the forty-part photo series **Study of Perspective** (1995–2011) on the wallpaper. Each image depicts a famous building, often one of cultural or national importance, including, for example, the White House, the Reichstag building, the Parliament Building in Bern, the Eiffel Tower, Tate Modern, and St. Peter's Basilica. To each of the buildings, Ai Weiwei "gives" the middle finger. In combination with **Odyssey** and **Life Cycle**, the series can be understood as an indictment of political and social decision-makers that they face up to their responsibility towards refugees.

Next to **Life Cycle**, Ai Weiwei has placed a marble surveillance camera and life buoy. The stone life preserver is, however, not a cynical play between light and heavy. Rather, Ai Weiwei performs a translation in material which, through the costly medium, heightens the life buoy into a symbol. This also applies to the surveillance camera. It is derived from the time of Ai Weiwei's house arrest and follows the same logic regarding material. Here, however, it is aimed at the boat and alludes to the surveillance technologies that are intended to keep refugees away at the borders.

1

Klaus J. Bade, **Europa in Bewegung. Migration vom späten 18. Jahrhundert bis zur Gegenwart** (Munich 2000), p. 11, quoted in: Jochen Oltmer, **Migration. Geschichte und Zukunft der Gegenwart** (Darmstadt 2017), p. 9 [translated].

2

Data files of the International Organization for Migration are available at: https:// missingmigrants.iom.int/ global-figures/all/xls (last accessed on March 4, 2019).

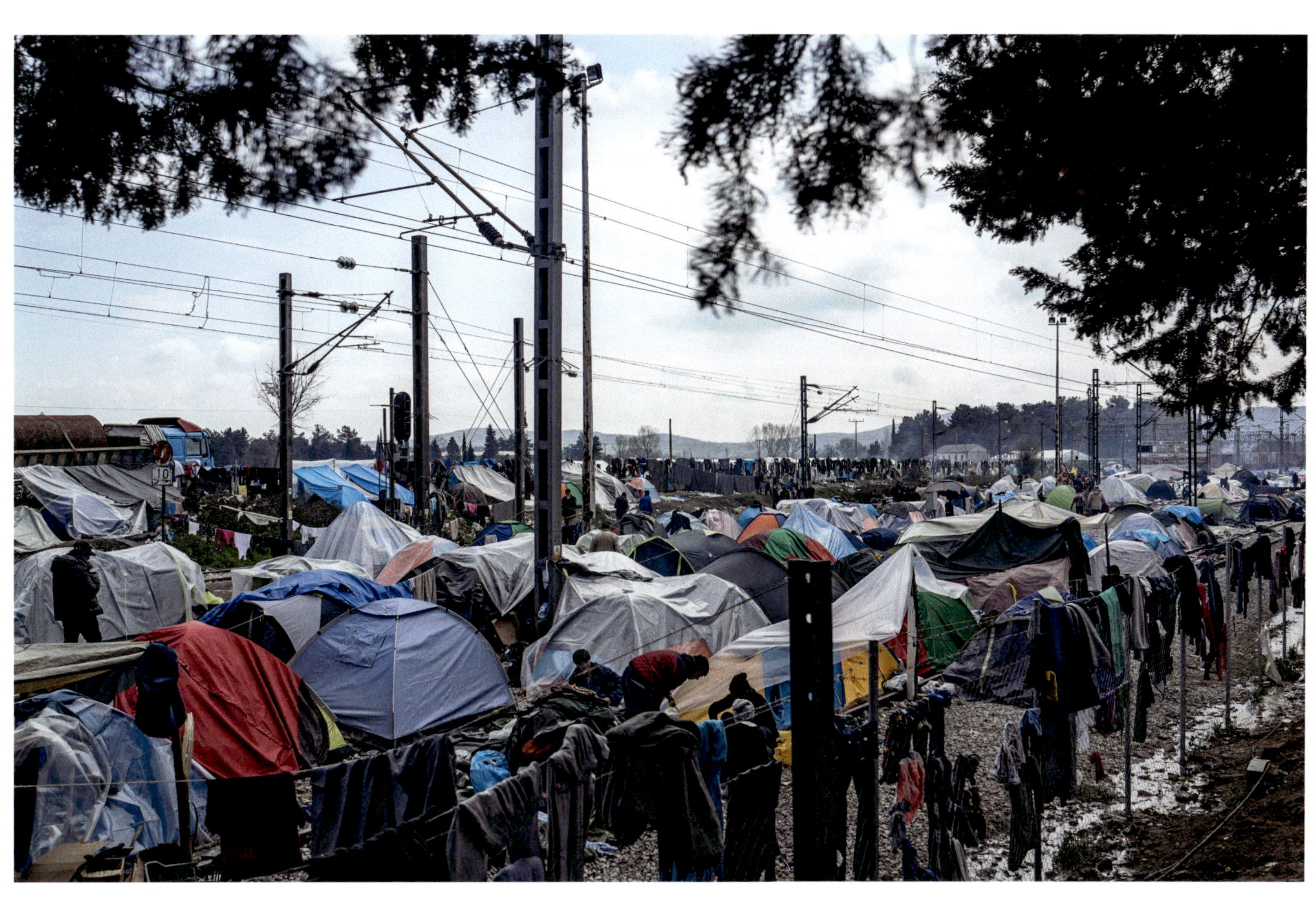

Idomeni makeshift camp,
Greece, 2016

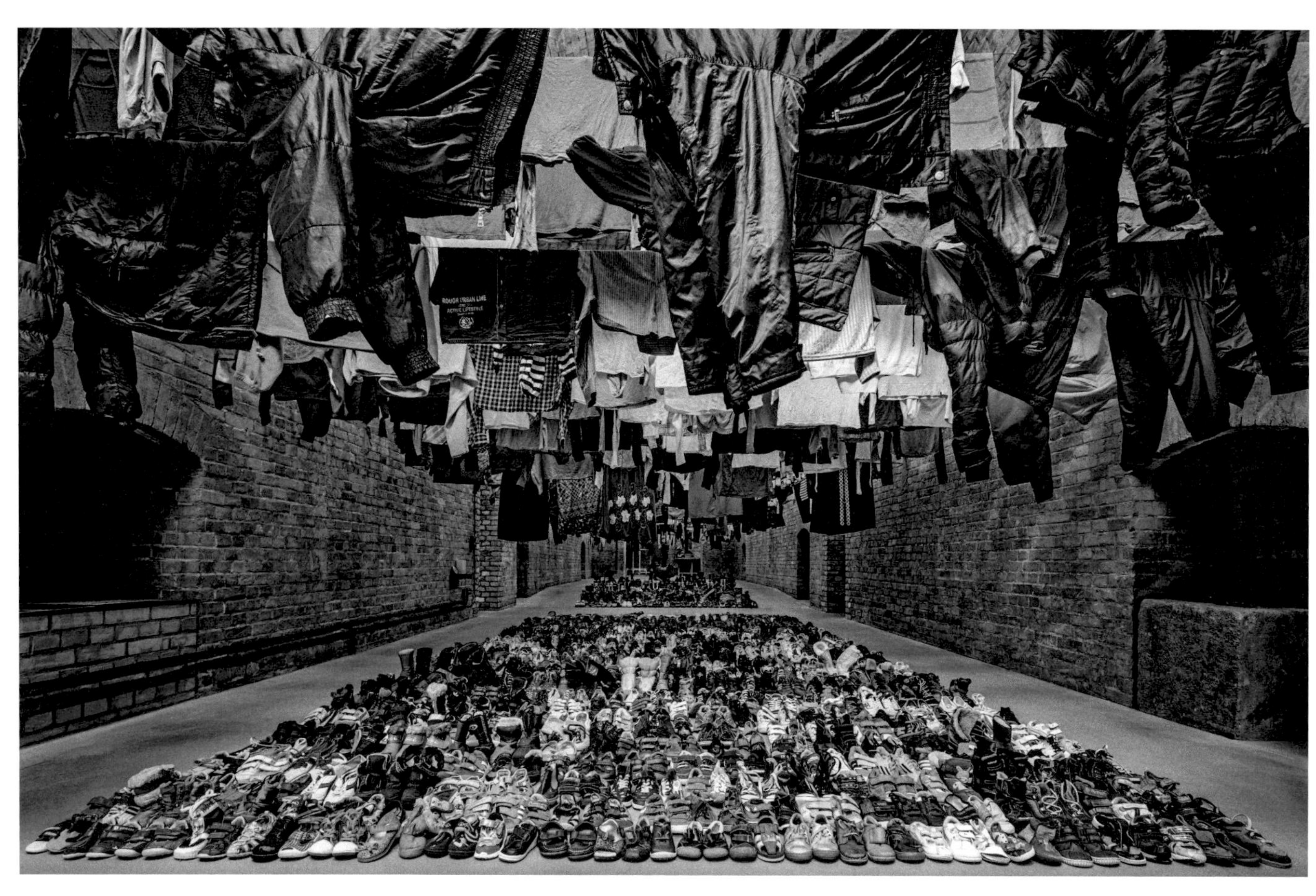

Production of **Laundromat** in
Ai Weiwei's Studio in Berlin,
2016

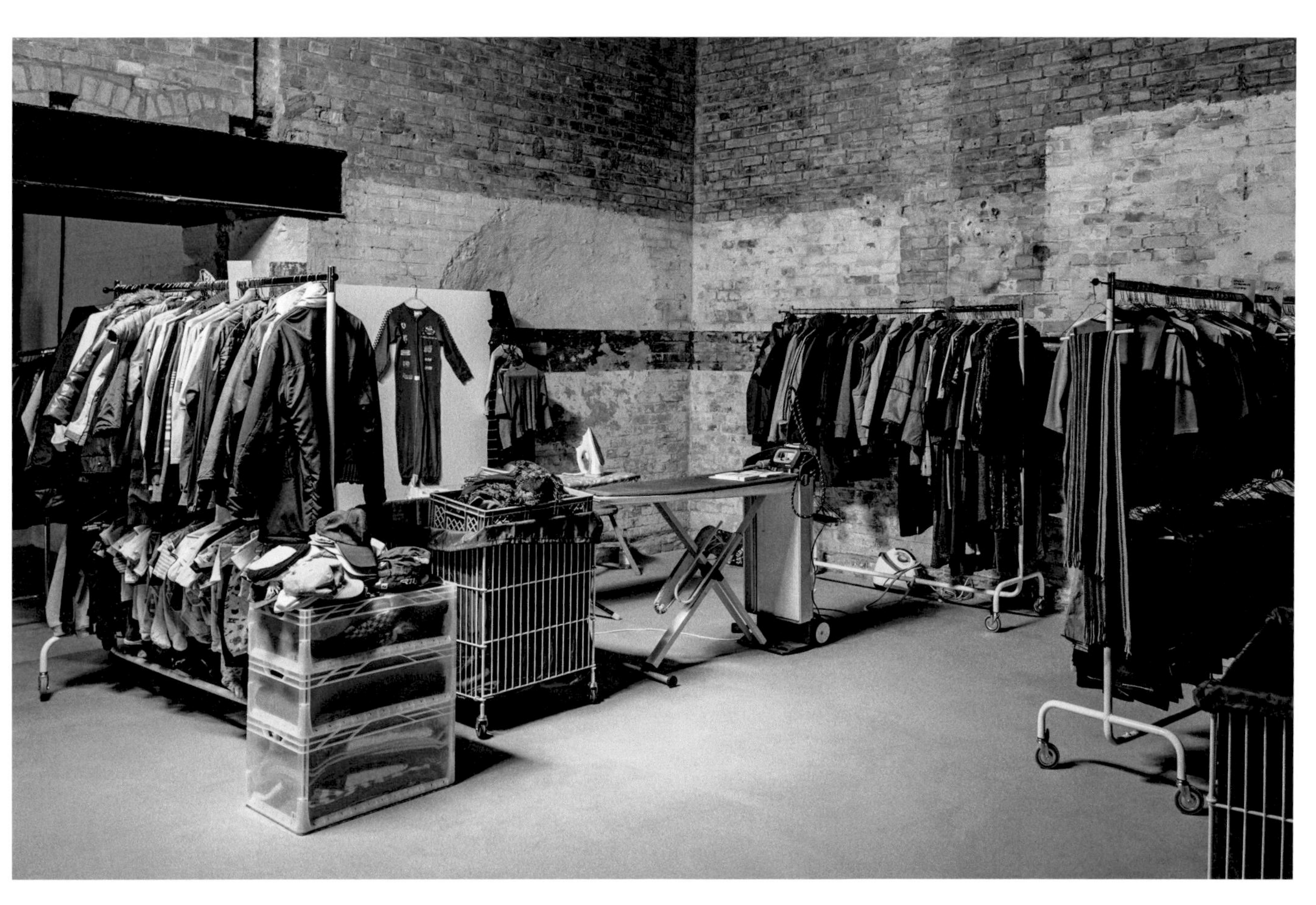

Laundromat, 2016
40 clothing racks,
2,046 clothing items.
Installation view,
Jeffrey Deitch, 2016

97

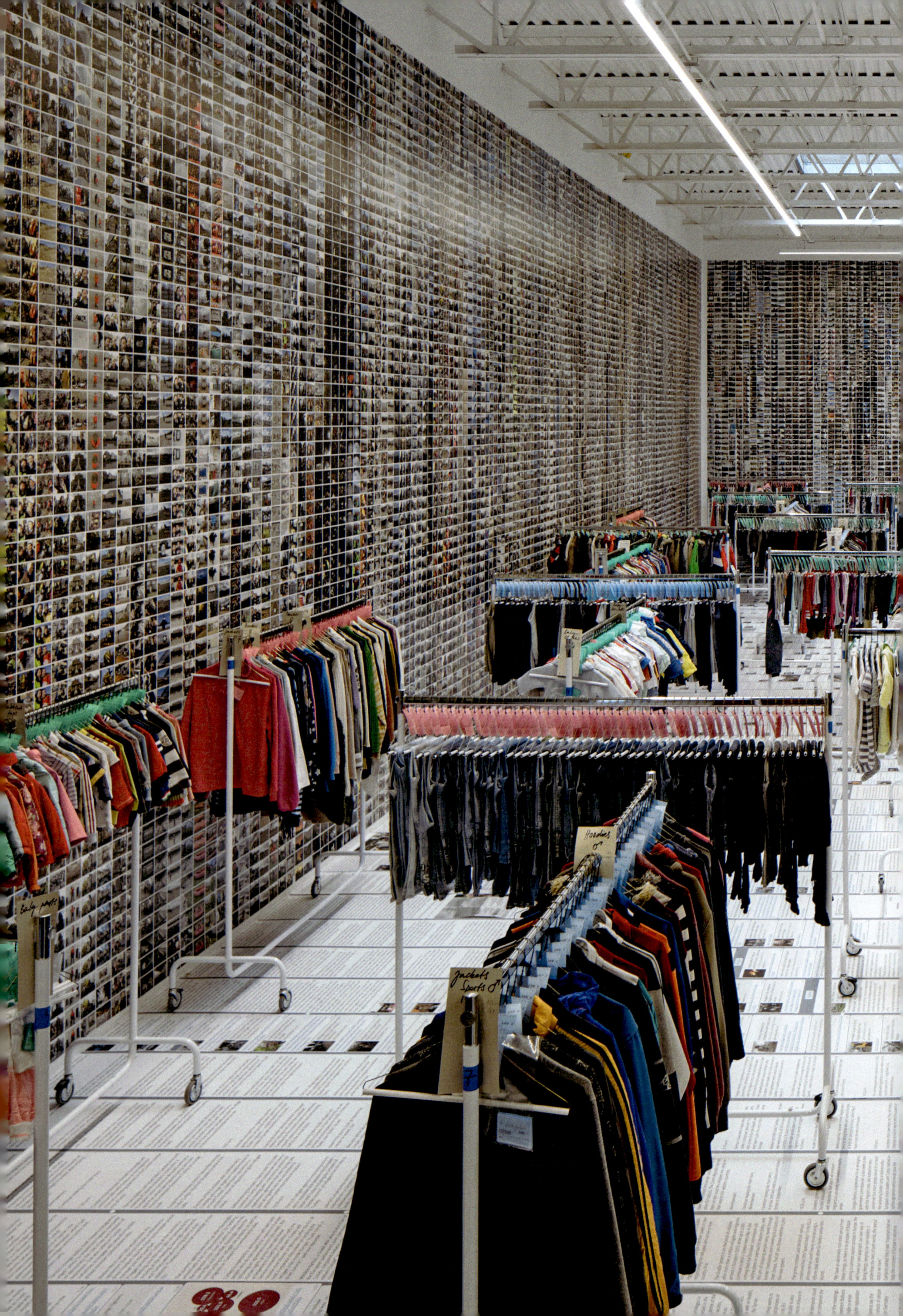

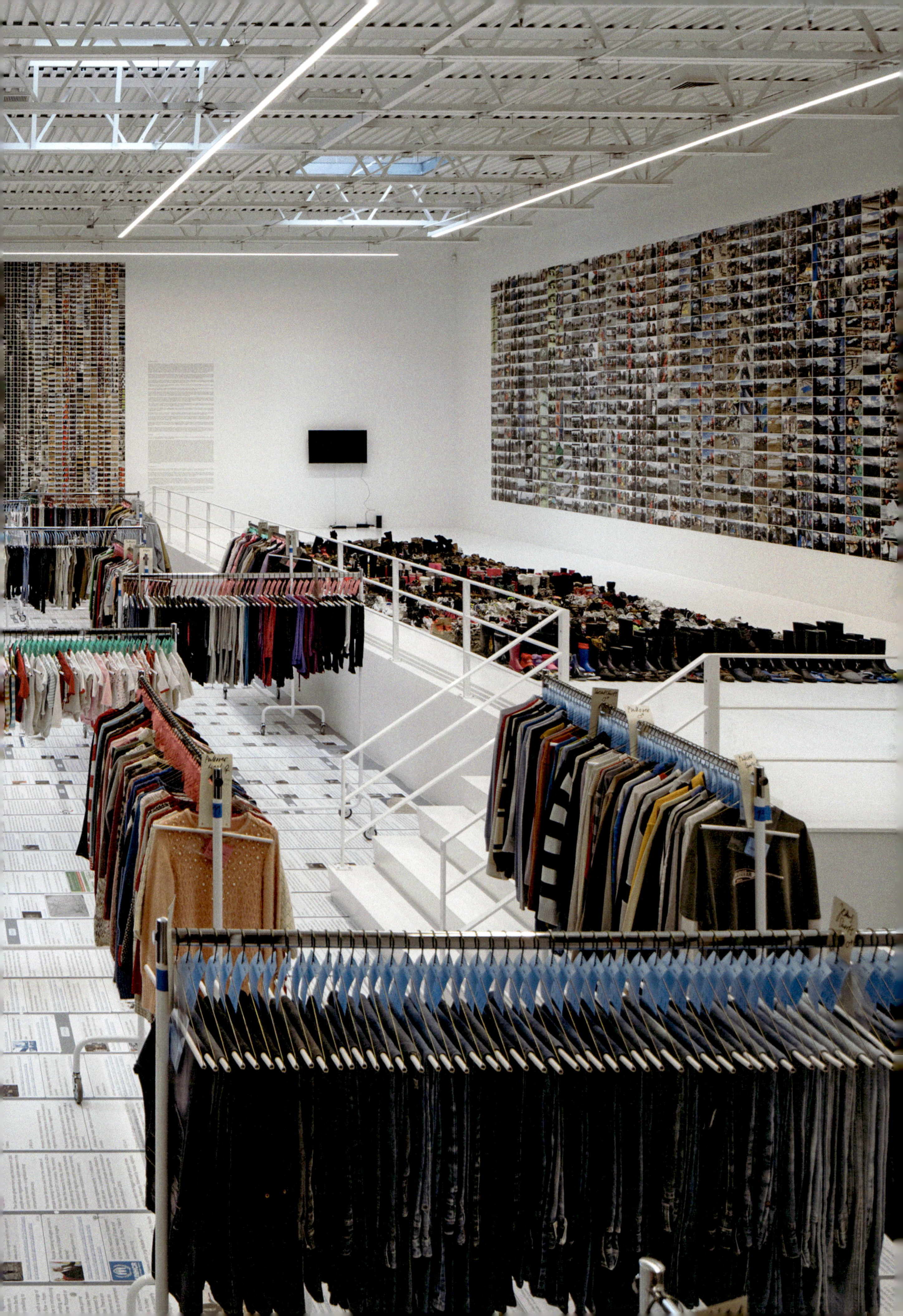

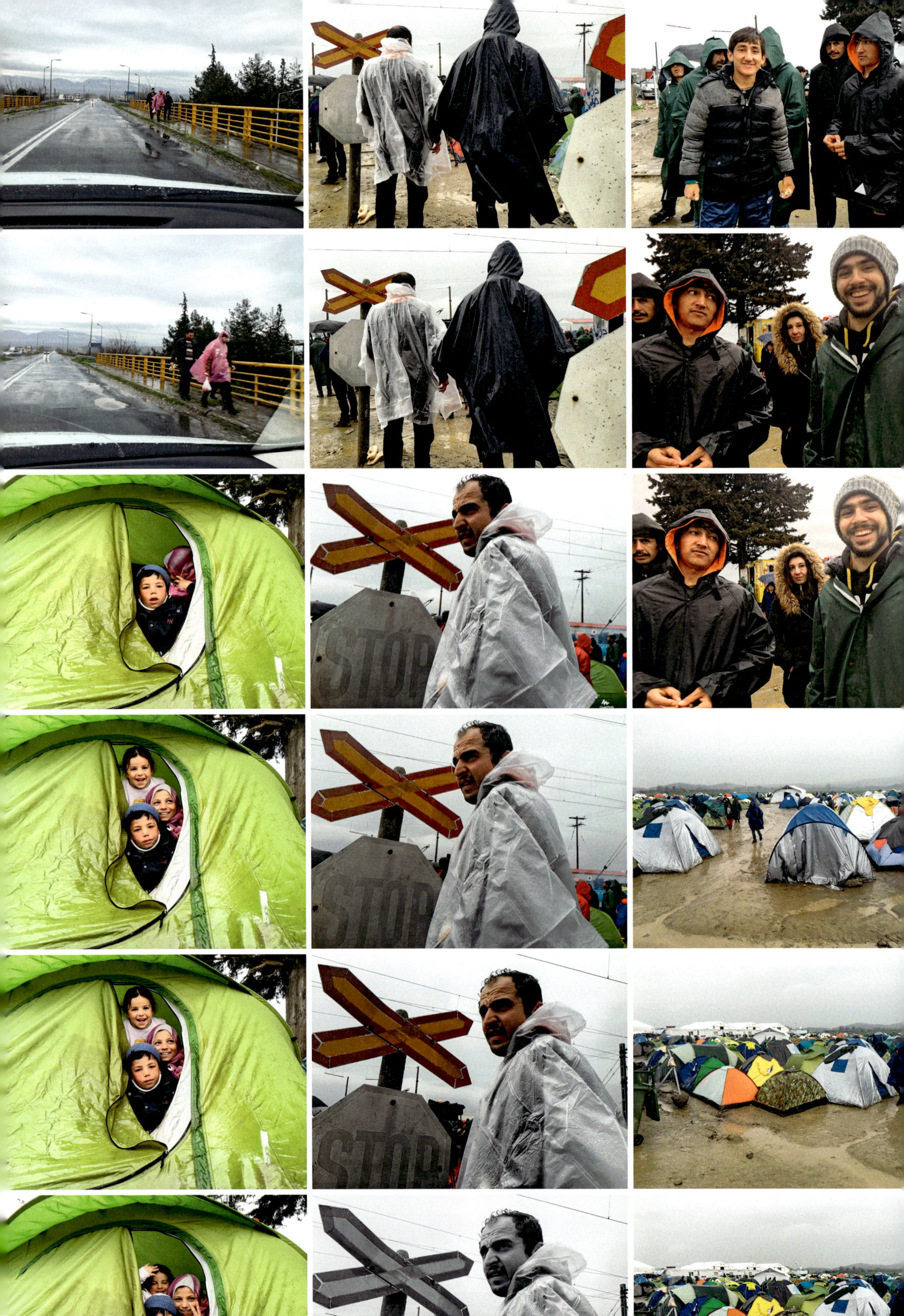

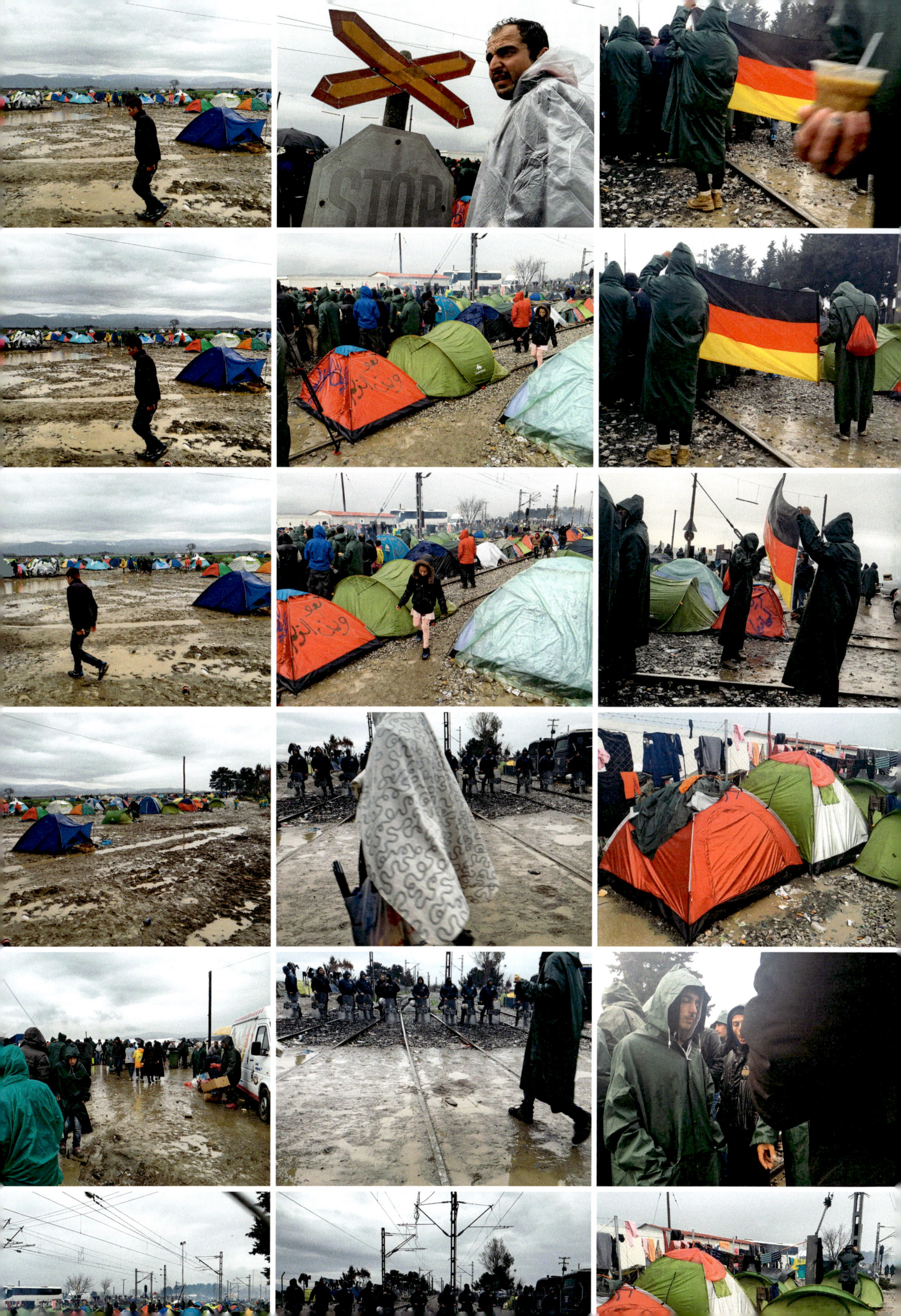

Idomeni, 2016
Wallpaper
Dimensions variable

The Newsfeed, 2016
Floor paper
Dimensions variable

**17'232 Photos
Relating to Refugees,
01.12.–09.08.2016, 2016**
Wallpaper
Dimensions variable

https://vimeo.com/150493039
Jan. 21, 2016

Why is it so Difficult for Syrian Refugees to Get into the U.S.? - NY Times

http://www.nytimes.com/2016/01/24/magazine/why-is-it-so-difficult-for-syrian-refugees-to-get-into-the-us.html?hp&action=click&pgtype=Homepage&clickSource=story-heading&module=second-column-region®ion=top-news&WT.nav=top-news
Jan. 21, 2016

5 Years in 60 Seconds, Watching 60 Seconds is Unbearable, Living 157,680,000 Unimaginable - Twitter

https://twitter.com/doruntineuk/status/690222571816620032
Jan. 22, 2016

Dozens Drown off Greek Islands in Deadliest January for Refugees - The Guardian

Search and rescue efforts ongoing.

http://www.theguardian.com/world/2016/jan/22/dozens-dead-as-two-boats-sink-off-greece
Jan. 22, 2016

London2Calais: Coach to Refugees Welcome Demonstration, Calais 23 Jan – Eventbrite

https://www.eventbrite.co.uk/e/london2calais-coach-to-refugees-welcome-demonstration-calais-23-jan-2016-tickets-20845532549
Jan. 22, 2016

EU Considers Ringfencing Greece to Stop Flow of Migrants - FT.com

EU leaders are weighing a drastic plan.

https://next.ft.com/content/c40504cc-c12b-11e5-9fdb-87b8d15baec2
Jan. 23, 2016

Protesting Migrants Storm French Port of Calais – CNN.com

http://edition.cnn.com/2016/01/23/europe/france-port-calais-jungle-migrant-crisis/
Jan.24, 2016

Banksy's New Artwork Criticizes Uses of Teargas in Calais Refugee Camp – The Guardian

http://www.theguardian.com/artanddesign/2016/jan/24/banksy-uses-new-artwork-to-criticise-use-of-teargas-in-calais-refugee-camp
Jan.25, 2016

Asylum Seekers Made to Wear Coloured Wristbands in Cardiff – The Guardian

Refugees say they were forced.

http://www.theguardian.com/uk-news/2016/jan/24/asylum-seekers-made-to-wear-coloured-wristbands-cardiff
Jan. 25, 2016

Denmark can now Legally Search Refugees and Seize Their Money and Jewellery – Independent

http://www.independent.co.uk/news/world/europe/denmark-approves-controversial-refugee-bill-allowing-police-to-seize-asylum-seekers-cash-and-a6834581.html
Jan. 26, 2016

UK 'Using Misleading Information' to Return Eritrean Asylum Seekers – The Guardian

http://www.theguardian.com/uk-news/2016/jan/22/uk-using-misleading-information-return-eritrean-asylum-seekers-home-office-guidance
Jan. 27, 2016

Junker Drops Greece, Bets on Macedonia - Politico

http://www.politico.eu/article/juncker-drops-greece-bets-on-macedonia-eu-migration-refugees-asylum-

Feb. 2, 2016

Shakespeare's Globe Actors Perform Hamlet in the Calais Jungle – Getty Images

http://www.gettyimages.co.uk/detail/news-photo/actors-from-shakespeares-globe-perform-hamlet-to-migrants-news-photo/508168804
Feb. 4, 2016

Syria Refugee Crisis: Six Charts That Show How Europe is Struggling to Respond – The Guardian

London conference this week aims to raise $9bn for Syrian refugees; to date, UNHCR appeal has fallen well short of target.

http://www.theguardian.com/world/datablog/2016/feb/03/syria-refugee-crisis-and-international-aid-in-numbers?CMP=share_btn_fb
Feb. 4, 2016

Refugee Children Forced into Labor in Turkey – CBS News

CBS News goes undercover in…

http://www.cbsnews.com/news/refugee-children-forced-into-labor-in-turkey/
Feb. 4, 2016

Churches Offer Sanctuary to Asylum Seekers Facing Deportation to Nauru – The Guardian

Anglican Dean of Brisbane says he is prepared to be charged with obstruction and calls conditions in offshore detention 'tantamount to state-sanctioned abuse'.

http://www.theguardian.com/australia-news/2016/feb/04/churches-offer-sanctuary-to-asylum-seekers-facing-deportation-to-nauru
Feb. 4, 2016

Fake Life Vests Soak Up Chances of Survival for Shipwrecked Refugees- Ekathimerini

FAKE LIFE VESTS being sold and produced on Turkish coast (Izmir) - Life vest manufacturing has become a booming industry and lack of sufficient quality checks means many vests are being made out of non-buoyant materials, causing the wearer to sink when wet.

http://www.ekathimerini.com/205666/gallery/ekathimerini/special-report/fake-life-vests-soak-up-chances-of-survival-for-shipwrecked-refugees
Feb. 5, 2016

Syrian Girl with Eye Cancer First to Use 'Humanitarian Corridor' to Italy – ABC

http://www.abc.net.au/news/2016-02-05/syrian-child-with-cancer-first-to-use-new-humanitarian-corridor/7142332
Feb. 6, 2016

Davos Boss Warns Refugee Crisis Could Be Precursor to Something Much Bigger – Bloomberg

http://www.bloomberg.com/news/articles/2016-01-18/wef-boss-schwab-warns-commodities-rout-could-spur-more-migration
Feb. 6, 2016

Thousands March Through Melbourne to Demand Asylum Seekers be Allowed to Stay – SMH

http://www.dailylife.com.au/news-and-views/news-features/thousands-march-through-melbourne-to-demand-asylum-seekers-be-allowed-to-stay-20160204-gmm4r5.html
Feb. 6, 2016

Malala Yousafzai Launches Campaign in Support of Refugee Children – NY Times

http://nytlive.nytimes.com/womenintheworld/2016/02/04/malala-yousafzai-launches-campaign-in-support-of-refugee-children/
Feb. 6, 2016

What a Quid Pro Quo Could do for Syrian Refugees – Devex

https://www.devex.com/news/what-a-quid-pro-quo-could-do-for-syrian-refugees-87707#.VrTHZH9f0eE.facebook
Feb. 6, 2016

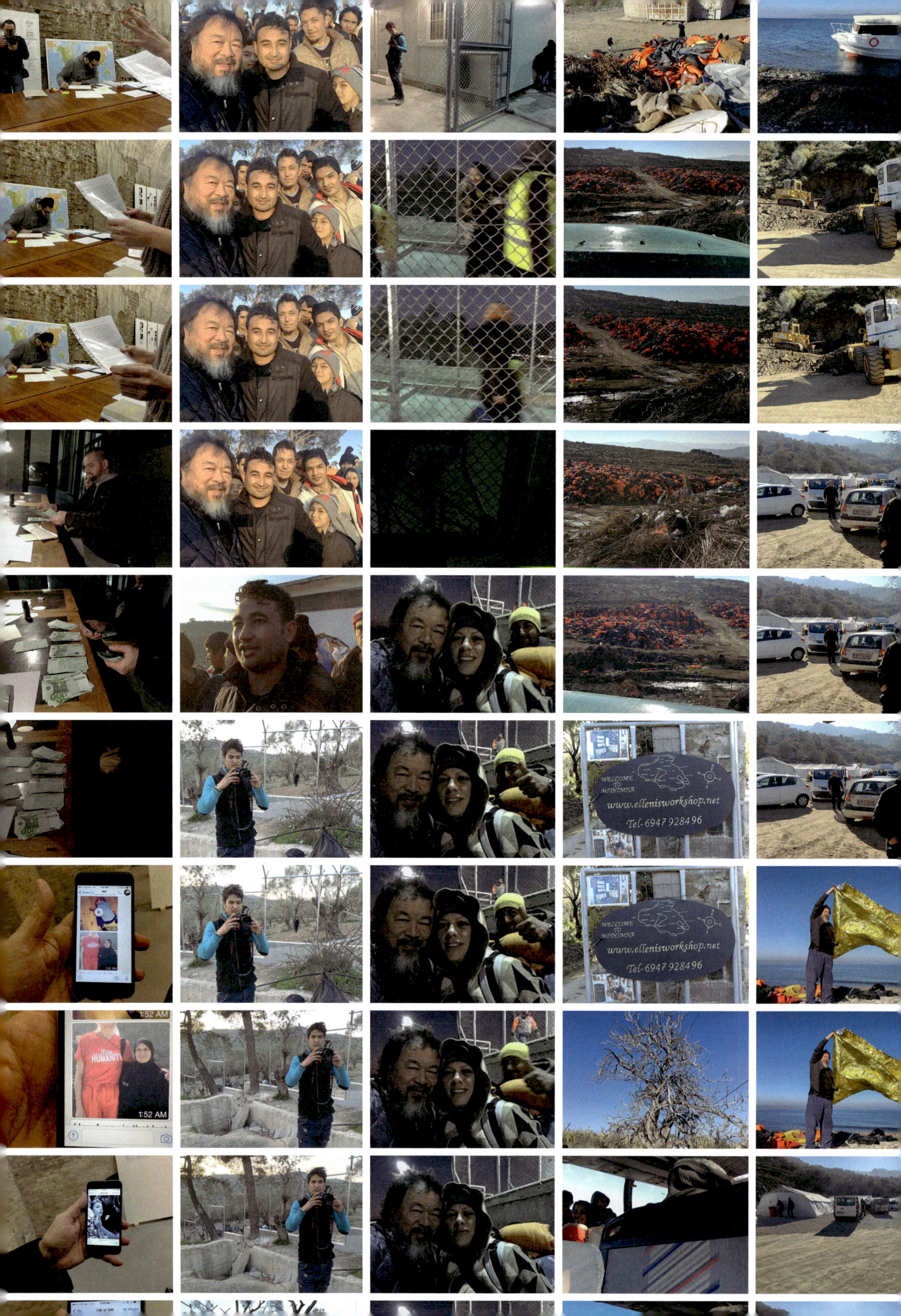

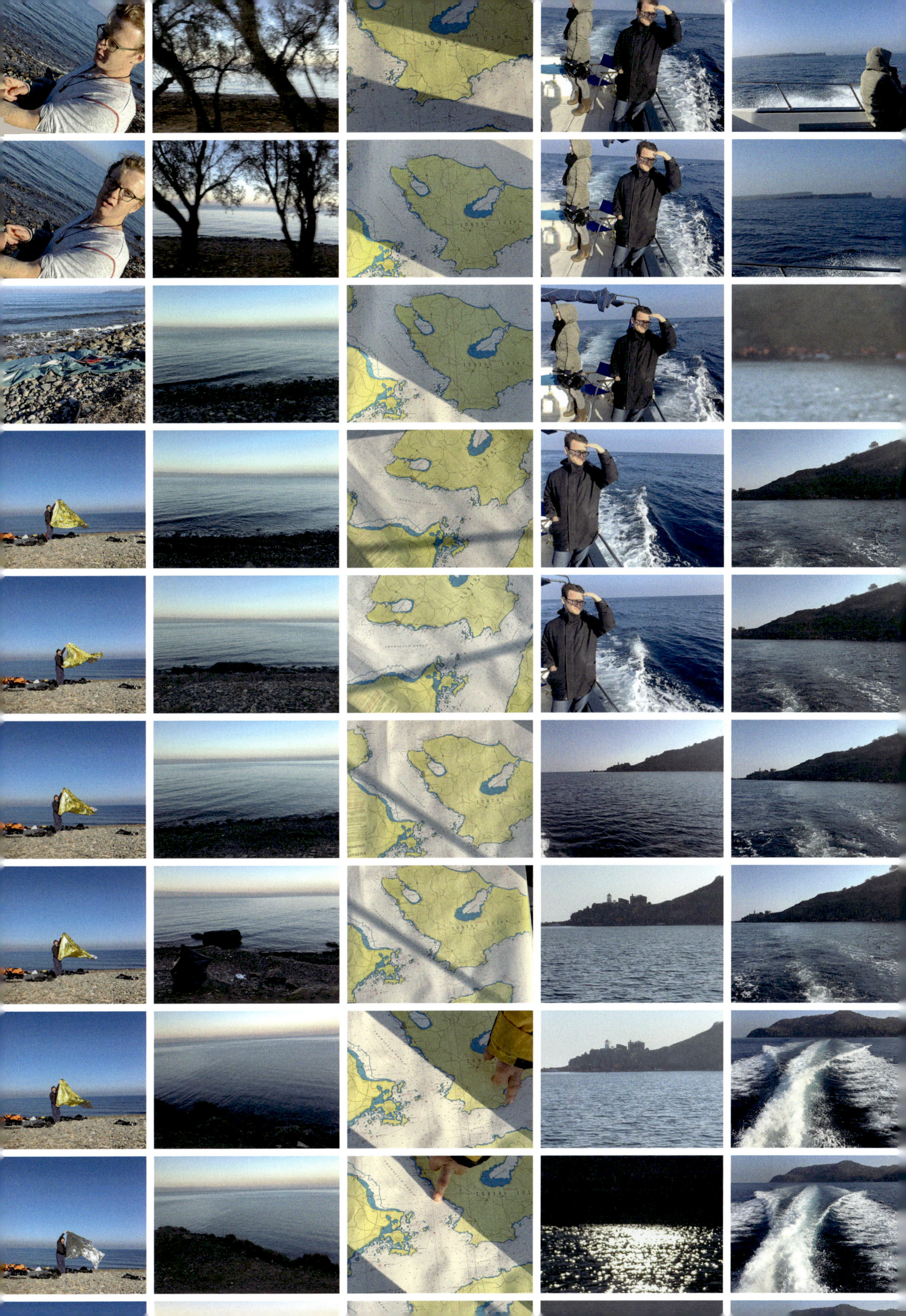

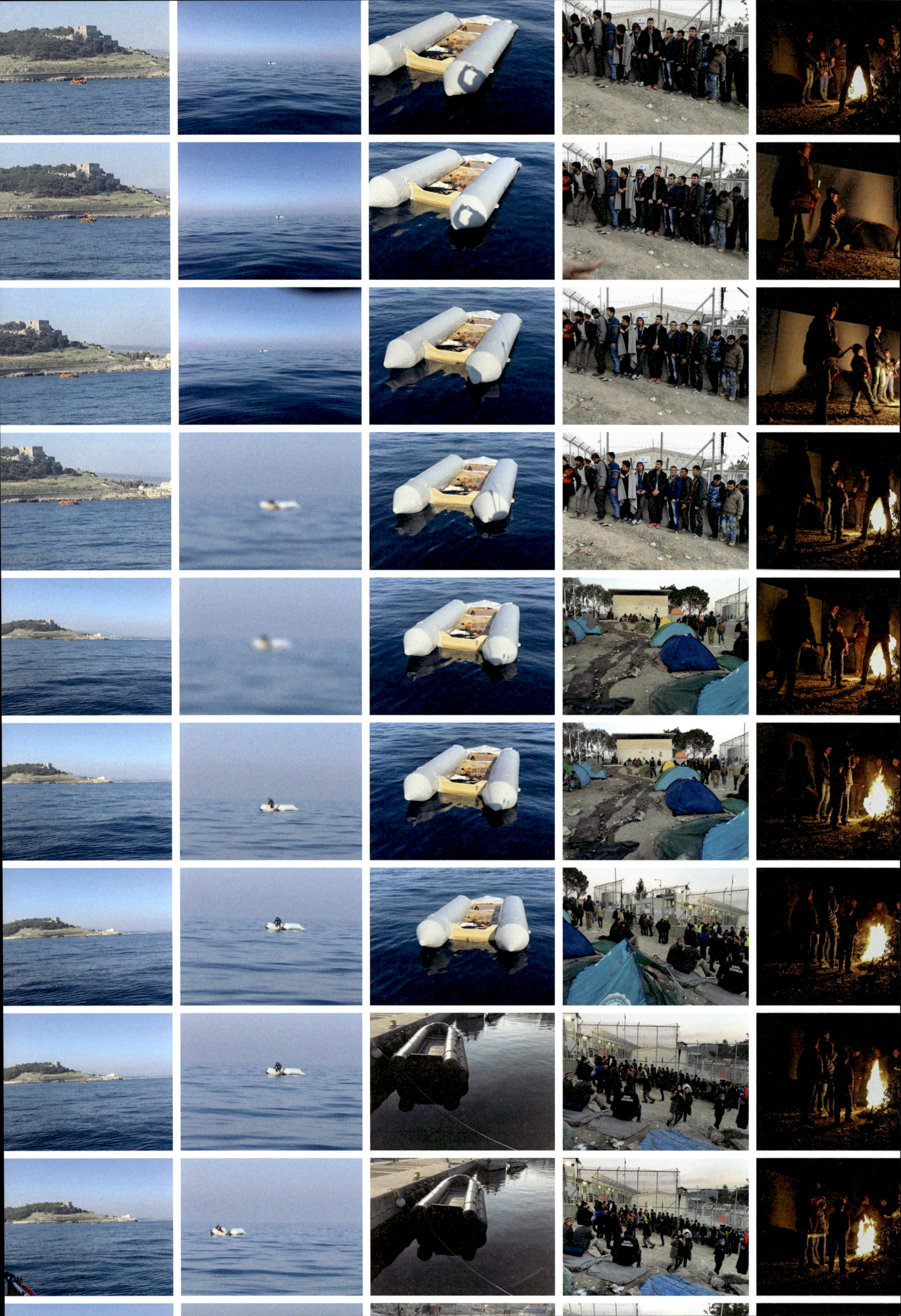

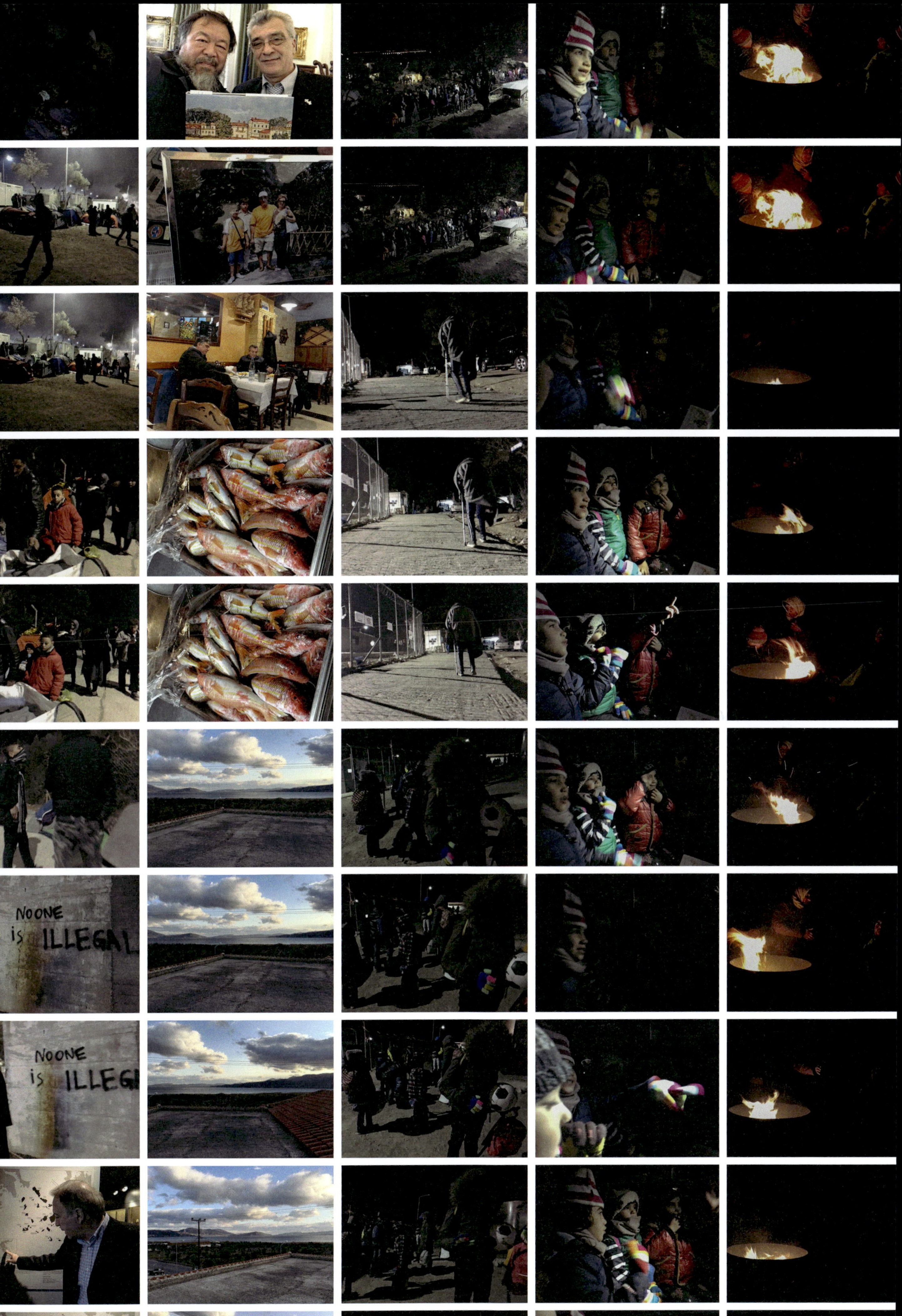

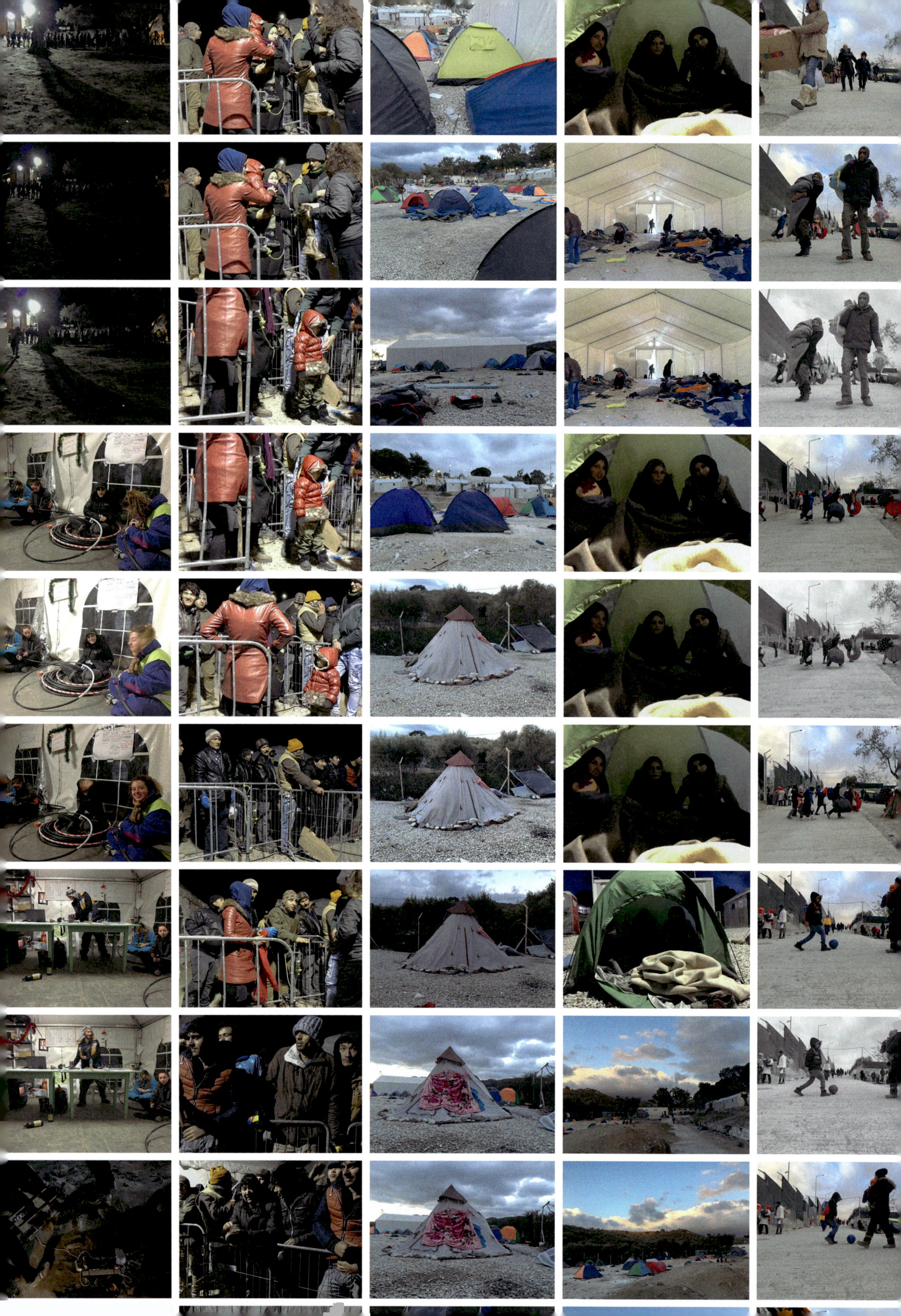

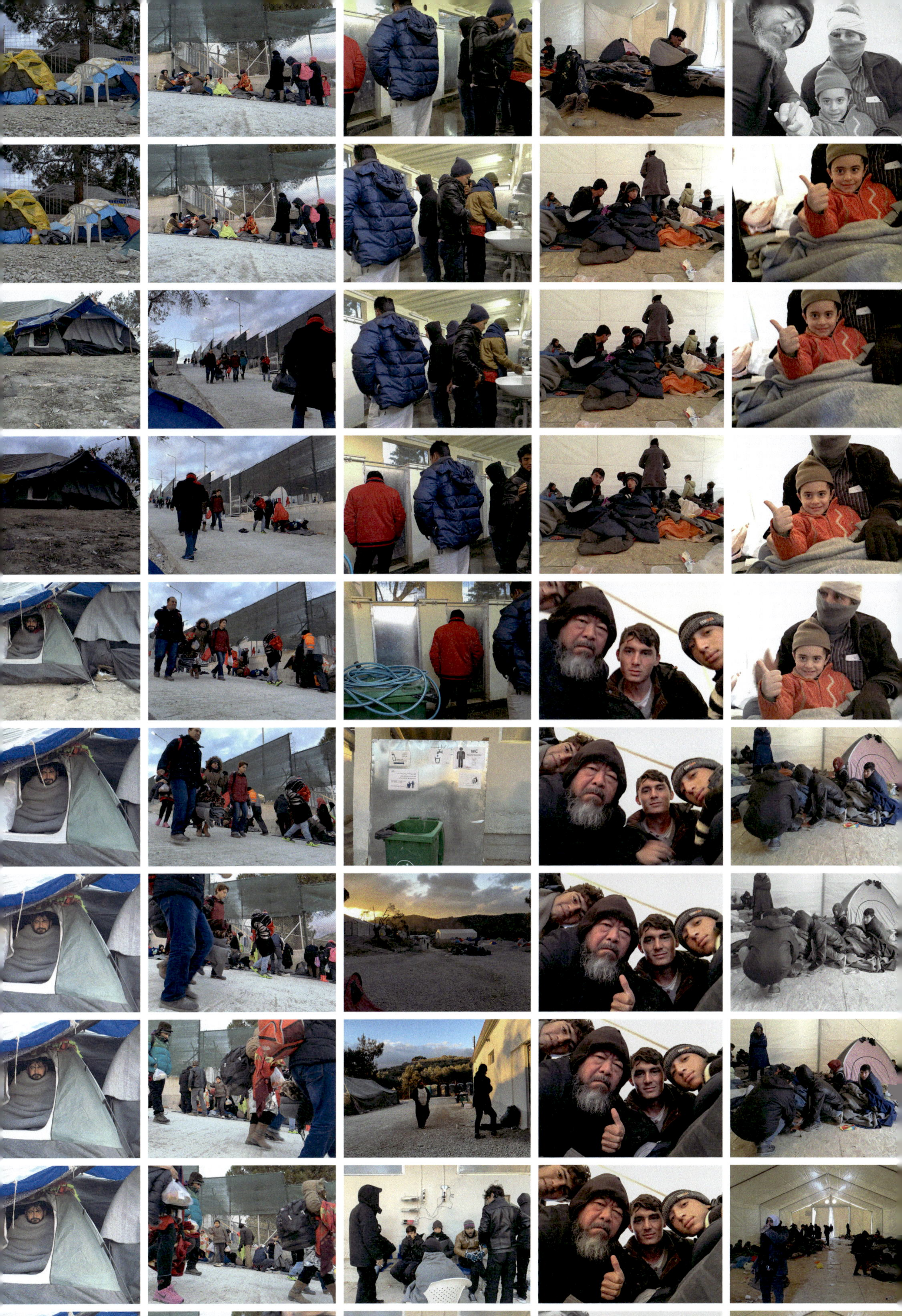

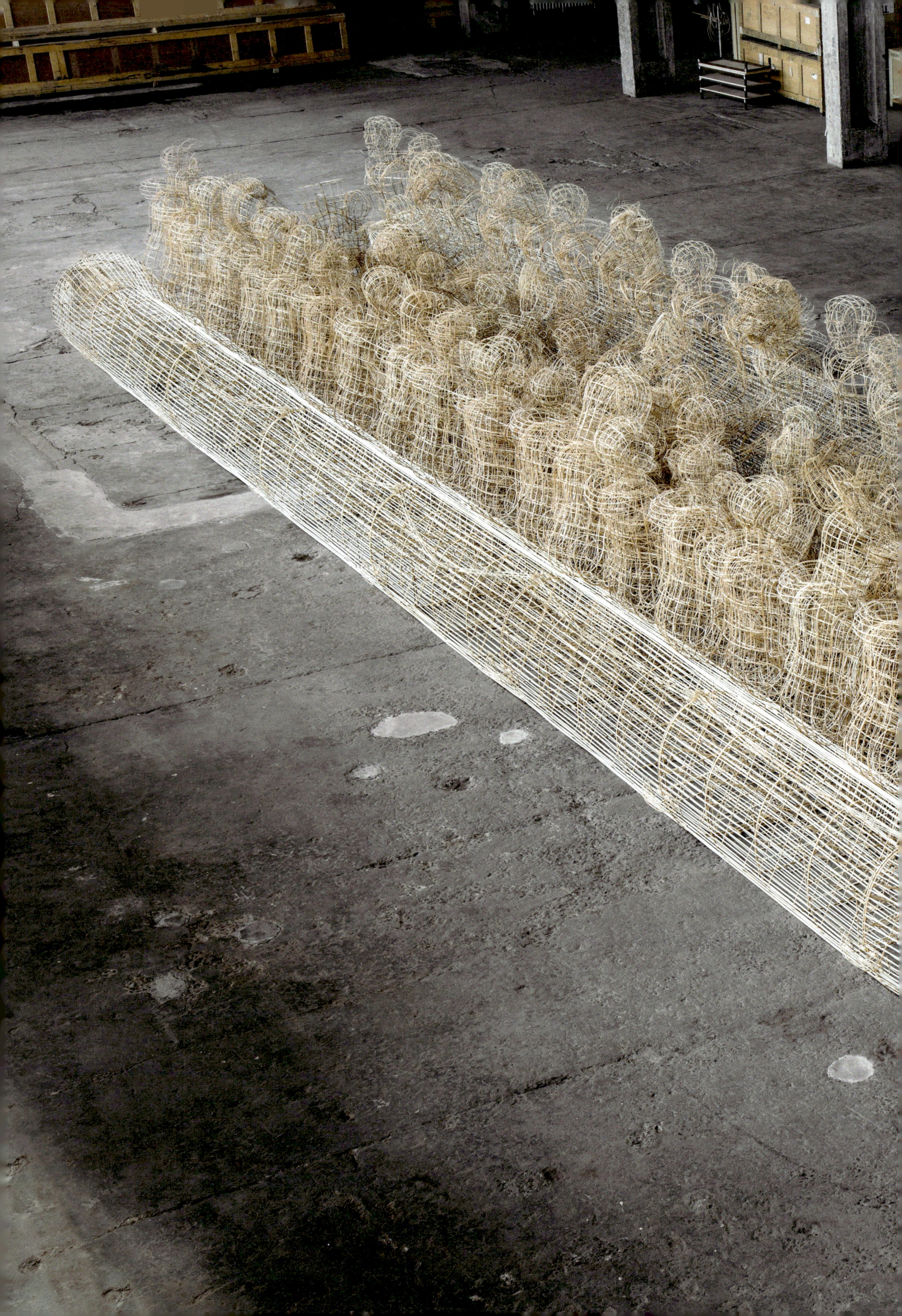

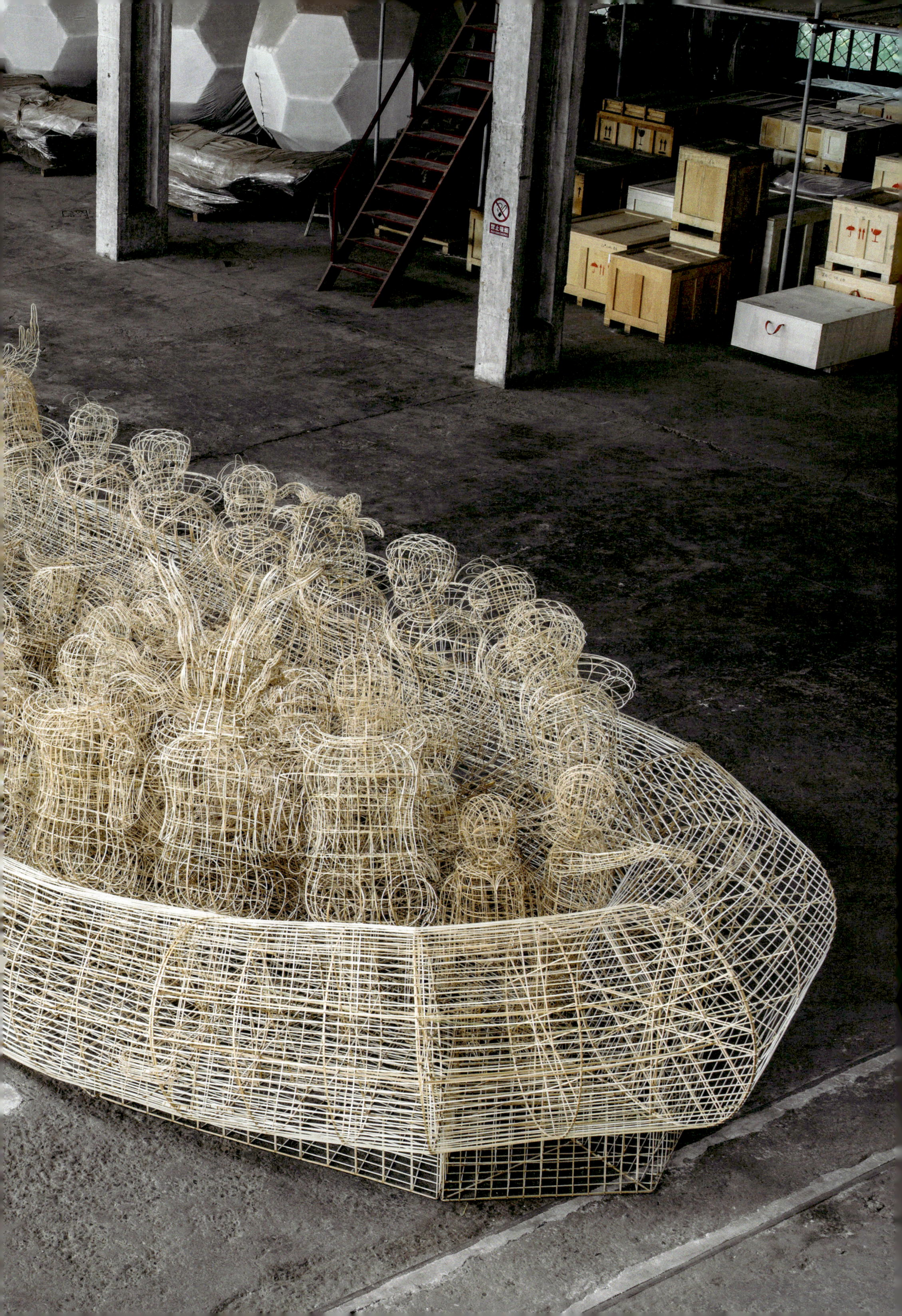

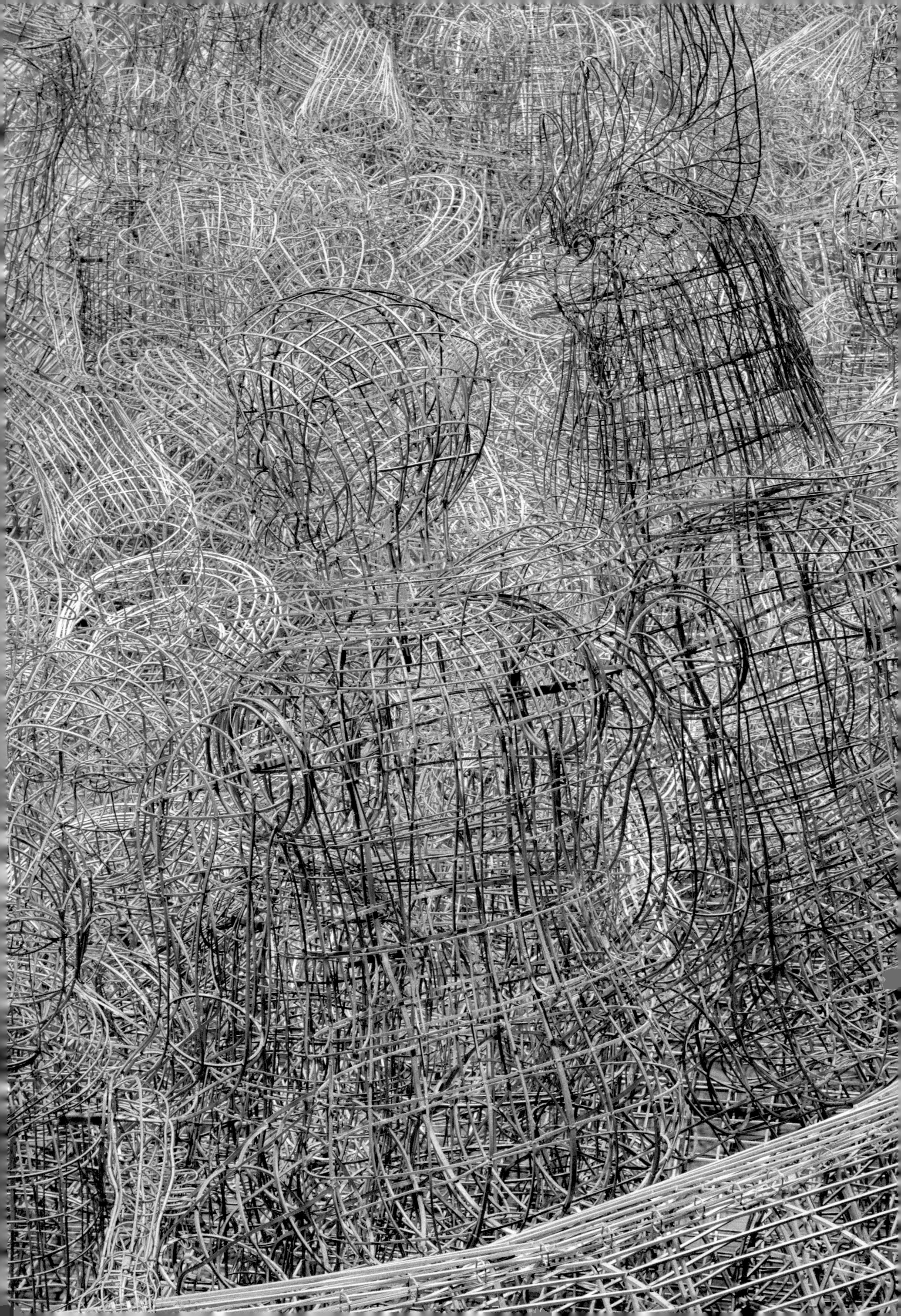

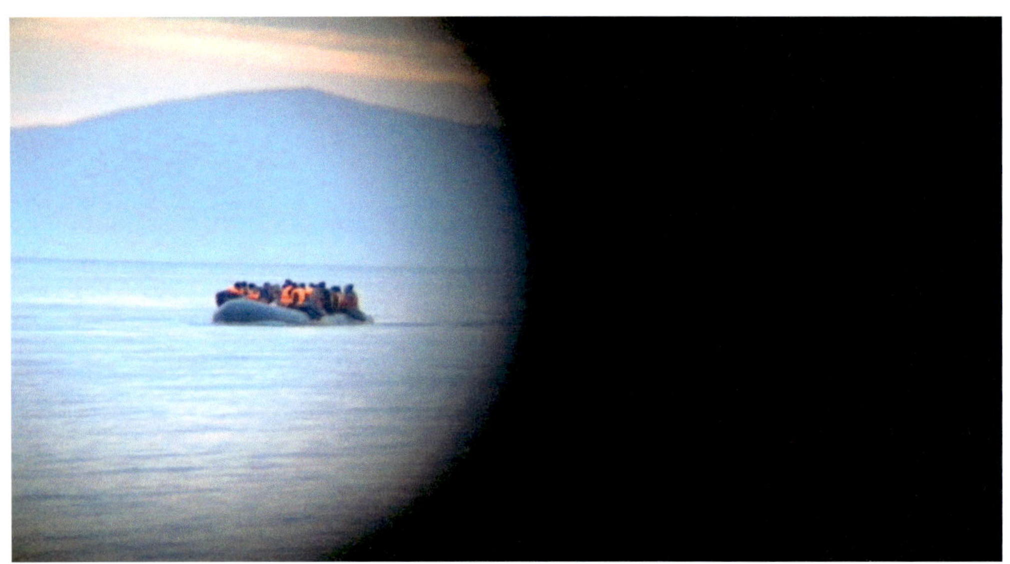

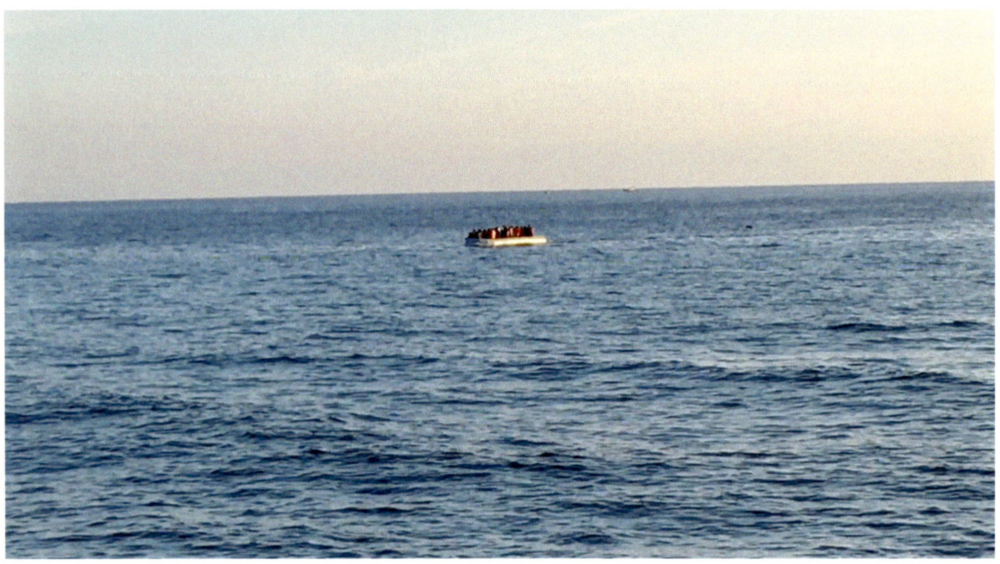

At Sea, 2016
Video, color, sound, 4'8"

114

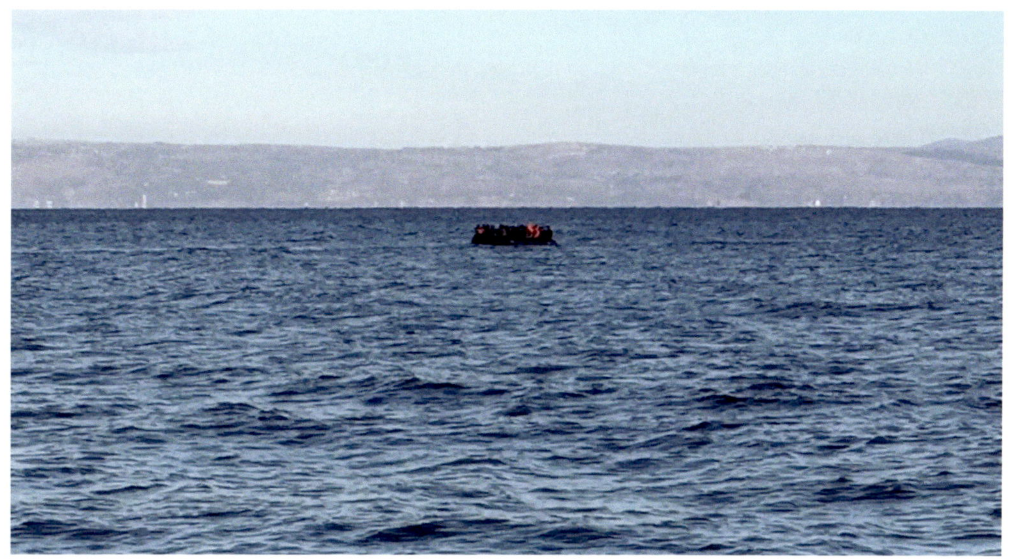

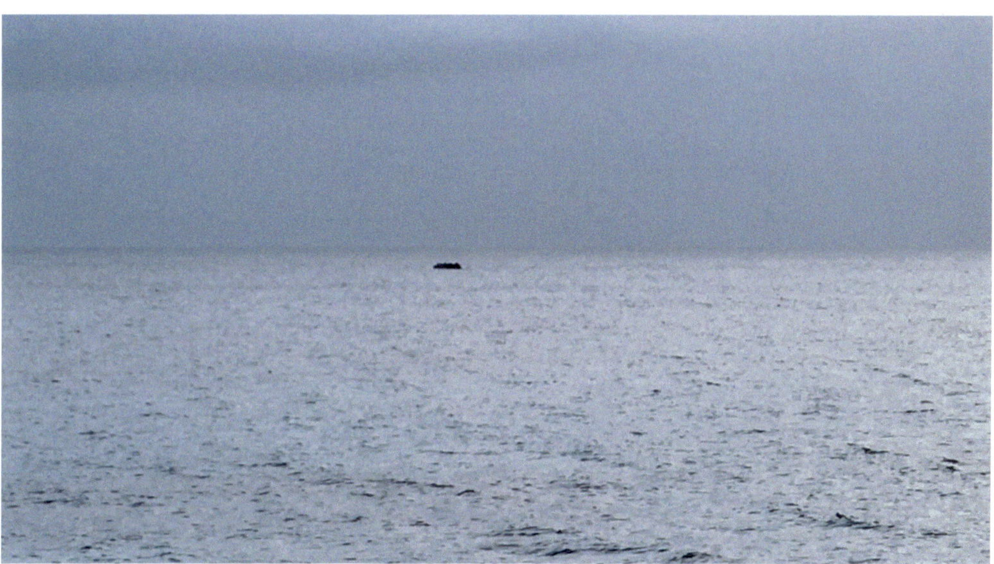

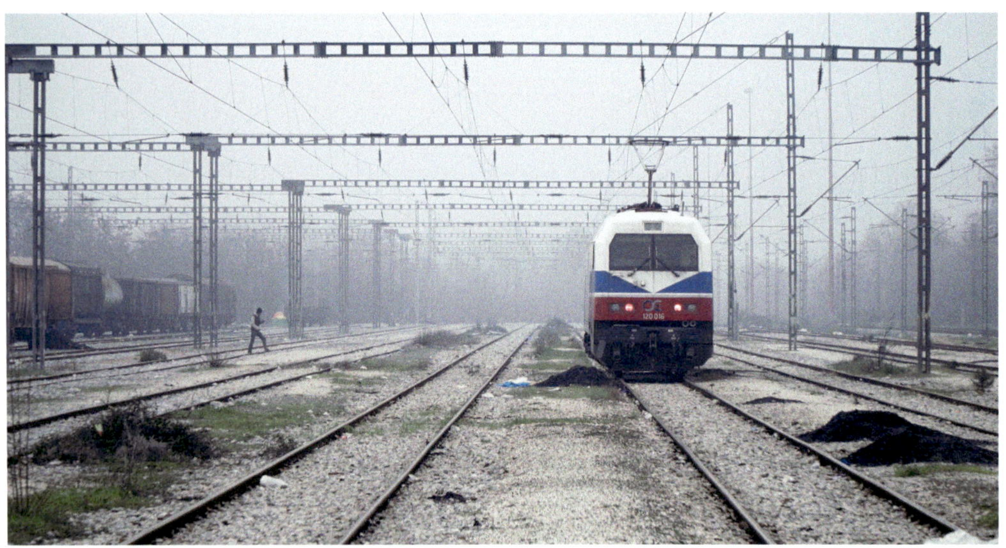

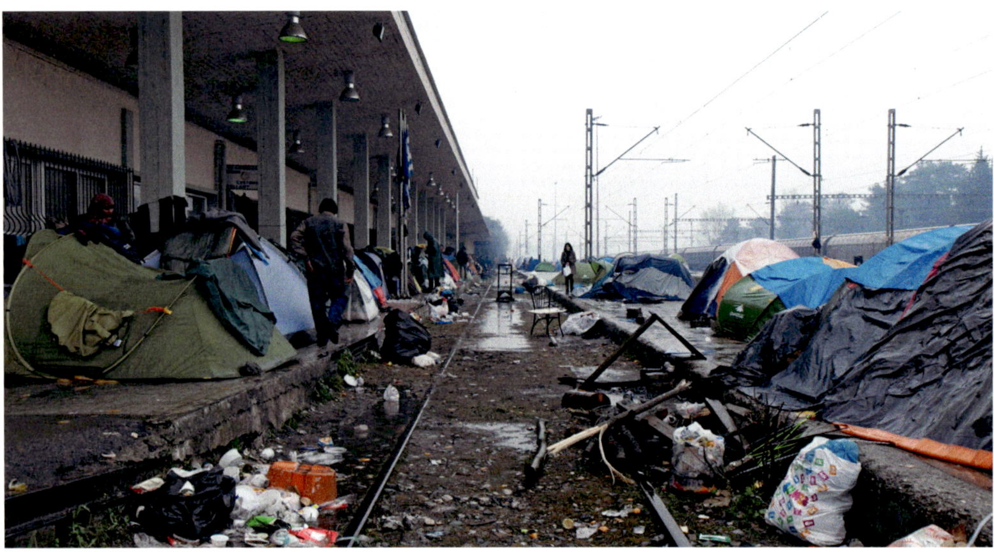

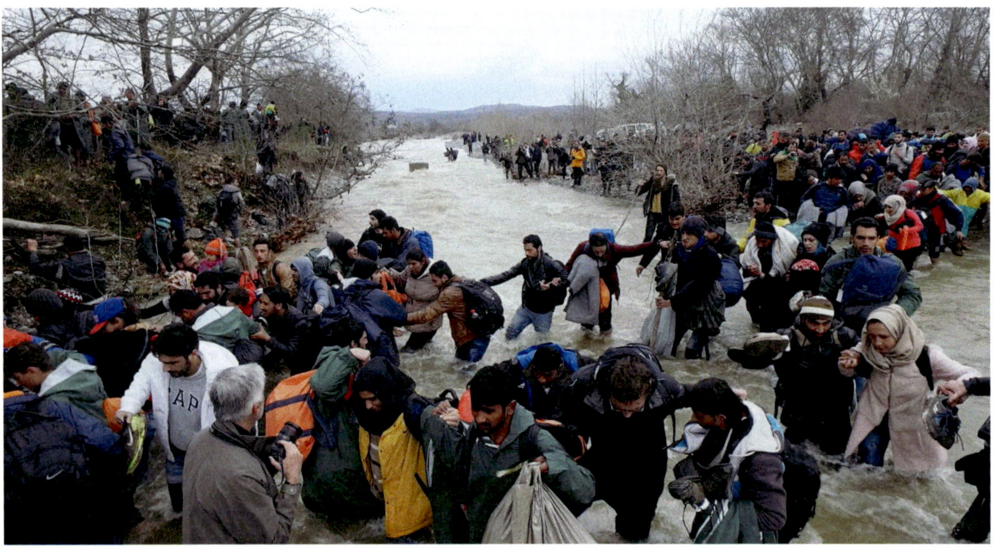

Idomeni, 2016
Video, color, sound, 17'22"

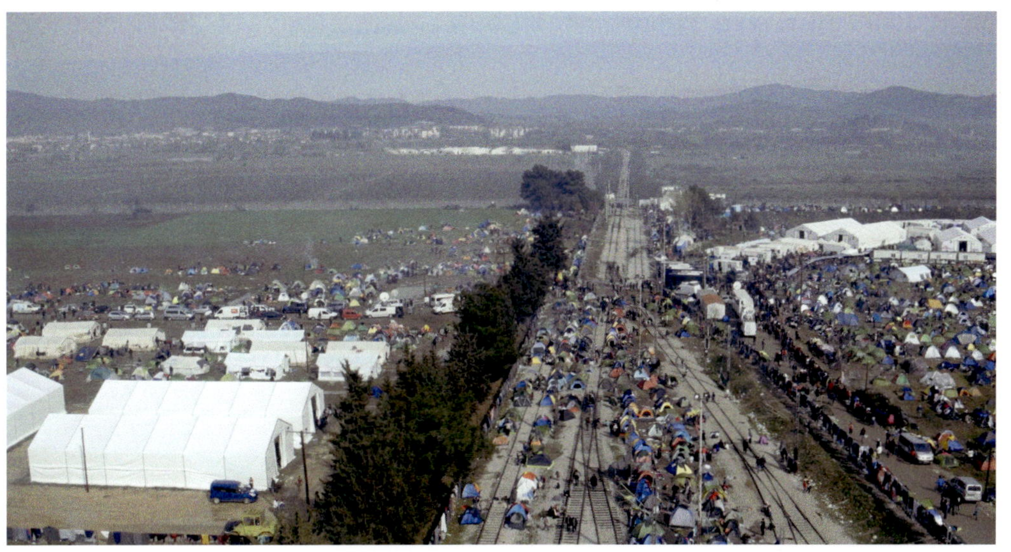

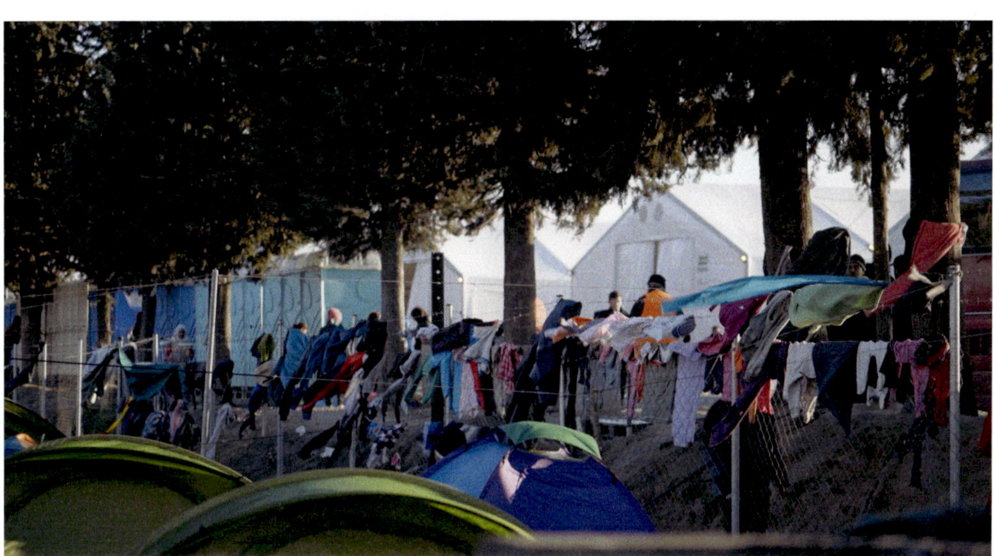

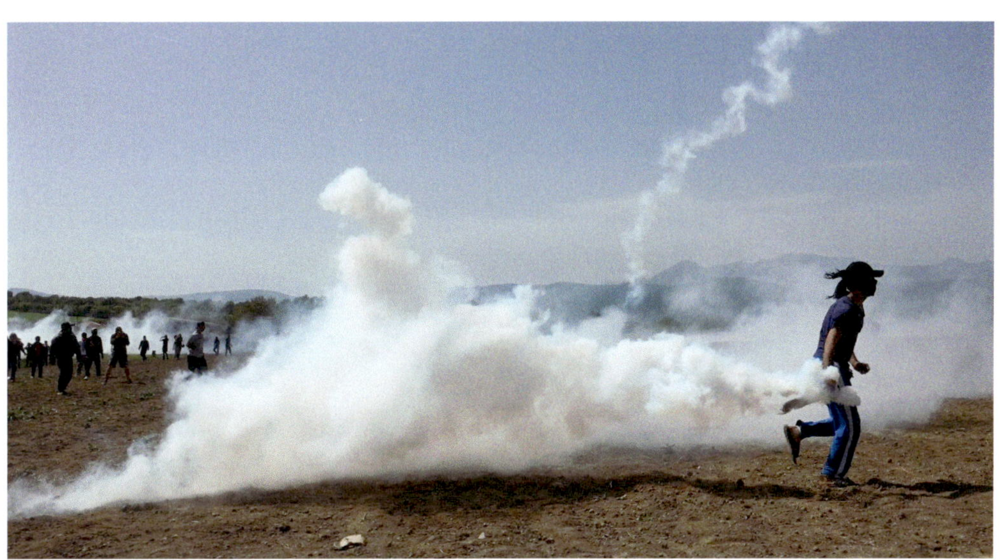

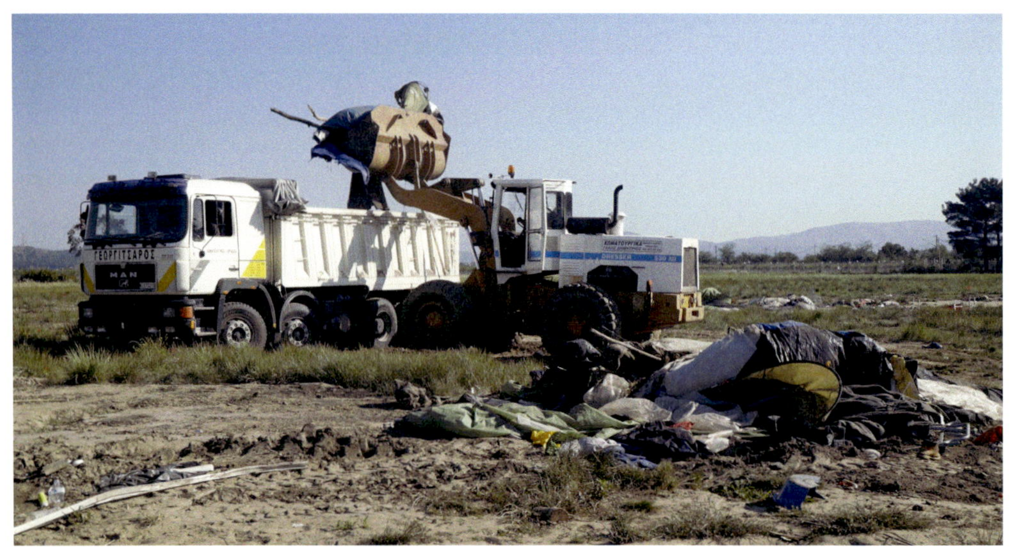

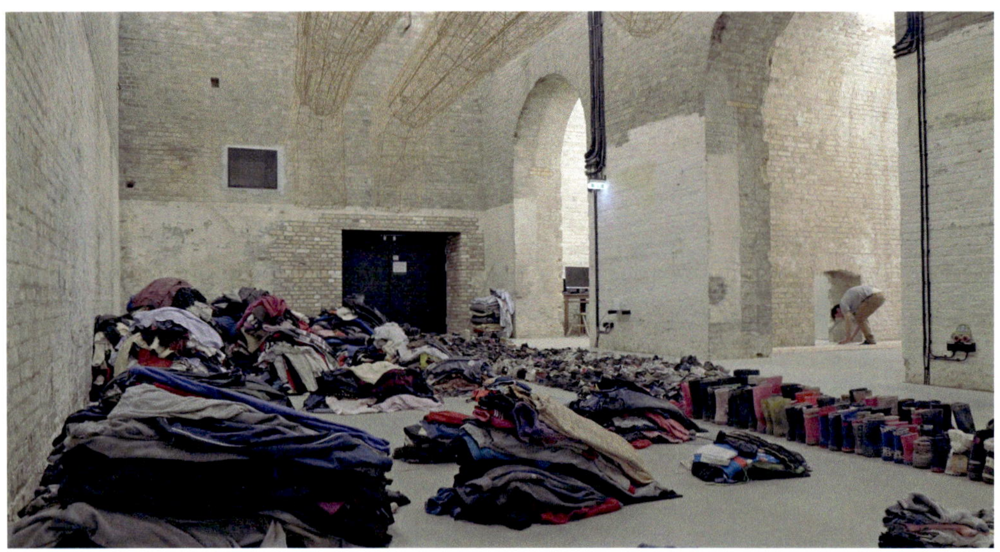

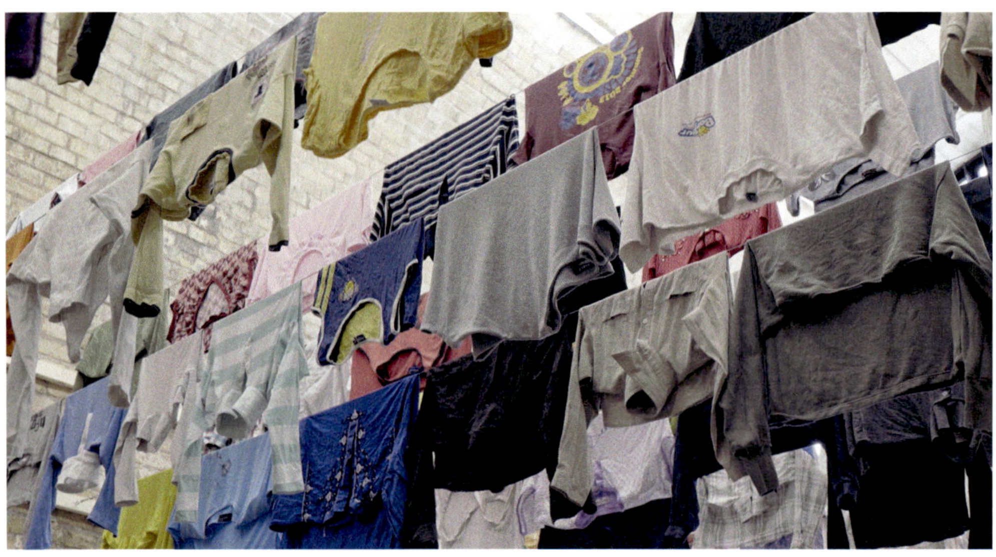

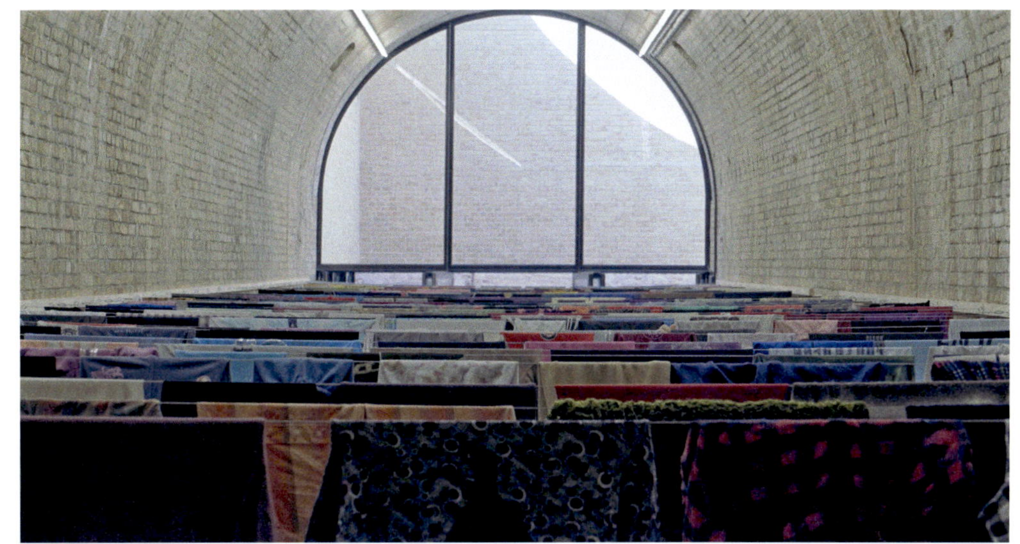

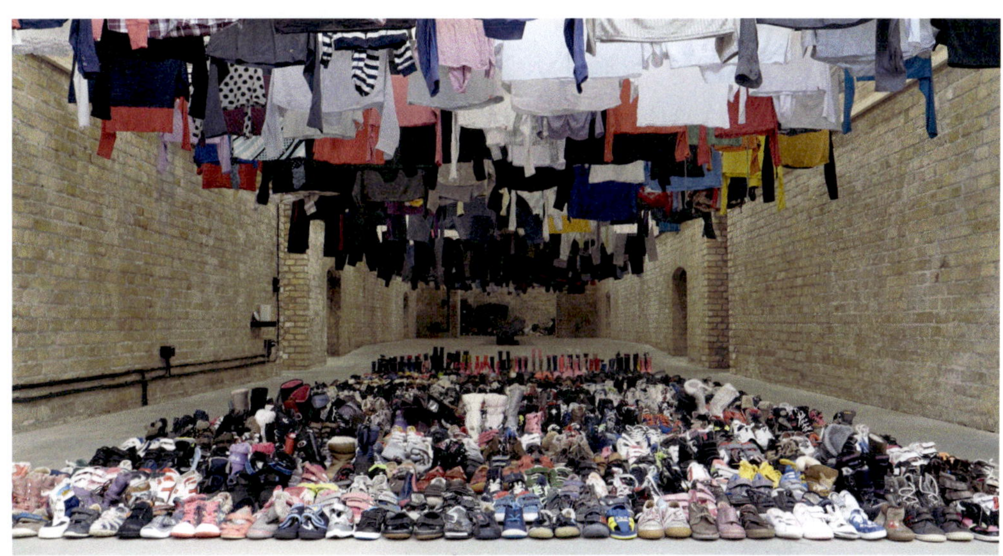

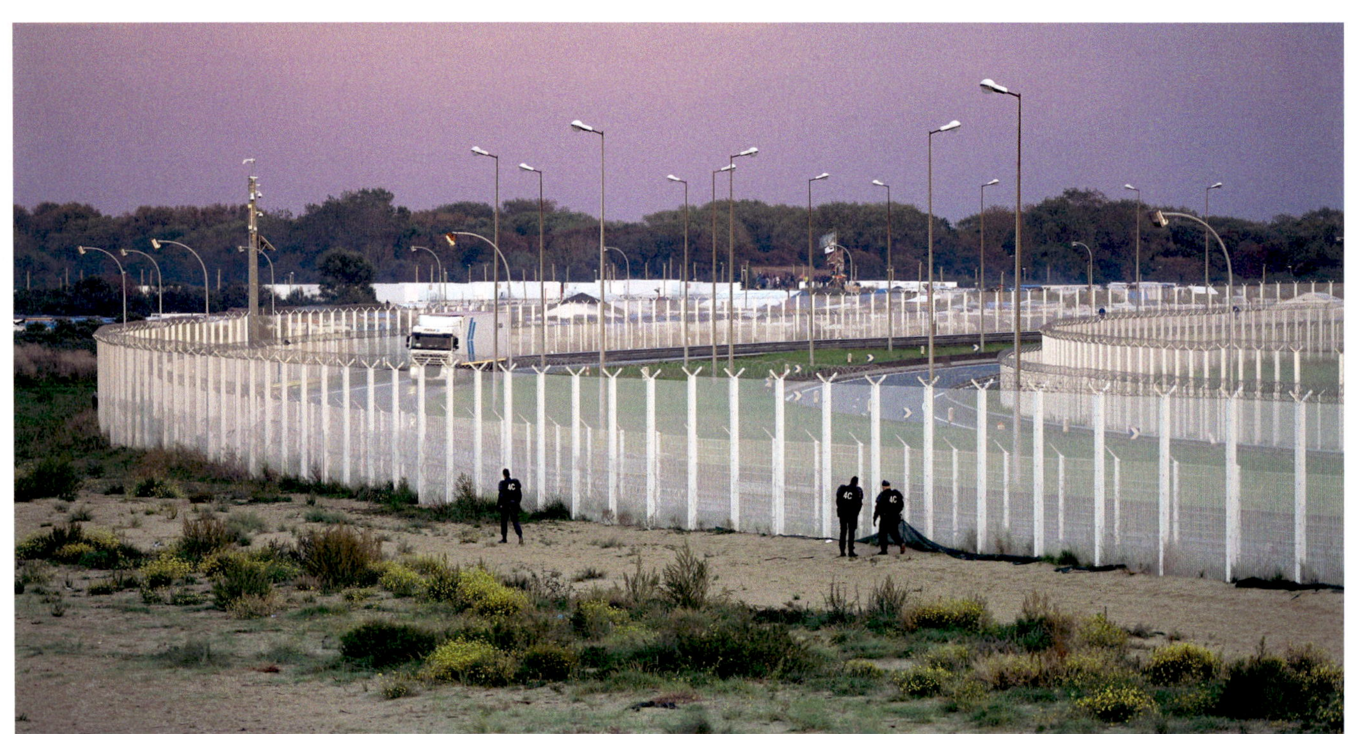

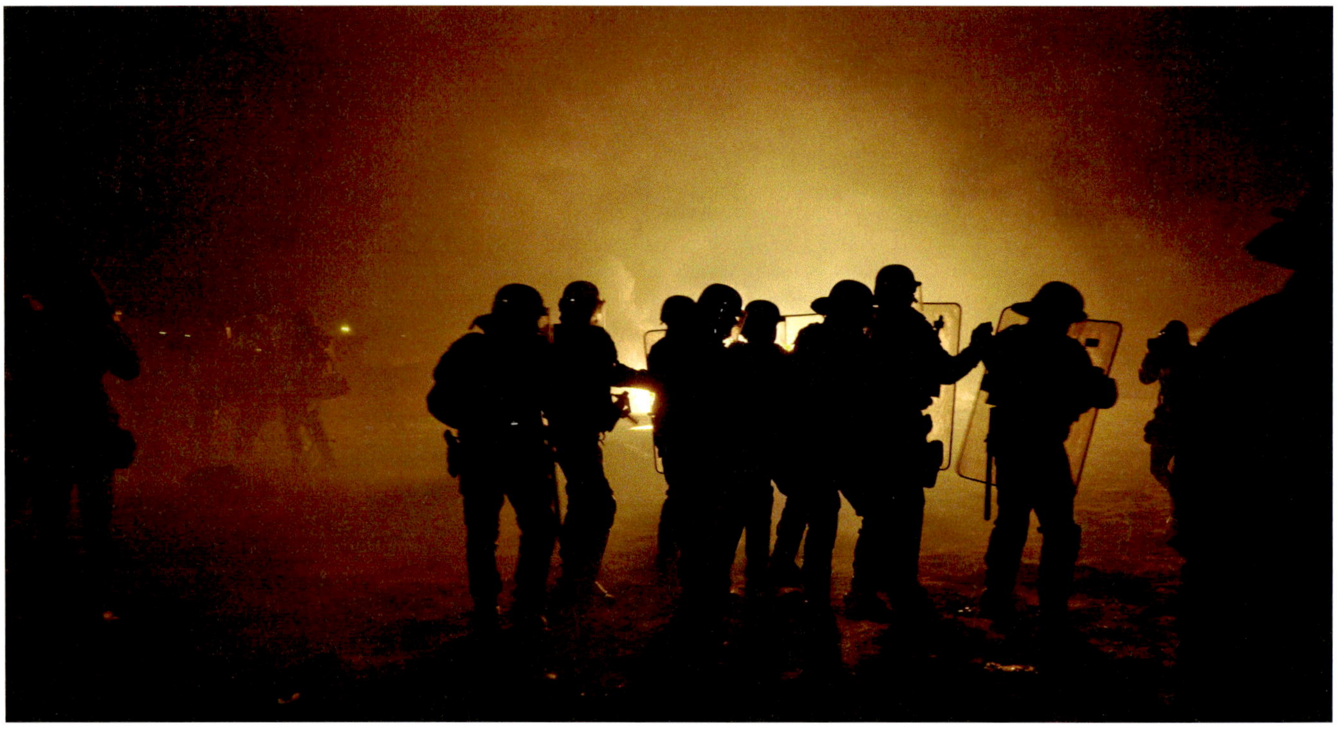

Calais, 2018
Video, color, sound, 18'41"

120

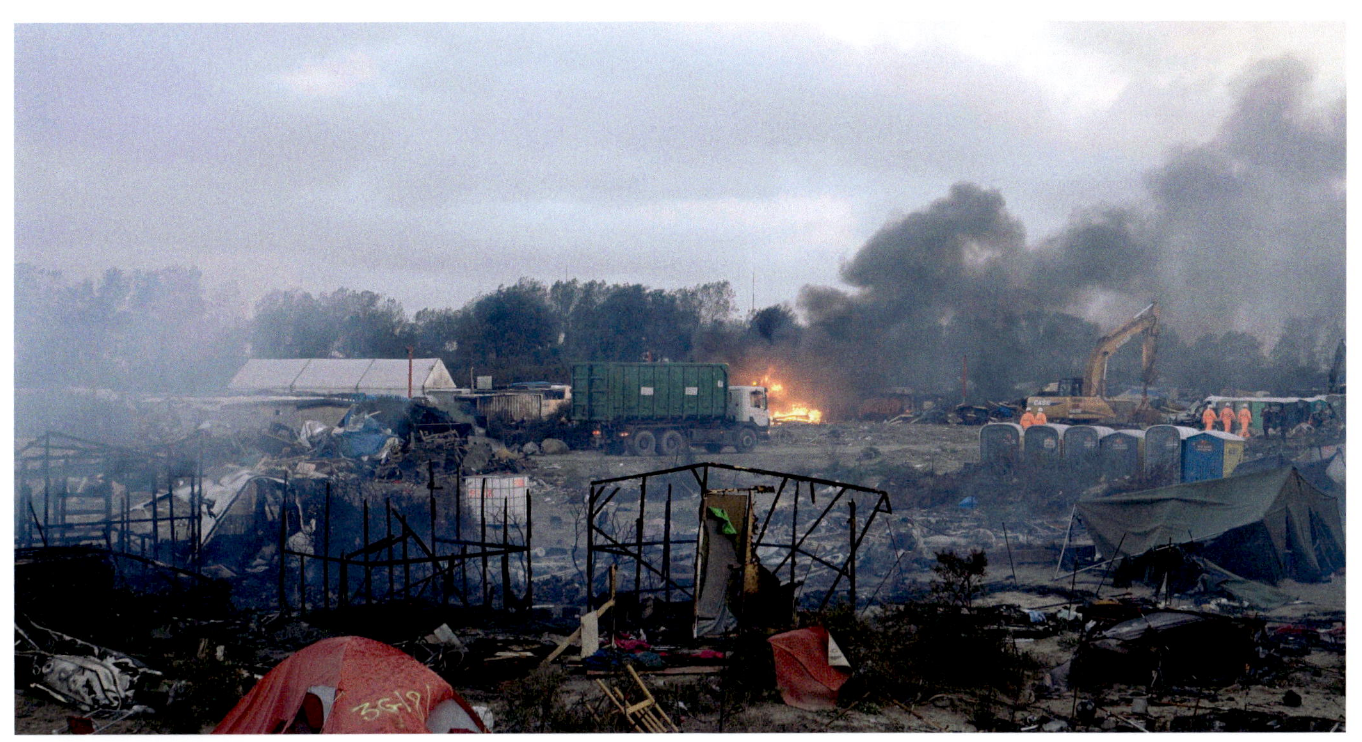

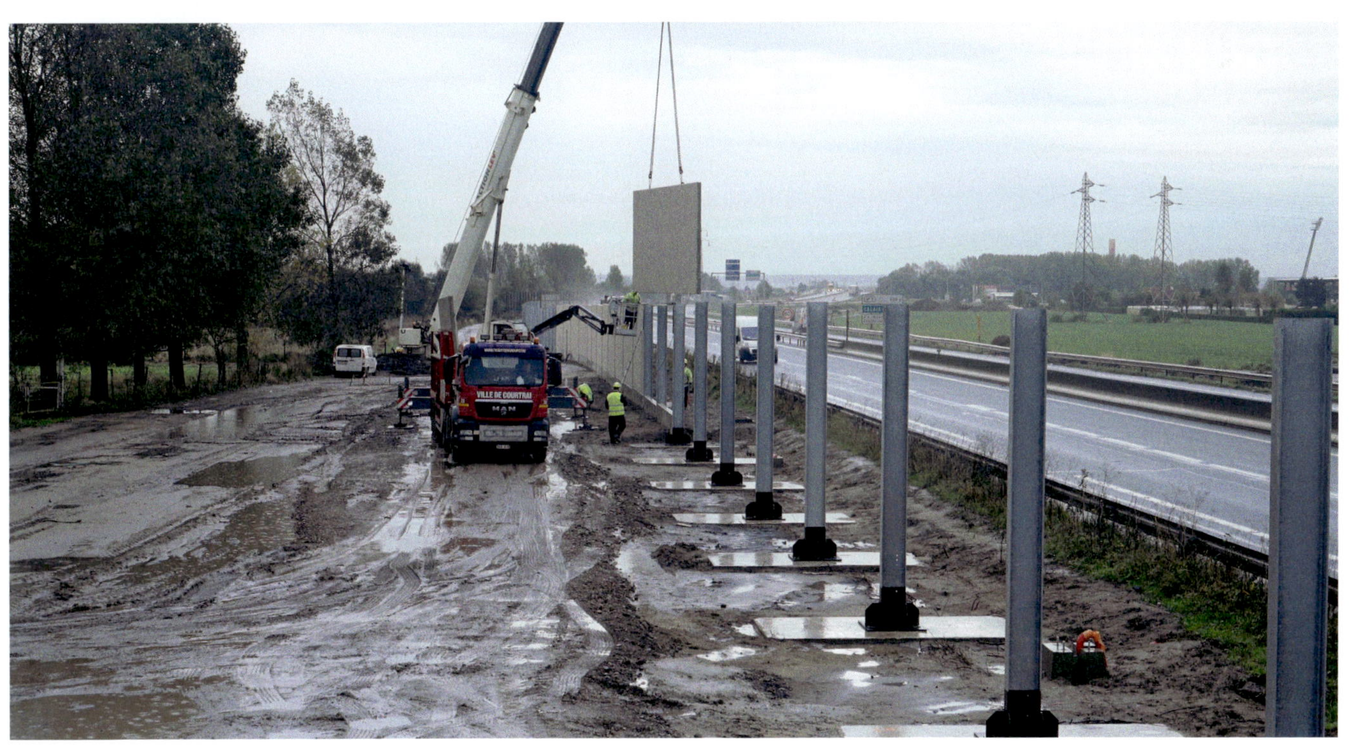

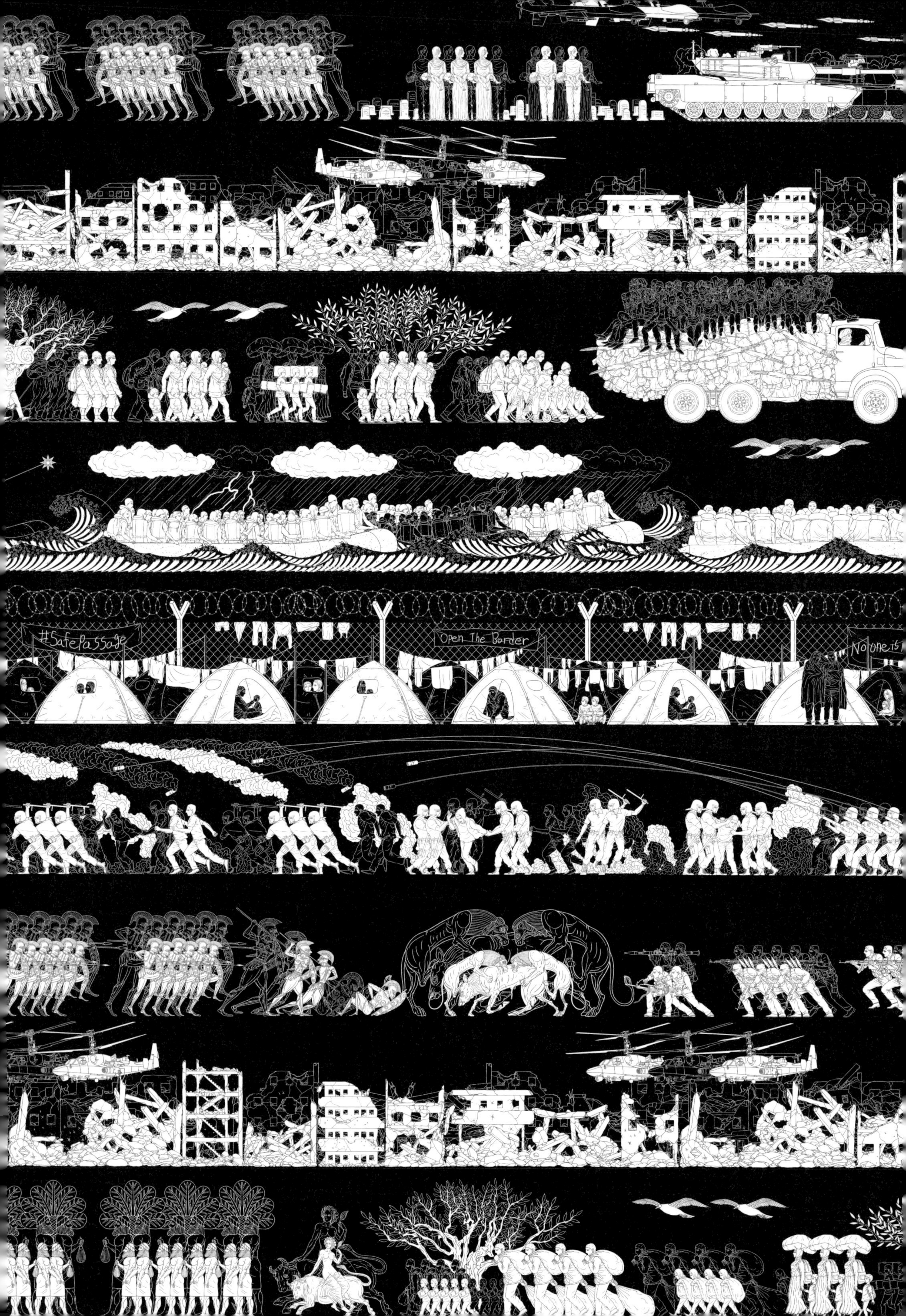
#SafePassage
Open The Border
No one is

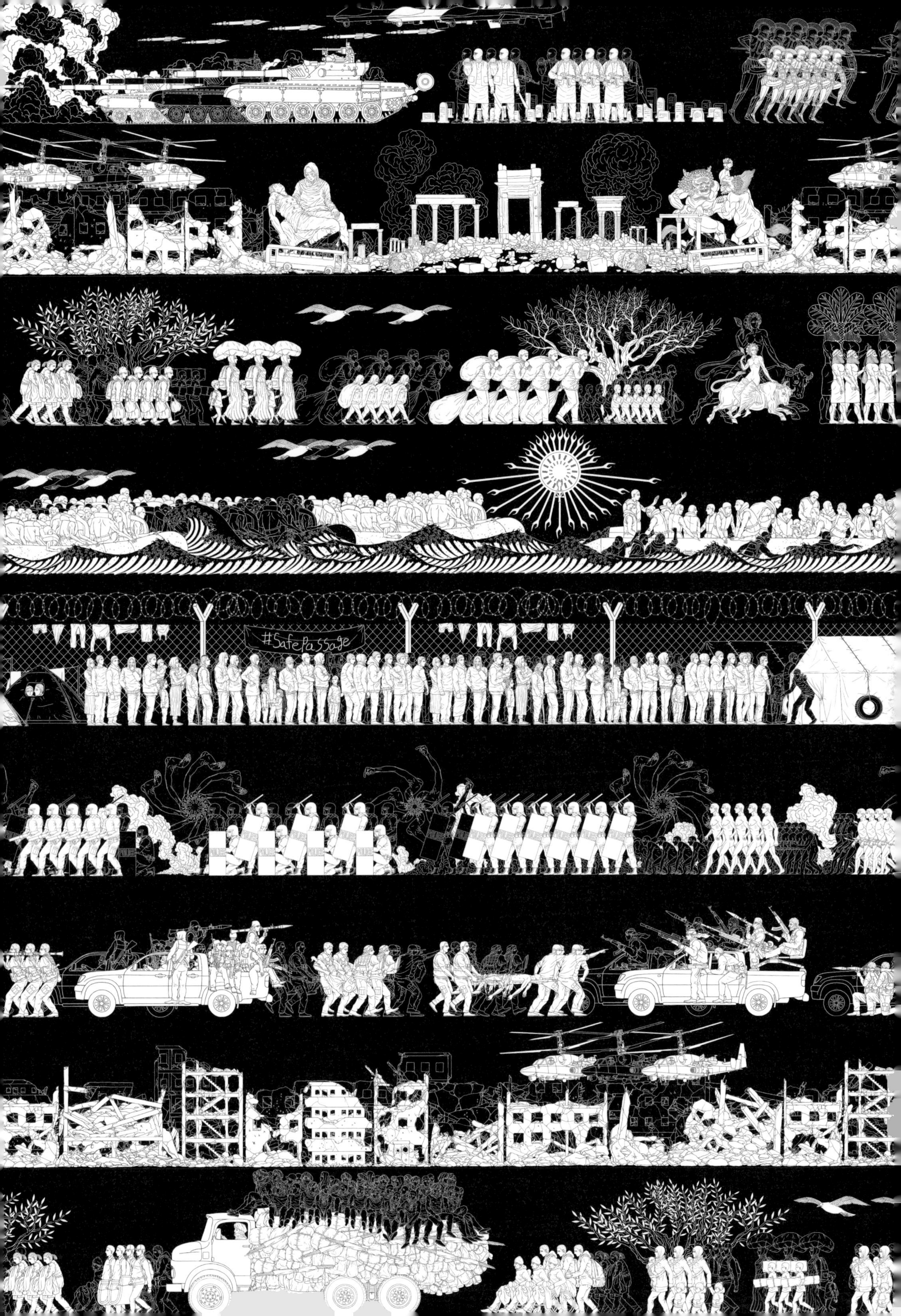
#SafePassage

Odyssey, 2016
Wallpaper
Dimensions variable

Study of Perspective,
1995–2011/2014
40 framed photographs
Height 50 cm, width
66.6–75.7cm

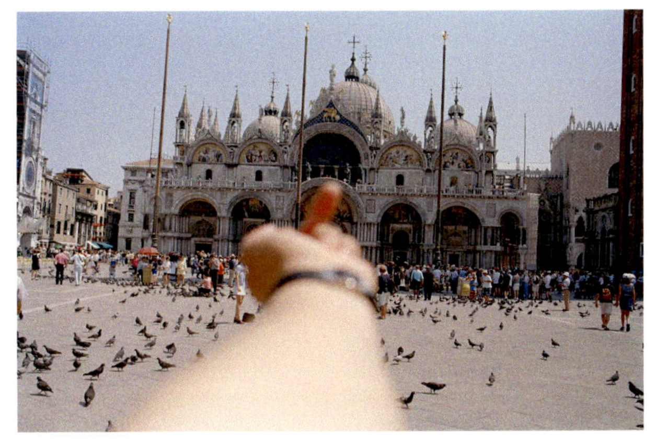
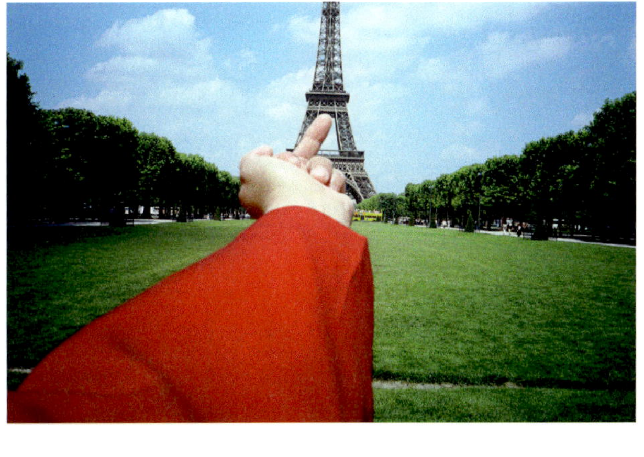
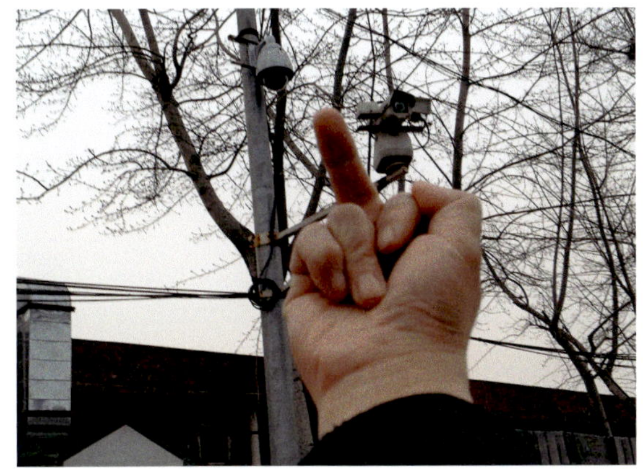
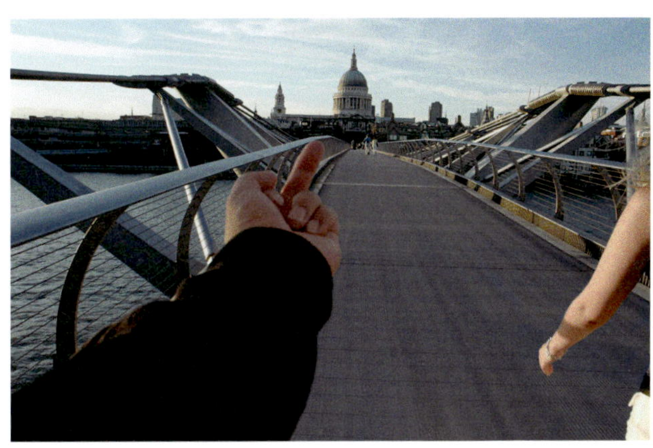
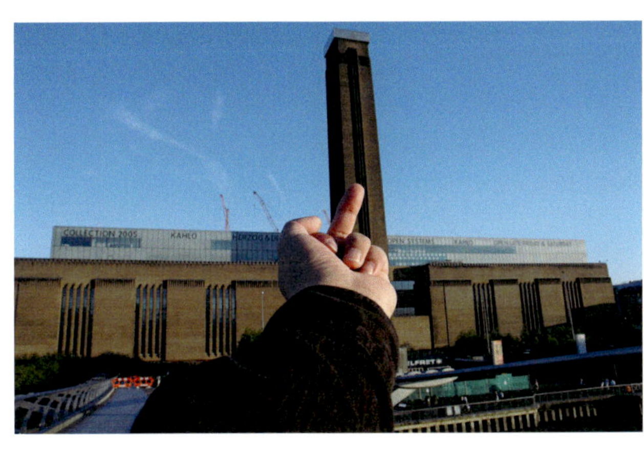
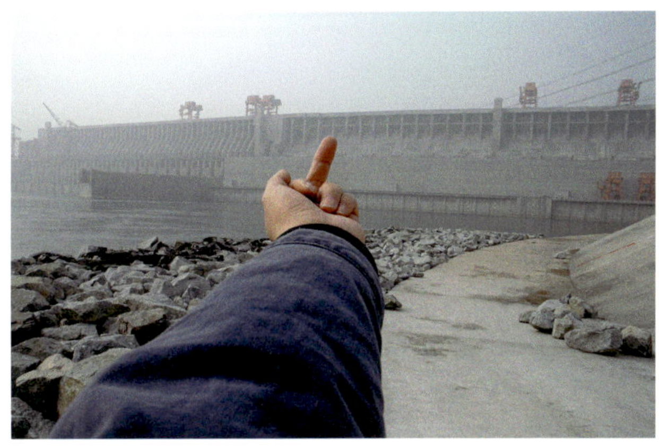
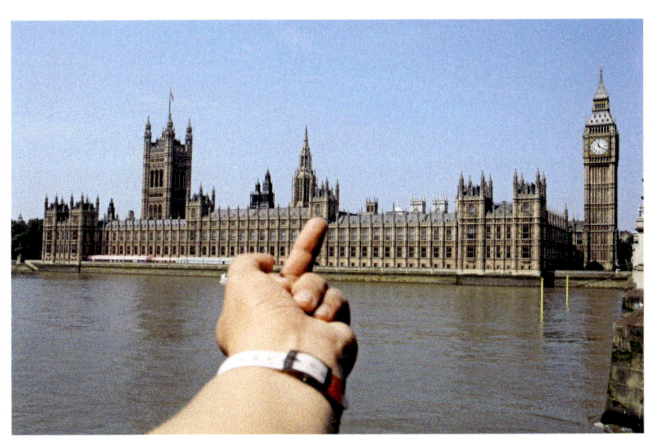
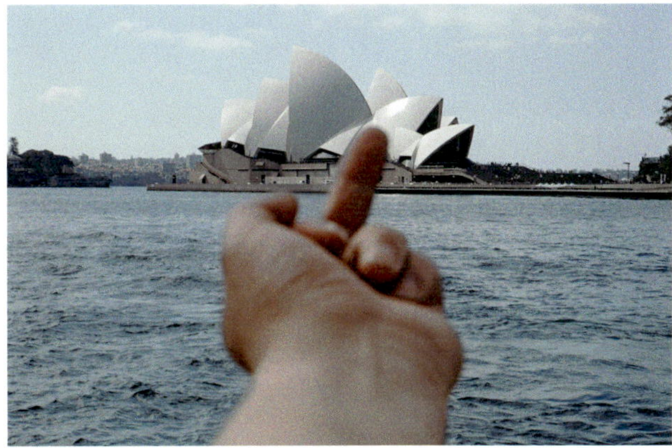

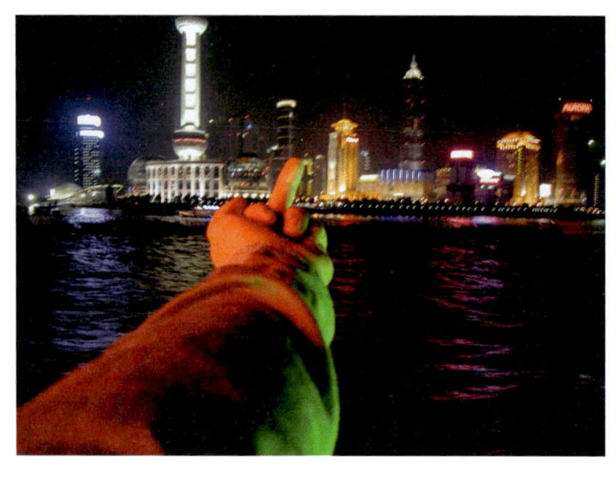
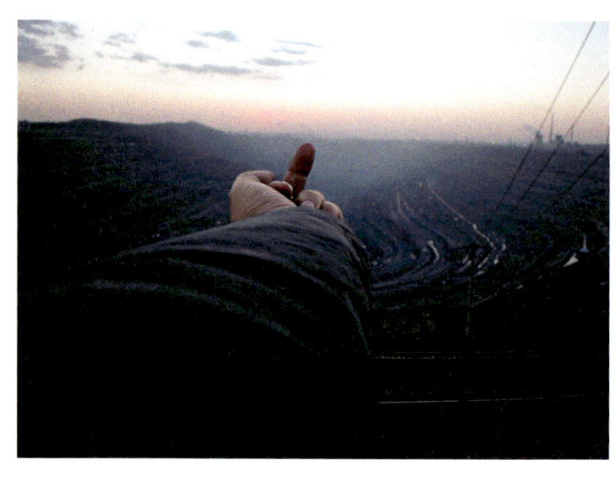
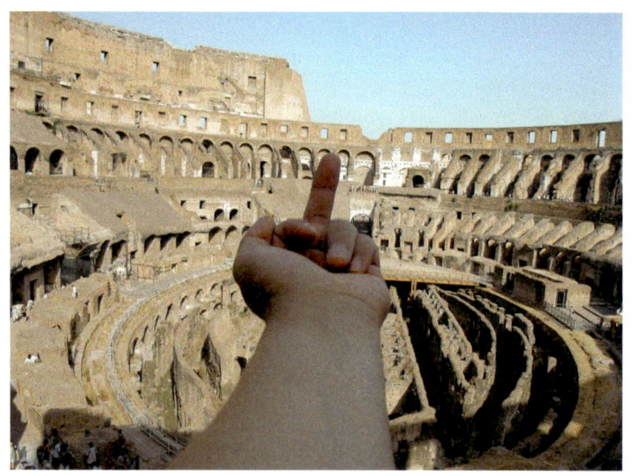
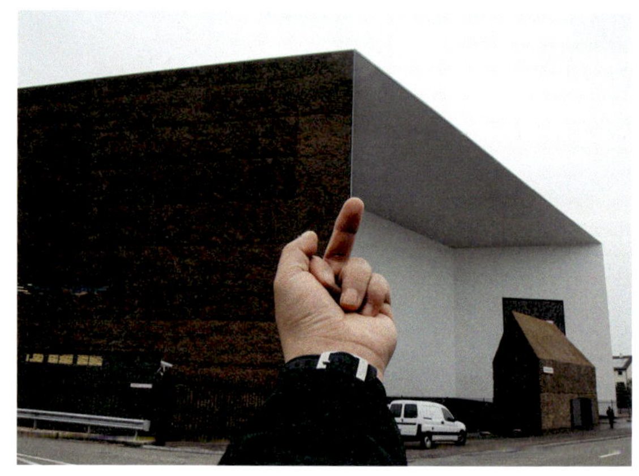
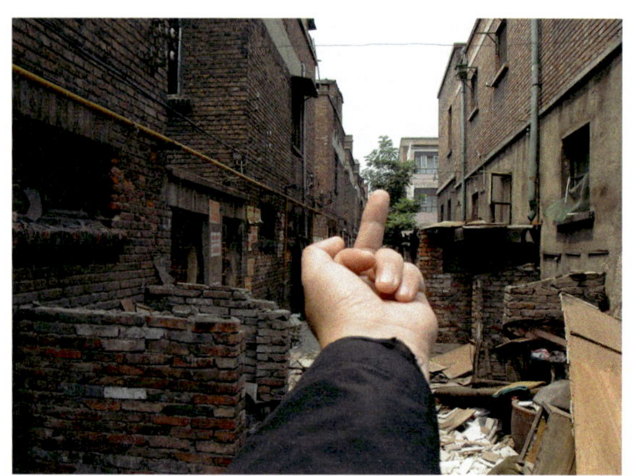
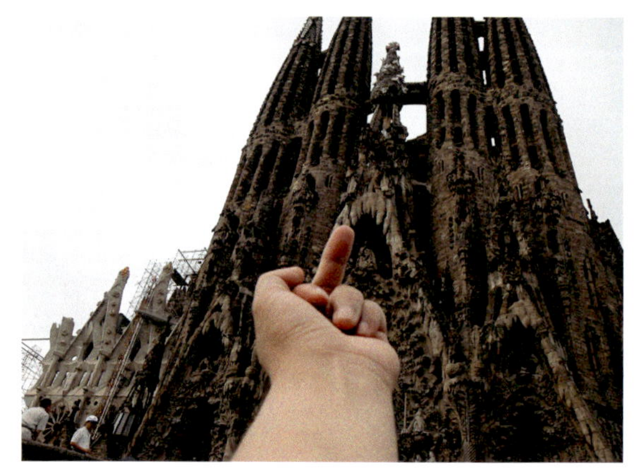
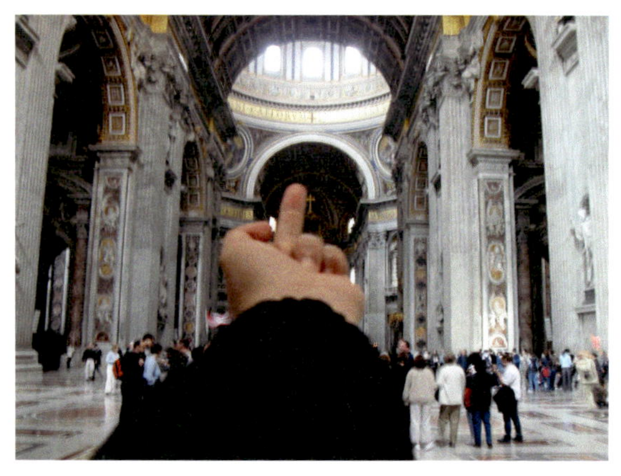
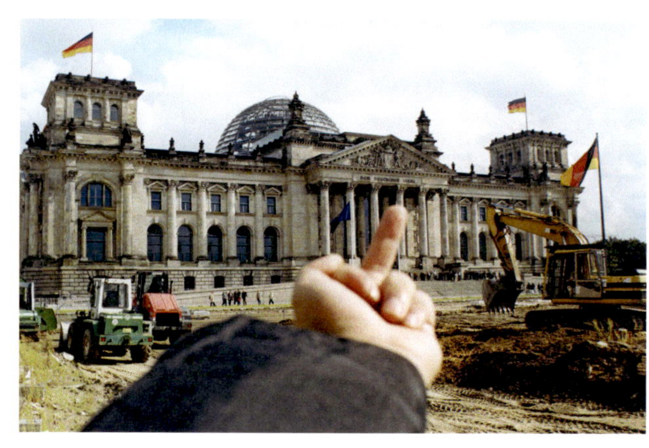

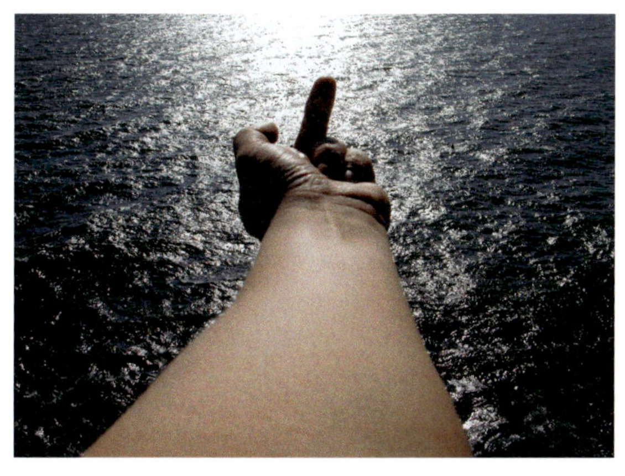
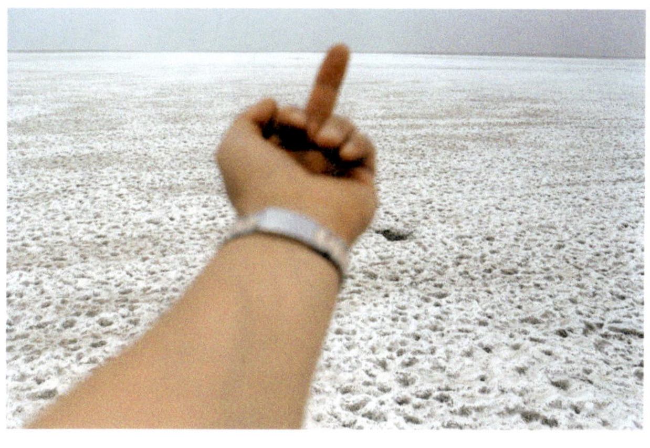
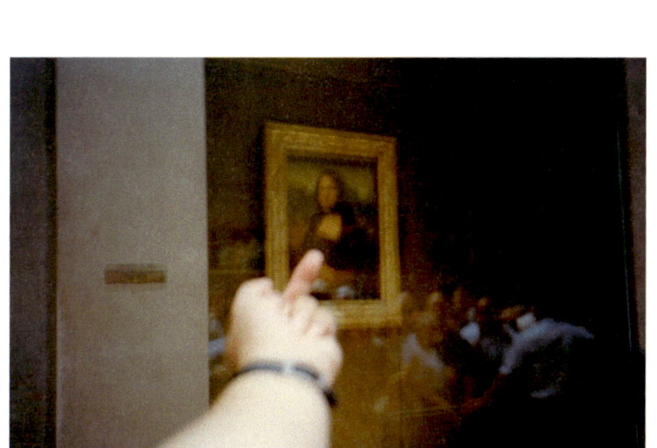
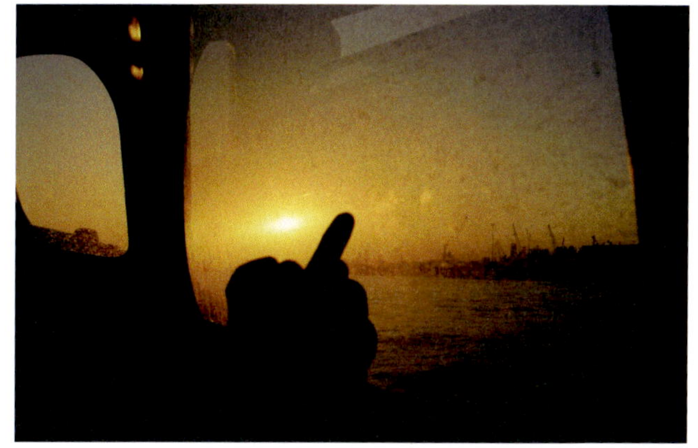
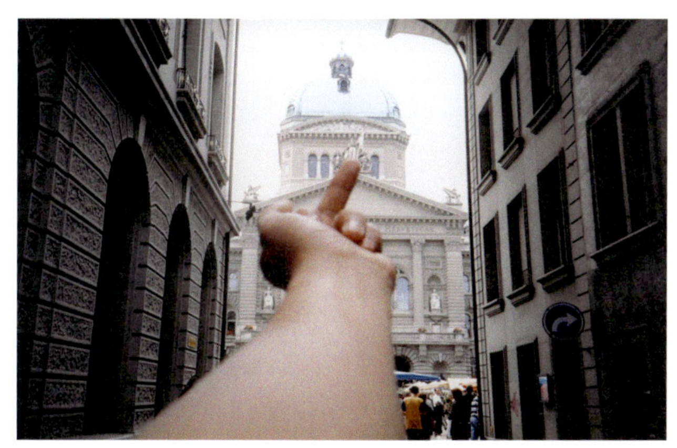
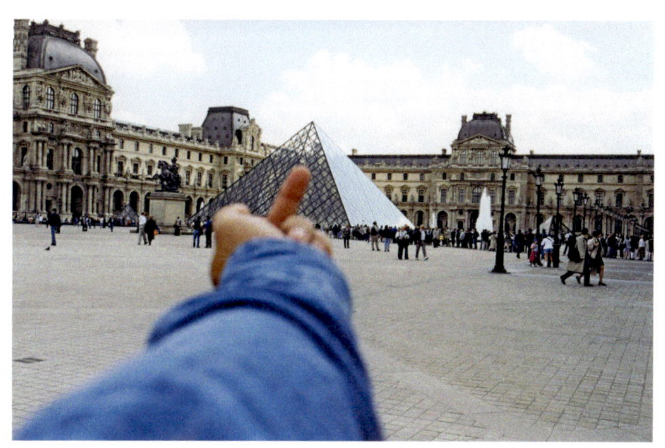
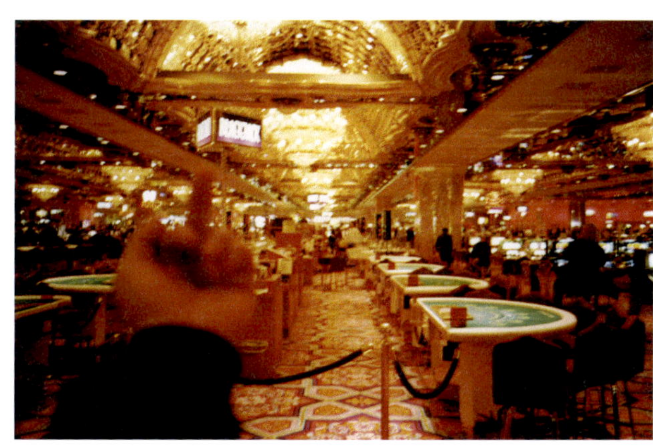
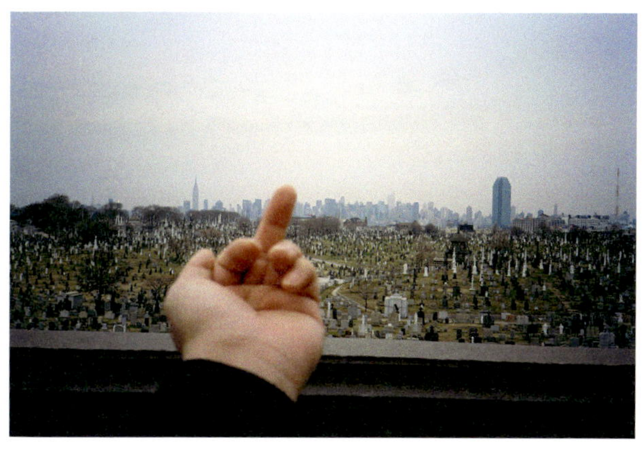

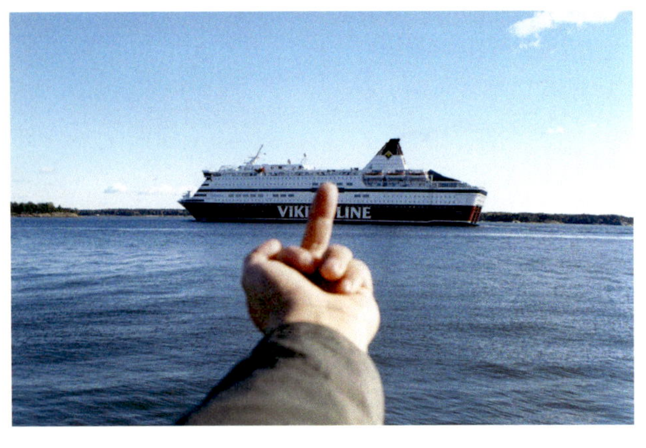
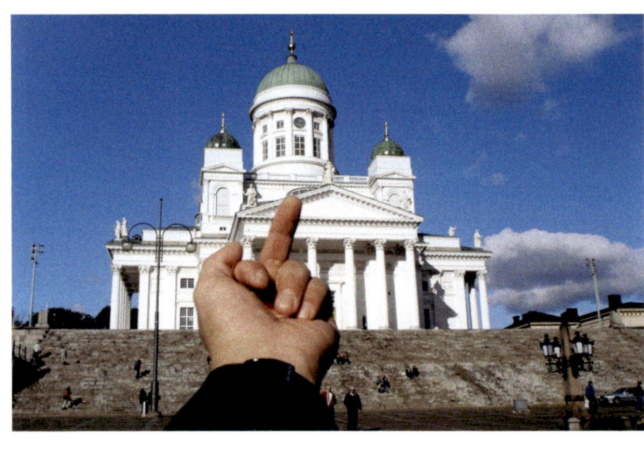
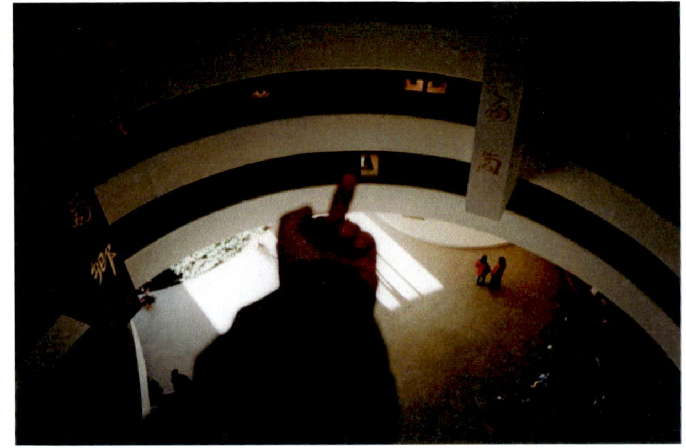
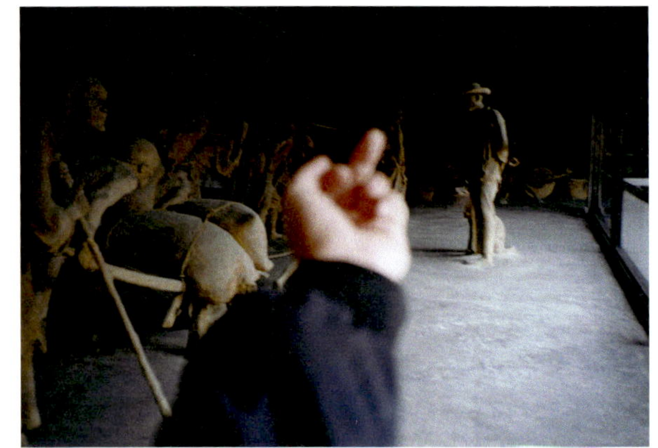
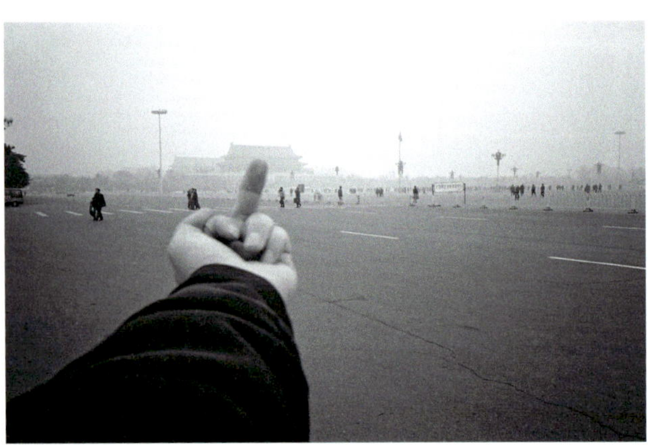
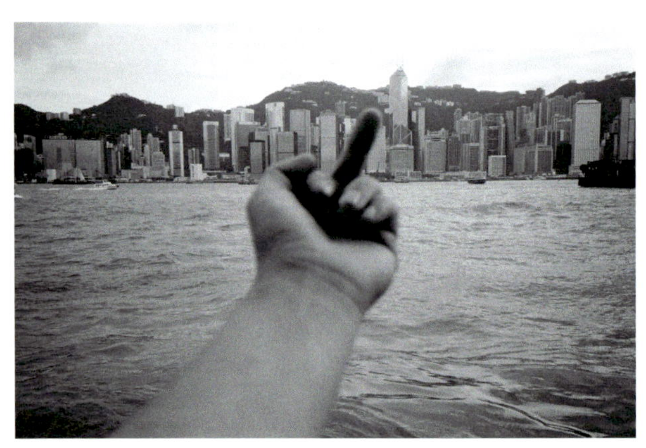
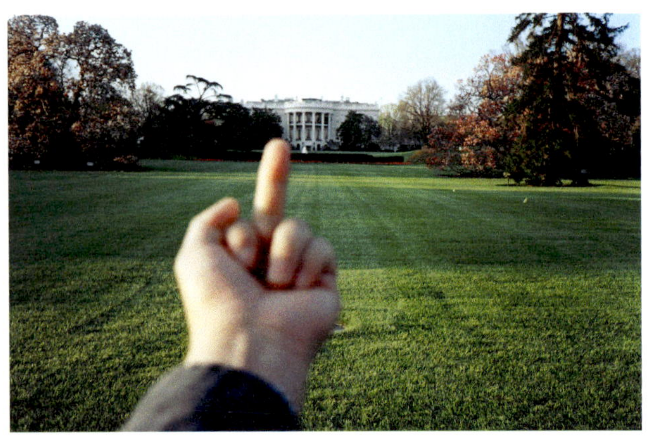
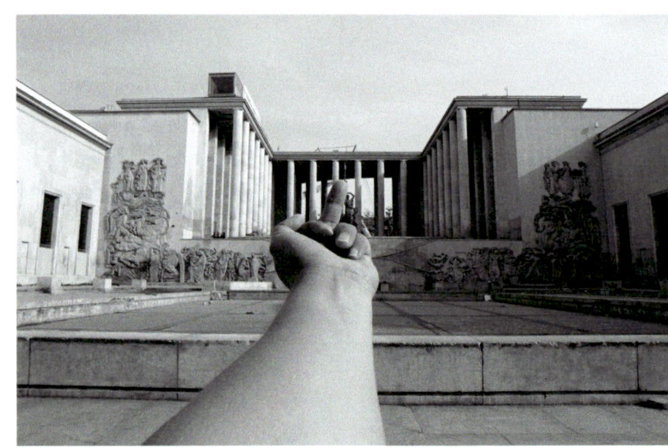

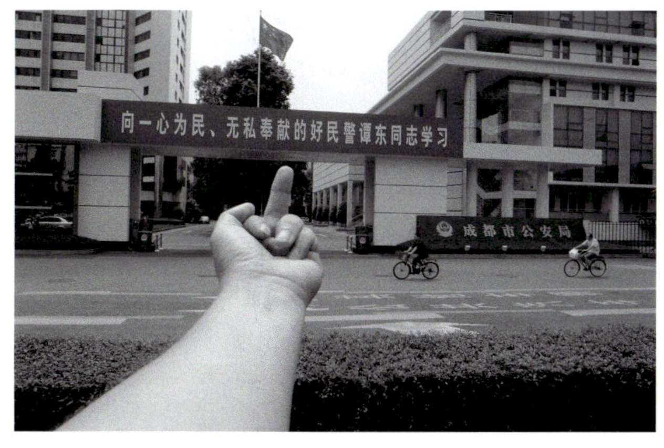

向一心为民、无私奉献的好民警谭东同志学习
成都市公安局

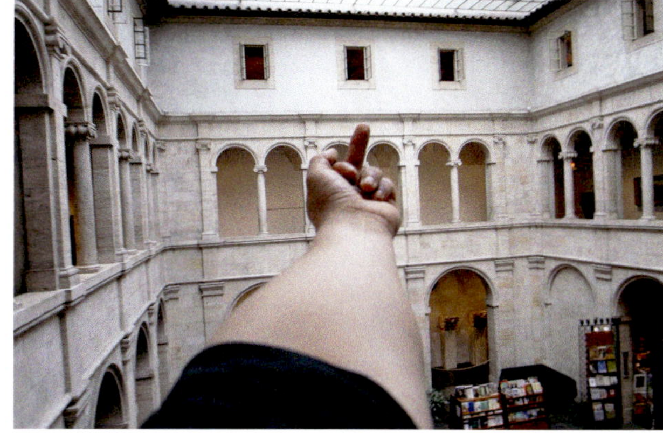

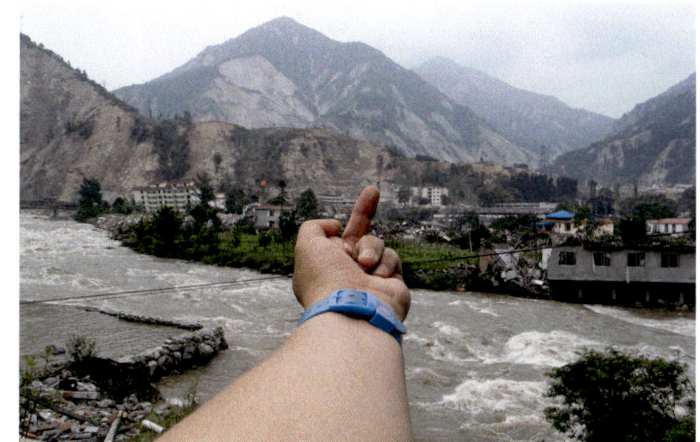

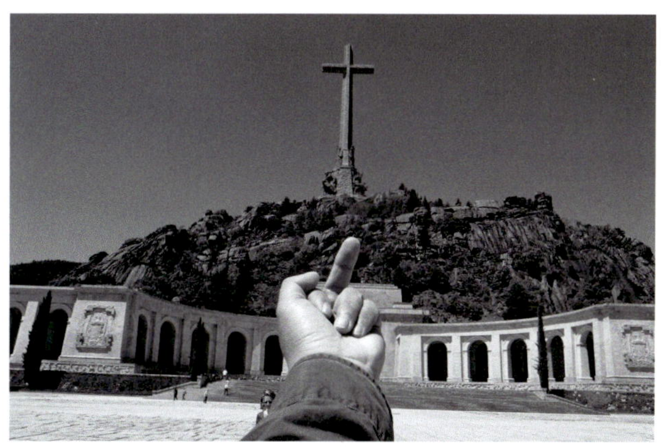

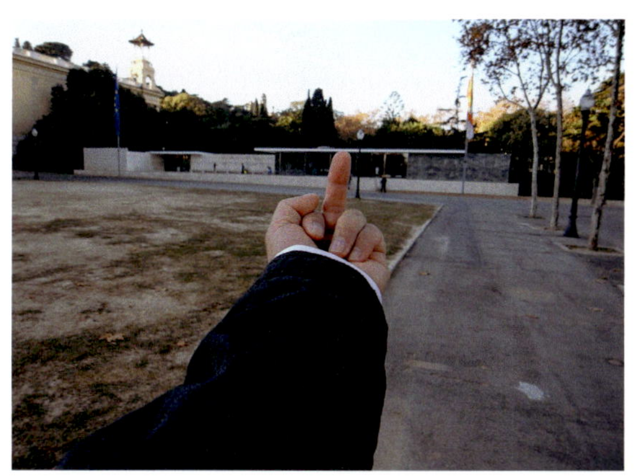

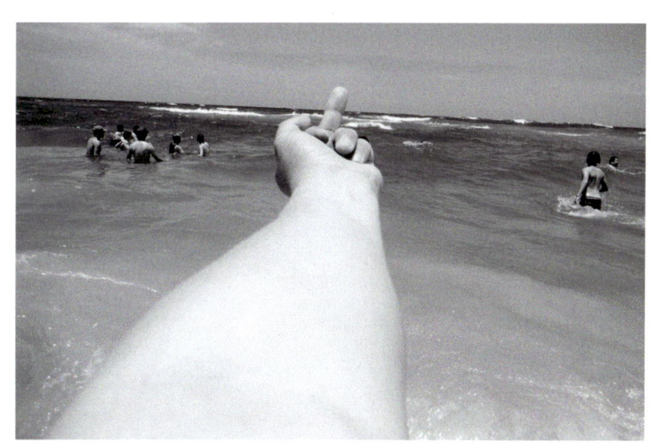

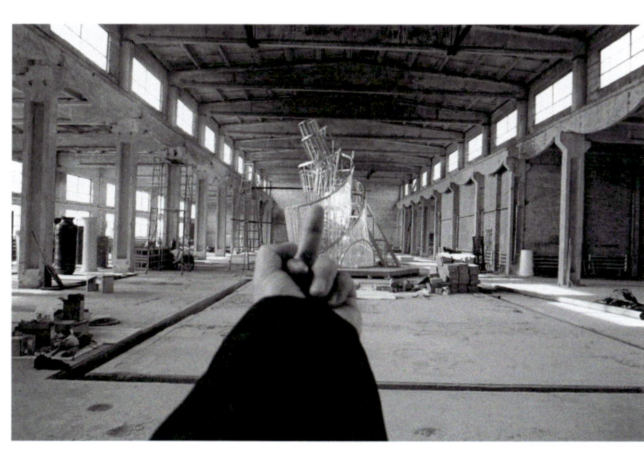

向一心为民、无私奉献的好民警谭东同志学习

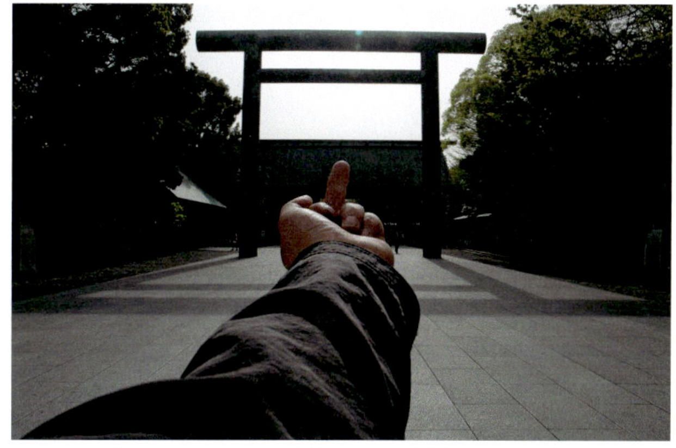

**Blue-and-White
Porcelain Plate** (**War**), 2017
Porcelain
74 × 74 × 12 cm

**Blue-and-White
Porcelain Plate** (**Ruins**), 2017
Porcelain
74 × 74 × 12 cm

**Blue-and-White
Porcelain Plate
(The Journey)**, 2017
Porcelain
74 × 74 × 12 cm

**Blue-and-White
Porcelain Plate
(Crossing the Sea)**, 2017
Porcelain
74 × 74 × 12 cm

**Blue-and-White
Porcelain Plate
(Refugee Camp)**, 2017
Porcelain
74 × 74 × 12 cm

**Blue-and-White
Porcelain Plate
(Demonstrations)**, 2017
Porcelain
74 × 74 × 12 cm

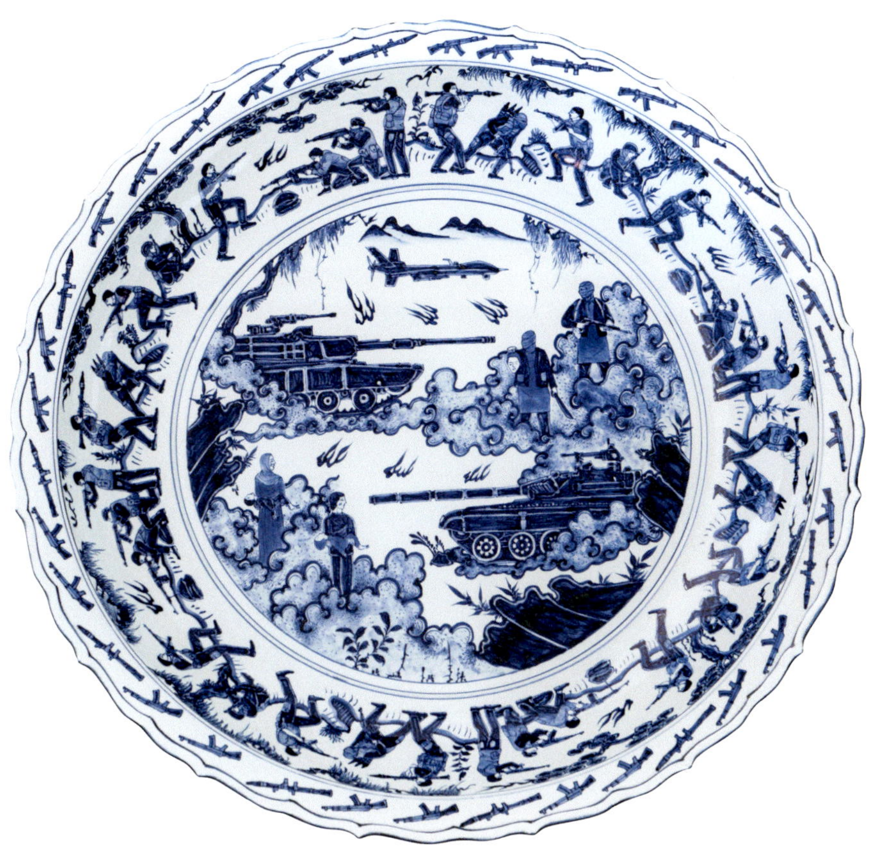

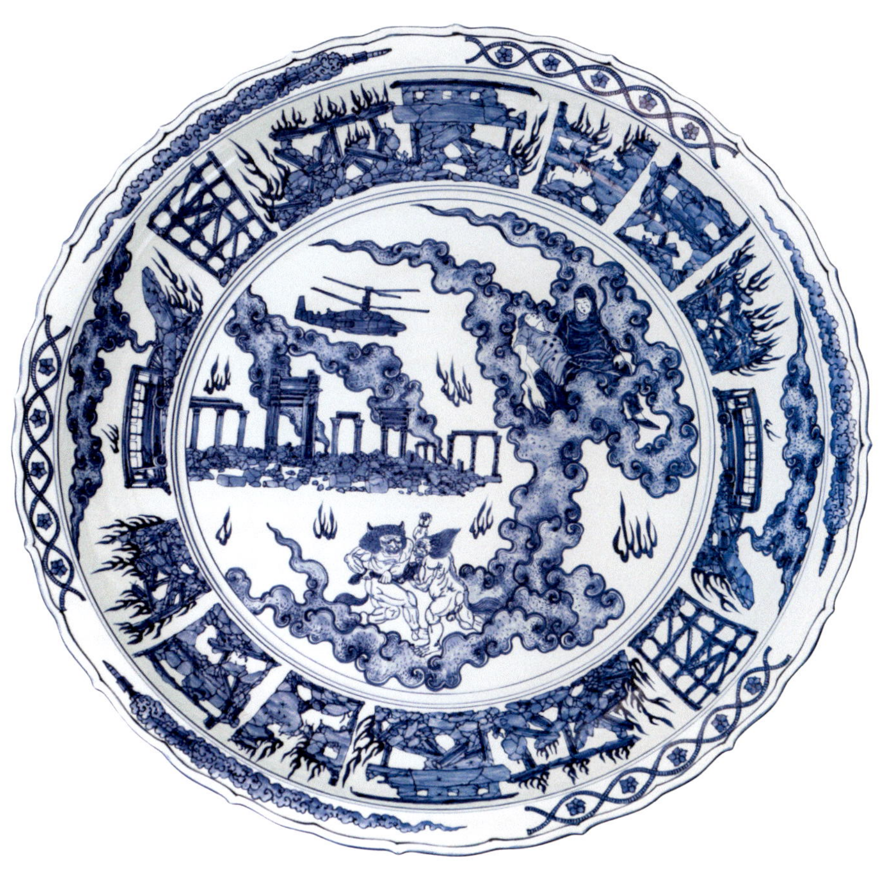

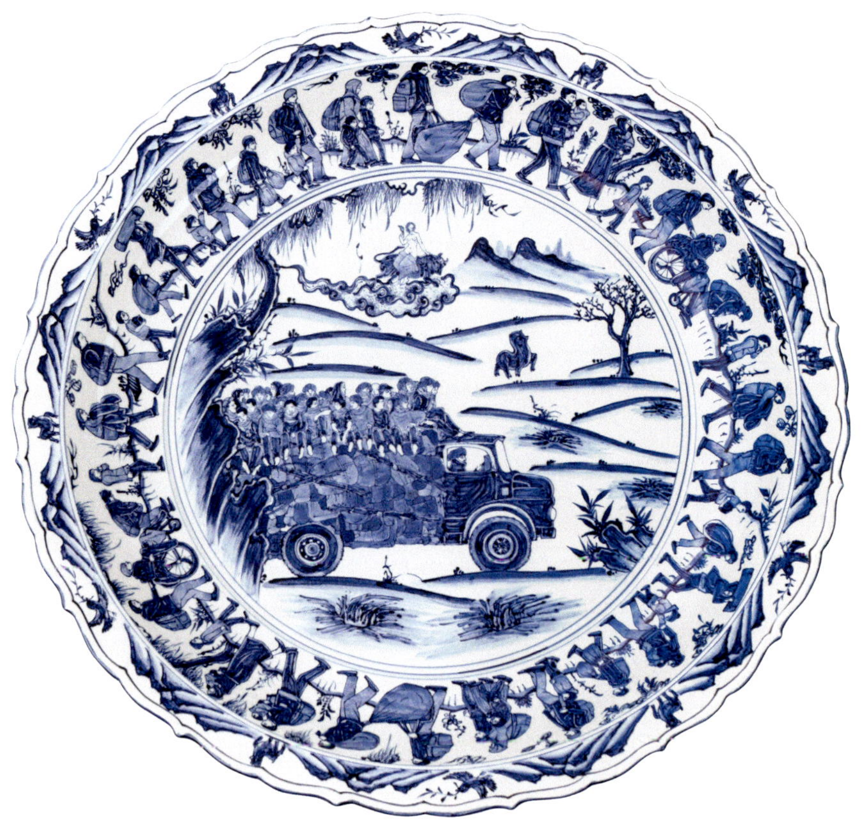

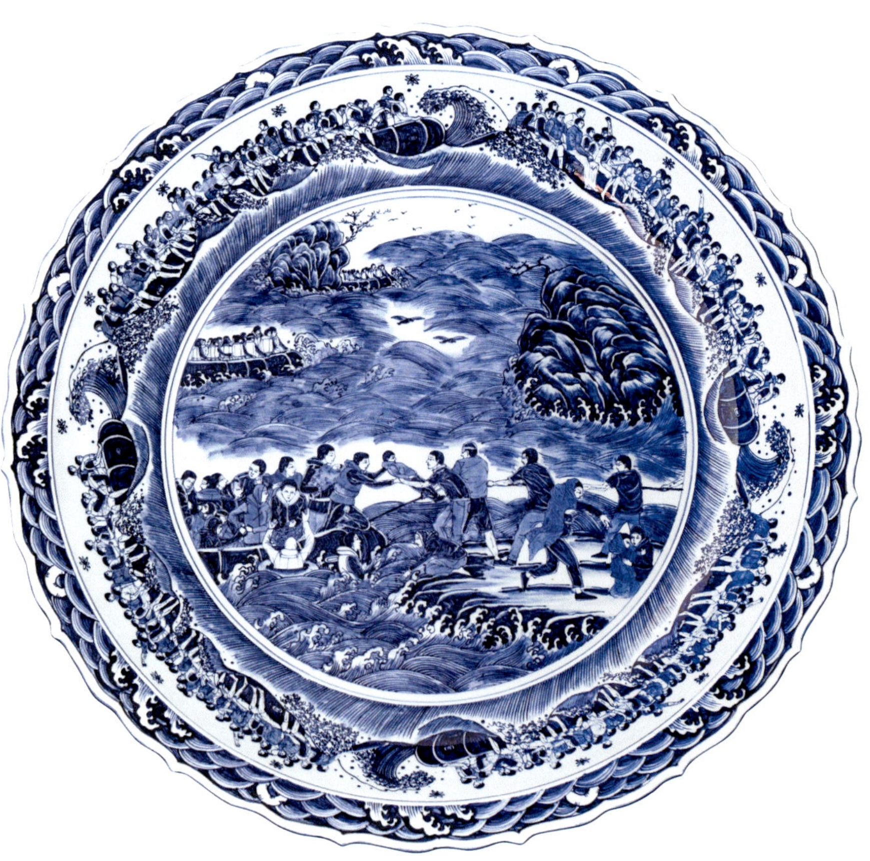

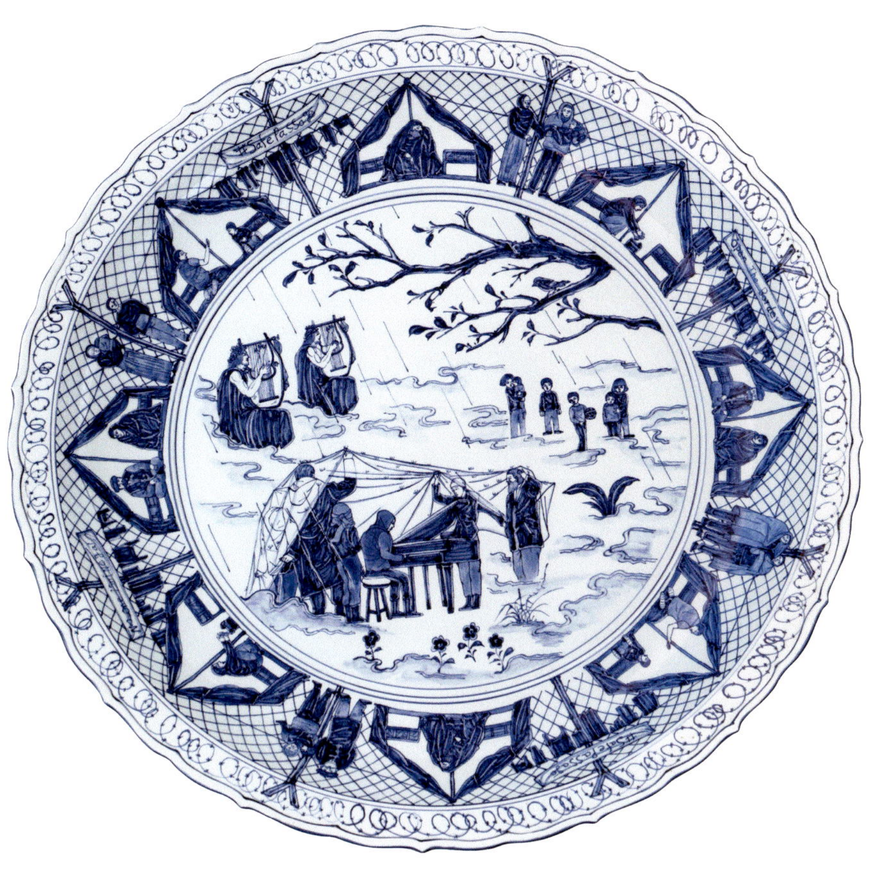

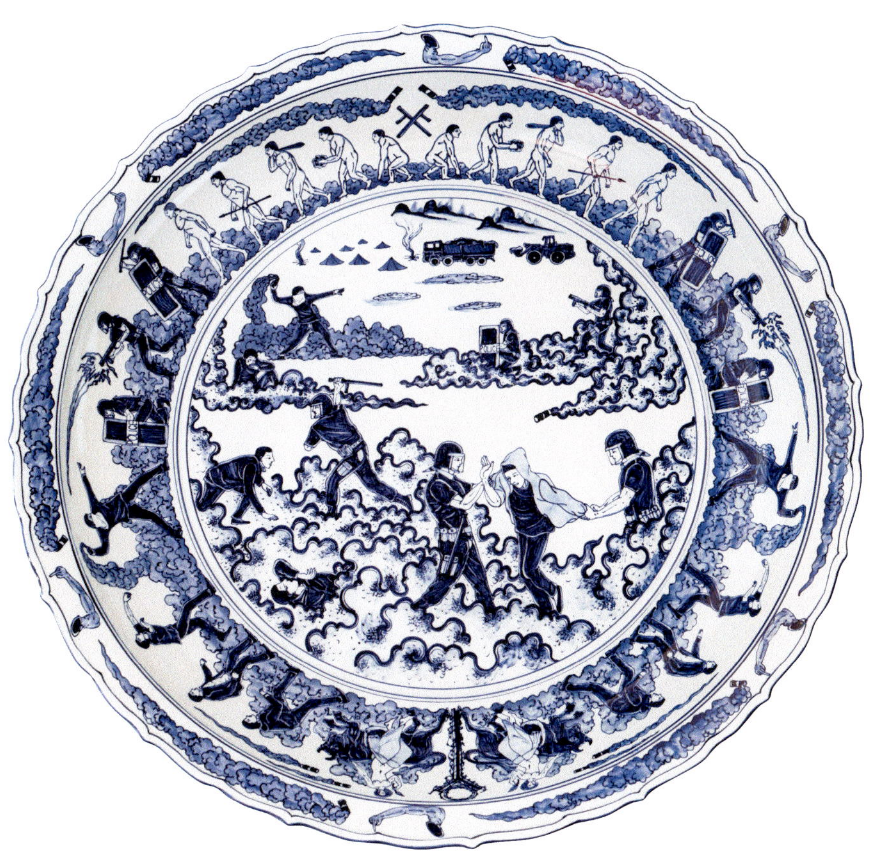

**Blue-and-White
Porcelain Vases**, 2017
Porcelain
6 vases,
each: 52 × 52 × 50.5 cm

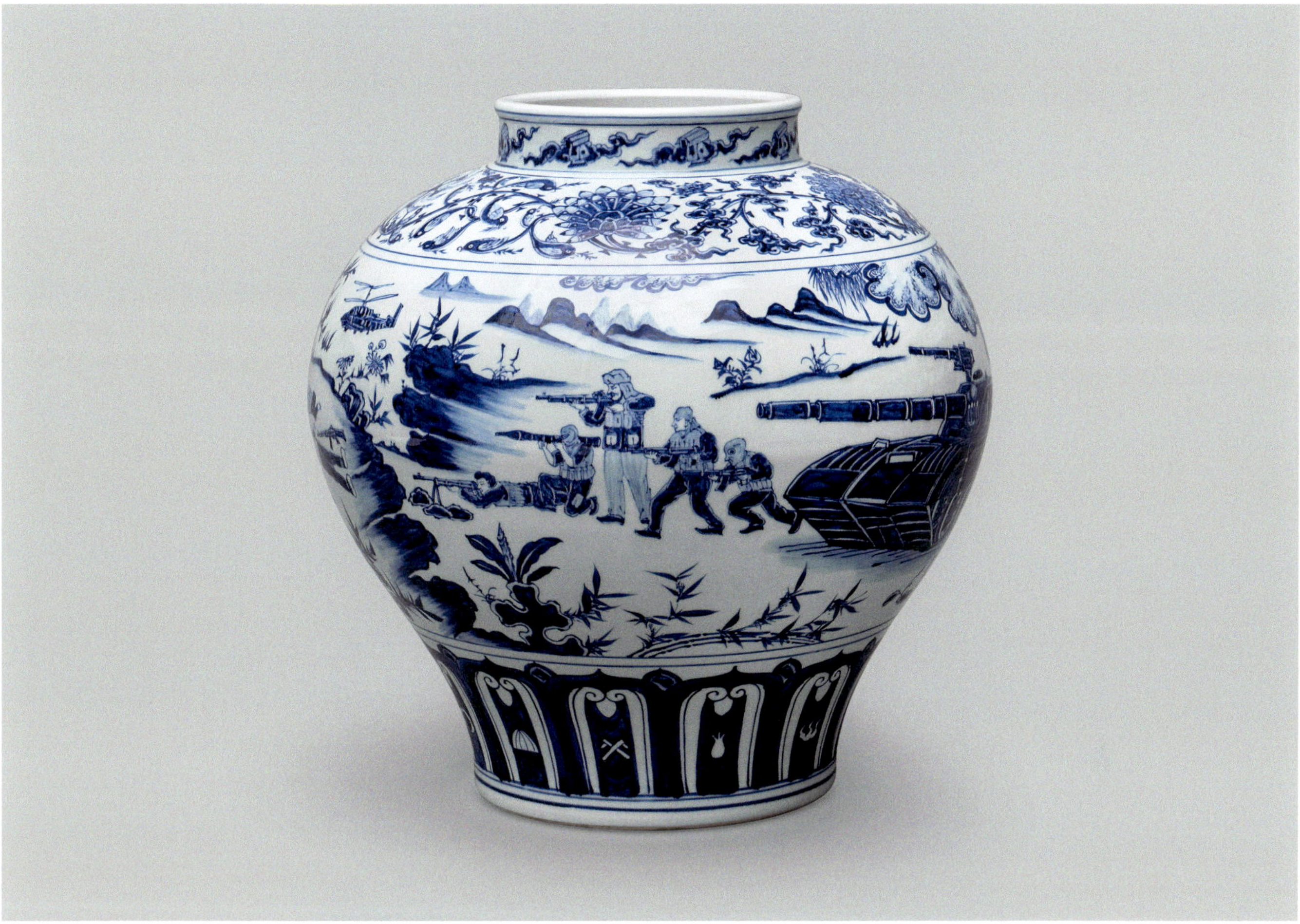

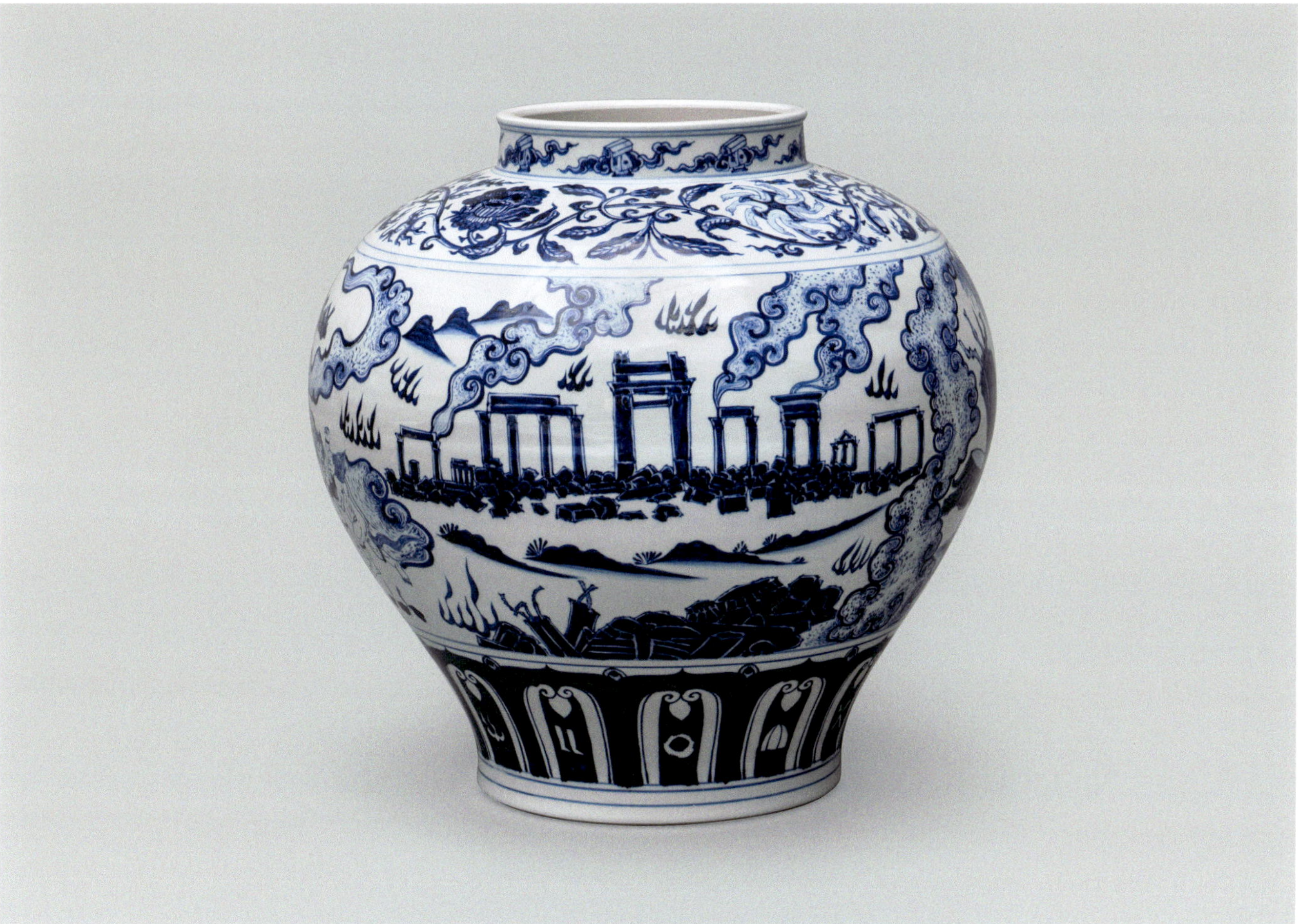

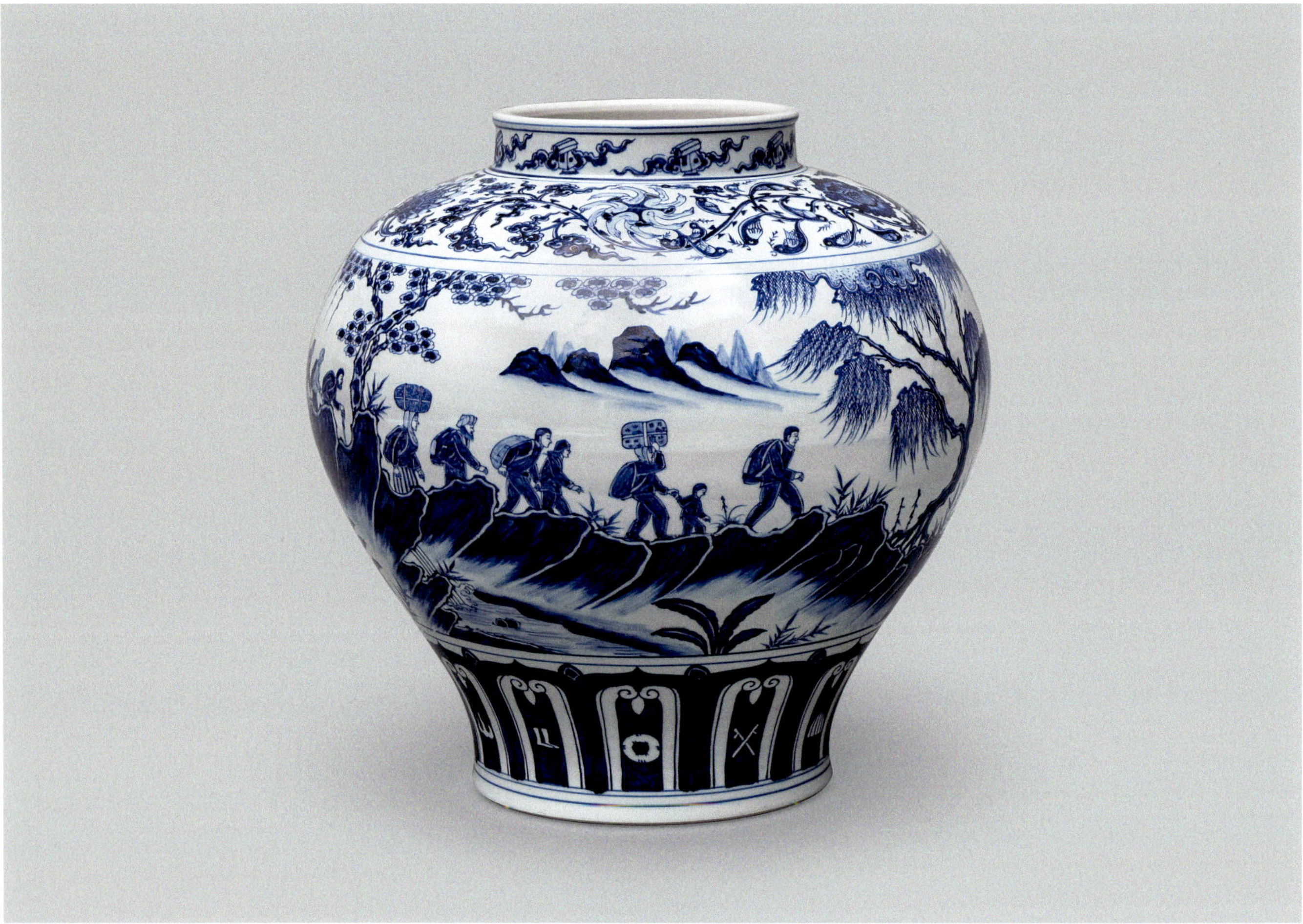

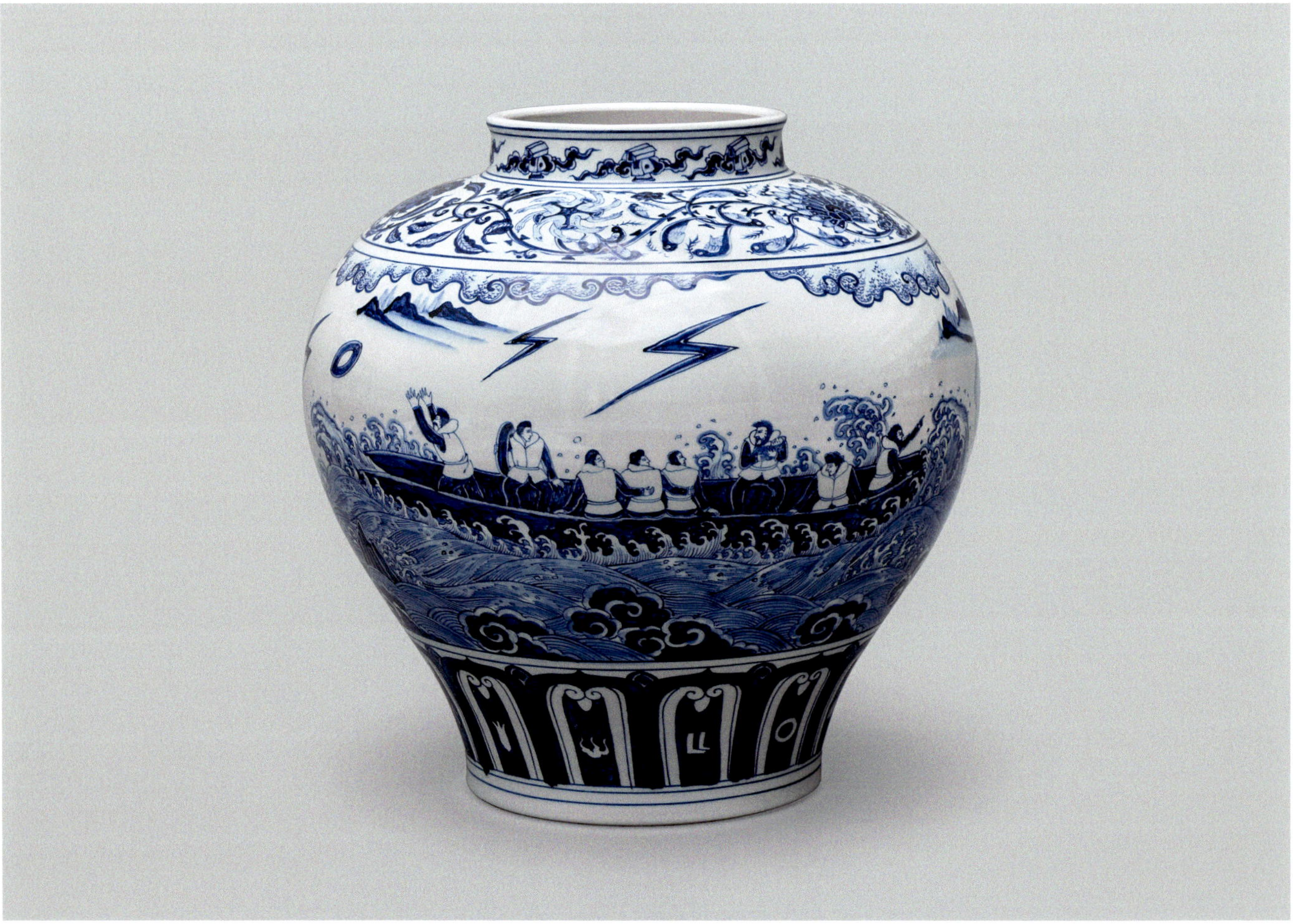

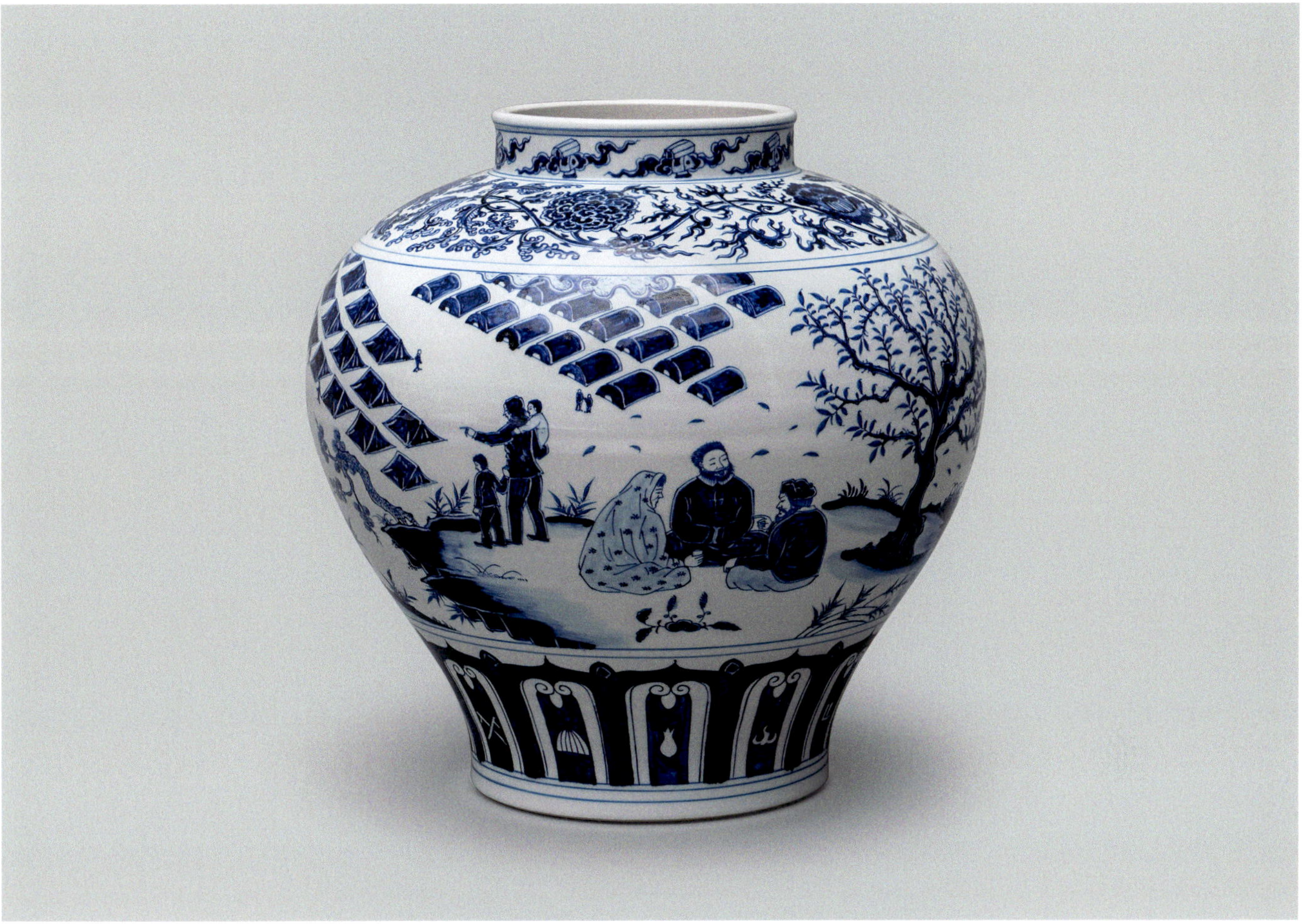

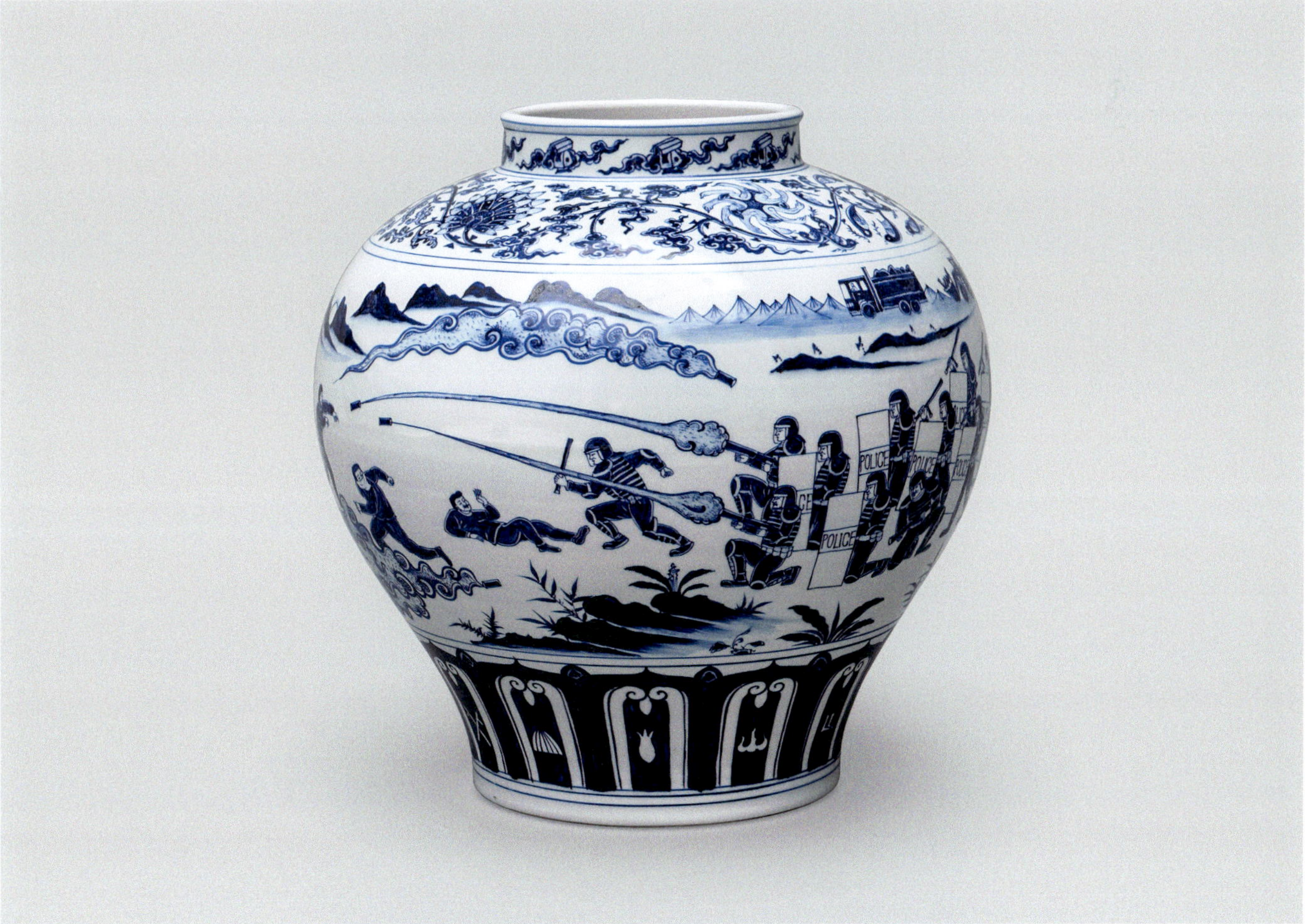

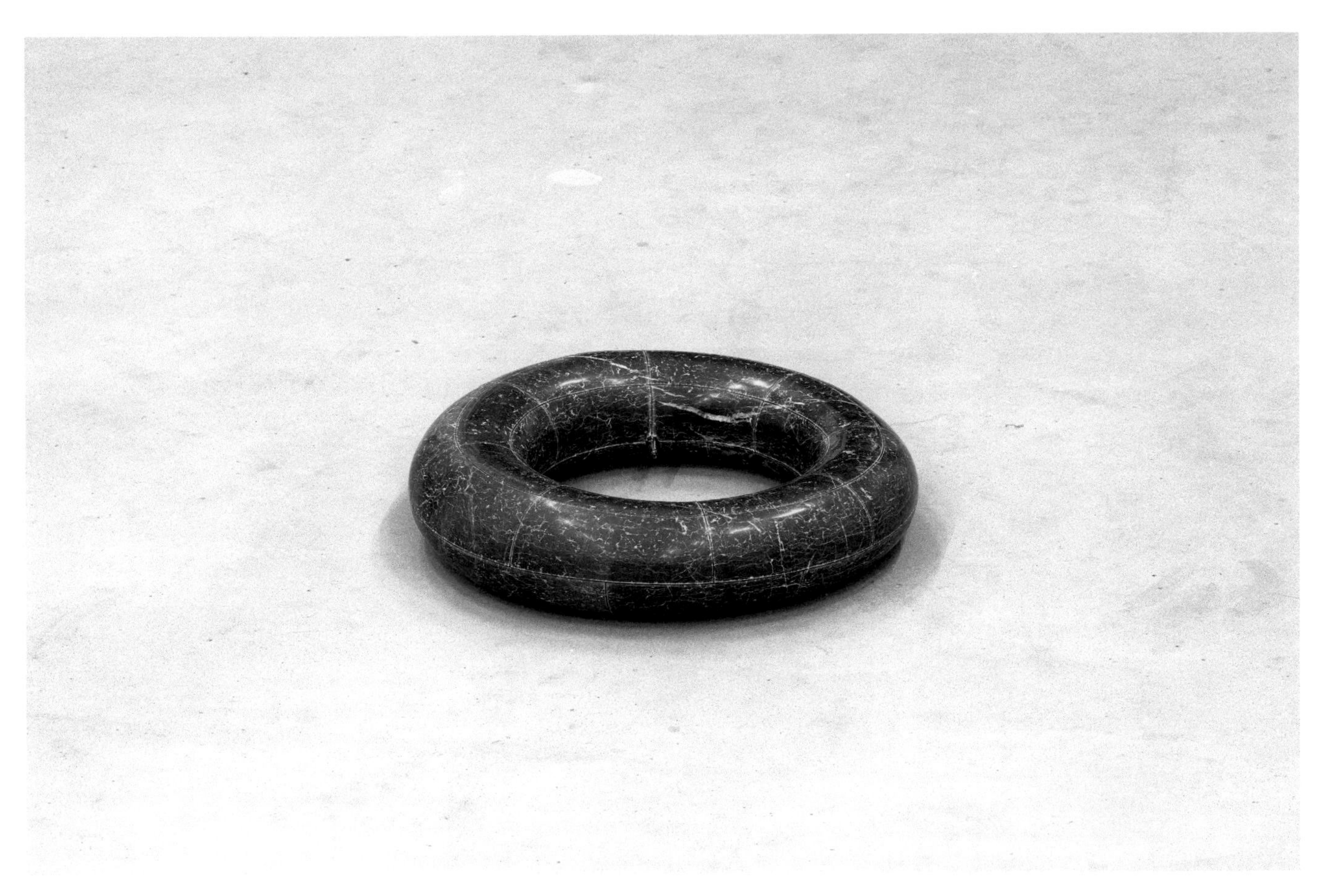

Tyre, 2016
Marble
80 × 75 × 35 cm

Camera with Plinth, 2015
Marble
52 × 52 × 120 cm

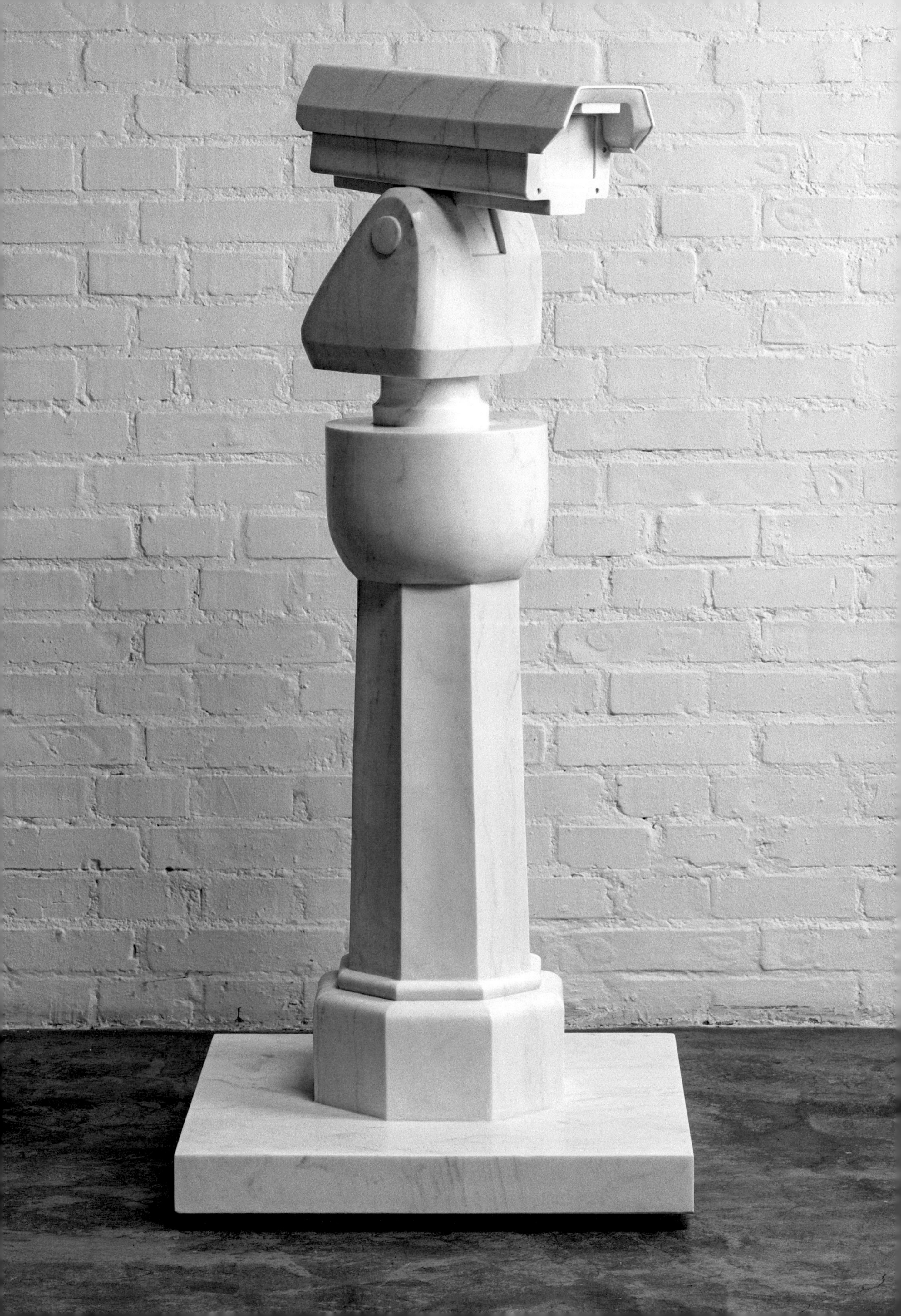

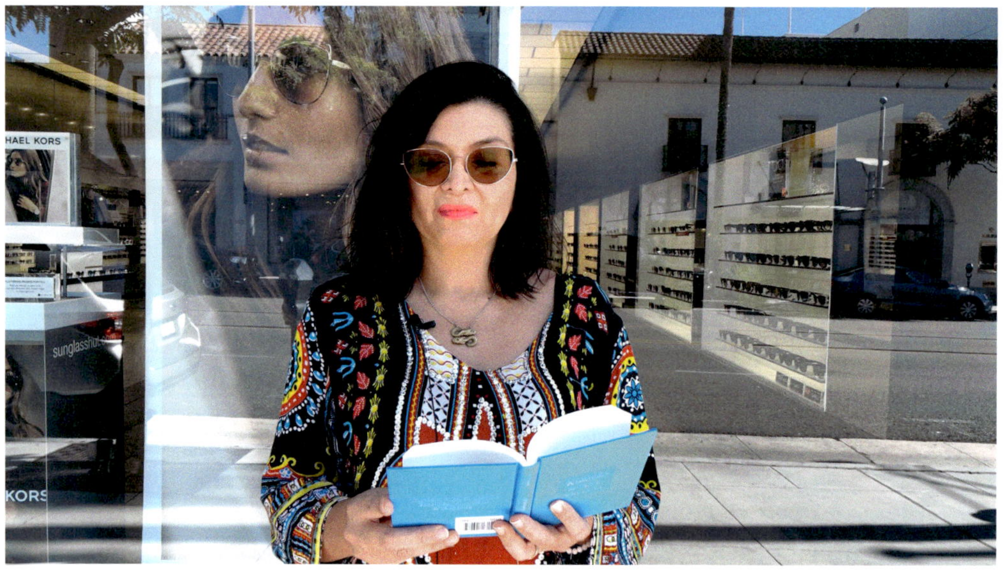

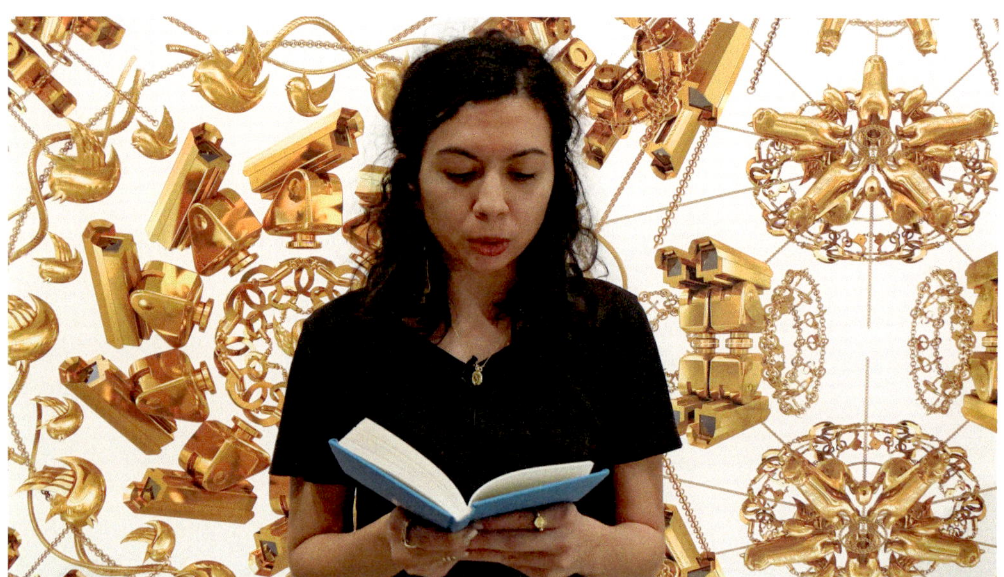

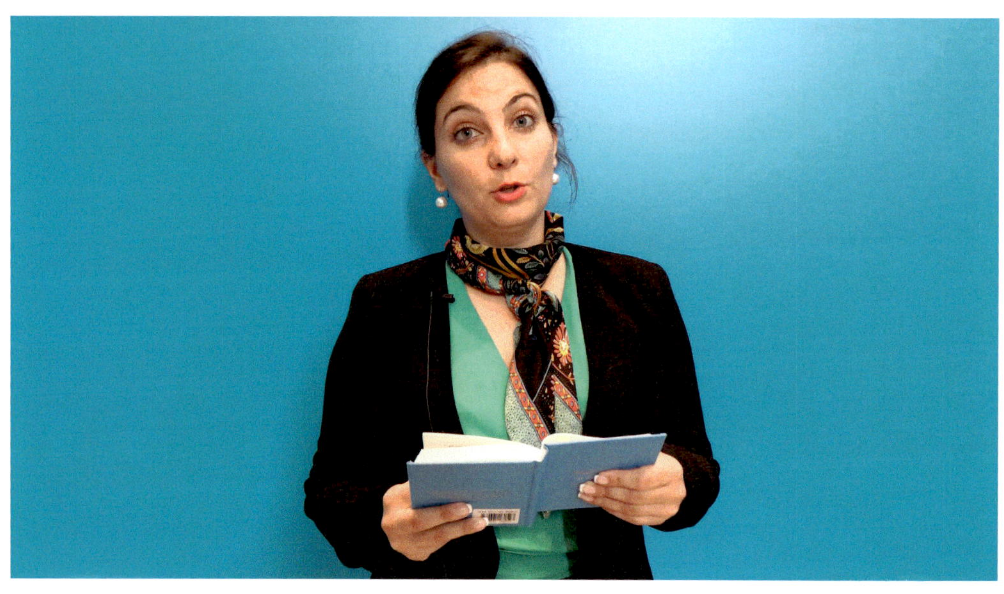

Humanity, 2018
Video, color, sound, 182'

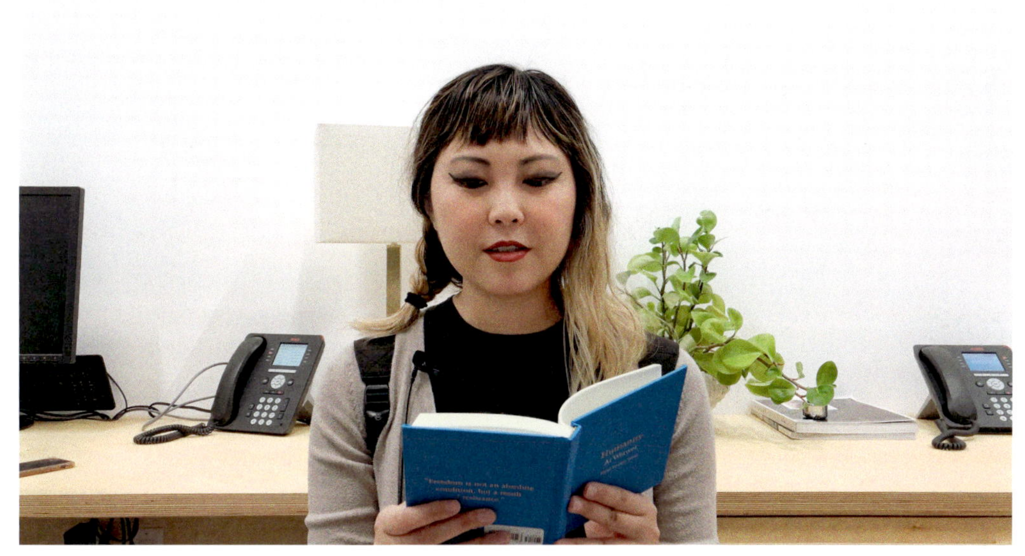

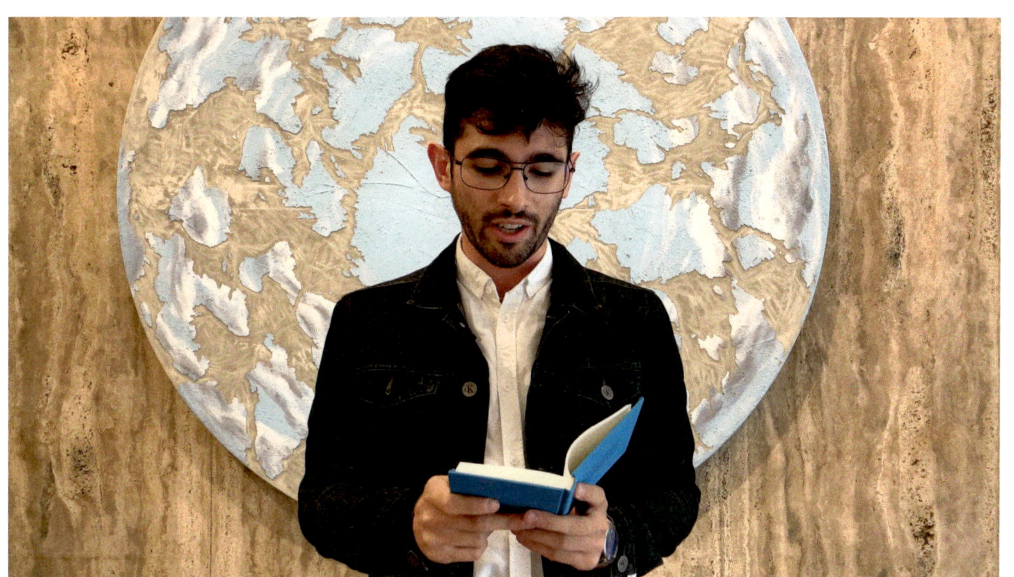

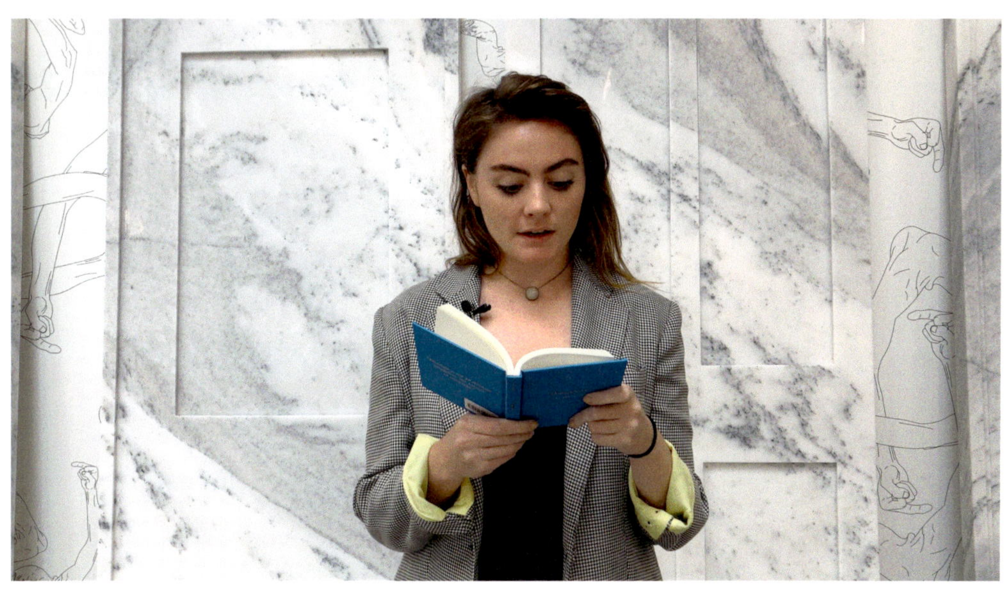

Ai Weiwei and the Politics of Life

Friederike Sigler

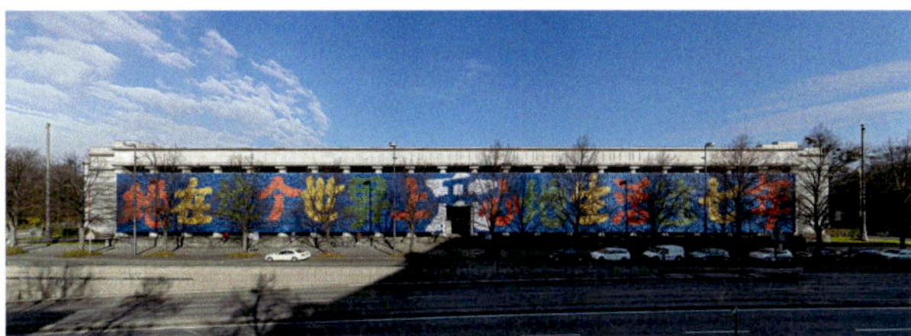

1
Remembering, 2009,
8,783 backpacks, metal
structure, 919.8 × 10,600 cm,
installation on the façade of
the Haus der Kunst, Munich

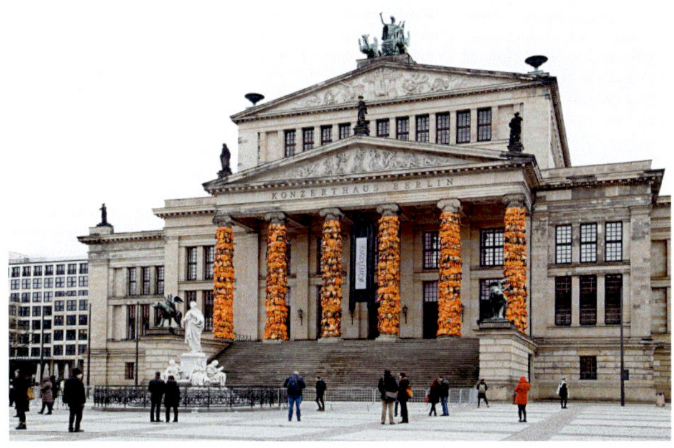

2
Safe Passage, 2016, life
jackets, inflatable raft,
dimensions variable.
Installation view,
Konzerthaus Berlin, 2016

In 2009, Ai Weiwei had roughly nine thousand children's backpacks attached to the colossal rectangular façade of the Haus der Kunst in Munich, a colorful arrangement which read in Mandarin, "She lived happily for seven years in this world." The title **Remembering** was intended to remind us of the more than five thousand schoolchildren who, in 2008, fell victim to an earthquake in the southern Chinese province of Sichuan. In 2016, Ai Weiwei took on another façade, this time the monumental columns of the Konzerthaus Berlin, around which more than three thousand orange life jackets were wrapped that the artist had had transported to Germany from the Greek island of Lesbos. Together with an inflatable boat hanging from the ceiling, on which "#safepassage" was written, they were intended to commemorate all those refugees who had undertaken the dangerous passage across the Mediterranean. In recent years, one might say that Ai Weiwei has often been conspicuously present wherever urgent help is needed: in Sichuan, in Idomeni, in Calais — in other words, at those places where human rights violations are systematically committed before the eyes of the world. With symbol-laden installations, he denounces, indeed publicly accuses, the governments of the world for the "collateral damage" of their deadly policies, the victims of which often do not even become numbers. What is more, his installations reveal the governmental means that tolerate countless human victims: from the corruption of Chinese building authorities and their concealment tactics to the European refugee policy that has made the Mediterranean the deadliest border in the world. For this, Ai Weiwei successfully relies on a great deal of media attention which, in the case of **Remembering**, led not least of all to his detention and subsequent house arrest. He, for his part, seems consistently to accept such "collateral damage." In 2016, barely a year after his release, Ai Weiwei began filming **Human Flow** (2017), thus again entering upon dangerous territory. For even in "modern Europe," saving human lives is subject to high prison sentences; rescue at sea has long been regarded as an organized crime and preventing deportation can occasionally, as in the case of the Stansted 15, lead to a criminal charge of terrorism.

Ai Weiwei has received great honors as both an artist and a human rights activist. The fact, however, that **Art Review** has already named him the most important artist in the world in addition to having received the Ambassador of Conscience Award from Amnesty International highlights the ambivalent position he occupies within art. To this day, art history and art criticism disagree on whether and, if so, to what extent these two roles are and can be compatible. Is Ai Weiwei an artist and an activist or an art activist, and can his art truly be regarded as being political? This debate is complicated by the fact that his artistic practice is difficult to reduce to one common denominator, that it is often perceived as somewhat naïve or even clumsy, and that the topics he deals with, in turn, give rise to complex ethical discussions. In the case of the Berlin life jacket installation, the art historian Wolfgang Ullrich felt a certain "unease."[1] He saw the mass of vests as a "particularly unsuitable means of making the suffering and hardship of each individual concerned tangible," as well as posing the danger of "nourishing fear of foreign infiltration" in such politically precarious times.[2] With a view toward recent years, the label "political" seems generally to have fallen into disrepute in art; European art history in particular finds it difficult to reconcile its traditional parameters with those of new "artivist" movements, such as the Peng! Collective and the Center for Political Beauty.[3] Art criticism is more receptive in this regard and, together with numerous exhibition projects, more often demands for an art propelled by highly political times such as ours.[4] In the midst of this often abstractly conducted cut and thrust, however, concrete examples are always neglected. And thus, the attempt to derive concrete criteria for that which is political also falls short. This question is therefore central: Is Ai Weiwei's artistic practice political, and how can this be determined?

So Sorry

Ai Weiwei's concern for the earthquake victims of Sichuan began in 2008.[5] One month after the devastating tremor, he traveled to the disaster area. Emergency care seemed to be adequate; even UN Secretary-General Ban Ki-moon had praised it. Yet the government was not forth-coming with the death toll and the identities of thousands of schoolchildren. What is more, rumor spread that they were actually the victims of corruption in the construction industry or, more precisely, of the use of inferior building materials. Fourteen schools had collapsed in the earthquake, while more than one hundred other schools in the same region, significantly made of a different building material, had withstood the quake.[6] Experts confirmed this theory based on photos of the "tofu-dregs buildings," as the unstable structures are commonly called.[7] Those who commissioned their construction were now considered responsible for the brutal deaths of thousands of schoolchildren. In the area, numerous parents had already joined together to demand that the circumstances be clarified. Yet the authorities remained silent. Shortly thereafter, Ai Weiwei with roughly fifty supporters initiated a "Citizens' Investigation."[8] The aim was to uncover the number and names of the victims. For over a year, the team canvassed houses and communities to find out who the victims were, speaking with desperate and grieving parents, relatives, and neighbors. Ai Weiwei posted requests for information on his blog, where he also regularly published the latest findings. At the same time, his team persistently contacted the local authorities. "We made 200 calls to various departments—the police, the civil affairs department, the construction department, the education department— just to ask simple questions. They asked almost 10,000 questions, and still we didn't get one answer."[9] Their many efforts were not only ignored by the authorities, but they were also strategically obstructed. For the nationwide "echo chamber," Premier Wen Jiabao made an emotional appeal to the population, stating that it was essential to come together and begin rescue and rebuilding efforts, as well as mourning. Yet behind the scenes, Ai Weiwei's blog was deleted and he, his team, and local activists were prevented by force from continuing their investigations.[10] Nevertheless, they did not desist and, through May 3, 2009, successively published their results: the names of 5,219 dead children. The government found itself forced to its knees and quickly followed up with its own list with the names of 5,335 children.

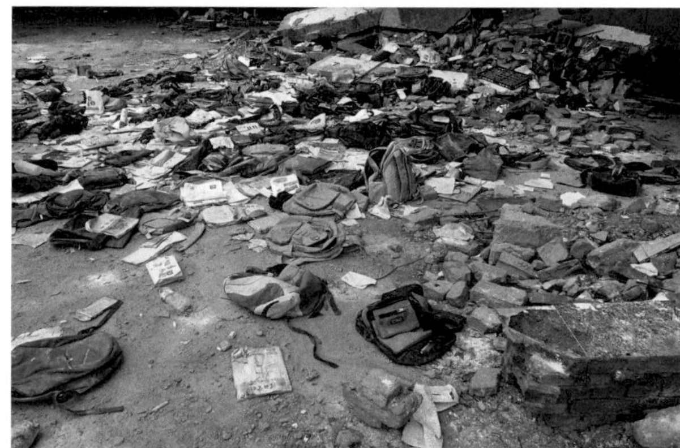

3
**Sichuan Earthquake
Photographs**, 2008,
black-and-white photographs

As public pressure on the Chinese author-ities grew, Ai Weiwei had already process-ed the lengthy research into his artistic practice and sent it on a journey around the world. These included, first and fore-most, the virtual list of the names of the dead children and an analog version which, like the installation **Straight** (pp. 63–73), for which he collected tons of rebar from collapsed school buildings, is now on view in K20, as well as numerous other works thematically dedicated to the deaths of the schoolchildren which were exhibited in Hong Kong, London, Washington, D.C., Venice, Ontario, Paris, etc.[11] To a certain extent, his detainment and subsequent house arrest were also part of this and have been reflected in a variety of his artistic practices; the flimsy allegations of tax evasion were presumably much more an attempt to stop the artist and his research in Sichuan for good through pressure from the state.[12] In this context, understanding **Remembering** as a strat-egy of representing the murder of over five thousand children with the help of backpacks falls short. Instead, the ex-pansion within art history, which, for some time, has replaced the notion of the "artwork" with that of "artistic practice," would seem to be more suitable for Ai Weiwei's investigation into the death of the schoolchildren. **Remembering** is thus part of a conglomerate or network of works that are thematically linked and, in their growing scope, pose a constant threat to the Chinese government. This network begins with the fact that Ai Weiwei launched and promoted a socio-critical movement on site, which quickly gained publicity through his blog and with which he also intervened in political processes. The artist thus acts, if you will, as a political activist, a social worker, a contact person, and a public voice. With the preliminary results, the number and names of the 5,219 children, a local community—which he helped to form—of all those who strove to solve the crime, not only put the government under pressure but also found itself participating in two acts: namely in the narrative of the earthquake and that of mourning. With the "Citizens' Investiga-tion," Ai Weiwei and his team undermined the official narrative which propagated the earthquake not as a "manmade catas-trophe" but as a "natural disaster" and thus strategically sought to evade any responsibility.[13] The act of mourning was also transformed by the artist and his allies by referring to those people killed in measurable quantities, such as numbers, or even by their names. The philosopher Judith Butler has prominently pointed out that the "grievability" of people is based on political mechanisms.[14] The decision as to who is mourned and who is not depends on the endangerment to which a life is exposed and equally corresponds to a judgement regarding its value.[15] At the same time, according to the sociologist Didier Fassin who continues her line of thinking, grievability can also be used to draw conclusions about the politics of life.[16] Thus, although the Chinese government may have initiated an act of mourning, it obscured the different values of the lives affected by the catastrophe. With the network of works on the Sichuan earthquake, Ai Weiwei revealed these deadly governmental strategies. On the façade of the Haus der Kunst in Munich, the artist once again sent a clear signal regarding the politics of life: "she," a seven-year-old girl who fell victim to cutbacks in construction, "lived happily for seven years in this world" he quotes the mother, and, according to the subtext, "had a happy life ahead of her."

Never Sorry

Reinforced by the façade installation, Ai Weiwei's political-artistic practice is to be located on the threshold between artistic space and public space. Instead of being absorbed in an object, it lies in the play between the arena of the artistic capacity for action and the crossing over into politics in order to establish itself there permanently as an actor which will avoid one thing in particular: letting up. In 2016, Ai Weiwei once again made use of a façade installation. With **Safe Passage**, he—at first glance—remembered the victims of the European refugee policy. In contrast to **Remembering**, it remains open here whether those who once wore these life jackets reached the Greek island alive or dead, just as clues regarding their subsequent fate are lacking. The number of vests is not congruent with a relevant political number; it is and represents an uncountable and constantly growing mass of people who risk their lives in order to reach Europe across

dangerous waters. The brutal reality is reflected especially in this indefinable magnitude. Nevertheless, as Wolfgang Ullrich has aptly pointed out, as mentioned already, the life jackets seem unsuitable for depicting the "refugee crisis," the complexity of which, as well as the unspeakable human suffering, simply elude such representation. Neither should the life jackets be confused with readymades, as is often done prematurely in the reception of the artist.[17] In contrast to the backpacks made especially for **Remembering**, these are found objects, although no further details about them are known. There is the possibility that among them are those that were never in working order. The trade in fake life vests, which increases the danger to life of those fleeing, disqualifies them for Marcel Duchamp's category. Upon closer inspection, it also does not appear as though they were hanging on the columns as individual items, but rather, that they were interwoven, connected, and entangled. In this way, the life jackets recede into the background as individual objects, allowing their solid and luminous color to stand out; it is their symbolic effect which Ai Weiwei strategically takes up in order to present them with their tragic and warning character.[18] After all, no other color has burned itself into the iconography of those crossings the Mediterranean as much as the bright orange that vibrantly marked Berlin's Gendarmenmarkt. But this is not the only symbol which Ai Weiwei used to take aim at Europe; like **Remembering**, this installation does not stand alone but is rather an integral part of a larger, thematically coherent network.

Since 2016, Ai Weiwei has dealt extensively with the living conditions of refugees all over the world; many of the relevant attitudes are represented in the Düsseldorf exhibition. These include the videos **At Sea** (2016), **Idomeni** (2016), and **Calais** (2018, pp. 117–121); as well as **Life Cycle** (2018, pp. 110–113), the monumental replica of an inflatable raft; **Laundromat** (2016, pp. 95–99), a collection of cleaned garments once belonging to refugees; and the self-explanatory **17'232 Photos Relating to Refugees, 1.12.–09.08.2016** (2016, pp. 104–109). Here as well, Ai Weiwei is onsite, travels to hotspots, takes a close look at the miserable conditions in the camps, talks to refugees, talks to activists, documents, shows solidarity, and gets involved. The resulting network of works relates to his experiences in exactly the same way as it relates to the stance he takes towards them. In contrast to **Remembering** and the works associated with it, there cannot be an official number of missing persons here, let alone a list of names that can lift the dead out of anonymity. In his comments on the value of life, Didier Fassin explains that this can additionally be determined by the economic measurability and countability of human beings.[19] His examples mainly concern payments of compensation, which, however, are not (and cannot) be applied to the wearers of the life jackets. In contrast to the victims of bomb attacks or civilians killed in war, there is no state responsibility here, which would then generate the necessary figures and monetary values. In the case of the refugees, such as those who, in some situations, are forced to spend weeks at sea with their rescuers, the access to ports is strategically denied to them and, with this, the framework that would also make the refugees legal entities and the potential bearers of value. With the Berlin life jacket installation, Ai Weiwei reformulates the biopolitical and necropolitical governmental strategies that permit people to take on the life-threatening risk of crossing the Mediterranean, during which many of them drown every day, into an appeal to rethink the politics of life.[20] The many dead but also the survivors who are then stuck for years at Idomeni or some other camp; who, having arrived on dry land, must fight their way through the confusion of European asylum policy; who, confronted with strengthened rightwing movements, must once again fear for their lives, only to face the high possibility of being deported again—Ai Weiwei makes their lives, as well as the politics that determine these lives, visible. This is what he does and what he can do. His art builds a bridge between personal encounters, between individual fates, concrete political examples, and the absolute value of life that European societies have lost. Ai Weiwei is concerned with humanity, with human rights, with universal values, and thus with the simple but central questions of the present day, which he

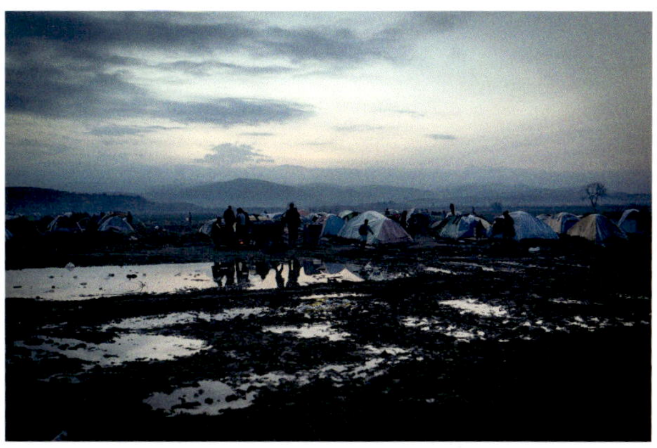

4

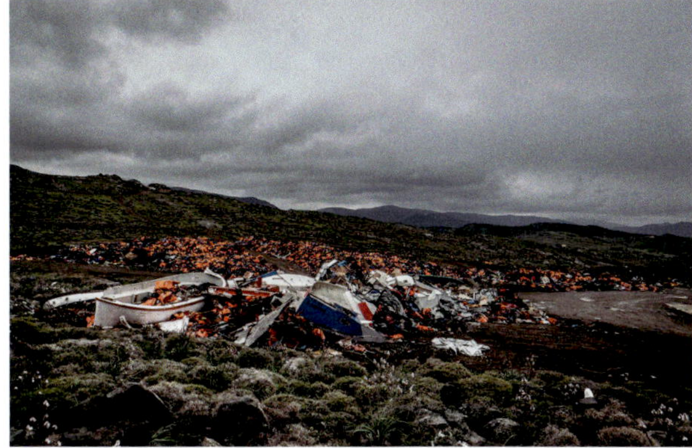

5

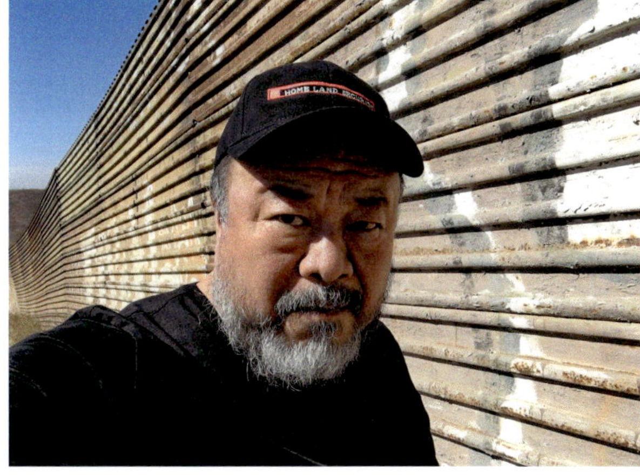

6

4
Idomeni makeshift camp,
Greece, March 18, 2016

5
Lesbos, Greece,
March 14, 2016

6
Ai Weiwei at the U.S.-
Mexico border, 2016

raises and confronts with consistency and tenacity. The fact that the artistic practices he uses for this are so variable and, because of that, seem to cause so many difficulties for art history may be due to Ai Weiwei's own biography. Much has been written about the artist growing up during Mao Zedong's Cultural Revolution and about his father, the poet Ai Qing, being banished and sentenced to hard labor precisely because he did not subordinate his art to the Maoist dictum.[21] To follow or even establish a style of political art must therefore be repugnant to the artist.[22] The naïveté and clumsiness described at the beginning, which seems to underlie many of his works, is part of this heterogeneous strategy — and can, in particular moments, develop a unique potential.

Ai Weiwei's art is political because it reacts to contemporary politics, because it intervenes in political processes, because it stands up for those who are endangered or excluded by these politics, and because the artist thereby demonstrates an unalterable interest in making the violence, which is inflicted on people for the basest reasons, public. Both the façade installations and the frequent use of virtual platforms — from his blog to Twitter and Instagram — stand for his striving to move beyond the realm of art, as does his recourse to media such as film, which, as the example of **Human Flow** demonstrates, strives to reach broader audiences — from social media junkies and people who walk past museums to moviegoers. Especially in an age when politics has become so clumsy that it allows itself to simplify and falsify complicated facts in such a way that fear can suddenly become a governmental policy that decides the fate of thousands of people at the drop of a hat and uses polemics to achieve this, which some time ago would not even have been conceivable within this sphere. Such politics are opposed by Ai Weiwei with an art that occasionally participates with comparable methods, having simply understood that in politically precarious times exactly the same means are occasionally necessary to counteract their popularization. In short, the political aspect of Ai Weiwei's art is the recourse to symbol-laden and symbolically powerful installations that aim precisely at where rightwing

populism strive, namely at an affective, emotional, and therefore immediate effect. Visitors to the exhibition, passersby, and all those who walk under the portal of the Konzerthaus Berlin should feel uneasy; they should feel bad and in this way be reminded of the most fundamental statutes of a democracy which invokes "inviolable human dignity" and is in the process of selling out universal ideals of human rights in favor of personal and nationalistic interests to those who would like to have these immediately removed from the Basic Law. It is therefore necessary to convey to the addressees with pathos that something is being destroyed here which will undoubtedly never again be able to be corrected and that the public space as well as the space of art, the threshold between which is marked by the façade, should feel equally responsible to change this state of affairs as quickly as possible. One may argue over the political sustainability of such (art-)populist strategies, but the fact that Ai Weiwei has been successful in pointing out and bringing charges against human rights violations with and through art for years remains undeniable. Under the heading "Familiar Curse Words," Ai Weiwei wrote in his blog on August 20, 2006, "Human life is sovereign, and we are born into the rights and dignity that are inherent to it. These are superior to any power save of death, either spiritual or physical./The above statement is complete bullshit. Human beings have never been sovereign, they have always lived under oppression, and they must constantly remind each other of this, or there will be an even higher price to pay. This is the history of civilization."[23] Today, thirteen years later, the question as to whether Ai Weiwei is an artist or an activist or both, and whether that is possible at all, is also bullshit. As long as the history of civilization continues like this and he uses all the means available to change it, there is hardly anything less important.

1
Wolfgang Ullrich, "Kunst
und Flüchtlinge. Ausbeutung
statt Einfühlung," in: **perlen-
taucher**.de: **Das Kunst-
magazin**, June 20, 2016,
https://www.perlentaucher.
de/essay/wolfgang-ullrich-
ueber-kunst-und-fluechtlinge.
html (last accessed on
March 8, 2019) [translated].

2
Ibid.

3
This is particularly evident
in comparison with U.S. art
history in which the issue of
political art has been flour-
ishing for some time.

4
Prime examples of this are
critical art platforms such as
e-flux and **TEXTE ZUR
KUNST**, as well as exhibitions
ranging from the most recent
Documenta to **POWER TO
THE PEOPLE** in the Schirn
Kunsthalle Frankfurt, both of
which have put the search
for the political in art on their
agendas.

5
The most detailed and reliable
descriptions of Ai Weiwei's
approach and its political
foundation can be found in:
Christian P. Sorace, "China's
Last Communist: Ai Weiwei,"
in: **Critical Inquiry**, vol. 40,
no. 2 (Winter 2014), pp. 396–
419, esp. pp. 412–5; Hans
Werner Holzwarth (ed.),
Ai Weiwei (Cologne 2016),
pp. 352–9.

6
See: Holzwarth 2016
(see note 5), p. 354.

7
See: Sorace 2014
(see note 5), p. 412.

8
See: Mark Siemons,
"China as Readymade: On
the Ai Weiwei System," in:
Ai Weiwei: **So Sorry**, exh.
cat. Haus der Kunst, Munich
(Munich et al. 2009),
pp. 22–8, here p. 28.

9
William A. Callahan, "The Art
of Politics," in: Holzwarth
2016 (see note 5), pp. 461–6,
here p. 462.

10
Ai Weiwei's blog entries were
regularly deleted since the
public announcement of his
research on the earthquake
victims, and the approaching
twentieth anniversary of the
Tiananmen Square Massacre
(presumably) led to the blog's
final closure on May 28, 2009.
Until then, the authorities had
harassed Ai Weiwei, his family,
and allies in various ways.
"[...] tensions increased," says
art historian Lee Ambrozy,
"as police tapped Ai's phone,
intercepted text messages,
and monitored his house, with
two conspicuous cameras
pointed at his door and the
occasional minivan stakeout.
In Sichuan, police detained
the volunteers, delivering
messages to Ai through them:
'Say hi to Ai Weiwei for us,
but he's not welcome here,
don't let us see him here.'
On May 26 [...] plainclothes
officers harassed his mother
in her home, then attempted
to interrogate Ai when he
arrived on the scene [...]" See:
Lee Ambrozy, "Introduction,"
in: Ai Weiwei, **Ai Weiwei's
Blog**: **Writings**, **Interviews**,
and Digital Rants, **2006–
2009**, ed. and trans. Lee
Ambrozy (Cambridge, MA
2011), pp. xvi–xxviii, here
pp. xxiii–xxiv.

11
These include an audio file
available online for which
volunteers read, for hours,
the names of those killed; a
string of 123 documents from
Chinese authorities that Ai
Weiwei and his team received
in response to their inquiries,
exhibited at the Art Fair in
Hong Kong in 2012; the installation **Remembering** in
Munich, incorporating the
statement of one of the
mothers who had lost her
child; a similar version, **Snake
Ceiling**, for which Ai Weiwei
attached countless black-
and-gray backpacks in the
shape of a snake to the ceiling
of the Mori Art Museum in
Tokyo; a series of photographs
shown at the Jeu de Paume
in Paris; and the photographs
documenting the operation
he underwent as a result of a
blow to the head by a police
officer leading up to the trial
of an accused activist in
Sichuan—and thus also **Brain
Inflation on Plate** (2012)
here in the Düsseldorf
exhibition, a ceramic plate

with a scan of Ai Weiwei's
brain hemorrhage. Even the
evidence of all the donations
that Ai Weiwei received after
his detainment in 2011 and
which are on view in Düsseldorf as **I.O.U. Wallpaper**
(2011–2013), contain symbolic
sums, equal to the number of
dead schoolchildren, with
which the donors showed
their support for the artist.

12
Ai Weiwei and those collabo-
rating with him, as well as
human rights organizations
such as the Human Rights
Watch and Amnesty Inter-
national, have long been of
this opinion.

13
The political scientist
Christian P. Sorace discusses
the political strategy to
distinguish between these
two categories in his extensive
study on the earthquake and
reveals their roots in Maoist
propaganda. See: Christian P.
Sorace, **Shaken Authority**:
**China's Communist Party
and the 2008 Sichuan Earthquake** (Ithaka, NY/London
2017), pp. 1–6.

14
See: Judith Butler, **Frames of
War**: **When Is Life Grievable**
(London/New York 2009),
pp. 1–32.

15
See: ibid., pp. 14f. "[...]
grievability is a presupposition
for the life that matters,"
Butler writes, for "[w]ithout
grievability, there is no life,
or, rather, there is something
living that is other than life."

16
See: Didier Fassin, **Life**:
A Critical User's Manual
(Cambridge/Medford,
MA 2018), pp. 84–120.

17
Such an analogy is reinforced
by Ai Weiwei himself, who
never tires of speaking of his
role model Marcel Duchamp.
See, for example: John J.
Curley, "Readymade Disas-
ters: The Art and Politics of
Andy Warhol and Ai Weiwei,"
in: **Andy Warhol/Ai Weiwei**,
exh. cat. National Gallery of
Victoria, Melbourne and
The Andy Warhol Museum,
Pittsburgh (Victoria 2015),
pp. 141–54.

18
The work has this in common
with **Remembering**, for which
Ai Weiwei drew upon the blue-
yellow logo of Toys "R" Us.

19
See: Fassin 2018 (see note
16), pp. 92–101.

20
For more on biopolitics, see:
Michel Foucault, **The Birth of
Biopolitics**: **Lectures at the
Collège de France, 1978–
1979**, ed. Michel Senellart,
trans. Graham Burchell (New
York 2008); for more on
necropolitics, see: Achille
Mbembe, "Necropolitics,"
trans. Libby Meintjes, in:
Public Culture, vol. 15, no. 1
(2003), pp. 11–40.

21
See: Karen Smith, "Ai Weiwei:
Freedom in Action," in:
Ai Weiwei. **Libero**, exh. cat.
Fondazione Palazzo Strozzi,
Florence (Florence 2016),
pp. 16–61, here pp. 32–4.

22
Christian P. Sorace argues
that Ai Weiwei necessarily
refers to Mao Zedong's
politics, namely by reversing
these politics for his art.
This is particularly evident in
Ai Weiwei's tendency towards
an "aesthetics of radical
transparency and a political
ethics of unrelenting criticism." See: Sorace 2014 (see
note 5), p. 404.

23
Ai Weiwei, "Familiar Curse
Words: Posted on August 20,
2006" in: Ai Weiwei 2011
(see note 10), pp. 93f.,
here p. 93.

CHAPTER IV

Chapter IV

The eighty-one days from April 3 to June 22, 2011, during which Ai Weiwei was detained in an unknown location in Beijing without charge and initially without the notification of his relatives, have produced several works in which the artist comes to term with and addresses his traumatic experiences with Chinese state power. The most important and largest work in this group is the installation **S.A.C.R.E.D.** (2011–2013), which is comprised of six large iron boxes. Inside each of the boxes, an exemplary scene from the period of confinement is depicted as a three-dimensional figurative image in the style of a diorama. Through small openings, one looks into the cell, illuminated with electric ceiling light, in which Ai Weiwei was detained under the permanent watch of two guards. Fiberglass figures, roughly at one-third scale, depict the prisoner Ai Weiwei and the two officials. The two guards wear the green uniform of the Chinese military and, as one sees, follow the prisoner at every moment, from eating and sleeping to using the shower and toilet. The depiction of the cell's barren interior with its meticulously represented details—the few pieces of clothing in the wardrobe, the padded cladding of the walls, and the jumble of colorful plastic bottles for washing in the bathroom—is so realistic that it is hard to imagine that the sets were not realized using photographs or drawings made on site. But during his two and a half months detainment, Ai Weiwei was not permitted to draw or write anything down; he thus had the cell and the figures modeled afterwards based solely on his recollections. He worked for several months with a large team on the extensive project, and because one of the many police requirements after release was his silence about the period of detention, this was done clandestinely. Since both written and verbal narration had been forbidden, the act of showing came into play as a narrative strategy whereby the desire for a demonstrative clarity of representation outweighs any reservations regarding a stylistic proximity to Socialist Realism.

S.A.C.R.E.D. was first exhibited in the Baroque church of Sant'Antonin, in the summer of 2013, during the Venice Biennale and, within the context of the world's oldest recurring art exhibition, broke all conventions of visual art at the beginning of the twenty-first century. **S.A.C.R.E.D.** is a colossal, incommensurable work that comes in the harmless didactic form of natural history showcases which provide information about exotic animals or past customs and traditions. The six catafalque-like boxes contain a dramatic self-portrait of the artist and, at the same time, act as a burning plea for the preservation of human rights. The work's title is an acronym consisting of six letters that correspond to six scenes and the actions represented therein from the prisoner's everyday life: S (Supper) shows the prisoner eating under the watchful gaze of his guards; A (Accusers) depicts the interrogation to which Ai Weiwei was exposed several times a day; C (Cleansing) refers to washing of the body in the shower; R (Ritual) stands for the ritualized movement, pacing back and forth in the cell; E (Entropy) depicts the prisoner in the entropic state of sleep; and D (Doubt) depicts the prisoner sitting on the toilet, while the guards stand unashamedly next to him. Here, the English word "sacred" does not solely point to a religious interpretation, although the work's presentation in a Christian church certainly suggests this reading. The location of Sant'Antonin was, it should be noted, chosen randomly; so **S.A.C.R.E.D.** primarily refers to the figure in ancient Roman law of the "Homo sacer" who stands outside the law. The Italian philosopher Giorgio Agamben described this figure in his influential book **Homo Sacer: Sovereign Power and Bare Life**,[1] with reference to Guantánamo Bay and other systems of injustice, as a type that has survived into the enlightened modern age. With **S.A.C.R.E.D.**, Ai Weiwei follows in this tradition. He identifies his situation in the cell as one lacking completely in protection and rights and makes his own body into a symbol of bare existence. With the sober depiction, like a model, he presents his "self" as an example and thus shares this state of being, thrown back into a state of bare existence, with all other detained dissidents in totalitarian regimes. Any Chinese citizen (as well as any citizen of Turkey, Brazil, Egypt, etc.) could disappear into such a box.

The music video **Dumbass**, which Ai Weiwei produced in the autumn of 2011 for his heavy metal album **The Divine Comedy** together with the musician Zuoxiao Zuzhou, presents an almost opposite form of grappling with his detainment in terms of self-empowerment and design. In the five-minute video which was shot in a full-sized reconstruction of the cell, Ai Weiwei becomes an unbound agent. He speaks, sings, nimbly dances, and acts in various roles in front of the camera of Christopher Doyle, a cameraman made famous for his collaboration with the Hong Kong star filmmaker Wong Kar-Wai. When Ai Weiwei romps about the shower as a prisoner, when he thrashes his guards as a whip-wielding tormentor, or when the officers teasingly throw themselves at the prisoner as seductive ladies in miniskirts, the role reversal and the living out of fantasies suggest the possibility of catharsis, even if the absurd, provocative song provoked further problems with the censor, such as when, in the refrain, China is described as a country that "puts out like a hooker."

In another music video, **Chaoyang Park** (2013), Ai Weiwei is again proactive in taking the initiative by removing the memory card from a police officer's camera. Upon viewing the contents of the card, he was horrified to discover that, even after his release, he and his family continued to be in the focus of the authorities. He processed this into a song that is also included on the album **The Divine Comedy**. Ai Weiwei incorporates his confrontations with state power and the dominance of themes around surveillance in the years 2011 to 2015, sometimes unfiltered, into his artistic practice. Listening devices from the walls of Ai Weiwei's Beijing studio, a full ashtray that testifies to how long the smoking informers had been on the lookout, and, above all, countless photos taken by Ai Weiwei of the plainclothes police watching him around the clock, prove that, for Ai Weiwei, anything that has to do with politics can also be art.

The beginning of the conflict between Ai Weiwei and the Chinese Ministry of State Security is marked by a selfie from 2009, which, in this exhibition, in the form of a large wallpaper image titled **Illumination**, is directly opposite the six boxes of **S.A.C.R.E.D.** The photo was taken in the early morning of August 12, 2009 in the mirrored elevator of the

Hotel Anyi in Chengdu, Sichuan province, when Ai Weiwei was detained by the police. The scene was preceded by the police breaking into Ai Weiwei's hotel room, during which he sustained a head injury. On the next day, he was to testify for the writer Tan Zuoren, who had been arrested for his activities while researching the victims of the Sichuan earthquake. The smartphone photo, which depicts Ai Weiwei, illuminated by the camera's flash, in the middle of musician Zuoxiao Zuzhou as well as two police officers, was quickly shown in a variety of contexts. At the large Ai Weiwei exhibition at the Haus der Kunst in Munich in the autumn of 2009, the picture was displayed as a monumental print in the entrance; shortly thereafter, it appeared in the German news magazine **Der Spiegel** to illustrate an article on the "Smartphone Revolution." The ironically ennobling title **Illumination** underpins the almost iconic position which the snapshot has attained in the meantime. The blow to the head on that August night caused a brain injury which Ai Weiwei was only able to have treated at a clinic in Munich in the autumn. An MRI image of his head, created at the clinic, was also used as the motif for an artistic work: **Brain Inflation on Plate** (2012).

The wallpaper with the enigmatic title **The Animal That Looks Like a Llama but Is Really an Alpaca** also refers to his 2011 imprisonment. The complex composition kaleidoscopically combines the logo of Twitter, surveillance cameras, chains, and handcuffs and was created (in one version) for the 2015 exhibition at the Royal Academy in London. The glamorous appearance of the pattern printed in gold on white is, however, as misleading as the lengthy title of the work. The alpaca mentioned in the title was born out of the creativity of Internet activism in China which has developed to circumvent the online censorship by state authorities. It is a symbol of freedom of expression. In 2006, one of the toughest measures allegedly against online vulgarity took place. A series of blogs, Internet forums, and platforms were closed, against which various forms of protest were given shape. The alpaca was identified with its relative, the "Grass Mud Horse," the Chinese name of which, **cao ni ma**, when pronounced in a certain way, sounds like a strong, sexualized insult (akin to "fuck your mother"). Parodies of this kind were developed online with fervor and inventiveness and planted into the most diverse contexts. The gold-white wallpaper, as a luxury article, with its reflections and repetitively arranged details, may be interpreted as an allusion to the nouveaux riches of China, but it actually contains multiple harsh innuendos. On closer inspection, for example, Ai Weiwei can be seen jumping naked into the air, covering his genitals with a stuffed animal in the shape of a Grass Mud Horse. The same stuffed animal also appears in a brief shot in the video **Dumbass**, where it takes the place of the accused in the interrogation scene. Another hidden reference can be found on the wallpaper in the depiction of a detail from Marcel Duchamp's installation **Étant donnés : 1. La chute d'eau, 2. Le gaz d'éclairage** (1946–1966) in the collection of the Philadelphia Museum of Art. The scene of a nude woman lying on a bed of foliage with her legs spread-eagle, which can only be seen through two knotholes in a wooden door, makes visual desire and forbidden voyeurism its themes and violates all standards of Modern art. With Duchamp, Ai Weiwei's central reference figure, we once again come back to **S.A.C.R.E.D.**, which, in addition to the experience of imprisonment, also deals with the limitations of visibility and the ambivalent relationship between observer and observed.

The heads of the signs of the Chinese zodiac, arranged in a semicircle in front of the camouflage wallpaper, find their origins in sculptures from the Old Summer Palace destroyed in the Second Opium War in 1860, which are encountered for the third time in the exhibition. The gilded sculptures reference the large bronze group **Circle of Animals** which was installed at the Pulitzer Fountain in New York City in May 2011. At that time, Ai Weiwei had disappeared, and the broad public was concerned about his whereabouts. While Ai Weiwei was detained in a small cell in Beijing and interrogated about his connections to the international art scene, a number of artists, including Olafur Eliasson, Jenny Holzer, Barbara Kruger, Rirkrit Tiravanija, Luc Tuymans, and Franz West, demanded with a worldwide poster campaign "Free Ai Weiwei."

1
Giorgio Agamben, **Homo
Sacer**: **Sovereign Power
and Bare Life** (1995), trans.
Daniel Heller-Roazen
(Stanford 1998).

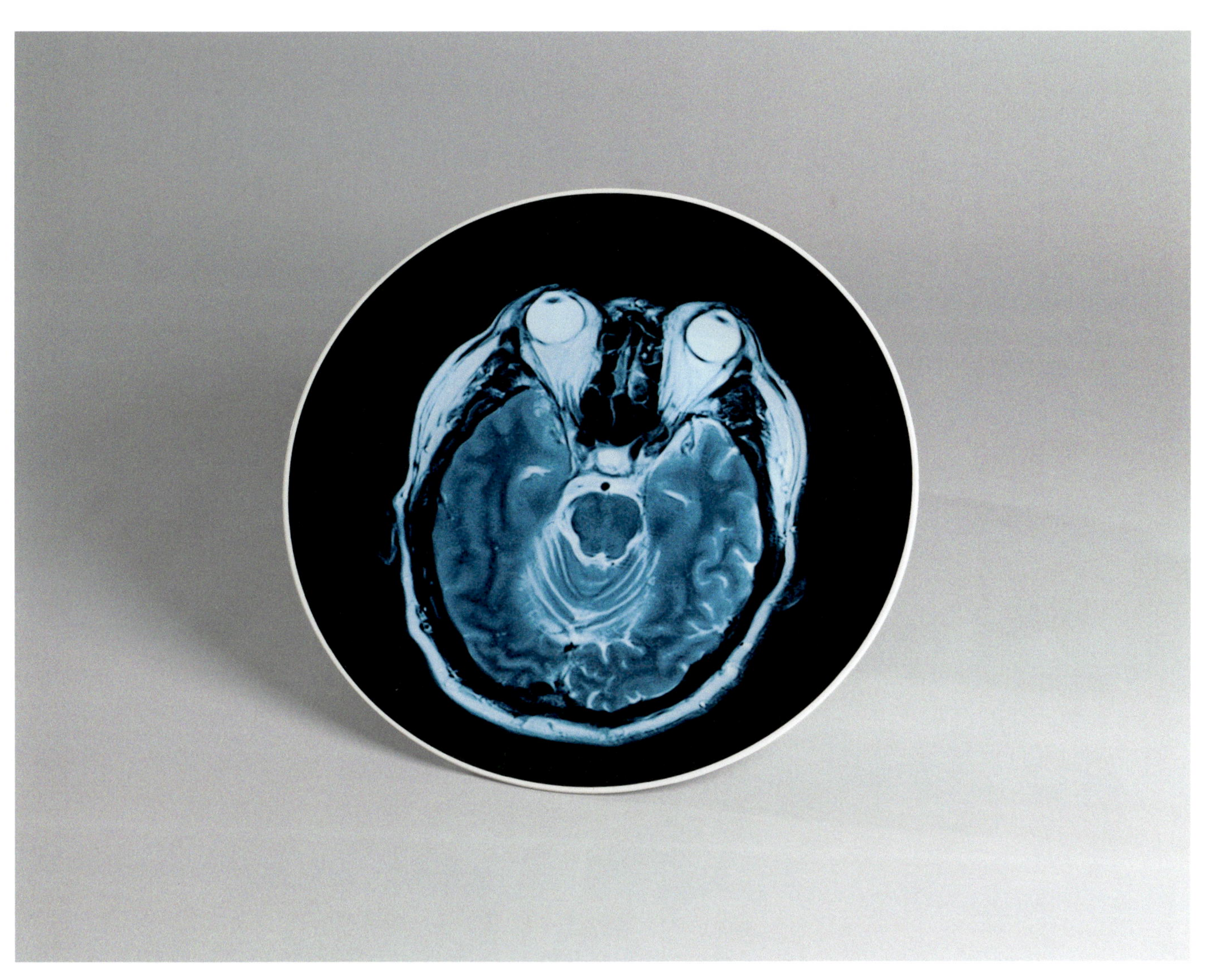

**Brain Inflation
on Plate**, 2012
Porcelain
40 × 40 × 4.5 cm

Illumination, 2009
Wallpaper
Dimensions variable

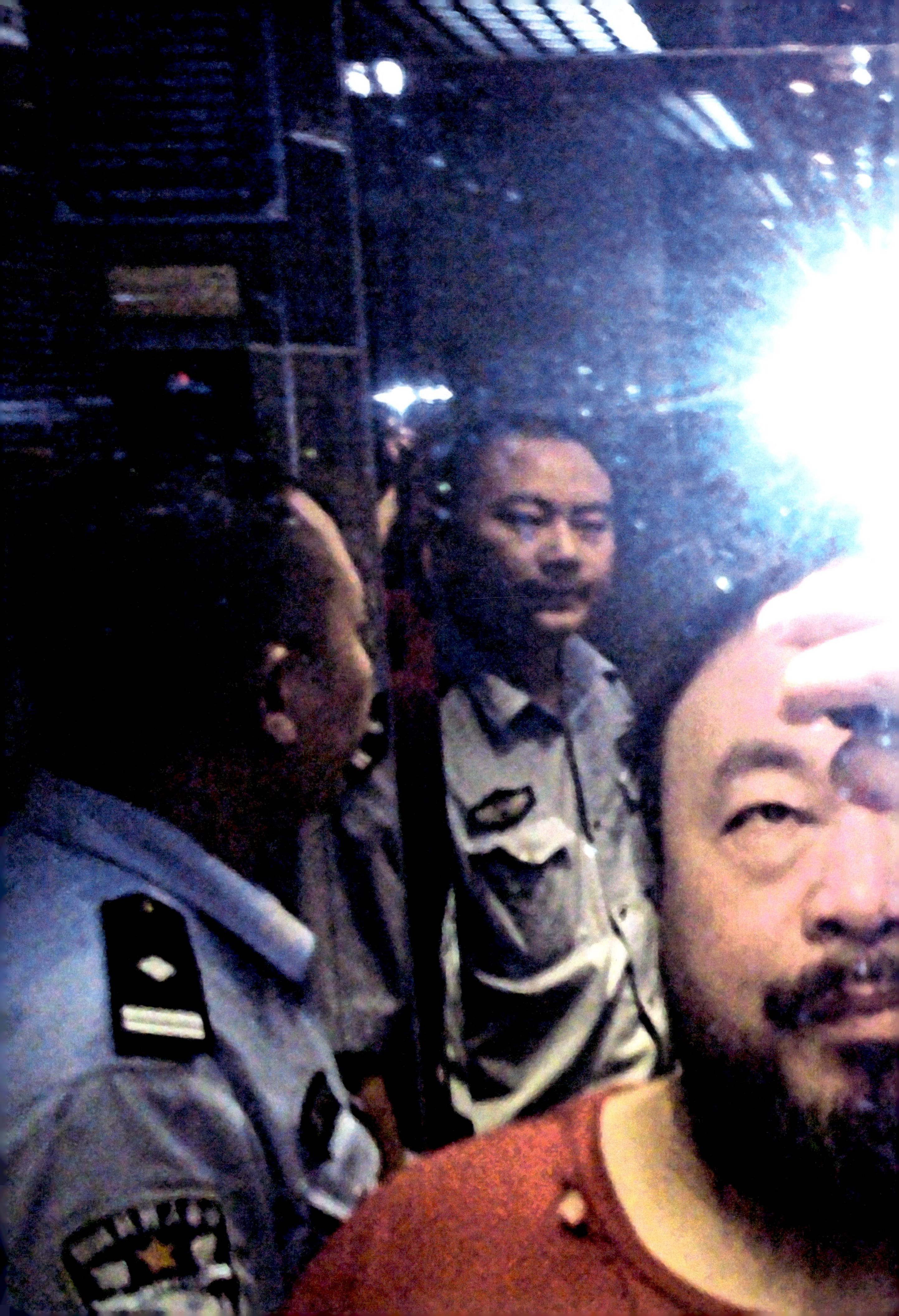

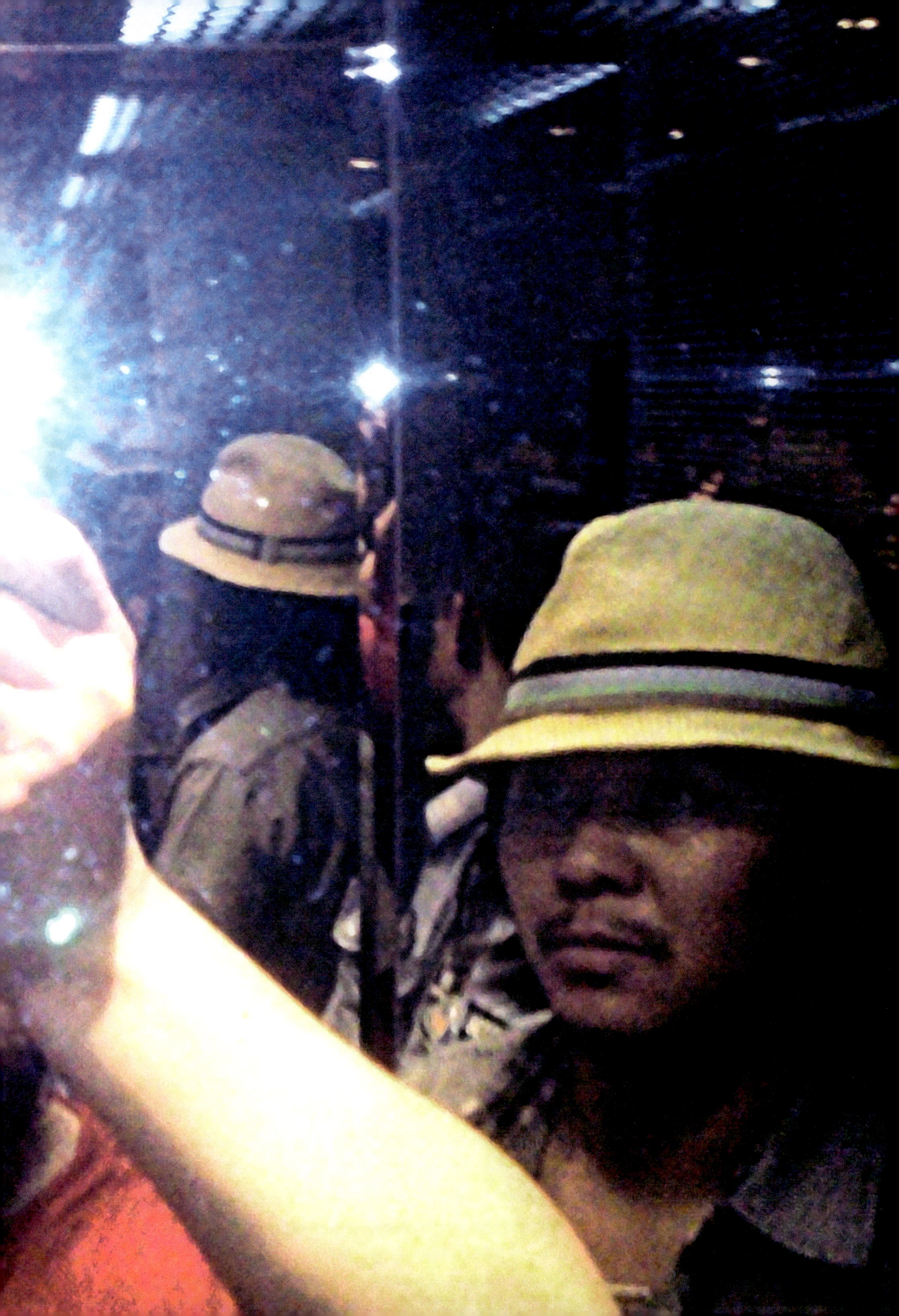

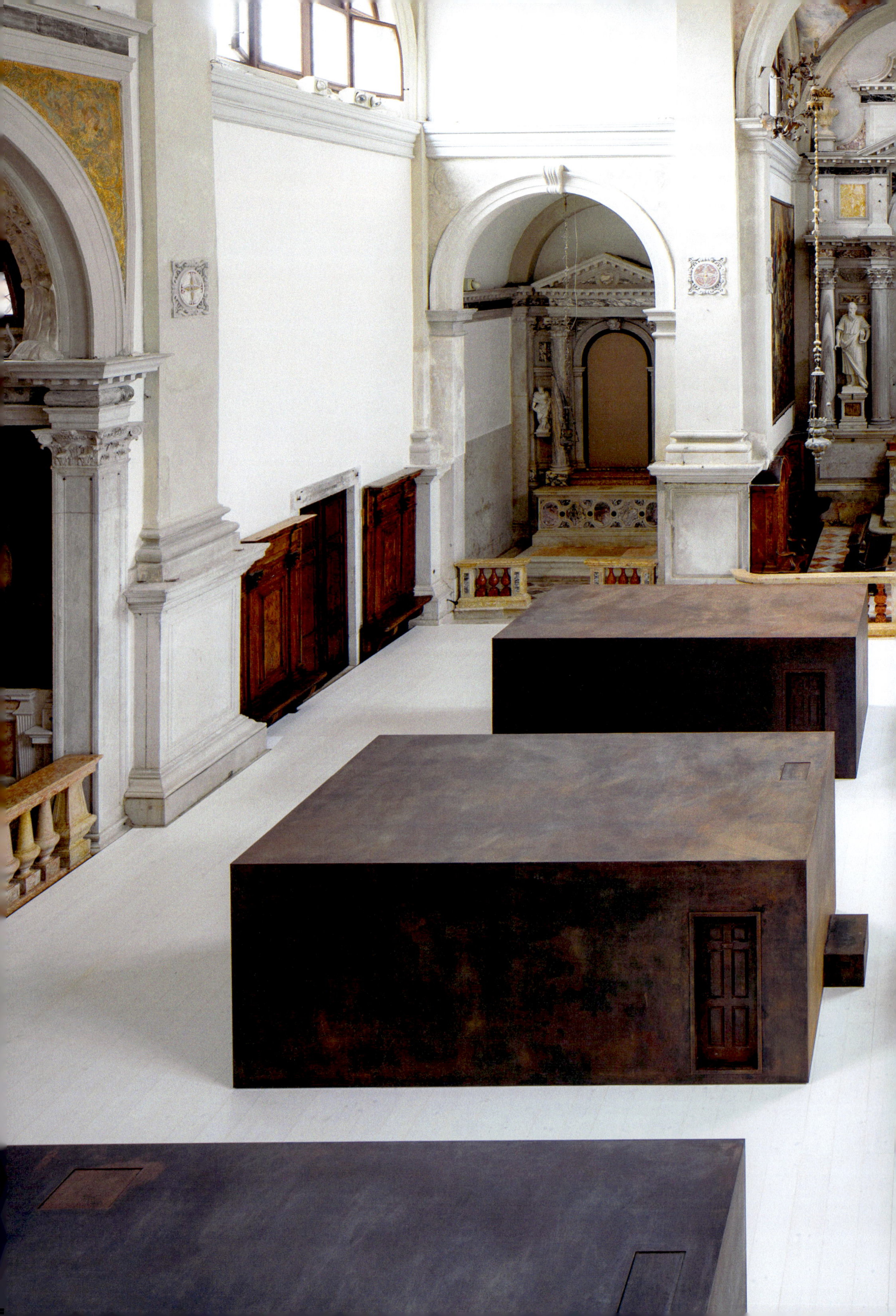

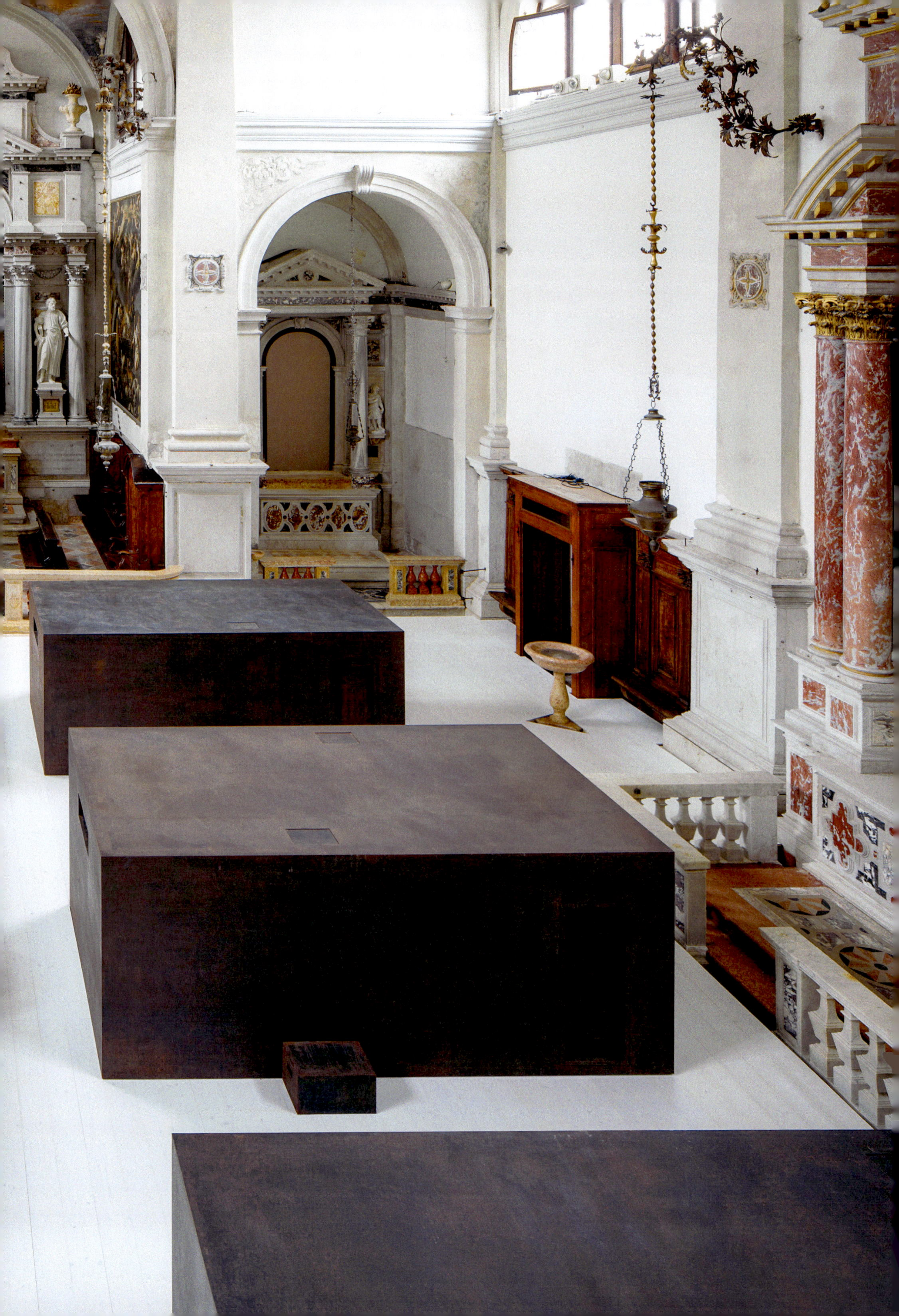

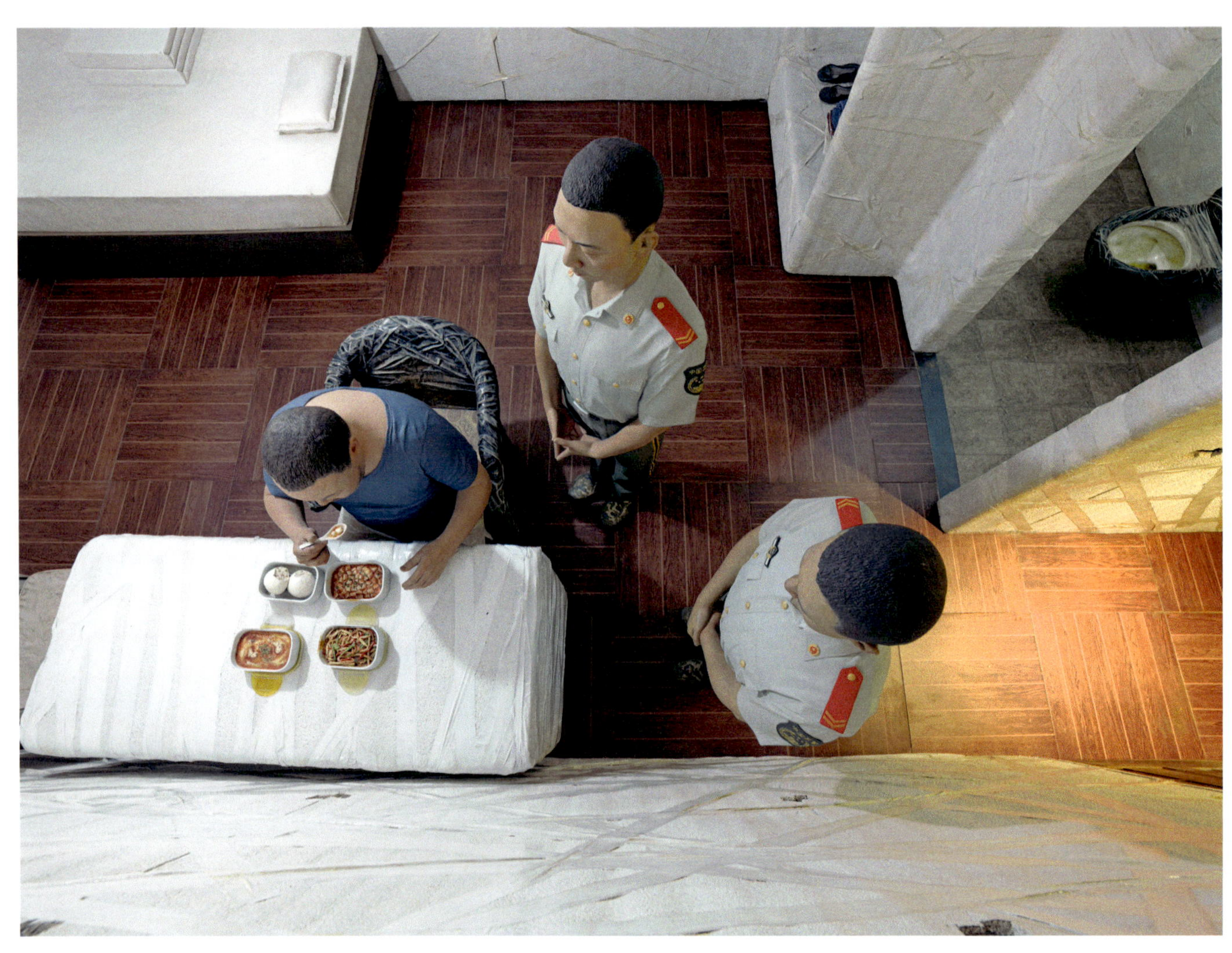

S.A.C.R.E.D., 2011–2013
Iron, fiberglass
Set of 6
(Supper, Accusers,
Cleansing, Ritual,
Entropy, Doubt),
each: 377 × 197 × 148.4 cm

pp. 164–165, 172–173:
Installation view
Sant'Antonin, Venice, 2013

166

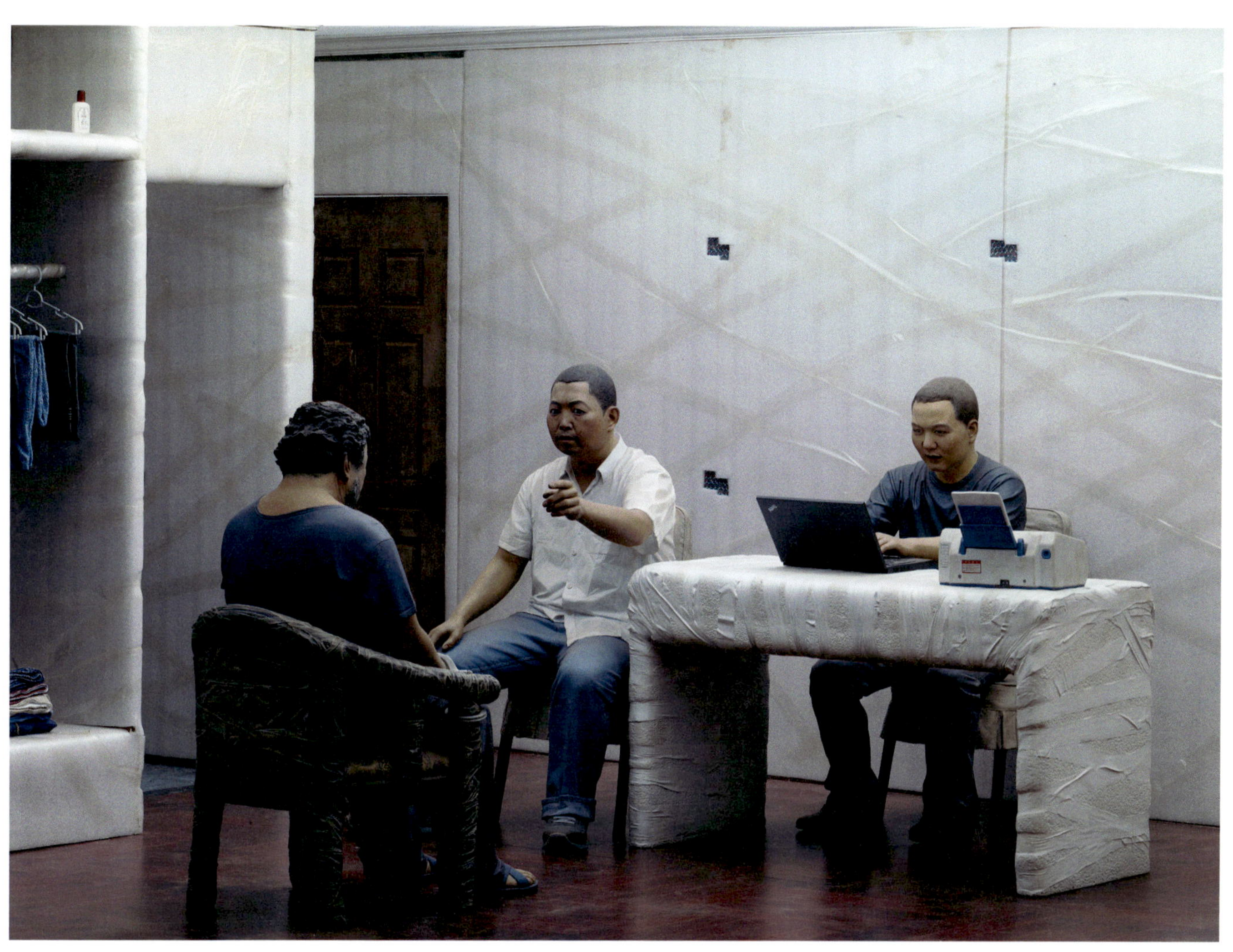

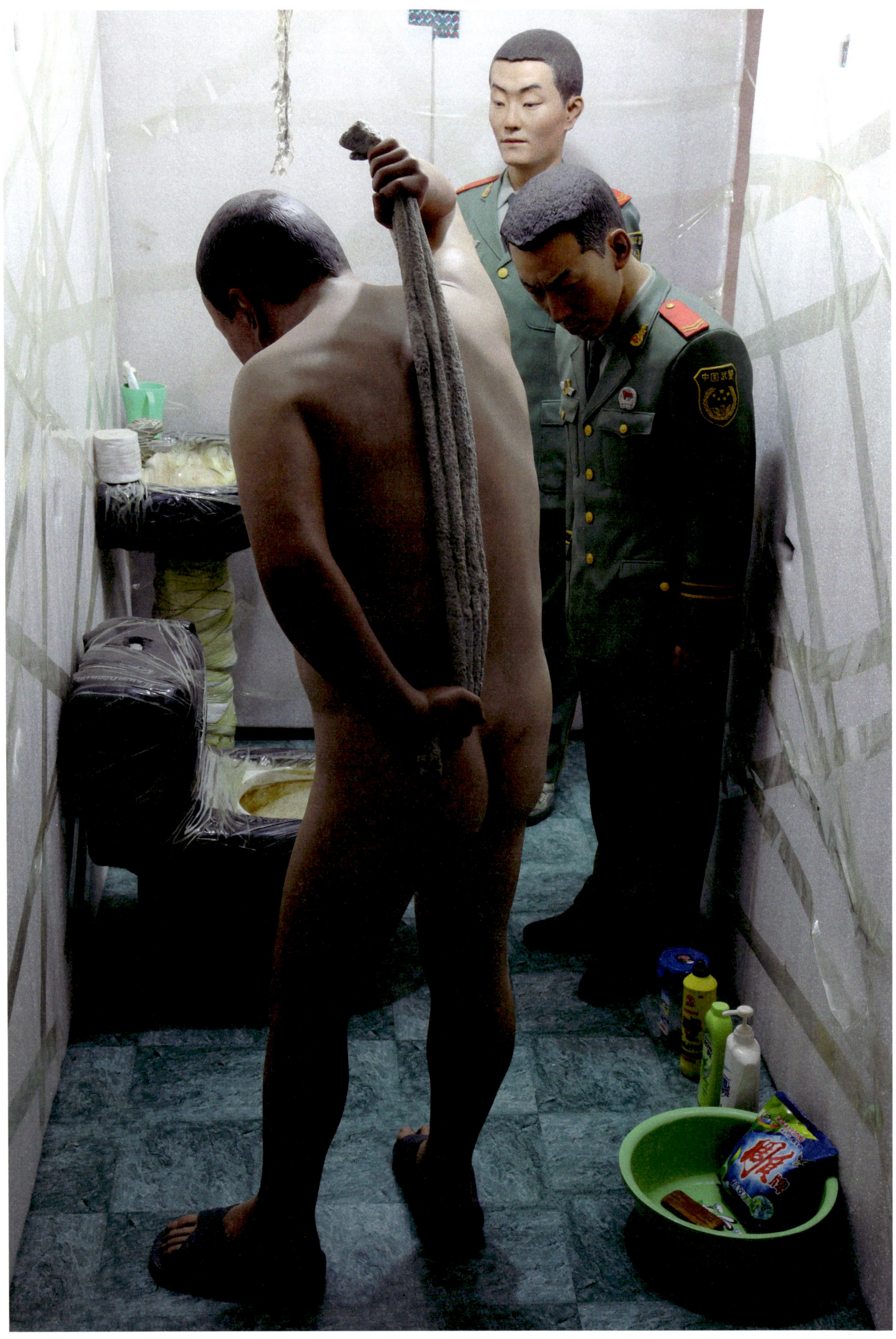

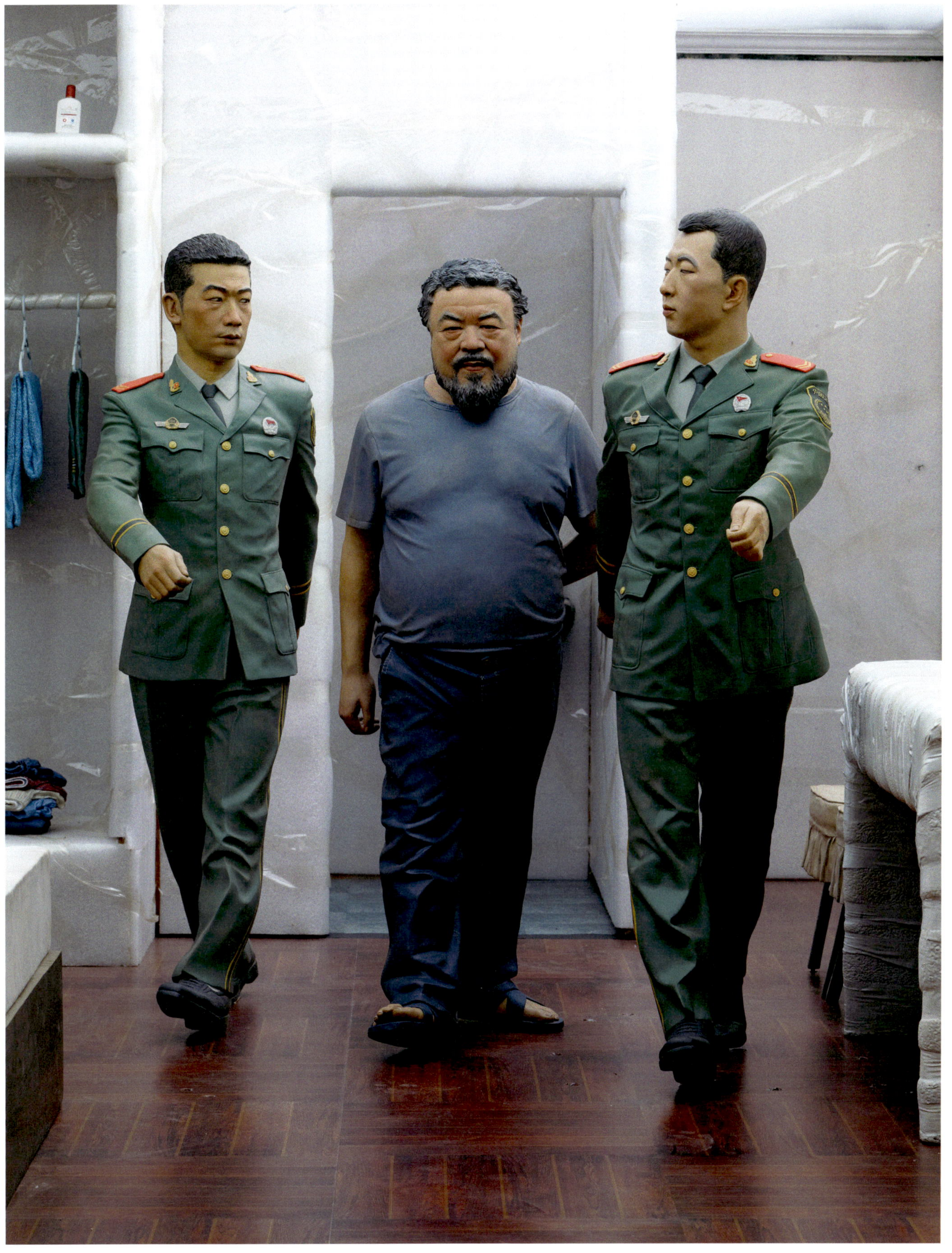

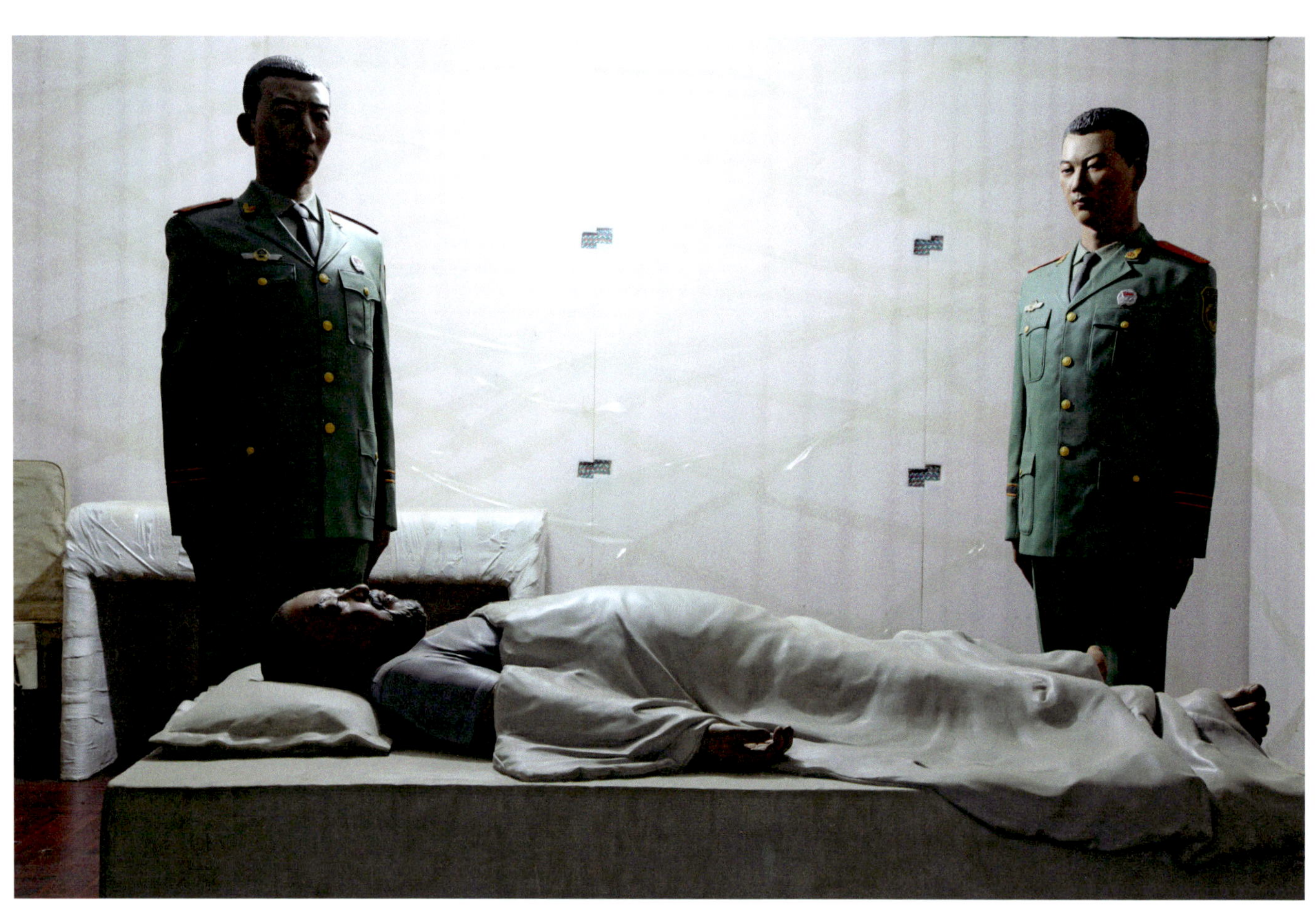

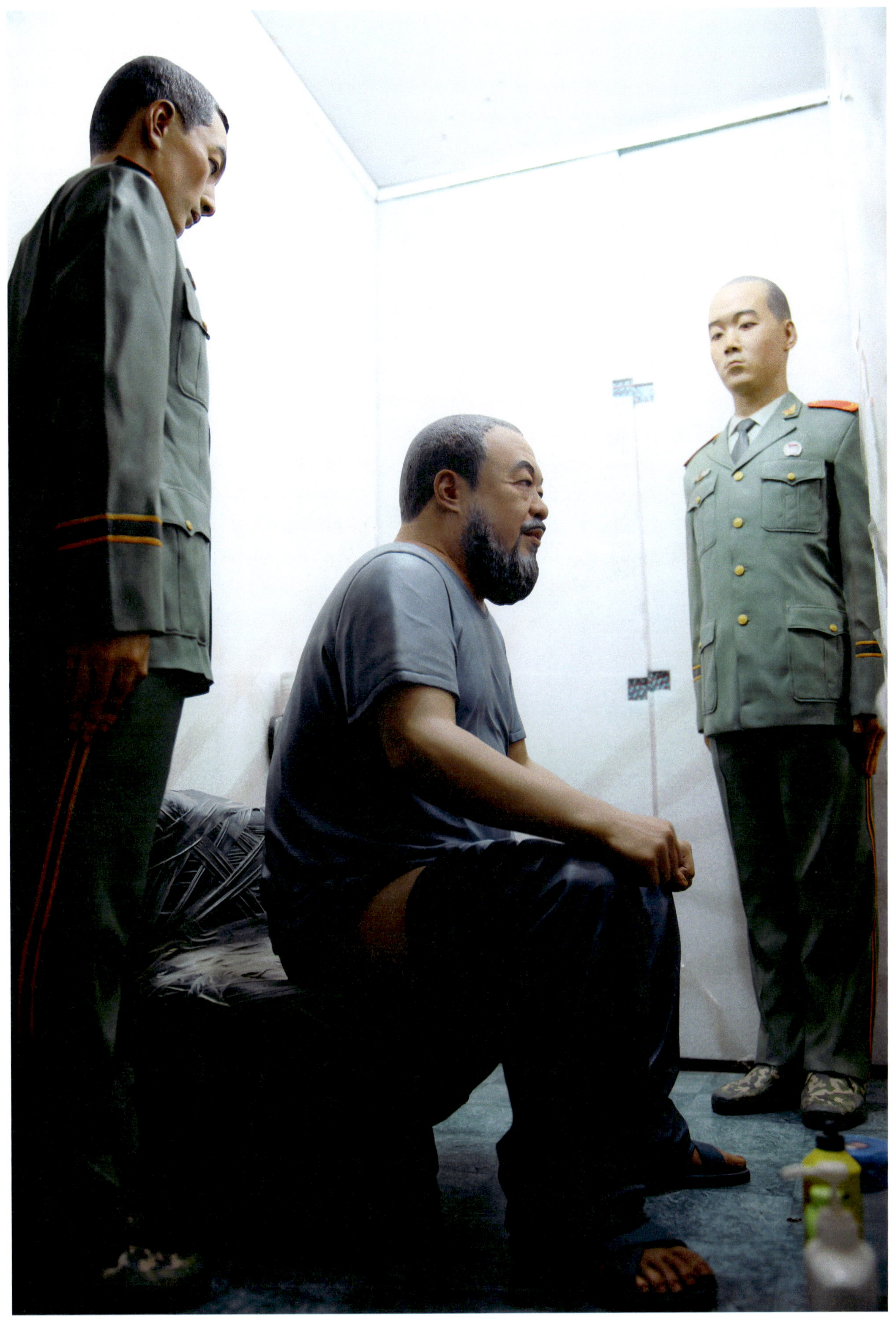

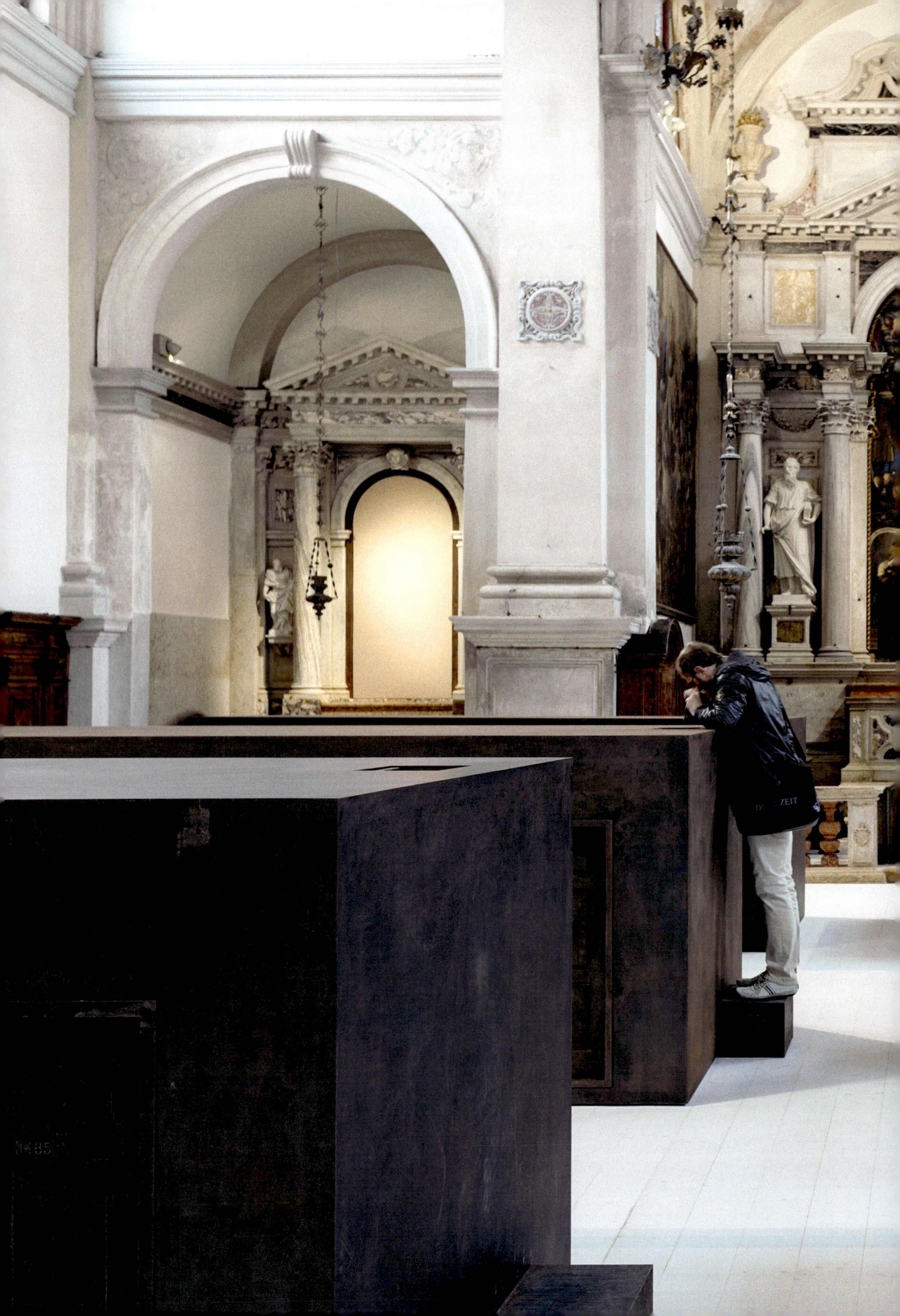

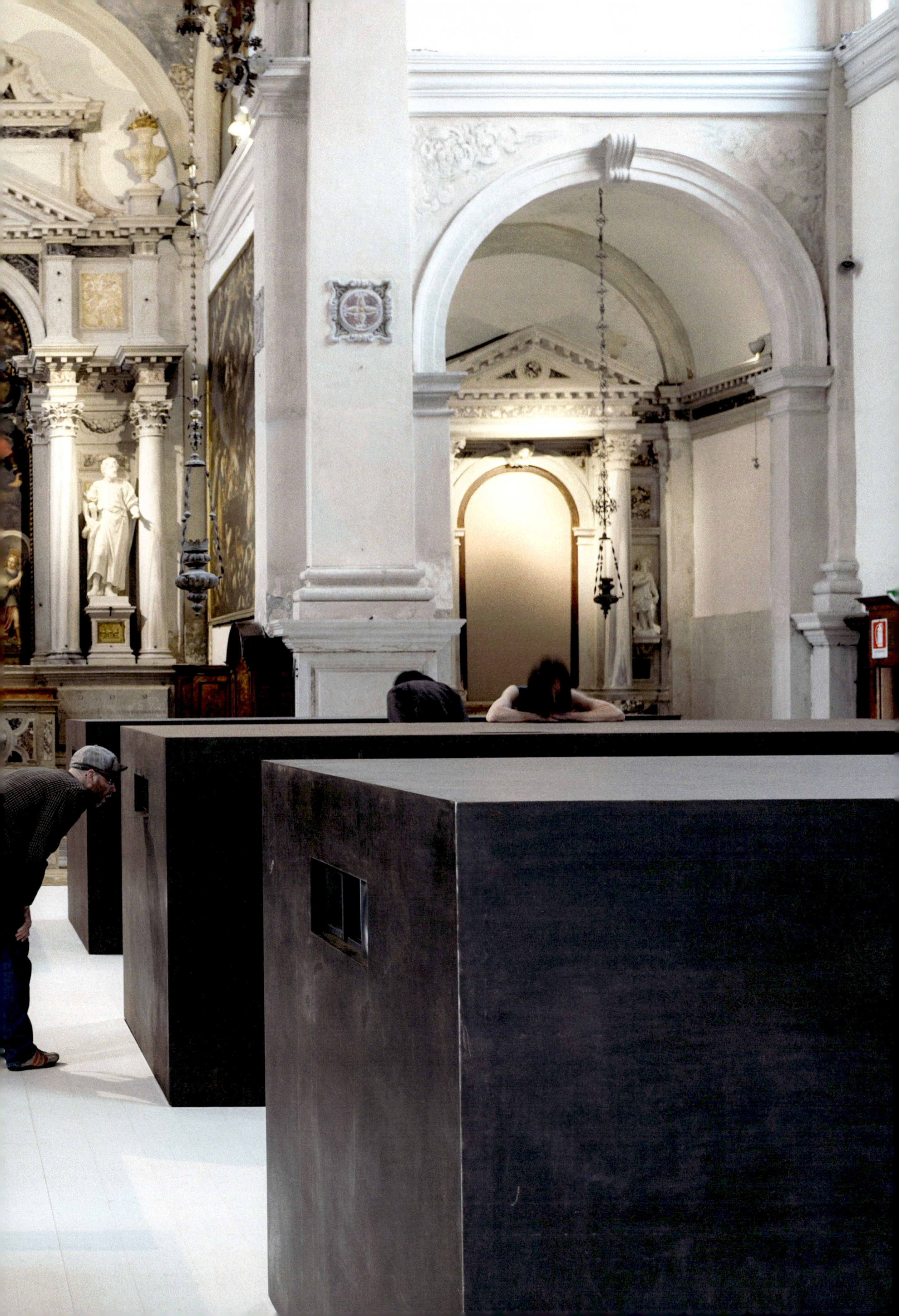

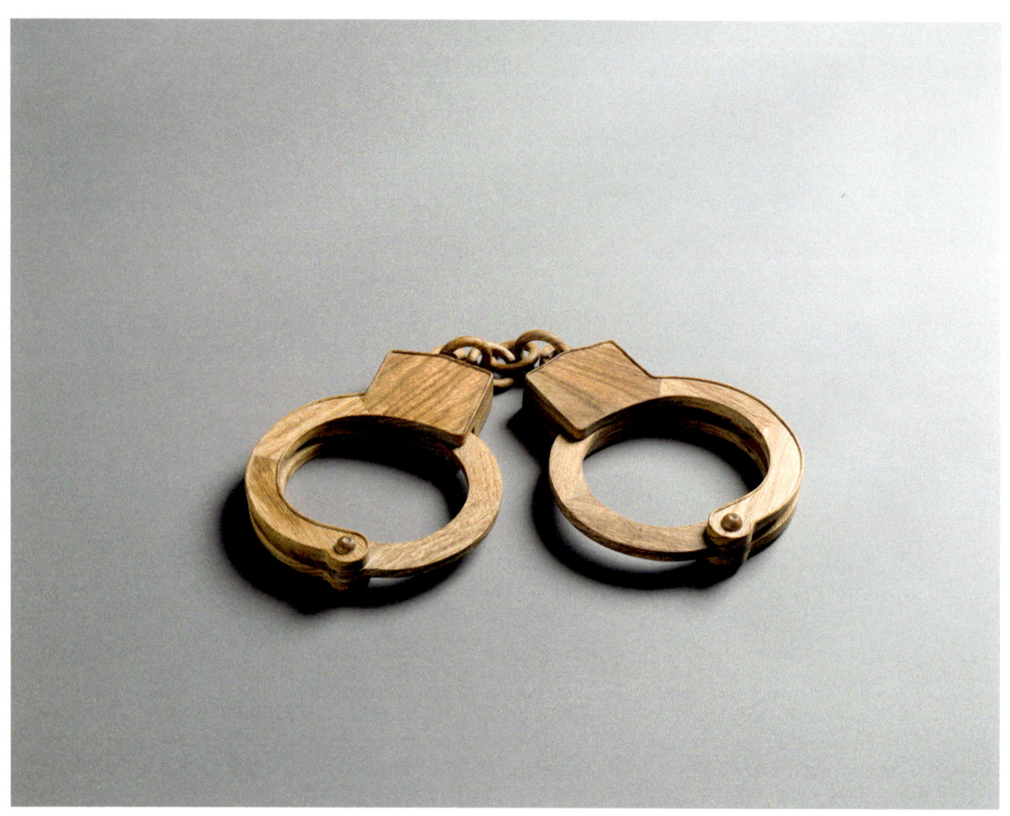

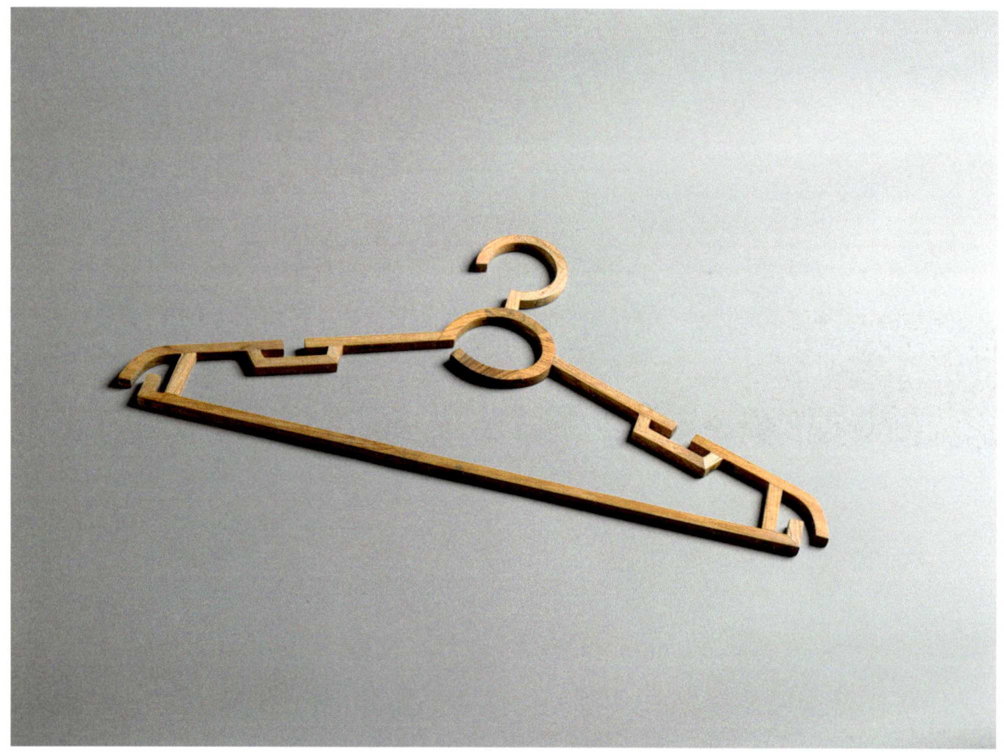

Handcuffs, 2015
Wood
40 × 13 × 2.5 cm

Hanger, 2011
Wood
50 × 24 × 0.8 cm

174

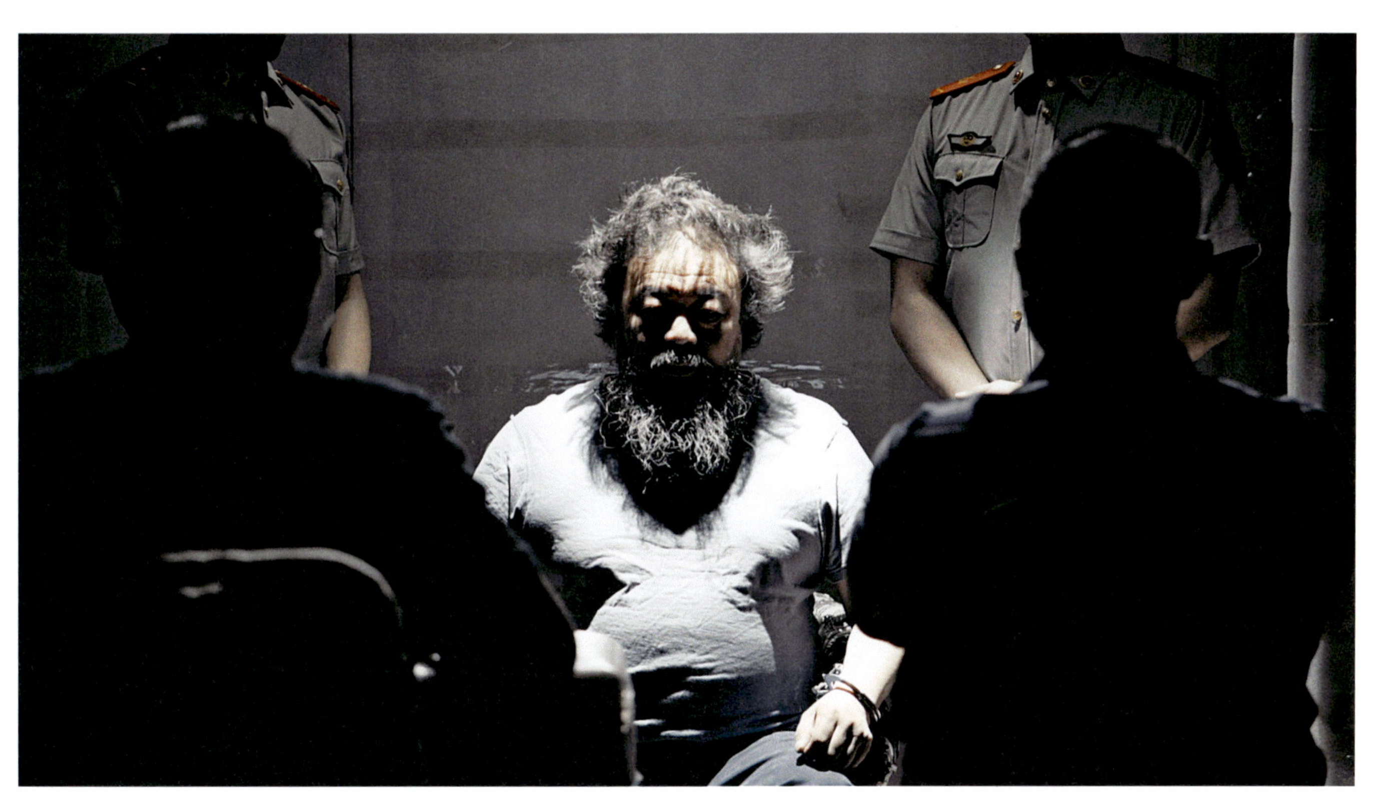

Dumbass, 2013
Video, color, sound, 5'12"

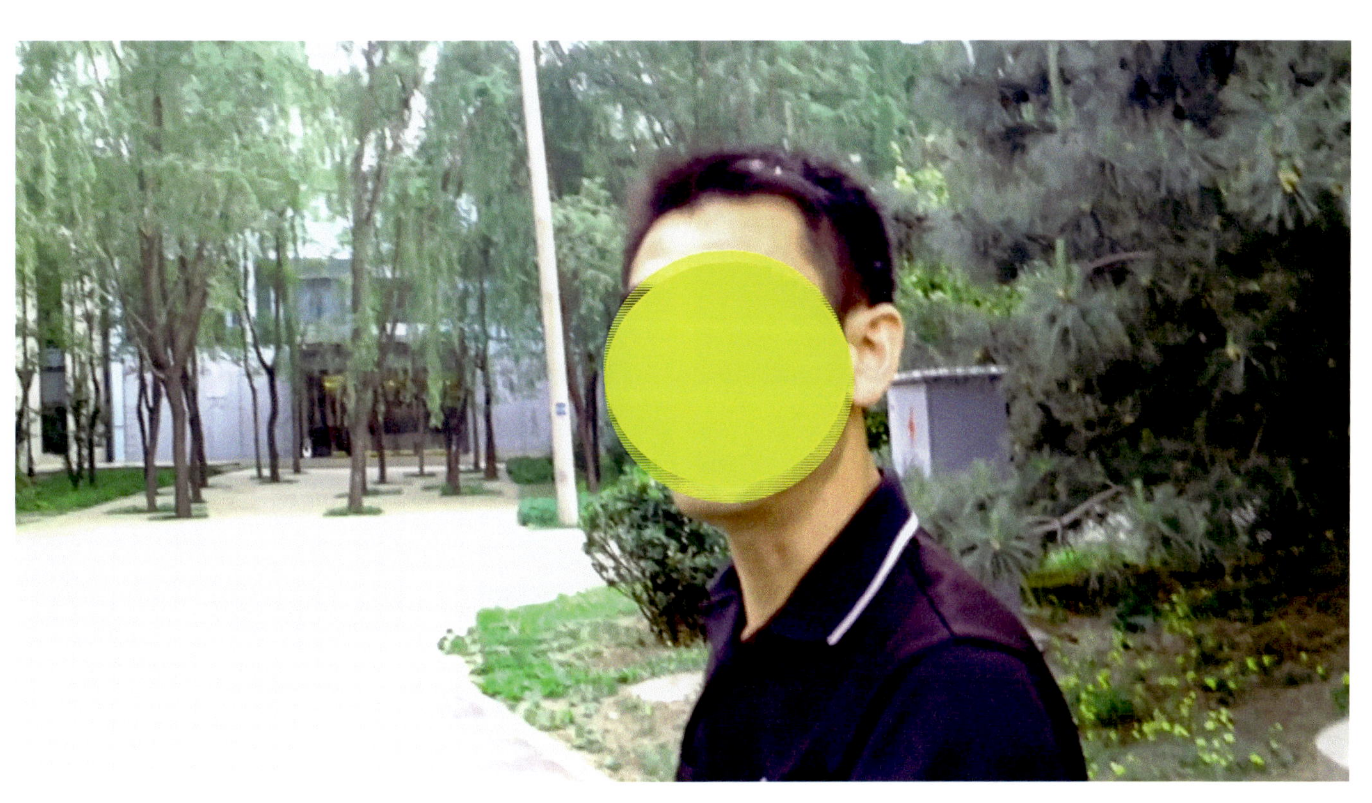

Chaoyang Park, 2013
Video, color, sound, 3'50"

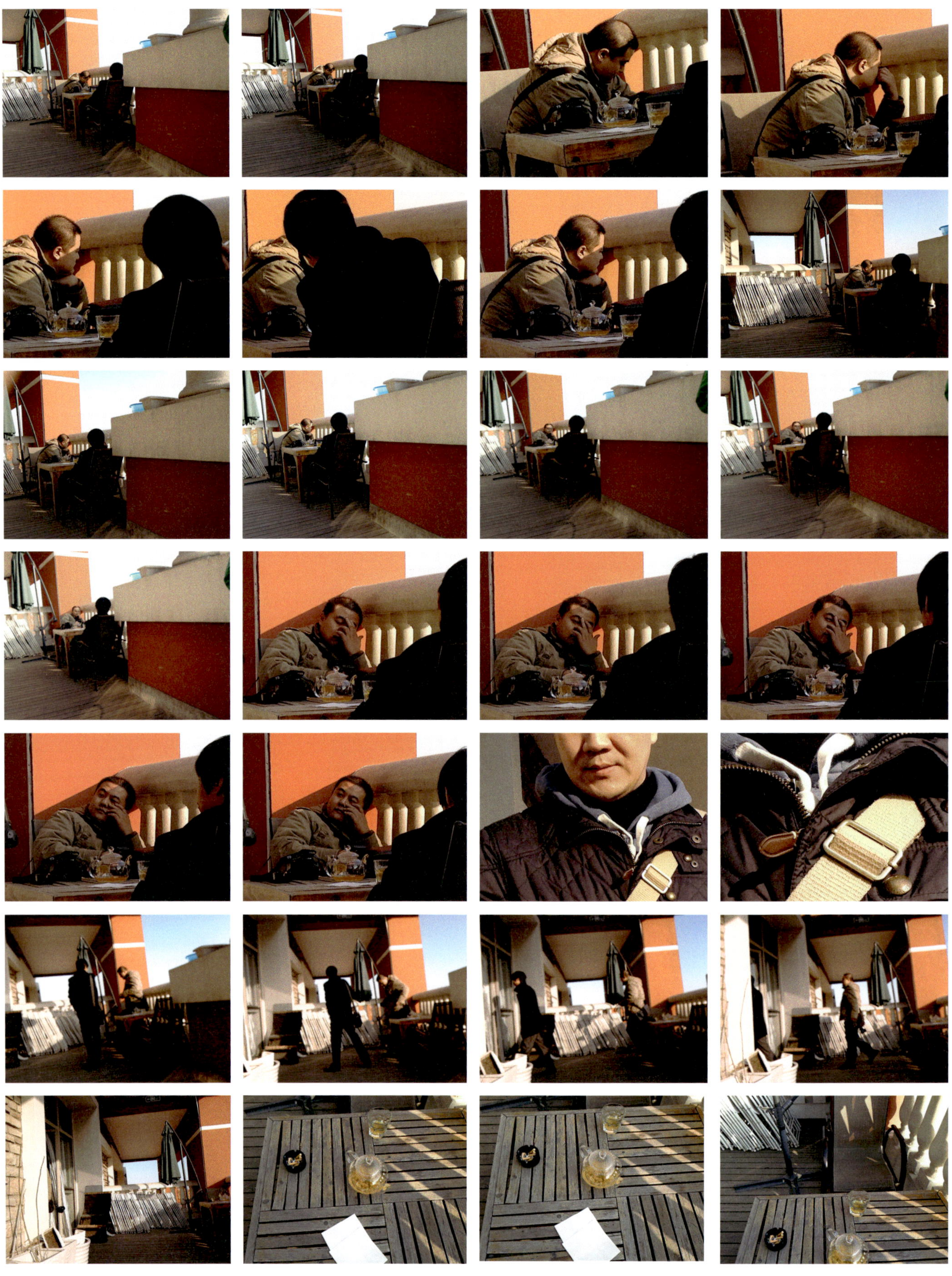

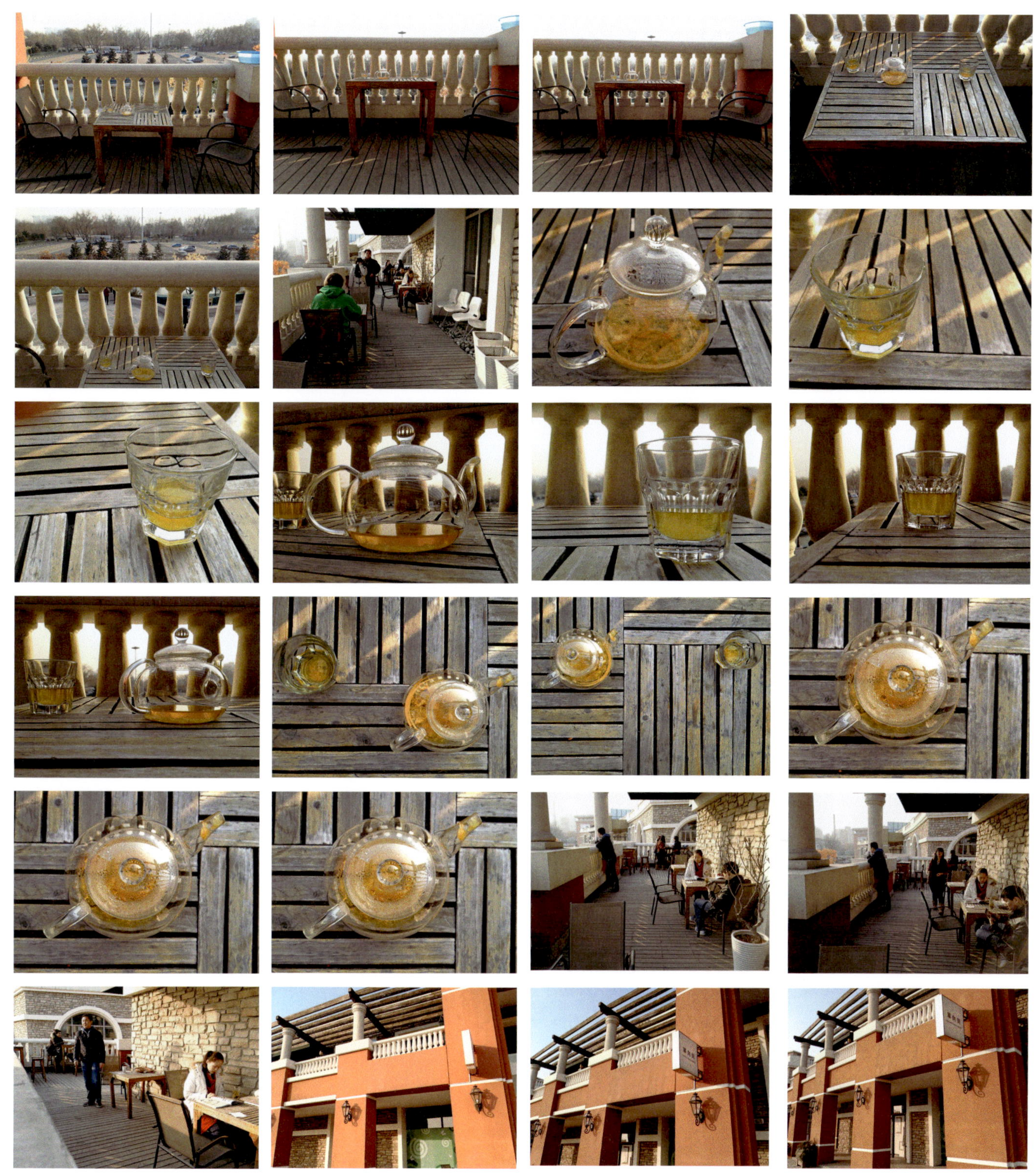

Photographs of Surveillance, 2010–2015
Wallpaper
349 photographs,
each: 12 × 16 cm

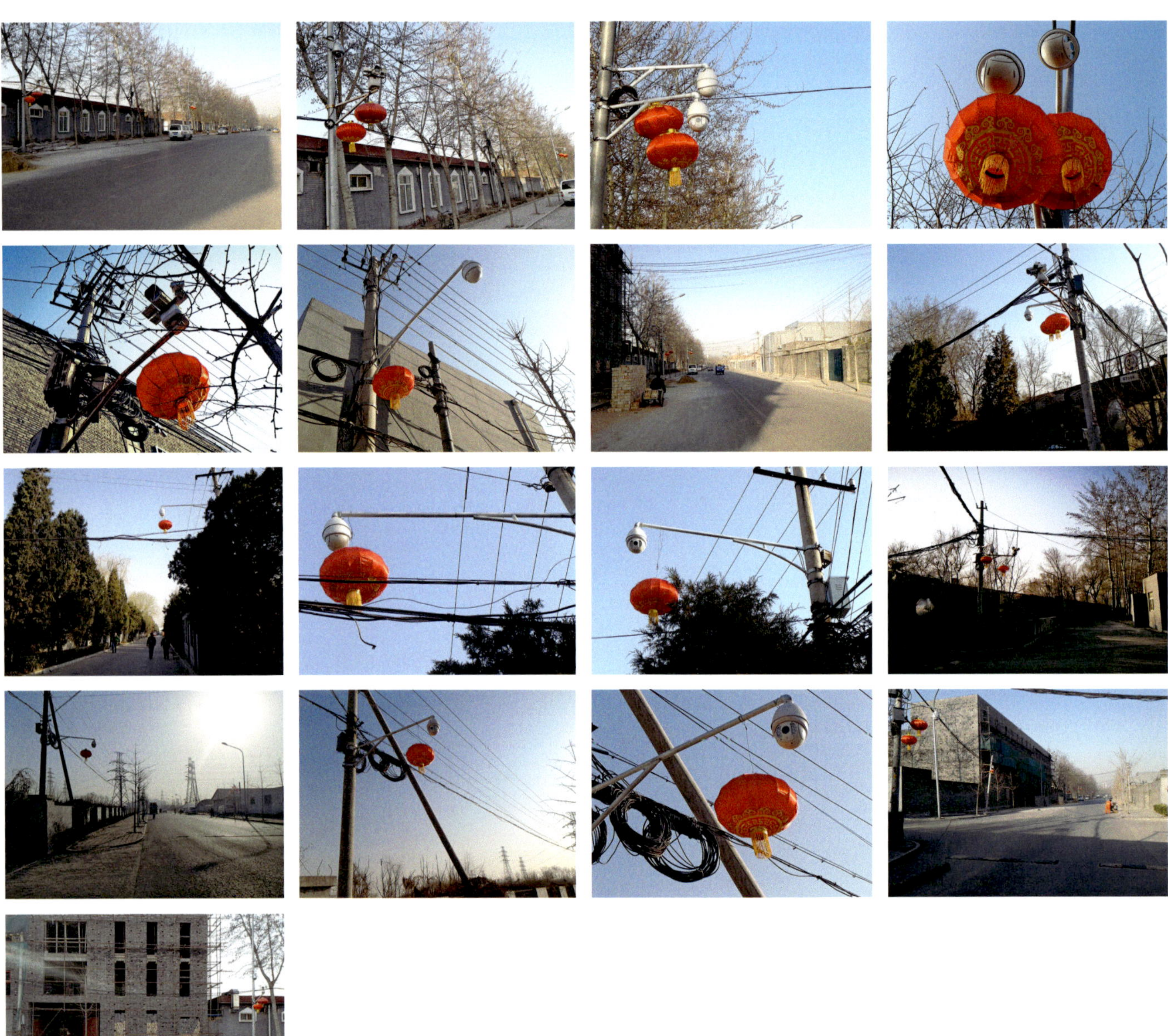

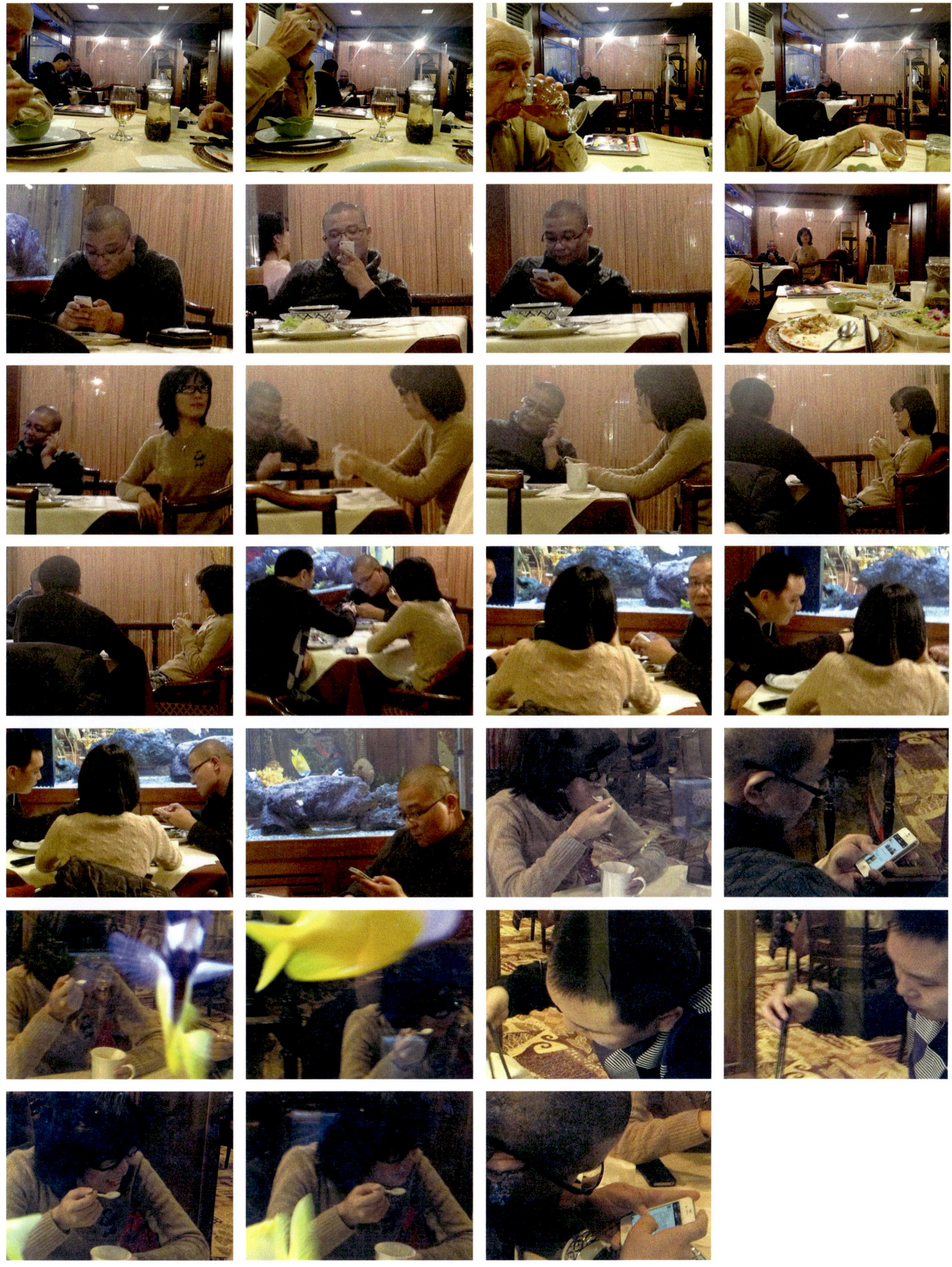

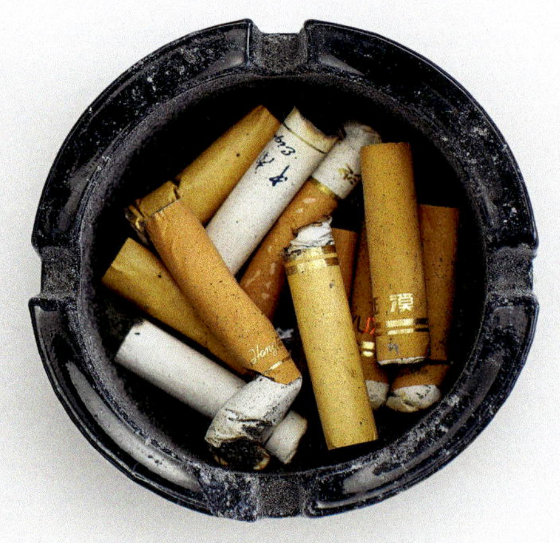

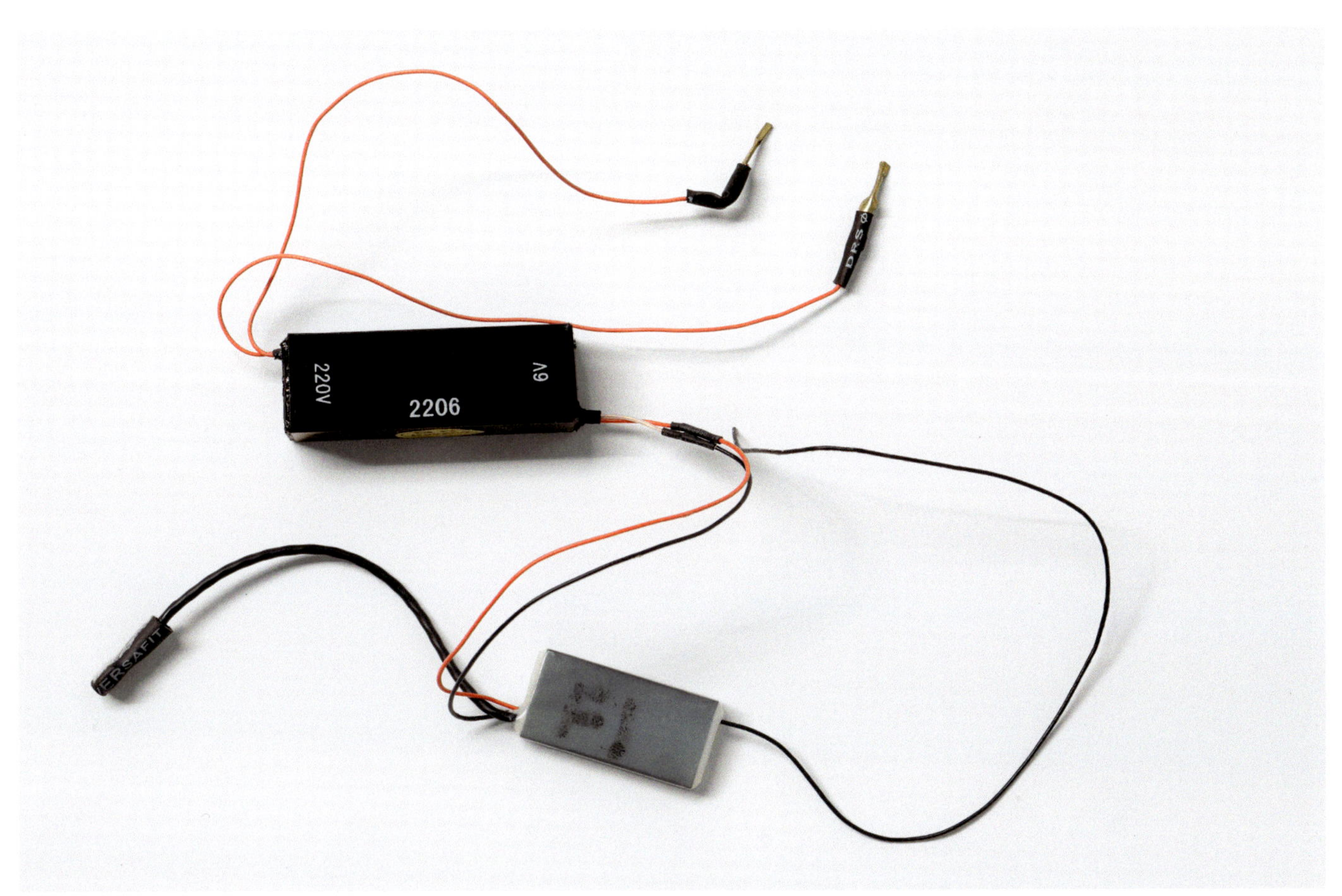

**Ashtray from Beijing's
Solana Bookstore**, 2011
Ashtray, cigarettes
7.5 × 7.5 × 3 cm

Bugs, 2015
Listening device
8.5 × 8.6 × 6 cm

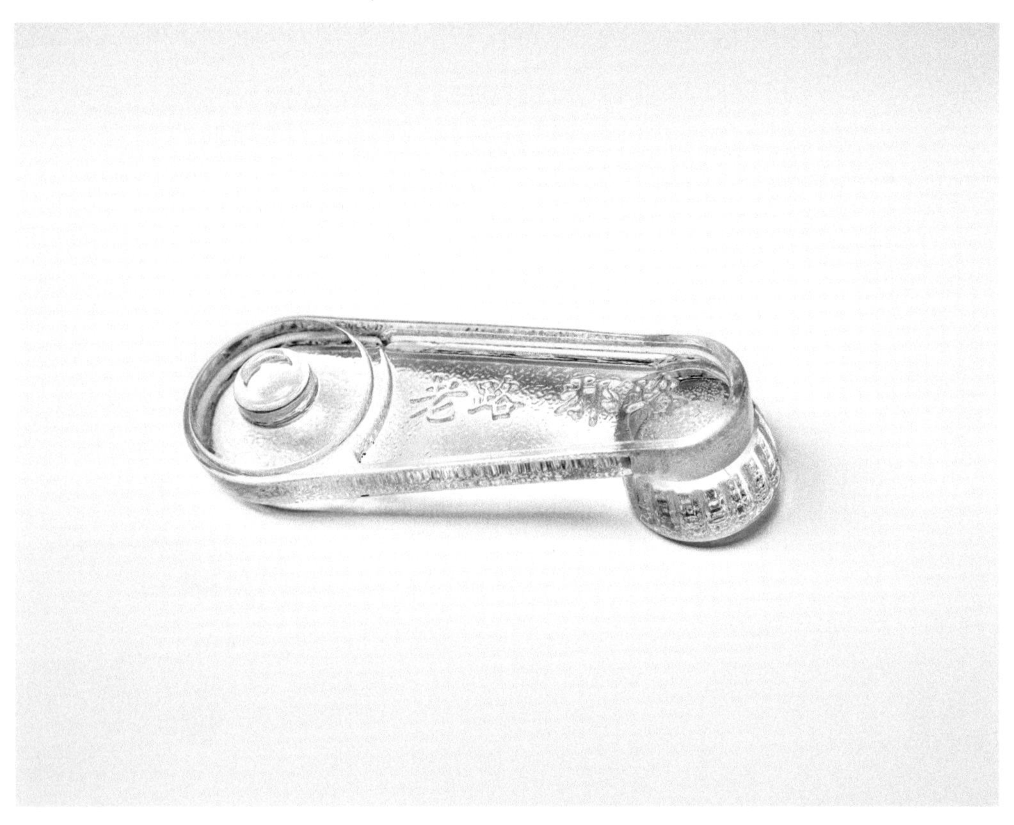

Taxi Window Crank, 2012
Glass
Set of 4,
each: 4 × 11.6 × 3.3 cm

**Discard the Old Path
of Closed Doors and
Rigidity and Reject Evil
Attempts to Change
the Party's Banner**, 2012
Video, color, sound, 18'35"

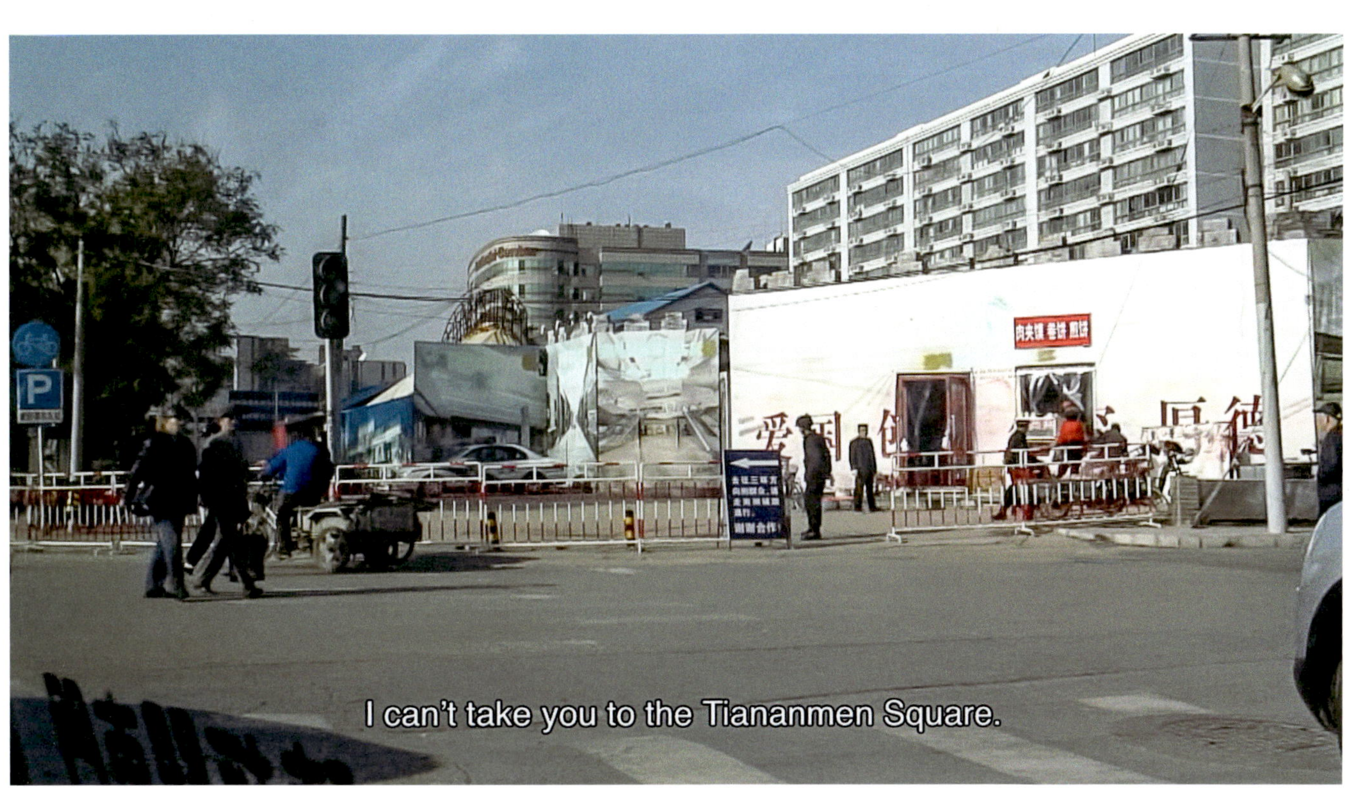

Circle of Animals, 2011
Bronze with gold plating;
stands: wood
Set of 12
Rat: 56 × 35 × 73 cm
Ox: 48 × 48 × 76.5 cm
Tiger: 40 × 33 × 70 cm
Rabbit: 47 × 33 × 77.5 cm
Dragon: 60 × 48 × 90 cm
Snake: 45 × 33 × 70 cm
Horse: 55 × 33 × 75 cm
Ram: 43 × 50 × 66 cm
Monkey: 39 × 33 × 70 cm
Rooster: 41 × 33 × 88.5 cm
Dog: 55 × 38 × 63 cm
Pig: 50 × 35 × 70 cm
Stands: 50 × 50 × 80 cm

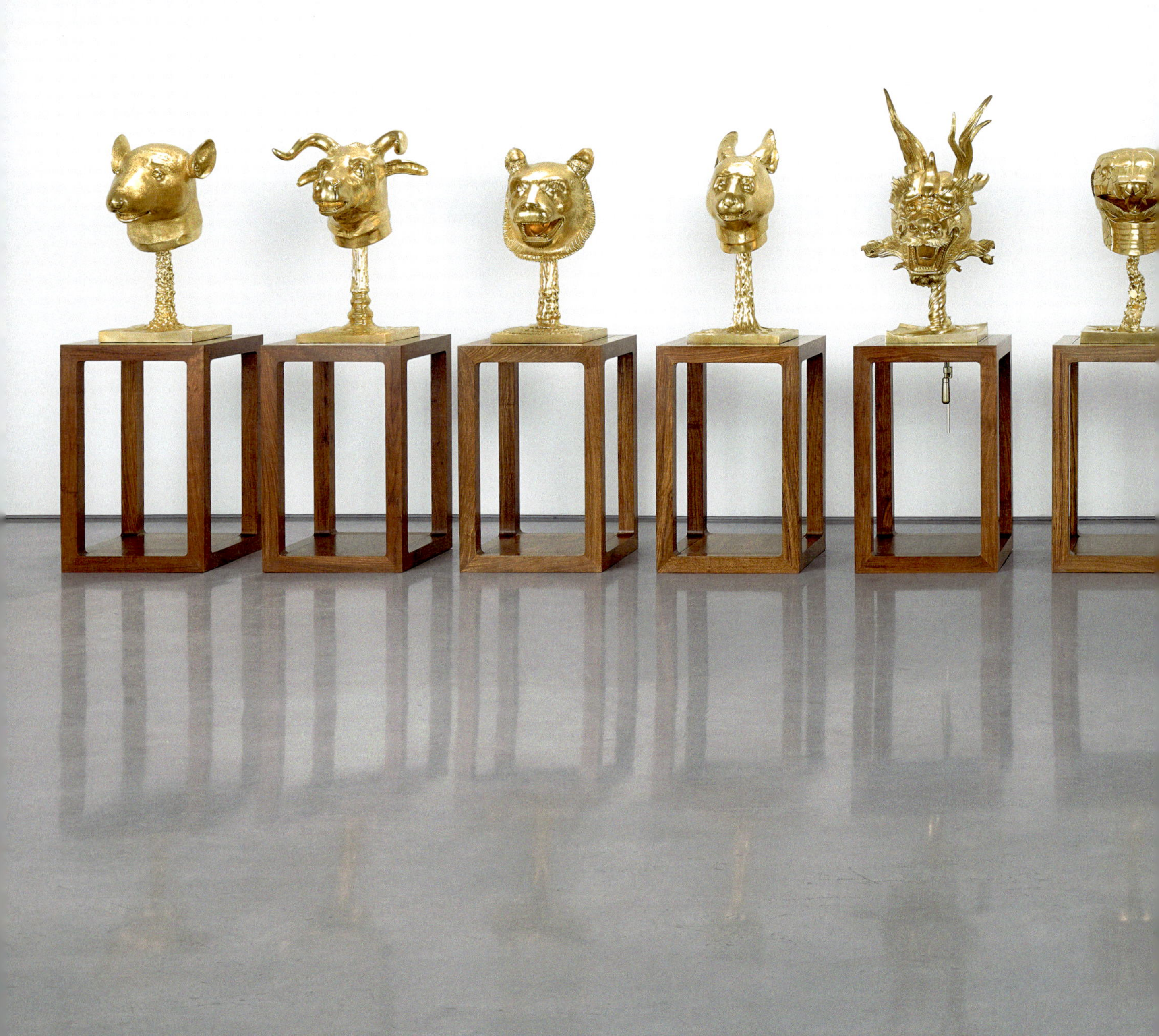

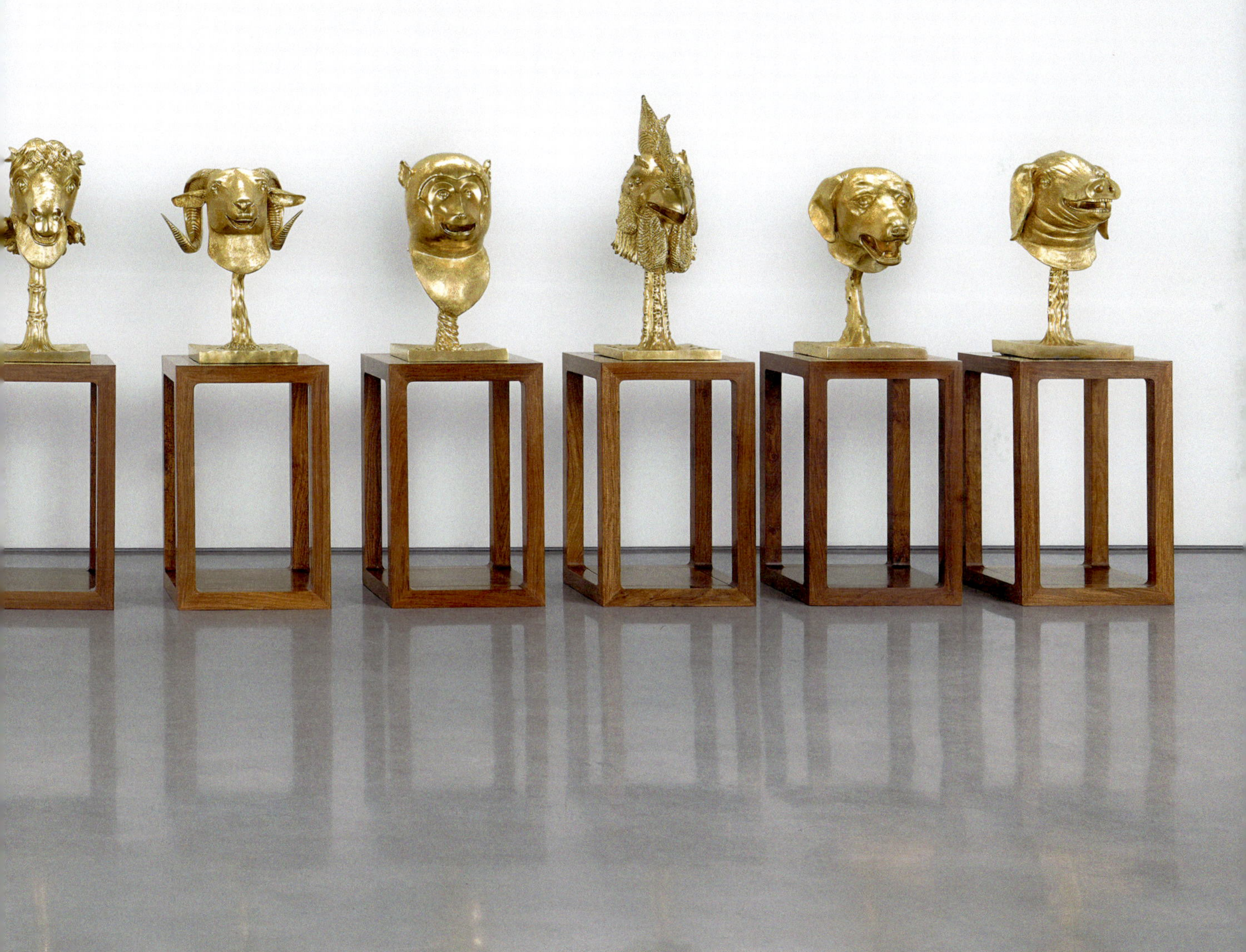

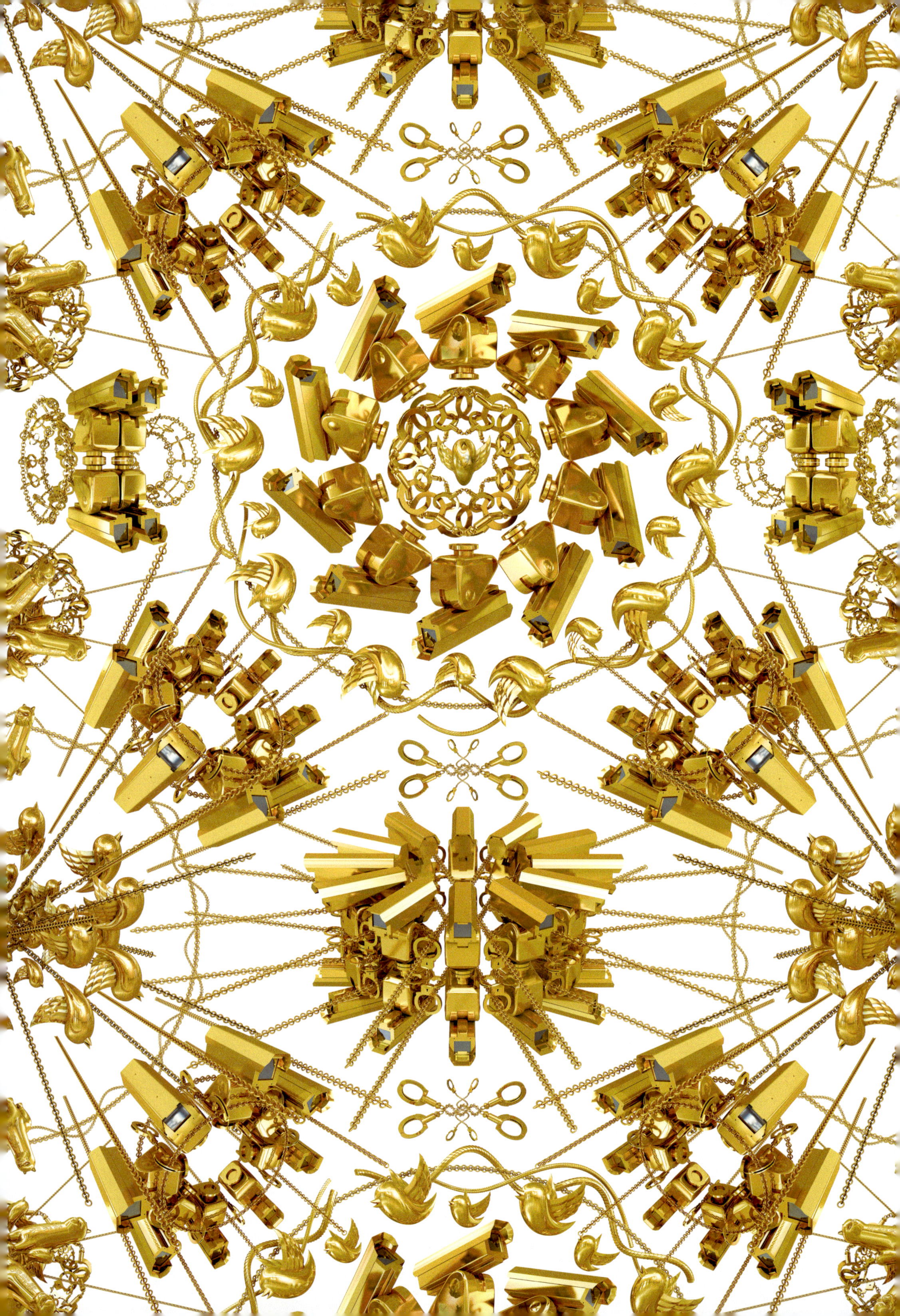

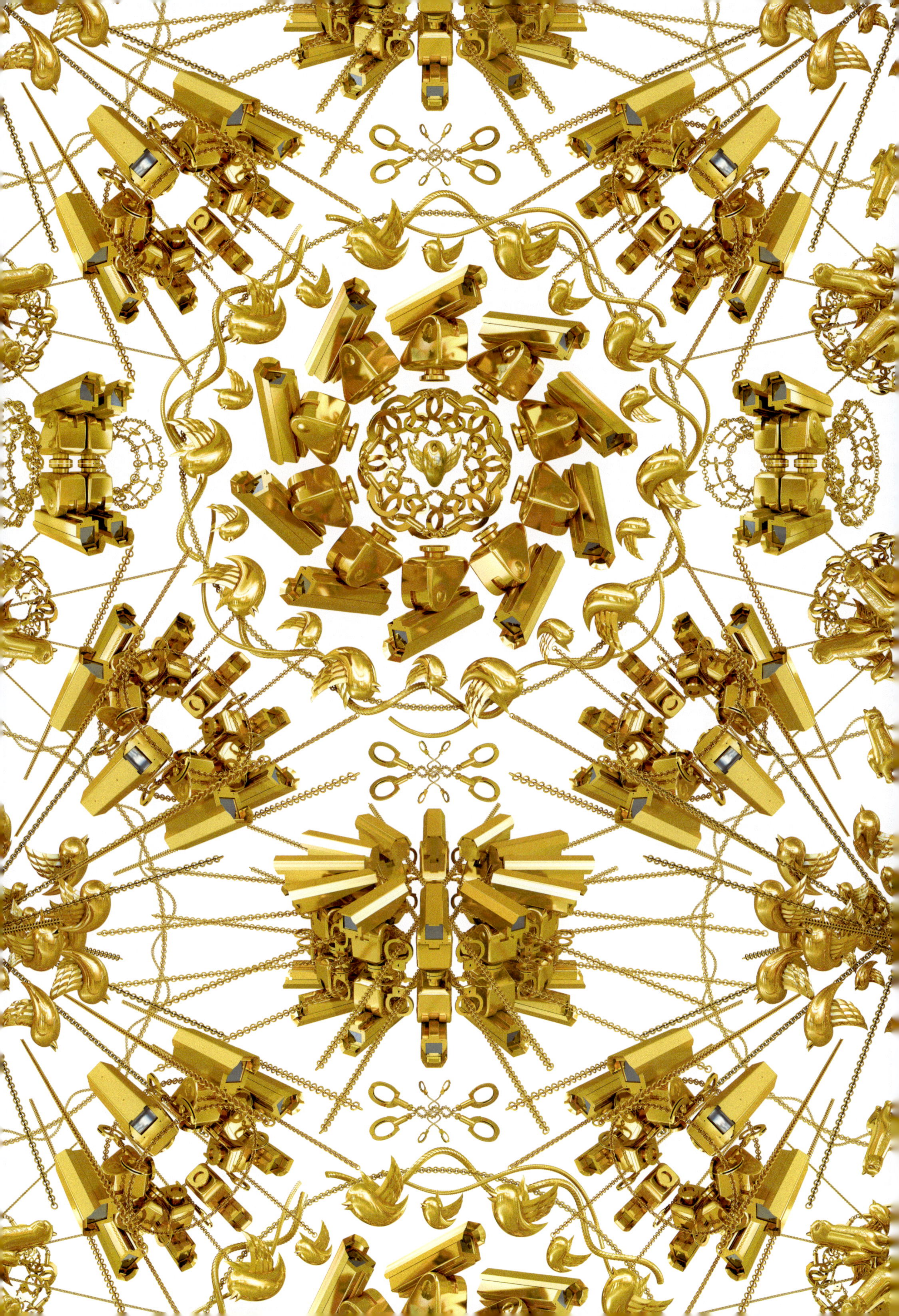

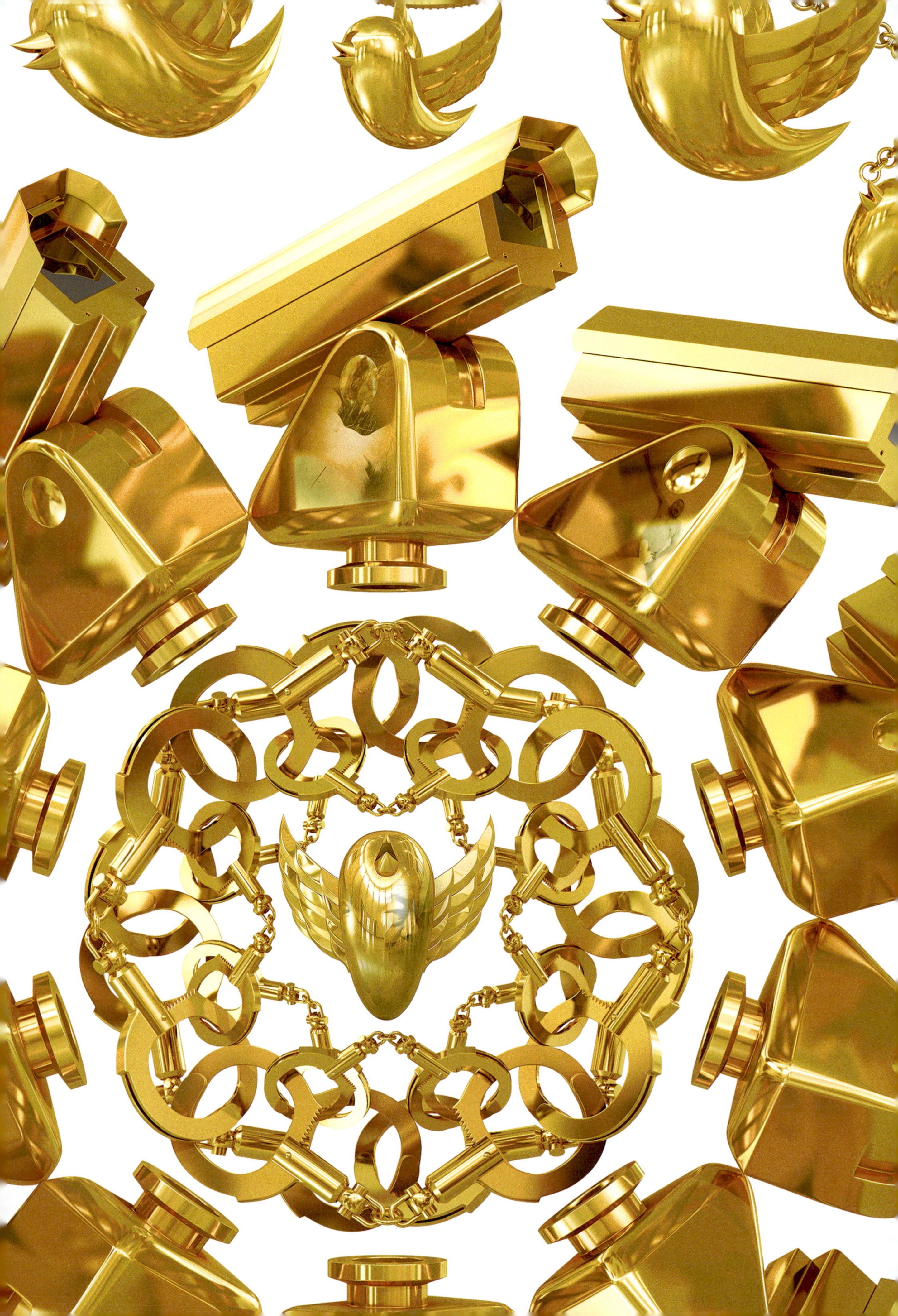

**The Animal That Looks
Like a Llama but Is
Really an Alpaca**, 2015
Wallpaper
Dimensions variable

"Don't harbor illusions about me"—Identity and Self-Staging in the Work of Ai Weiwei

Doris Krystof

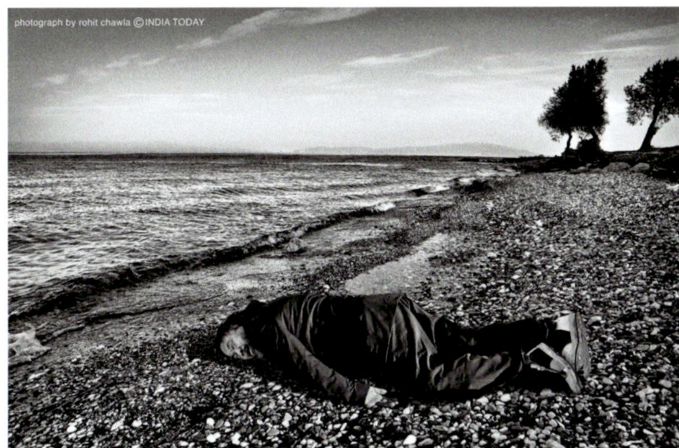

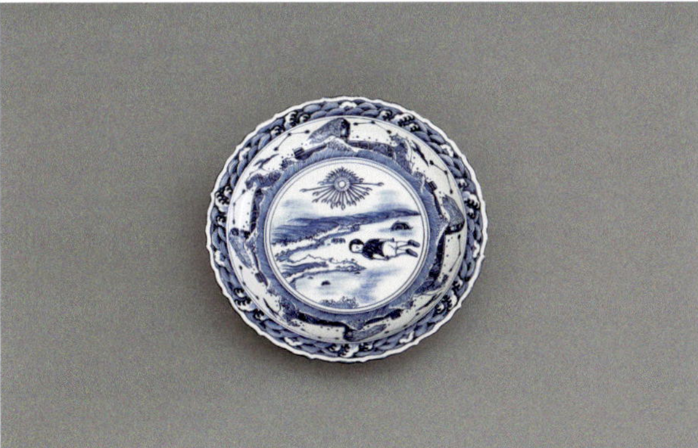

1
Rohit Chawla, **Ai Weiwei in Lesbos** for **India Today**, 2016

2
Blue-and-White Porcelain Plate (Crossing the Sea), 2017, porcelain
34 × 34 × 6.5 cm

The inclusion of his own person in his artistic work, the recourse to his own biography and his own body, form a constant in Ai Weiwei's work; and like other artists before him, who have often relentlessly included their "self" into their art—Yves Klein, James Lee Byars, Andy Warhol, and Joseph Beuys, for example—Ai Weiwei often risks life and limb by interweaving life and art. The similarity between the accusations against those so-called self-promoters among male artists (women artists are rarely affected), who are accused of craving recognition, egomania, narcissism, or charlatanry, are particularly striking, although such evaluations generally contain a good dose of ignorance with regard to the innovations that these artists have developed. Instead of addressing the challenges of developing novel forms in such work, critics tend to get caught up in personal details and trifles. This could be observed recently with regard to Ai Weiwei, for example, in German media reports, and especially in Berlin where Ai Weiwei has been living and working in exile since the summer of 2015. These include questions such as whether Ai Weiwei is abandoning Berlin or whether he is staying, why the human rights activist committed to issues related to refugees was available for a spontaneous selfie with the chairperson of a right-wing populist party, and why he is now also committed to animal welfare.[1] Already in the late summer of 2015, shortly after his arrival in Germany—where Ai Weiwei went after the return of his passport, which Chinese authorities had confiscated for more than four years—a number of critical articles appeared with the thrust that, after his imprisonment and house arrest in China, the artist was no longer the old militant dissident which had previously been celebrated.[2] The greatest indignation was caused by a black-and-white photo of Ai Weiwei, in which he allowed himself to be shown lying on his stomach on a Lesbos beach, at the turn of the year between 2015 and 2016, in the pose of the small boy Alan (not Aylan) Kurdi, who drowned in the Mediterranean Sea while fleeing the war in Syria with his parents. In doing so, he referenced the press photo taken by the Turkish journalist Nilüfer Demir on September 2, 2015, which depicts the toddler's body washed up on the Turkish

coast near Bodrum. [3] During a preliminary height in the tightening of European
migration policy, this disturbing photo
triggered a controversial debate about the
moral responsibility of politics and jour-
nalism and was explicitly not published
in various newspapers. Half a year later,
Ai Weiwei rekindled this debate by re-
enacting the motif for the Indian photo-
grapher Rohit Chawla. Apart from the
fact that Chawla created the picture as
an artistic work in his series of "tableaux
vivants," Ai Weiwei, in the pose of the
dead child, raised the issue as to whether
it would not be better for people to become upset about the political situation
in Syria and the numerous refugees
drowned in the Mediterranean than about
a photograph. He ultimately incorporated
the original motif into his art. In the
series **Blue-and-White Porcelain Plates**
(2017), one work, titled **Crossing the
Sea**, refers back to the press photo of
the dead boy. [4]

Who is Ai Weiwei, and how does he
represent himself? What roles does he
play in his art? What part does social
media play in his self-portrayal? Is he a
"Dada dandy," a "cellphone revolutionary," or "China's last communist," [5] to
name but a few of the numerous labels
of recent years? The former Swiss
Ambassador to the People's Republic of
China, Uli Sigg, a long-time associate
and supporter of Ai Weiwei, has described the artist's development in three
stages from "artist" via "artist-activist"
to "activist-artist." [6] But how is the large-
scale installation **S.A.C.R.E.D.** (2011–2013,
pp. 164–173) to be understood, in which
Ai Weiwei depicts himself, in the style
of a diorama, in the forced passive role
of a prisoner — martyr? saint? — during
his eighty-one-day detention in 2011?

At first glance, Ai Weiwei's identity as a
Chinese artist is evident in his decided
use of traditional Chinese materials and
themes. Porcelain, bamboo, wood, paper
kites, jade, and tea are all elements of his
œuvre, influenced by Conceptual and
Pop art. References to China's past and
present have shaped Ai Weiwei's work
from the very beginning — China is his
readymade, he once said. [7] His introduction to art began at a time of upheaval.
Mao Zedong's death in 1976 and the end
of the Chinese Cultural Revolution were

194

followed for a short time by a phase of openness and democratization. In his late teens, Ai Weiwei, the son of the highly respected poet Ai Qing, who had fallen from grace during a Communist purge, returned to Beijing with his family from exile in Xinjiang. He began his studies at the Beijing Film Academy and, for a short time in 1979 and 1980, joined the Stars artists' group as its youngest member, which, after revolutionary Socialist Realism, reclaimed free expression of the artistic self. Every artist is a star, argued Ma Desheng,[8] one of the key protagonists of the Stars group, who aimed to strengthen the individual and oppose notions of uniformity and the depersonalization that emerged from the Cultural Revolution under Mao Zedong. The opening of China under the new "paramount leader" Deng Xiaoping lasted only briefly, however, and in the early 1980s many members of the Stars group and others involved in the cultural sector left the country. Ai Weiwei, for example, went to the USA in 1981 and from 1983 lived in New York for ten years. Photos from those years present him as a young bohemian who lives in the East Village, in the neighborhood of such greats as Allen Ginsberg, who roams the city, visits the major museums and countless exhibitions. He poses next to Andy Warhol's series of self-portraits from 1966, imitating his contemplative gesture with an index finger placed on his lips. He learned a great deal from Warhol in general—including, for example, the cooperative organization of artistic productivity in an extensive team within a studio, a catchy branding of one's own person, as well as the systematic undermining of an expressive self as a guarantor of personal authenticity. When the French philosopher François Jullien aptly notes that "Ai Weiwei does not represent, he does not even represent himself,"[9] this also refers to the influence of postmodern culture in New York in the 1980s, during which Warhol's Factory functioned as a lucrative image machine and the Pictures Generation around Cindy Sherman and Jack Goldstein questioned the reproducibility of reality, replacing it with the reality of pictures. The portrait, in particular the self-portrait as a guaranteed representative of identity, became diluted in those last years of the twentieth century, until a short time later, fueled by digital

media, it embarked on a global victory parade. Ai Weiwei recognized the potential of the transformation of the artistic self-portrait into a "face as an attention-grabbing machine"[10] at an early stage and has meanwhile become a prime example among the artists of his generation for the use of social media, especially Twitter and Instagram.

For the exhibition at the Kunstsammlung Nordrhein-Westfalen in the summer of 2019, Ai Weiwei has created a new photographic self-portrait, which depicts the sixty-two-year-old full-length in a brisk stride with his left arm bent. Dressed in a running jacket, he confronts the viewer head-on, and with his head raised, he directs his gaze into the distance. The dark background obscures the location and the direction from which he comes; only the large stone floor slabs can be clearly seen as the stable foundation under the figure as he steps forward. The question "**Wo ist die Revolution?**" (Where is the revolution?) is written in white at the bottom-right edge; above it is the name of the artist. With this self-portrait, Ai Weiwei pays homage to Joseph Beuys. He quotes the Düsseldorf-based artist's famous poster from 1971, **La rivoluzione siamo Noi** (We are the revolution), thus invoking an important chapter in the Western European tradition of political art after 1968. In 1971 (one year before his dismissal as professor at Düsseldorf's State Academy of Art), Beuys depicted himself as a resolutely forward-looking (avant-garde) artist and revolutionary leader.[11] The fact that the inscription is written in Italian is due to the place where the photograph was taken, Capri; however, it also reflects a romanticizing component inherent in the idea of the politically active artist. When Ai Weiwei reenacts Beuys's prominent photograph almost fifty years later, once again raising the question of revolution, his knowledge of the mythologizing perspective regarding the connection between art and politics resonates. By posing the question in German, he also makes it clear that this is happening outside China, where, at the time when Beuys had produced his poster, the Cultural Revolution was raging, which in turn had been highly romanticized by the Left in the West. And by replacing Beuys's handwritten inscription with a calligraphic

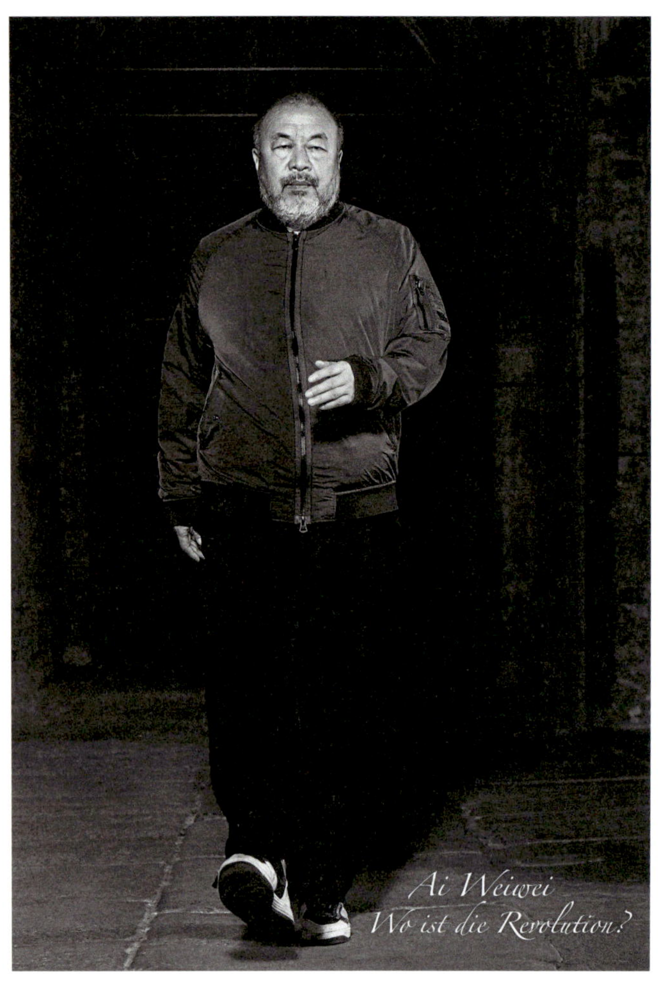

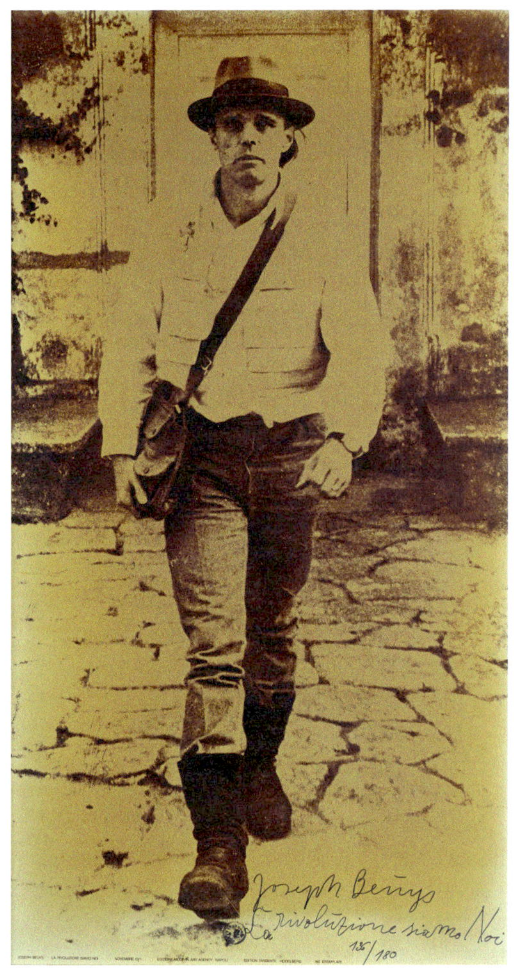

3

4

3
Wo ist die Revolution?, 2019,
black-and-white photograph

4
Joseph Beuys,
La rivoluzione siamo Noi,
1972, light impression/
polyester foil, 191 × 102 cm,
Hamburg, Hamburger Kunst-
halle, Kupferstichkabinett

196

script designed by Hermann Zapf, he gives the pathos of Beuys a nostalgic touch. [12]

Ai Weiwei's "Düsseldorf self-portrait" navigates through recent art history with dialectical twists and turns and proves once again that Ai Weiwei is difficult to pin down as a person between art and politics. The casually cautionary title of his penultimate post before his blog was shut down by the Chinese authorities on May 28, 2009, "Don't harbor illusions about me," [13] expresses the fluidity of the artist's self-image. This statement, made shortly before June 4, the twentieth anniversary of the Tiananmen Square Massacre, was directed towards the Chinese censorship authorities. "It's about that time of year again, and you must be busy these days," reads the provocative first sentence. In the "forbidden blog," edited by Lee Ambrozy as a book in 2011 and described by Hans Ulrich Obrist as "one of the greatest social sculptures of our time," [14] one can trace and comprehend the increasing severity of the artist's tone over the years. Ai Weiwei had launched his blog on **sina**.com in the autumn of 2005 with topics relating to architecture, photography, and art. With the earthquake in Sichuan and the state propaganda surrounding the Beijing Olympics, the year 2008 marked a turning point that manifested itself in the increasing radicalization of Ai Weiwei's entries relating to political themes, which were being posted at a much higher frequency. According to the journalist Mark Siemons, Ai Weiwei's complementary demands for more transparency in public and personal responsibility touched at the heart of present-day China as the growing number of Chinese blog readers demonstrated. "So it would be completely wrong to say that Ai is citing the traditional Western model of the 'political artist'; rather, by taking part in the current changes in his country, he is one of the few artists in China to reestablish a relationship with the reality outside of their milieu, as was common in the 1980s. This is inseparable from the way he presents himself: 'I put myself as a readymade,' he says, 'in order to carry out investigations. Using yourself as an example becomes a purpose in life.'" [15]

After his blog was shutdown, Ai Weiwei took to Twitter and came into direct conflict with the state authority on several occasions. In addition to being placed under surveillance and facing exhibition bans, he was prevented by police, in August 2009, from participating in the trial of human rights activist Tan Zuoren in Chengdu, Sichuan province. In the night before the trial, police burst into Ai Weiwei's hotel room and seriously injured him with blows to the head. Captured in the hotel's mirrored elevator during his detention, the selfie depicting Ai Weiwei in a red T-shirt, drowsily blinking at the light of the flash, later became famous under the title **Illumination** (pp. 162–163). [16] In January 2011, Ai Weiwei's newly constructed studio building in Shanghai was demolished at the behest of the authorities, and on April 3, his arrest by police at Beijing's airport led to an eighty-one-day imprisonment without charge and initially without notification of his relatives. Ai Weiwei was detained at a secret location, interrogated and, after two weeks, transferred to a cell in a military facility, where two uniformed soldiers stood guard over him around the clock in three-hour shifts. On June 22, 2011, Ai Weiwei was unexpectedly, and without reason, released on bail. He was accused of tax evasion, the dissemination of pornography, and endangering national security and was not permitted to leave China for four years.

His conflicts with Chinese security authorities and the humiliations he faced while detained undoubtedly represent a turning point in Ai Weiwei's life, which he thematizes in several artistic works in various ways. In his personal act of coming to terms with the events, questions regarding the representability of traumatic experiences are mixed with questions regarding artistic means. Ai Weiwei is aware that, with his release and his relatively mild treatment during his detention—in contrast to many others detained in Chinese prisons, he was not beaten or physically tortured—he is a lucky exception. The memory of his father's experience of detainment—in the early 1930s, he spent several years in prison for political reasons—also helped him put his own experience into perspective. [17] It was not without a bit of gallows humor that, in search of a way to lend expression to his own situation, he resorted to the figure of the **Hanging Man** [18] in the form of his early filigree work from his time in New York, formed from a wire hanger representing Marcel Duchamp, making it available to the British writer Barnaby Martin as the cover motif for his book based on numerous interviews conducted shortly after his imprisonment. In the autumn of 2012, a first major international show picked up on the period before his imprisonment. The exhibition **According to What?**, which was first presented at the Hirshhorn Museum in Washington, D.C., and then toured North America and Canada for several years, was largely based on the 2009 exhibition presented at the Mori Art Museum in Tokyo. In the catalog, Ai Weiwei describes how, after his imprisonment, he renegotiated his understanding of himself between art and politics. Perhaps he is now an "undercover artist in the disguise of a dissident," he states; ultimately, however, such labels could not be less important for him. [19]

In the summer of 2013, Ai Weiwei returned to the stage of the international art world and presented three major works in three different locations at the Venice Biennale. He was represented in the German Pavilion [20] with the installation **Bang**, comprised of 886 Chinese wooden stools, and the Zuecca Project Space presented two further works as part of the "Collateral Events" distributed throughout the city: in its exhibition space on Giudecca, the work **Straight** was on view, consisting of 150 tons of straightened rebar from buildings that collapsed during the earthquake in Sichuan; and **S.A.C.R.E.D.**, with six large iron boxes, was shown in the Baroque Church of Sant'Antonin not far from St Mark's Square. Each of the three works required a monumental, expansive setting, with which Ai Weiwei drew on his earlier artistic practice. To reference Uli Sigg's triad again, **Bang** returns to the artist as a collector of Chinese antiques and cultural artifacts, while **Straight** picks up on the civil rights and artist-activist who is committed to solving an immense corruption scandal. What remains is **S.A.C.R.E.D.** and the activist-artist—who may be faced with the question as to the extent to which the self

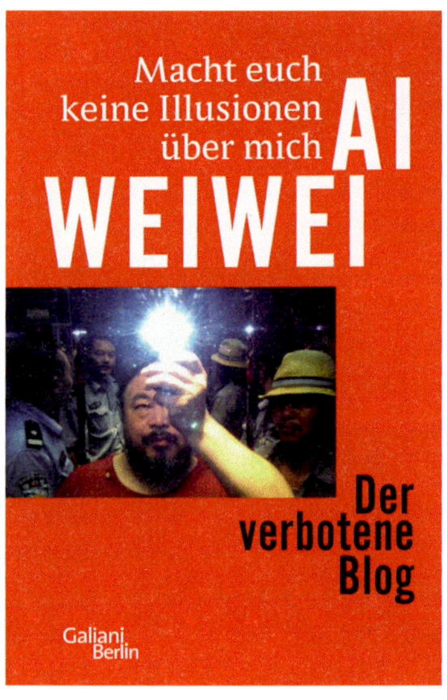

5

6

as a readymade can withstand the traumas of the excesses of governmental violence.

With the unabashed representation of his personal history in the form of a diorama, Ai Weiwei breaks all conventions of art at the beginning of the twenty-first century. The three-dimensional scenes installed inside large iron boxes, reminiscent of catafalques, with figures made of fiberglass, roughly at one-third scale, illustrate the detainee's everyday life in an uncanny, realistic way. "An Artist Depicts His Demons," read **The New York Times** after the opening in May 2013. Elsewhere, there was talk of "horrifying mockups of his 2011 detention" and that, "Watching this series of horrific tableaux is nausea-inducing." [21] In each interior scene, which can be viewed through small openings in the boxes, two young uniformed soldiers stand as guards right next to Ai Weiwei, even at night when he sleeps and then even when he is in the small bathroom. In one scene, the prisoner is manacled to the armrest of a chair with handcuffs; while in another, he walks back and forth in the cell, flanked by his guards, with bright radiant light always burning throughout. "Every second is so long when I was in there," Ai Weiwei reported shortly after his release. "It was endless and it was terrifying because everything was so distorted. It's torture to put a human being in such a hopeless condition. You feel you dropped into a hole and you will never be discovered again. You have no rights. You cannot contact anybody and you are totally cut off from reality [...]." [22] The scenic portrayal of the traumatic experience captures numerous details, and it seems unthinkable that they were not created from photographs or drawings made on site. However, as Ai Weiwei was forbidden to document anything during his detainment, the set of the cell was created entirely from memory, after the fact, as Ai Weiwei explained: "I memorised every crack in the ceiling, every mark on the wall. I am an artist and architect, so I have a good memory for these things." [23]

The scenic structure follows the six letters that form the title of the work as an acronym and designate the actions depicted within each box: S (Supper) shows the prisoner eating under the watchful gaze of his guards; A (Accusers) depicts the interrogation to which Ai Weiwei was exposed several times a day; C (Cleansing) refers to washing of the body in the shower; R (Ritual) stands for the ritualized movement, pacing back and forth in the cell; E (Entropy) depicts the prisoner in the entropic state of sleep; and D (Doubt) depicts the prisoner sitting on the toilet, while the guards stand suffocatingly close. Here, the English word "sacred" points less to a religious interpretation, although the work's presentation in a Christian church certainly suggests this reading; and Ai Weiwei's depiction of his imprisonment calls up several associations with Christian iconography of the Passion of Christ. [24] The location in the nave of Sant'Antonin was, however, chosen rather randomly; and thus, **S.A.C.R.E.D.** suggests more a reference to the figure in ancient Roman law of the "Homo sacer," who stands outside the law. The Italian philosopher Giorgio Agamben refers to this figure in his influential book **Homo Sacer: Sovereign Power and Bare Life** (1998, originally published in Italian in 1995) and describes him with references to Guantánamo Bay and other systems of injustice as a type that has survived into the enlightened modern age. [25] Ai Weiwei's cell appears as such a place of vulnerability and lawlessness described by Agamben, and the body held in it becomes—in the sense of Foucault, to whom Agamben refers—a symbol of "bare life." With the sober depiction, model-like, the artist makes his own person available as an example. In this respect, as Greg Hilty has explained, the images of imprisonment, with their rhythm, create less a specific story than a universal reality of myth, and the six stages of detention appear as "repeated, eternal presents, conditions of transformation rather than simply moments of existence." [26] Does Ai Weiwei make himself an exemplary case study in **S.A.C.R.E.D.**? The depiction of the wound which has been personally experienced does not only begin the process of personal-therapeutic coping, but an appeal is also made. Ai Weiwei's showpieces imply being thrown back into a state of bare existence as a common experience of all imprisoned dissidents in totalitarian regimes.

From a sculptural, artistic point of view, the relationship between the outside and the inside also plays a key role in this large-scale work. At first glance, the boxes arranged accurately in the space may be reminiscent of Minimal art objects. The implied doors on the outside, as well as the small windows in the walls and the openings in the ceilings, however, adjust the role of the audience (the media, the art world) in a way which is reminiscent of peep shows or, to remain within the realm of visual art, of Marcel Duchamp's **Étant donnés**: **1**. **La chute d'eau**, **2**. **Le gaz d'éclairage** (1946–1966) in the collection of the Philadelphia Museum of Art. With the realistic scene of a nude woman lying on a bed of foliage, which can only be seen through two knotholes in a wooden door, Duchamp addresses the desire for forbidden sight as well as the ambivalent relationship between the observer and the observed. In **S.A.C.R.E.D.**, one also looks as if through a keyhole and sees something that one does not otherwise get to see, and which one is actually not permitted to see. The ingenious twist of the piece is that it allows one to observe the two uniformed observers while they observe. By borrowing from the diorama and its proximity to natural history or ethnographic vitrines which teach about exotic animals or past customs and traditions in museums, **S.A.C.R.E.D.** makes observing its actual subject through an emphatically demonstrative and didactic form.

Visual narration in the sense of indoctrination is tied, at least from a Chinese perspective, to the sculptural figuration of socialist realism. With regard to **S.A.C.R.E.D.**, the comparison is striking with a famous example from the history of Chinese art, the **Rent Collection Courtyard**, which consists of more than one hundred sculptures and was realized in 1965 by an artists' collective at the Sichuan Fine Arts Institute in Chongqing. Created as a site-specific installation on the former estate of the landlord Liu Wencai (1887–1949) near Chengdu, Sichuan province, the sculptural panorama presents the merciless exploitation of the rural population in China's pre-Communist era. From 1966 onwards, the "model art work of the Cultural Revolution"[27] was presented in many places across China with massive crowds of visitors expressing profound emotional sympathy for the fate of the peasants. Several copies and versions were made of copper-plated fiberglass, a surviving one of which is on display today in the Museum of the Fine Arts Institute in Chongqing.[28] The **Rent Collection Courtyard** was also known in the West. Harald Szeemann wanted to present it at documenta 5 in 1972 but failed for financial and political reasons. To this day, the original clay group, declared a national cultural landmark in 1996, is installed at its original location, the former estate of the landlord Liu Wencai, now a popular and much advertised destination.

The **Rent Collection Courtyard** served Communist propaganda as education for the class struggle. The theoretical basis is Mao Zedong's **Talks at the Yan'an Forum on Literature and Art**, held at the famous Yan'an Forum in 1942, at which Ai Qing, the father of Ai Weiwei, also participated. The focus of the forum was the political subjugation of the arts and their need to serve the masses. In the sculptural realization from 1965, this intention is translated into a succession of narrative sequences intended to indoctrinate and captivate audiences with images. In **S.A.C.R.E.D.** as well, the dominant form of mediation is showing rather than narrating, the image rather than the text, the eye rather than the ear. Ai Weiwei's work—as with the **Rent Collection Courtyard**—lays claim to a general comprehensibility of the content through its figurative representation. A further reason for the primacy of showing in **S.A.C.R.E.D.** may lie in the fact that one of the conditions of his bail after his release was that Ai Weiwei was barred from speaking to the media for a year. It did not take long, however, for him to find a variety of forms in which to portray the entire reality of what had happened to him.[29]

As early as the autumn of 2011, Ai Weiwei went public with another almost opposite form of grappling with his detainment. The music video **Dumbass** was created in collaboration with the musician Zuoxiao Zuzhou for the heavy metal album **The Divine Comedy** and was recorded in an accurate 1:1 reconstruction of the cell.[30] Christopher Doyle was hired as the cameraman, famous for his collaboration with Wong Kar-Wai, the famed director of Hong Kong cinema. In contrast to the puppet-like appearance of the detainee in **S.A.C.R.E.D.**, Ai Weiwei presents himself in **Dumbass** as an unbound agent. The five-minute video begins dramatically with the removal of the black hood, revealing the pale face of the imprisoned Ai Weiwei. Gradually, the video picks up speed and accelerates into a nightmarish revue. When Ai Weiwei, free and boisterous, jumps up and down in his cell shower, when he thrashes his guards as a whip-wielding tormentor, when the soldiers transform into seductive female escorts wearing miniskirts, when sex dolls await the detainee under the sheets of his cot, or when he struts through his cell as a drag queen with his head shaved clean and in high heels, role reversal and the living out of fantasies provide possibilities for catharsis in the sense of Gestalt therapy. In the last sequence, Ai Weiwei steps out of his cell with a blow-dried hairstyle, an unbuttoned white shirt, a black sport coat, and a seductive woman on each arm—a playboy once again pulling all the strings.

In addition to dramatic fantasies of liberation, **Dumbass** (p. 175) provides several references to the subversive ways with which Chinese Internet users and netizens deal with the censorship authorities. The porcelain crabs in the toilet, for example, refer to a common linguistic distortion of the justification given by security authorities for their use of censorship for purposes of social "harmony," a word which, depending on pronunciation, can easily be confused with the Chinese word for crabs, **he xie**.[31] Another subversive symbol used in **Dumbass** is the so-called "Grass Mud Horse," an alpaca, which can be seen as a stuffed animal in a very short frame in the video in place of the accused during his interrogation. Its Chinese name, **cao ni ma**, sounds very similar to a strong, sexualized insult (akin to "fuck your mother"), which is why the alpaca has become a symbol of freedom of expression since 2006, when the toughest measures by authorities allegedly against vulgarity on the Internet banned numerous blogs, Internet forums, and platforms.[32] This tactful attack is also expressed in the wallpaper titled **The Animal That Looks Like a Llama but Is Really an Alpaca** (2015, pp. 188–190).

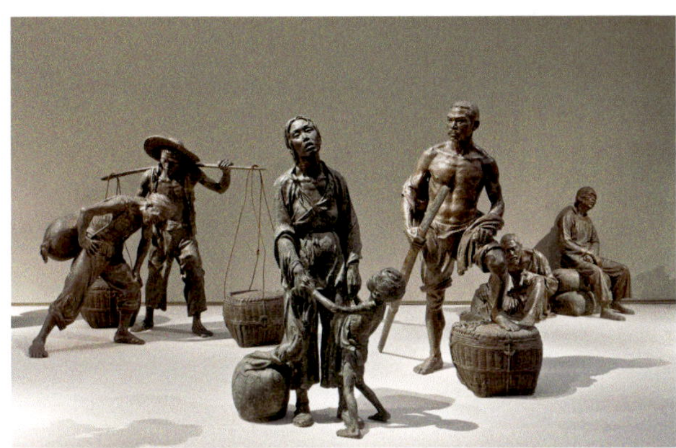

7

7
The Rent Collection Courtyard, fiberglass copies of the originals from 1965. Installation view, Schirn Kunsthalle, Frankfurt am Main, 2009

201

The complex composition kaleidoscopically combines the logo of Twitter,
surveillance cameras, rebar, chains,
handcuffs, and the Grass Mud Horse.
The glamorous appearance of the pattern
printed in gold on white is, however, just
as misleading as the title. The alleged
luxury items ostensibly refer to the
nouveaux riches of China, but when one
takes a closer look, various critical details can be found hiding in the shining
surfaces. A detail from Marcel Duchamp's
Étant Donnés is recognizable in the
golden sheen of a camera, once again
manifesting the artistic practice of revealing and concealing that emerged as
a reference to voyeurism implied by
S.A.C.R.E.D. In the reflective surface of
another camera, Ai Weiwei can be seen
jumping naked into the air, covering his
genitals with a stuffed Grass Mud Horse.
The artist presents himself in action with
the offensive prop and is reflected in,
of all things, a symbol of state surveillance.
However, he appears on the side of the
camera and is not captured by its lens. In
the symbols of oppression and liberty, the
different facets of Ai Weiwei, the artist
and the activist, are reflected. A self-
image is thus articulated that not only
intends a subjectivity turned outwards
but also nimbly sets itself in relationship
to social and political realities.

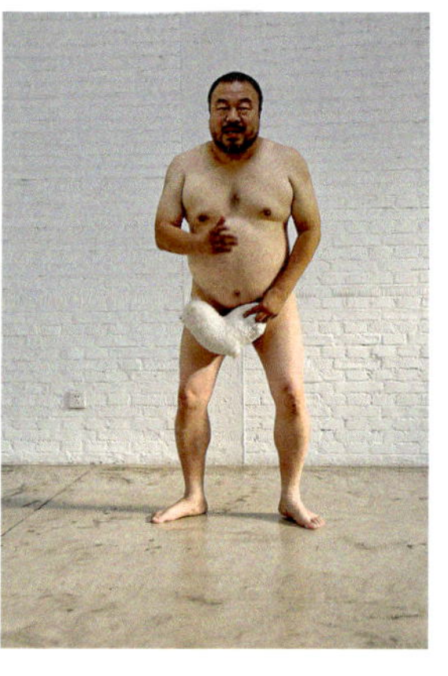
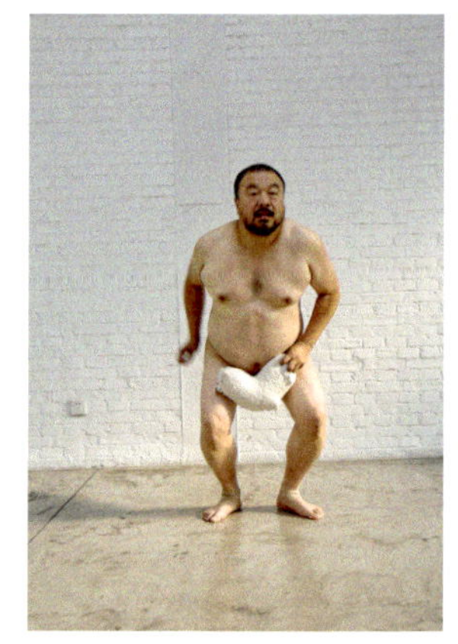
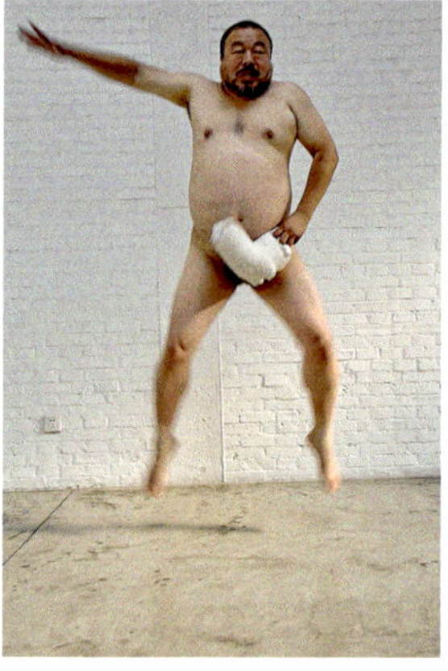
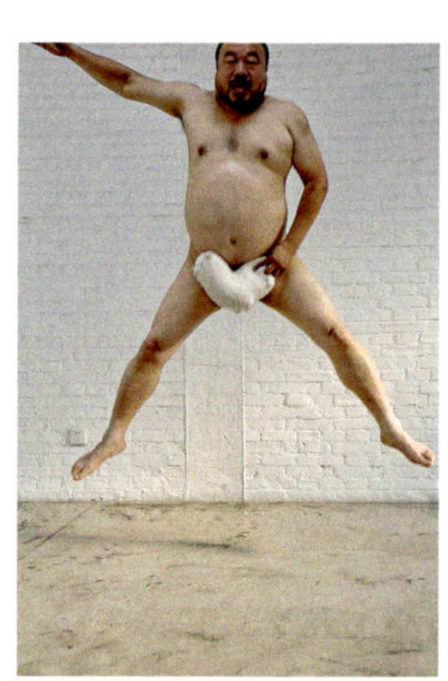

8

8
**Caonima Dang Zhongyang
(The Alpaca Blocks the
Middle)**, 2009, 4 color
photographs

1
See: Gabriela Walde, "Künstler Ai Weiwei will Berlin offenbar verlassen," in: **Berliner Morgenpost**, May 2, 2018; "Ai Weiwei verteidigt Selfie mit AfD-Fraktionschefin Weidel," in: **monopol**, April 20, 2018; Gesine Borcherdt, "Was kommt als Nächstes? Selbst-bildnisse aus Elfenbein?," in: **Die Welt**, July 16, 2018.

2
Two interviews in the **Süd-deutsche Zeitung** and **Die Zeit**, which subsequently were circulated and com-mented on repeatedly, contri-buted significantly to this change of opinion: "Gezeich-net von der Gängelung," Ai Weiwei in conversation with Jörg Häntzschel, in: **Süd-deutsche Zeitung**, August 5, 2015; "Kein Grund zu weinen," Ai Weiwei interviewed by Angela Köckritz and Miao Zhang, in: **Die Zeit**, no. 33/2015, August 13, 2015. See also: Christiane Peitz, "Plötzlich ist Ai Weiwei der Stinkstiefel," in: **Der Tages-spiegel**, August 19, 2015; Andraes Rosenfelder and Ronja von Rönne, "Das große Ai-Weiwei-Missverständnis," **Die Welt**, August 16, 2015.

3
See the following remarks: Alfred Weidinger, "Ai Weiwei Flies a Kite," in: Agnes Husslein-Arco and Alfred Weidinger (eds.), **Ai Weiwei: Translocation—Transfor-mation**, no. 4, Vienna 2016, p. 68. Examples of the controversial debate can be found in articles by: Swantje Karich, "Warum Ai Weiweis Flüchtlings-Foto schamlos ist," in: **Die Welt**, February 1, 2016; and Julia Voss, "Künstler Ai Weiwei: Ich bin Aylan Kurdi," in: **Frankfurter Allge-meine Zeitung**, February 3, 2016. A detailed and nuanced scholarly view is provided in the analysis of: Mette Mortensen, "Constructing, confirming, and contesting icons: the Alan Kurdi imagery appropriated by #humanity-washedashore, Ai Weiwei, and Charlie Hebdo," in: **Media Culture & Society**, vol. 39, no. 8, 2017, pp. 1142–61; and Abir Hamdar, "The Syrian corpse: the politics of dignity in visual and media representations of the Syrian revolution," in: **Journal for Cultural Research**, vol. 22, no. 1, 2018, pp. 73–89.

4
See: Norman Rosenthal, Stacey Pierson, and Hans Ulrich Obrist (eds.), **Ai Weiwei on Porcelain**, exh. cat. Sakip Sabanci Museum, Istanbul (Istanbul 2017), p. 129.

5
See: Peter Weibel, "The Dada Dandy," in: Agnes Husslein-Arco and Alfred Weidinger (eds.), **Ai Weiwei: Translocation—Transfor-mation**, no. 2, Vienna 2016; Susanne Beyer, "Der Han-dy-Revolutionär," in: **Der Spiegel**, no. 39, 2009, pp. 140–3; Christian P. Sorace, "China's Last Communist: Ai Weiwei," in: **Critical Injury**, no. 40 (Winter 2014), pp. 396–419.

6
Uli Sigg, "The Better Argument: A Portrait of Ai Weiwei," in: Hans Werner Holzwarth (ed.), **Ai Weiwei** (Cologne 2016), pp. 7–12, here p. 10.

7
Ai Weiwei explained: "Duchamp had the bicycle wheel. Warhol had the image of Mao. I have a totalitarian regime. It's my readymade," quoted in: Victor Maldonado, "Harming the Art: Ai Weiwei's Wicked Sense of Humor," quoted in: Sorace 2014 (see note 5), p. 396.

8
See: Barnaby Martin, **Hanging Man**: **The Arrest of Ai Weiwei** (London 2013), p. 45. On the following pages is a detailed descrip-tion of the art scene in Beijing around 1980.

9
"Ai Weiwei ne pose pas, ne se pose pas," see: François Jullien, "Ai Weiwei, ou l'art de la variation efficace," in: Susanne Gaensheimer (ed.), **Ai Weiwei, Romuald Karmakar, Santu Mofokeng, Dayanita Singh. Deutscher Pavillon 2013, 55. Inter-nationale Kunstausstellung La Biennale di Venezia**, exh. cat. Venice (Berlin 2013), pp. 207–9, here p. 209.

10
Valentin Groebner, **Ich-Plakate. Eine Geschichte des Gesichts als Aufmerk-samkeitsmaschine** (Frankfurt am Main 2015).

11
For more on Beuys's artistic practice of staging himself, see: Maria Müller-Schareck, "Joseph Beuys: 'Ich bin ein Sender, ich strahle,'" in: Armin Zweite (ed.), **Ich ist etwas anderes. Kunst am Ende des 20. Jahrhunderts**, exh. cat. Kunstsammlung Nordrhein-Westfalen, Düsseldorf, (Düsseldorf 2000), pp. 136–40.

12
A deeper examination of the relationship between Joseph Beuys and Ai Weiwei would be interesting but is still lacking: Joseph Beuys's political commitment and its continued effect in the visual arts (**Office of the Organi-zation for Direct Democracy by Referendum**, etc.) as well as in real politics (as a founding member of the Green Party in North Rhine-Westphalia) would be as important as the practice of large-scale sculptural instal-lations (compare Beuys's **7000 Oaks** at documenta 7, 1982, with Ai Weiwei's installations with trees). The "Mail Art" begun by Beuys (with Klaus Staeck) in 1968, in the sense of a mass distri-bution of texts and slogans, represents another reference point to Ai Weiwei's inces-sant transmission of visual and textual messages through the channels of social media. Finally, despite all the differ-ences in cultural contexts, Beuys's awareness of the unstoppable medialization in consumer society, which demands a pronounced culti-vation of one's own image and ubiquitous press work, can be compared with the practice of Ai Weiwei, who also makes no distinction between his private and public person. And with both artists, the origin myths of their art and their connection to national history play a central role. While Beuys derives his use of felt and fat from the traumatic experience of a plane crash, which he survived thanks to a group of Tartars who rescued him, Ai Weiwei's childhood and

youth spent in a Mongolian hole with his father exiled by the Communists represents a constant point of reference for his artistic practice.

13
See: Ai Weiwei, in "Don't Harbor Illusions about Me: Posted on May 28, 2009," in: Ai Weiwei, **Ai Weiwei's Blogs**: **Writings**, **Interviews**, **and Digital Rants, 2006– 2009**, ed. and trans. Lee Ambrozy (Cambridge, MA 2011), pp. 228–30, here p. 228.

14
Hans Ulrich Obrist, interview with Mathieu Wellner, "Ai Weiwei," **Mono-Kultur**, no. 22 (Autumn 2009), p. 5.

15
Originally in: Mark Siemons, "China als Ready-Made. Das System Ai Weiwei," in: **Frankfurter Allgemeine Zeitung**, April 29, 2009, translated in: Mark Siemons, "China as Readymade: On the Ai Weiei System," in: **Ai Weiwei**: **So Sorry**, exh. cat. Haus der Kunst, Munich, (Munich et al. 2009), p. 28.

16
See: Wolfgang Ullrich, "Selfies als Weltsprache," in: Pia Müller-Tamm (ed.), **Ich bin hier**! **Von Rembrandt zum Selfie**, exh. cat. Staat- liche Kunsthalle Karlsruhe, (Karlsruhe 2015), pp. 268–9.

17
Ai Weiwei in conversation with the author in Berlin on January 21, 2019.

18
Martin, **Hanging Man** (see note 8); for more on Ai Weiwei's allusions to Duchamp, see: Stefan Banz, "Hanging Man in Porcelain: Ai Weiwei's 'Homages' to Marcel Duchamp," in: **Ai Weiwei. D'ailleurs c'est toujours les autres**, exh. cat. Musée cantonal des Beaux-Arts de Lausanne (Milan 2017), pp. 188–91.

19
"In normal circumstances, I know it's undesirable for an artist to be labeled a political activist or dissident. But I've overcome that barrier. The suits that people dress you in are not as important as the content you put forth, so long as it gives meaning to new expression. The struggle is worthwhile if it provides new ways to communicate with people and society. […] Maybe I'm just an undercover artist in the disguise of a dissident; I couldn't care less about the implications." Kerry Brougher, "Reconsid- ering Reality: An Interview with Ai Weiwei," in: Mami Kataoka, Charles Merewether, and Kerry Brougher, **Ai Weiwei: According to What?**, exh. cat. Hirshhorn Museum and Sculpture Garden, Washington, D.C., (Munich et al. 2012), p. 39.

20
In 2013, Germany swapped pavilion buildings with France.

21
Edward Wong, "An Artist Depicts His Demons," in: **The New York Times**, May 26, 2013; Charlotte Higgins, "Ai Weiwei Shows Venice Biennale His Many Sides," in: **The Guardian**, May 30, 2013; Barnaby Martin, "Ai Weiwei, S.A.C.R.E.D., Venice Biennale – Review," in: **Financial Times**, May 27, 2013.

22
Ai Weiwei in: Martin, **Hanging Man** (see note 8), pp. 73f.

23
Ai Weiwei in: Martin, "Ai Weiwei, S.A.C.R.E.D." (see note 21).

24
Ai Weiwei explained that the memory of his father's "books about religion […] those religious images," gave him the idea of staging the situation in each cell as "a frozen moment," in: Holzwarth 2016 (see note 6), p. 530.

25
Giorgio Agamben, **Homo Sacer: Sovereign Power and Bare Life**, trans. Daniel Heller-Roazen (Stanford 1998). In the context of S.A.C.R.E.D., Roger M. Buergel provides the refer- ence to Agamben, to whom the question "What is bare life?" referred, which was at the center of documenta 12 in 2007, curated by Buergel and Ruth Noack. See: Roger M. Buergel, "The Mediator's Ways: The Freedom and Art of Ai Weiwei," in: Holzwarth 2016 (see note 6), pp. 171–9.

26
Greg Hilty, "S.A.C.R.E.D.," in: Maurizio Bortolotti (ed.), **Ai Weiwei**: **Disposition**, exh. cat. Venice (London 2014), p. 119.

27
"Musterkunstwerk der Kulturrevolution," see the extensive entry: "Der Hof für die Pachteinnahme," in: Wikipedia, https://de. wikipedia.org/wiki/Der_ Hof_f%C3%BCr_die_Pacht- einnahme (last accessed on March 30, 2019).

28
The monumental sculpture ensemble was presented at the Schirn Kunsthalle, Frankfurt am Main in 2009 in an exhibition titled **Art for the Millions**: **100 Sculptures from the Mao Era**, accom- panied by a publication of the same name edited by Max Hollein with numerous references to its history and reception.

29
In addition to S.A.C.R.E.D., a play by Howard Brenton about Ai Weiwei's imprison- ment, **#aiww**: **The Arrest of Ai Weiwei**, was created based on the interviews conducted in July 2011 by the writer Barnaby Martin (see note 8) and premiered at the Hampstead Theatre, London in the spring of 2013. See: Hilty 2014 (see note 26), p. 118. Since 2018, the maquettes of the sculptures produced for S.A.C.R.E.D. have also been exhibited; see: **Ai Weiwei Raiz**, exh. cat. Oca, São Paolo (São Paolo 2018), pp. 68–70.

30
The replica of the cell, in its original size, was on display in the Berlin exhibition at the Martin-Gropius-Bau in the spring of 2014 and is now in a New York private collec- tion. See: Gereon Sievernich (ed.), **Ai Weiwei**: **Evidence**, exh. cat. Martin-Gropius-Bau, Berlin (Munich et al. 2014), p. 145.

31
Ai Weiwei has stated in
reference to the symbolism
of the crab, which has
appeared in his work in
various forms since 2010,
"In Chinese, 'harmonious'
(a code word for state
censorship popular among
netizens) also sounds like
'crab,' so I asked my porcelain makers to make crabs to
bring the irony of the political situation into a physical,
everyday visual language that
people can understand. Later
I realized that the crab had
a long history as an object of
art in China—different
dynasties made them in jade,
or bamboo or onyx. In contemporary times, after the
Gang of Four was arrested
in 1976, many artists even
painted crabs to celebrate."
Quoted in: Holzwarth 2016
(see note 6), p. 478.

32
See: Ai Weiwei 2011 (see
note 13), p. 279, note 42.

CHAPTER V

Chapter V

Photographs from New York and Beijing serve as an introduction to a selection of rarely exhibited early works by Ai Weiwei. In 1981, Ai Weiwei went to the United States of America and lived from 1983 to 1993 in New York City. During this time, he studied at the Parsons School of Design. In this period, while executing his first paintings and later objects, and ultimately realizing his first solo exhibition, he captured his life in thousands of photographs. A very small portion of these photographs can now be seen at K21. Among these are photos that reflect his personal life as well as those that capture the social and political situation at the time in New York. There are also images that provide insight into the Chinese artist community in New York and the intellectual circle within which he was active. During this time, in which he was still unknown, living in the city, and in his mid-twenties, Ai Weiwei took in not only the current political movements but also the latest movements in art. One photograph taken at the Museum of Modern Art, for example, depicts him as an interested observer of the works of Marcel Duchamp—an artist whose influence is felt in Ai Weiwei's art. One of his most famous works from this period is **Hanging Man** (1985), a clothes hanger that he bent into the profile of Marcel Duchamp. As in the eponymous viewing instructions of Duchamp's work **To Be Looked at (from the Other Side of the Glass) with One Eye, Close to, for Almost an Hour** (p. 228), the hanger may also potentially be viewed from two sides, resulting in two mirror-inverted images. Both works, thus, potentially permit what is called "perspective"; the Latin word "perspicere" means "to look through."

A very early and never before exhibited painting, **Untitled (Yantai, Shandong)** (1977), depicts boats in the harbor of the north east Chinese seaport Yantai in Shandong province. It was painted in China, in 1977, after the rehabilitation of his father, the poet Ai Qing, and the family's return from exile to Beijing in 1976, and before Ai Weiwei enrolled at the Beijing Film Academy in 1978. Further paintings from his time in New York are also included in the exhibition: a head, a negative image of the **Mona Lisa**, a flower bud, and a picture made of text, **Coke Painting**, which anticipates the **Coca Cola Vase**, an equally exemplary work, also on view. Thus, explicit examples of artistic influences—such as Pop art, in particular, and to the progenitor of all Conceptual artists, Marcel Duchamp—can already be identified here.

In 1988, Ai Weiwei had his first solo exhibition, organized by the Art Waves Gallery in New York. It bore the title **Old Shoes - Safe Sex**. Here, Ai Weiwei presented several readymade objects. The work **Safe Sex** (1986), however, figured prominently: a raincoat with an attached condom. It was during this time that AIDS became a major public threat. New York was one of the cities in which AIDS first had a social impact and was, at the same time, reflected upon artistically. It is significant that Ai Weiwei was, already at this early point in his career, reflecting on social and political conditions in his art.

Also during this period, he created **Untitled** (**Fur Basketball**) in 1987: a basketball covered with fur. This makes reference, on the one hand, to Meret Oppenheim's fur-covered coffee cup and saucer, but also, on the other hand, to sculptures by Jeff Koons, who, in several works, presented basketballs in tanks of water, thus alluding to, among other things, the problem of an unstable social equilibrium. Ai Weiwei had seen the early exhibitions of Jeff Koons in New York. During this time, he experimented extensively with fur in connection with objects—such as a shovel—but also as a "natural picture" in which the fur was presented as a framed pictorial object.

Ai Weiwei returned to China in 1993, mainly due to the poor health of his father, who died in 1996. Upon his return, he processed his experiences with Pop and Conceptual art not only in new works, which slowly took form, but also in groundbreaking books, which were published below the radar of the system and made waves above all in artistic circles which almost completely lacked access to publications on contemporary art. Included in the exhibition is the **Black Cover Book** (1994), which presents pioneering works of twentieth-century art by artists such as Marcel Duchamp, Jeff Koons, and Andy Warhol, as well as the work of contemporary Chinese

artists. He would publish two additional books titled the **White Cover Book** (1995) and the **Grey Cover Book** (1997). In 2000, Ai Weiwei curated the exhibition **Fuck Off**, together with Feng Boyi, in which over forty contemporary Chinese artists participated.

At the same time, Ai Weiwei created objects that fed on his preoccupation with antique art objects which he began to collect after his return to China. **Fragments of Blue-and-White Dragon Bowl** from 1996 consists of the shattered fragments of a valuable porcelain vessel smashed by the artist with a hammer. Like the much more famous work **Dropping a Han Dynasty Urn** from 1995, the destruction of a valuable cultural artifact is, on the one hand, a provocation that challenges our perception of traditional art and value. On the other hand, it is a direct reflection on the manner in which art works were handled during the Cultural Revolution, when the destruction of antiquities was seen as tantamount to affirming a new future. Ai Weiwei, who had suffered greatly from the excesses of the Cultural Revolution, takes an ironic view of the movement.

Coca Cola Vase also belongs to this group of works: a vase from the Neolithic period (5000 to 3000 BC) to which Ai Weiwei has added the ubiquitous logo of the soft drinks manufacturer from Atlanta. In no other work from the 1990s does he connect the practices of Pop and Conceptual art, which he brought back with him to China from New York, so confrontationally with Chinese cultural tradition. As a result, a piece of pottery, more than five thousand years old, becomes a work of contemporary art.

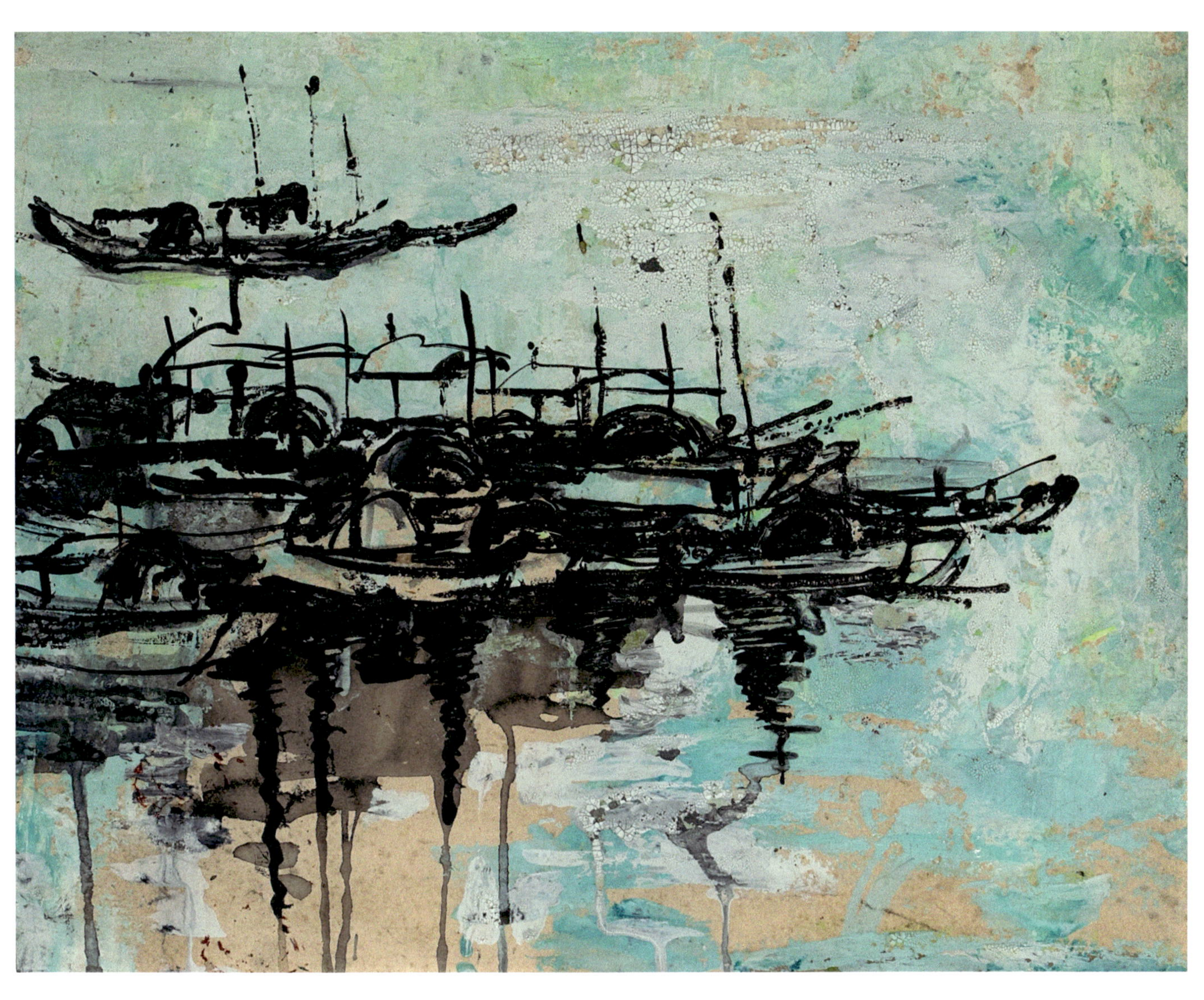

Untitled
(**Yantai, Shandong**), 1977
Oil on paper
41.5 × 35.5 cm

211

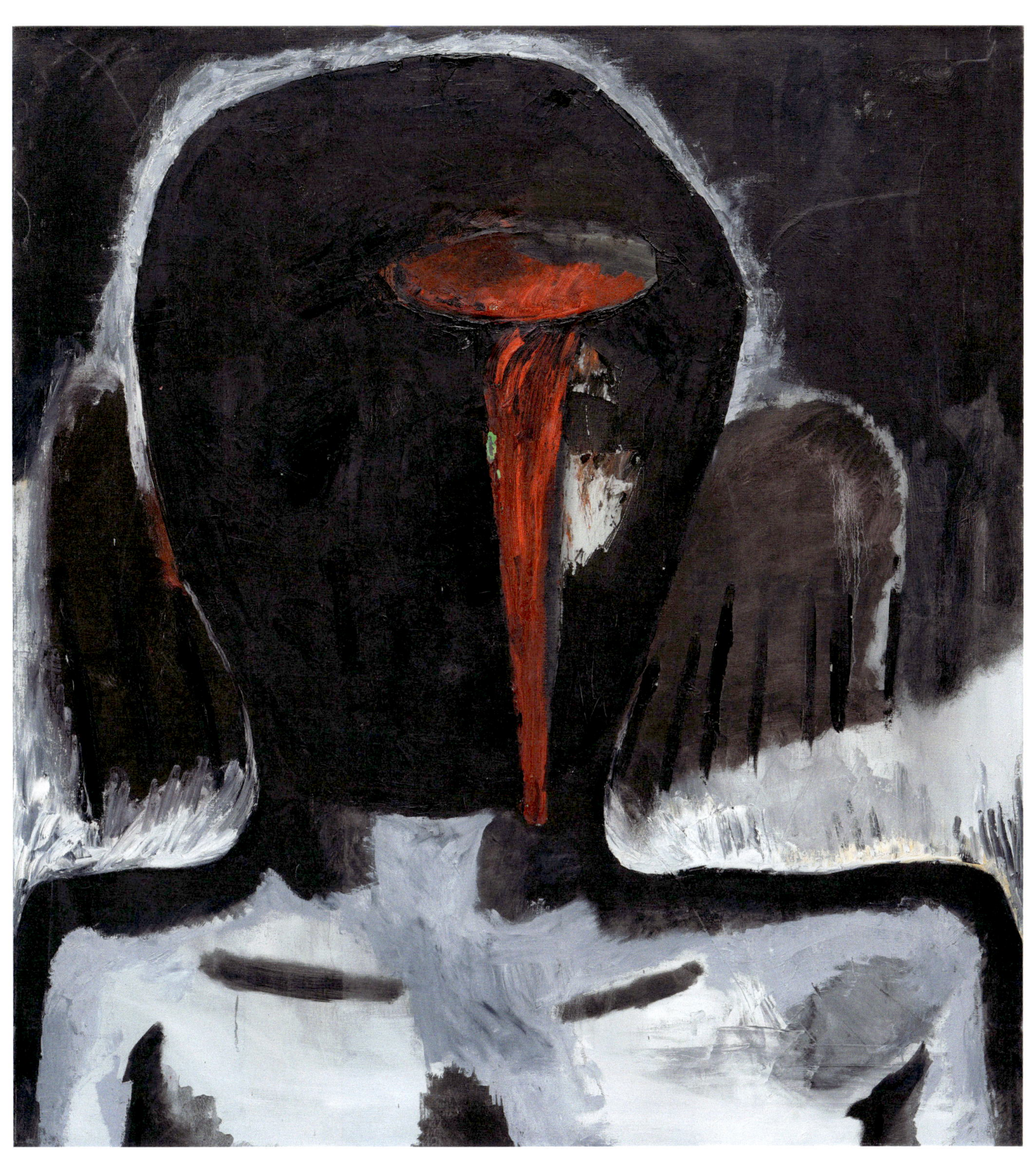

Untitled, 1980
Oil on canvas
141 × 126 cm

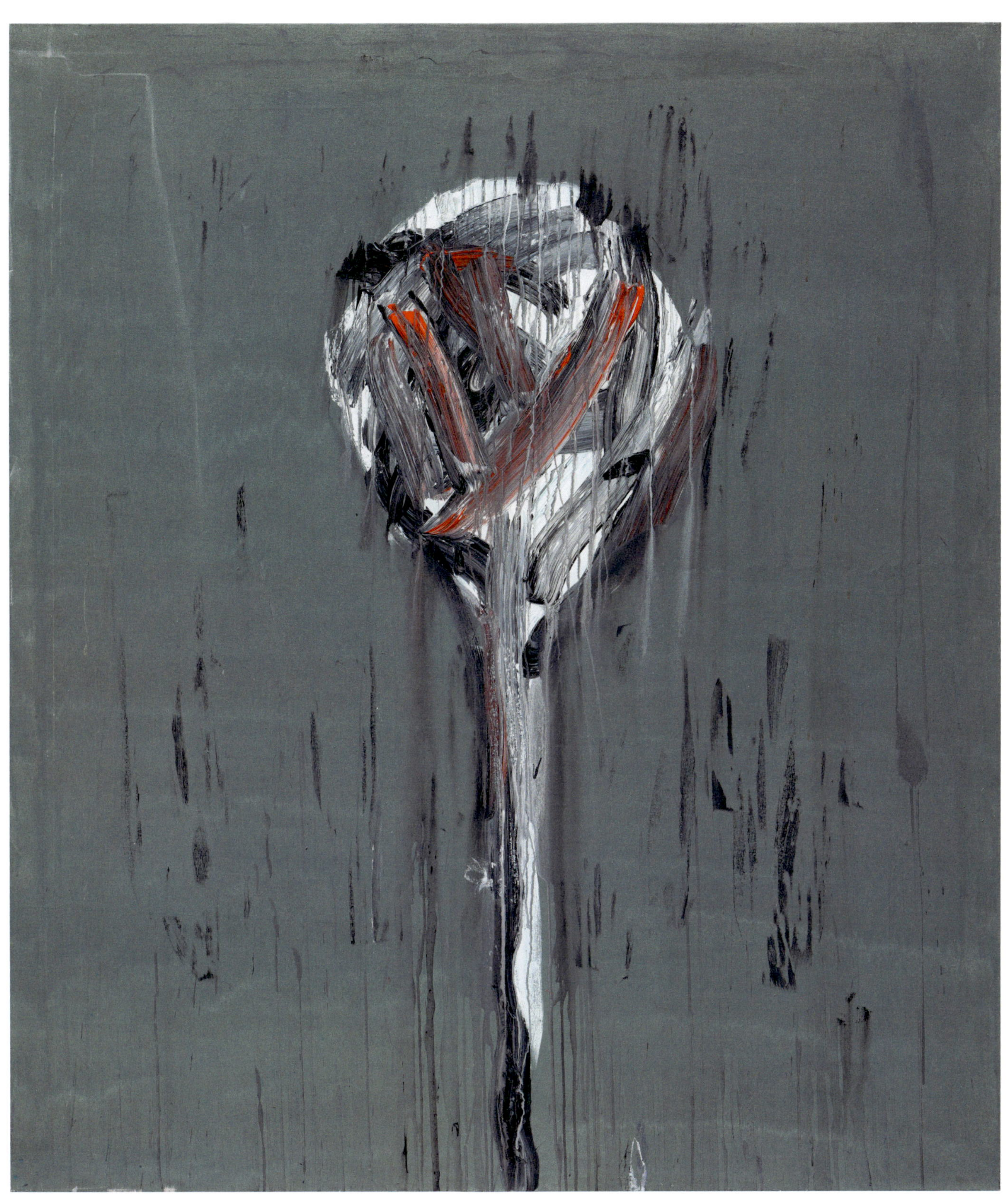

Untitled, 1980
Oil on canvas
168 × 142 cm

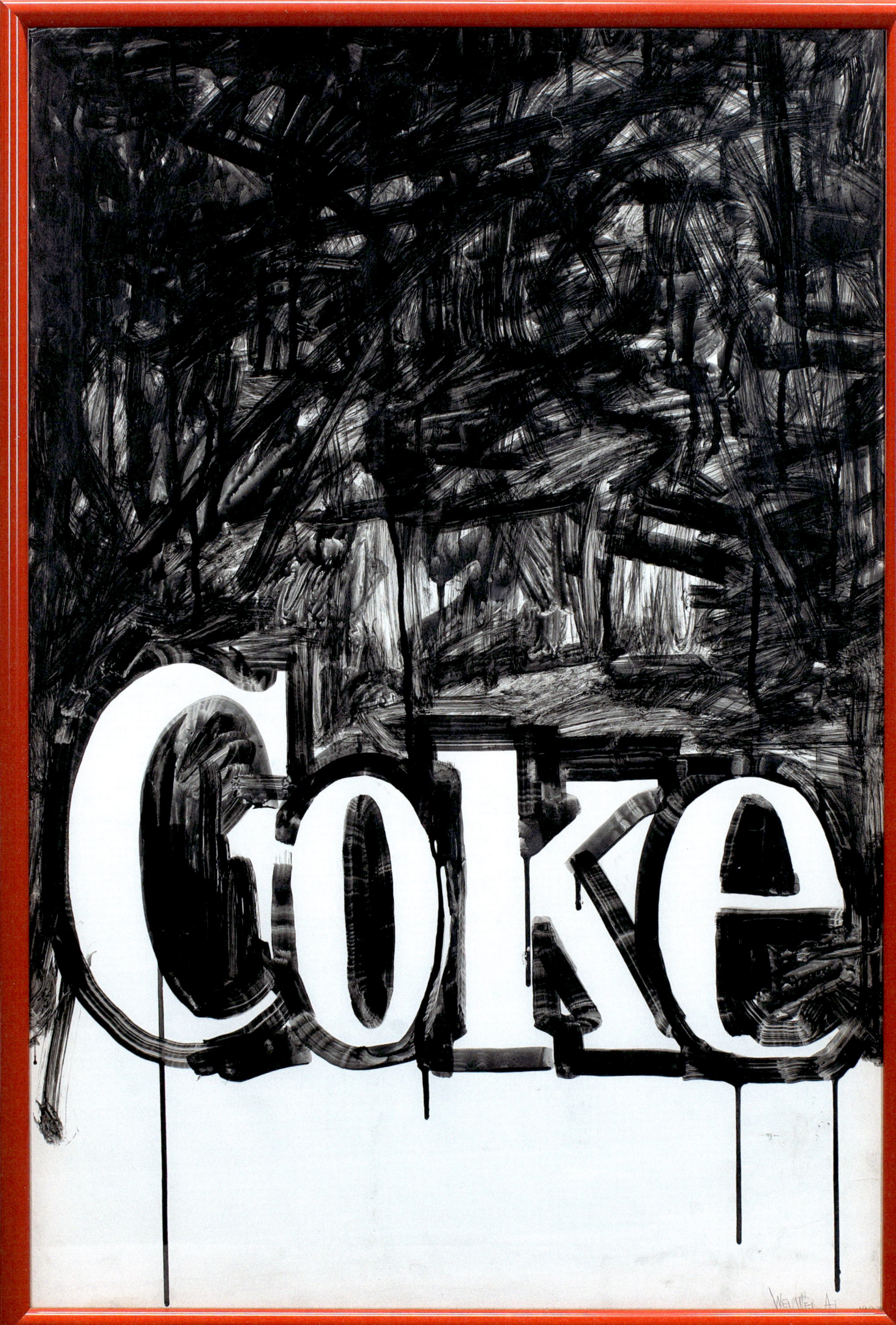
Coke

Coke Painting, 1982–1983
Ink on paper
91 × 63.5 cm

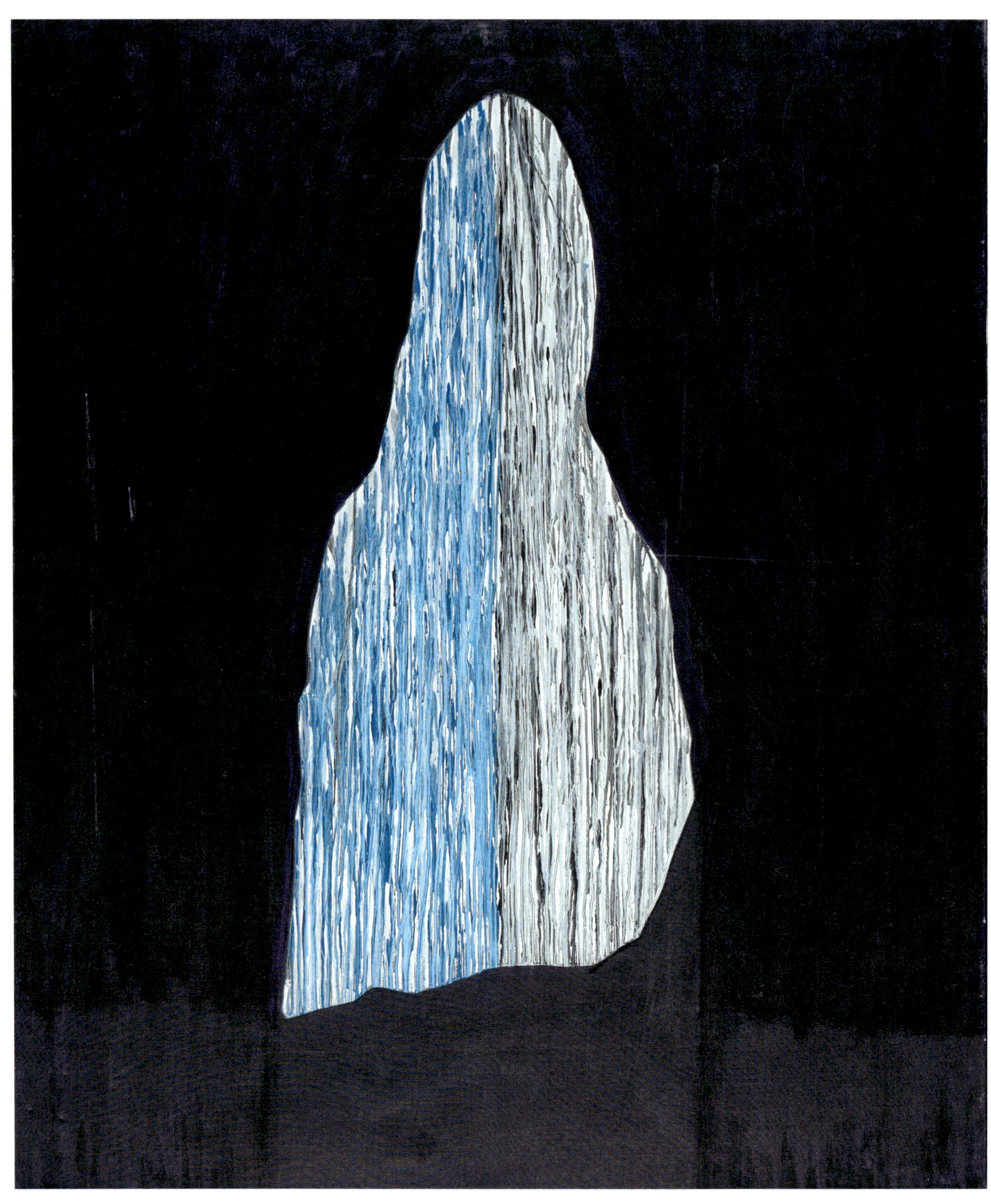

Untitled, 1986
Oil on canvas
172 × 142 cm

218

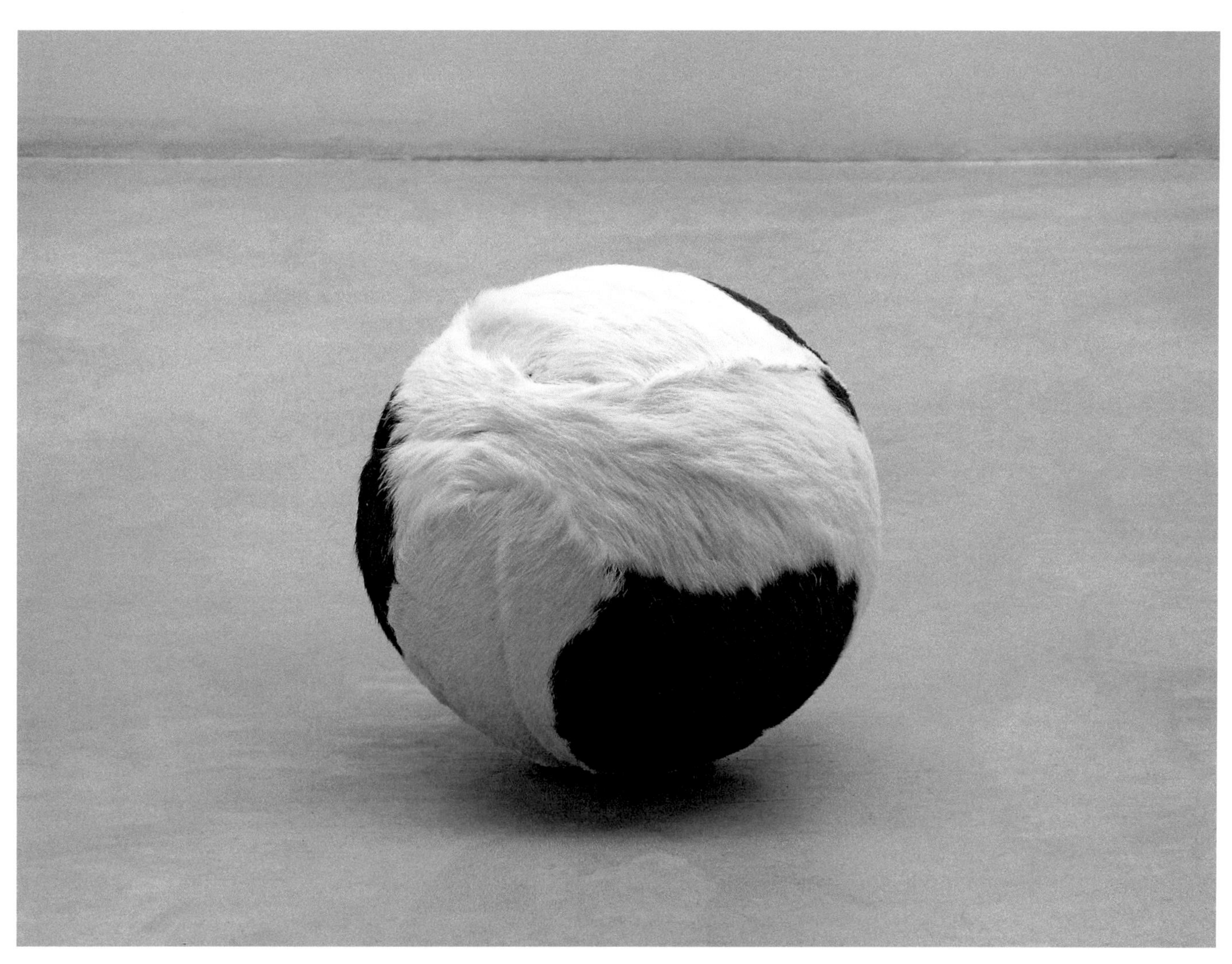

Untitled
(Fur Basketball), 1987
Fur, basketball
25 × 25 × 25 cm

Safe Sex, 1986
Rain coat, coat hanger,
condom
164 × 124 cm

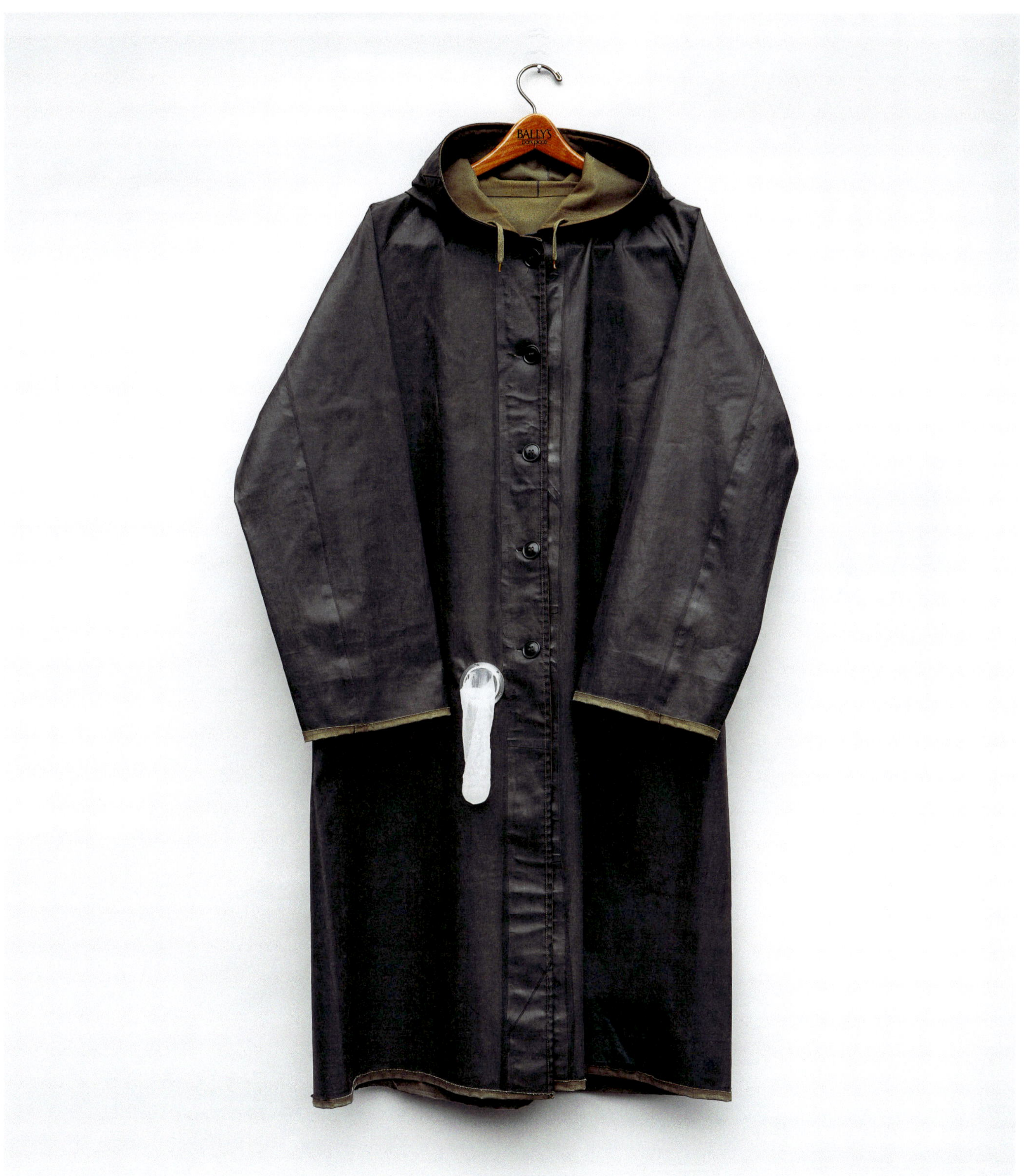

BALLY'S

New York Photographs,
1983–1993
57 framed photographs,
each: 50 × 50 cm

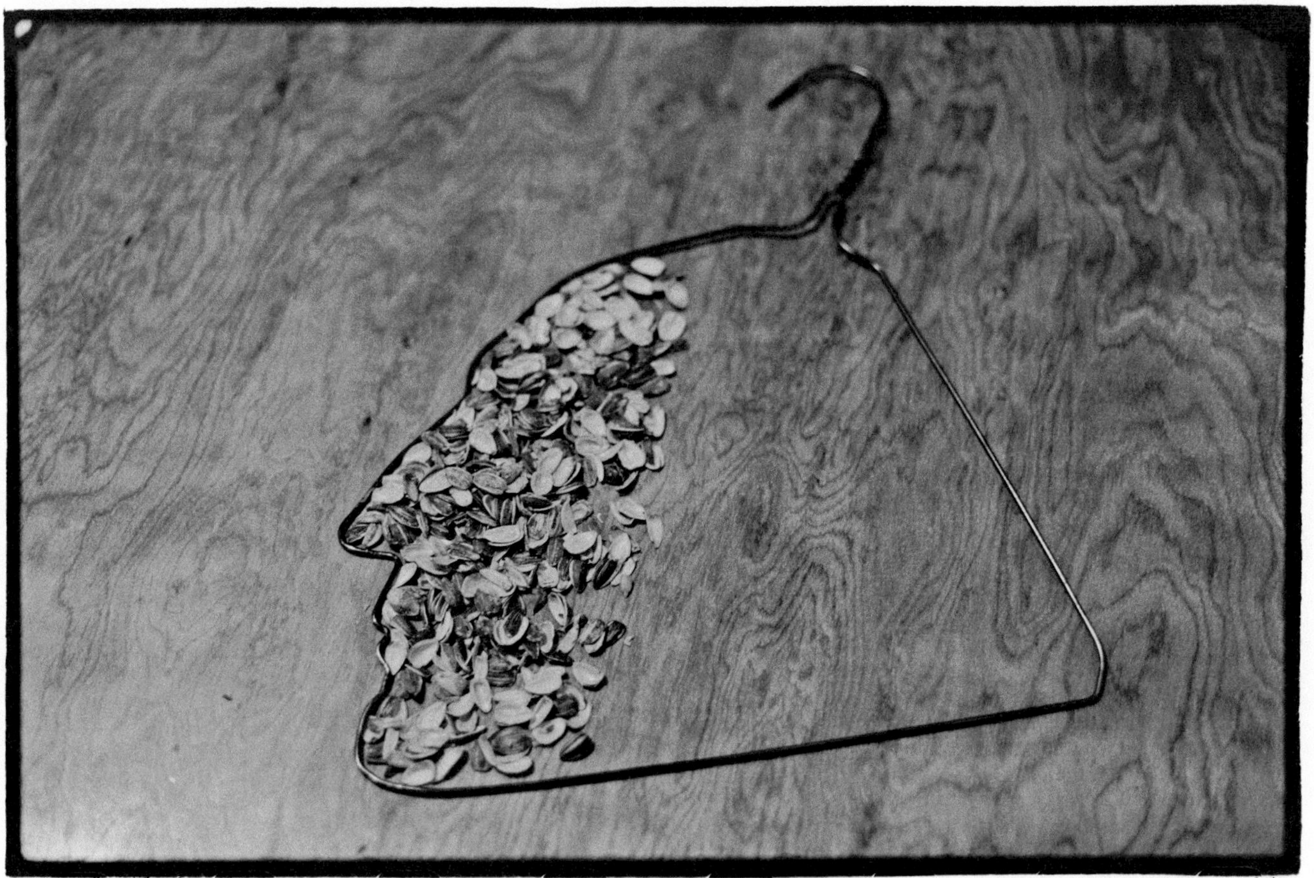

杜尚像. 葵花籽.   1983   Profile of Duchamp, Sunflower Seeds 1983

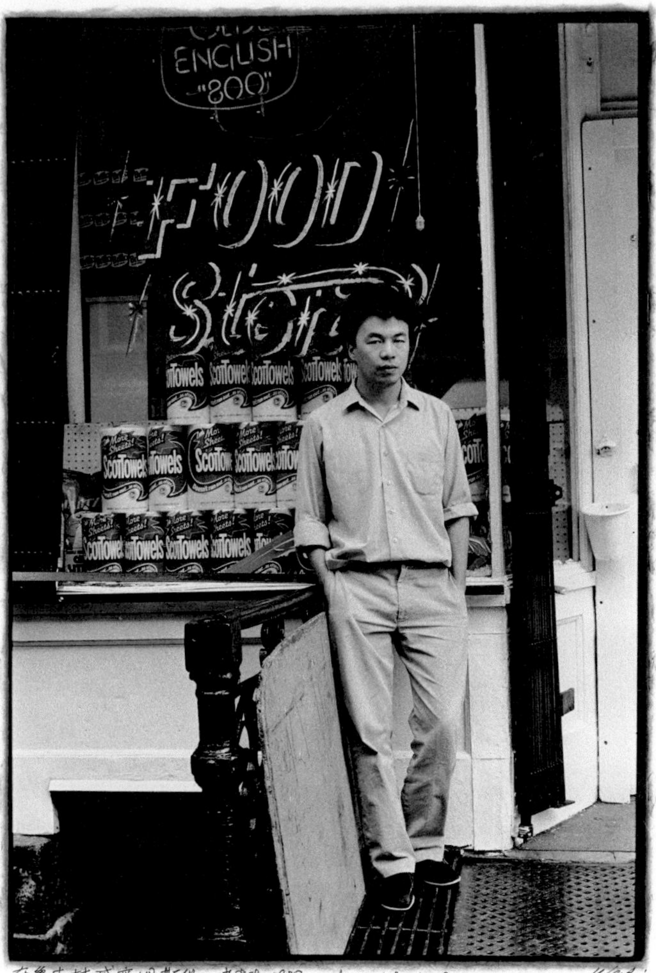

布魯克林威廉姆斯堡. 艾未未 1983   Ai Weiwei, Williamsburg, Brooklyn 1983

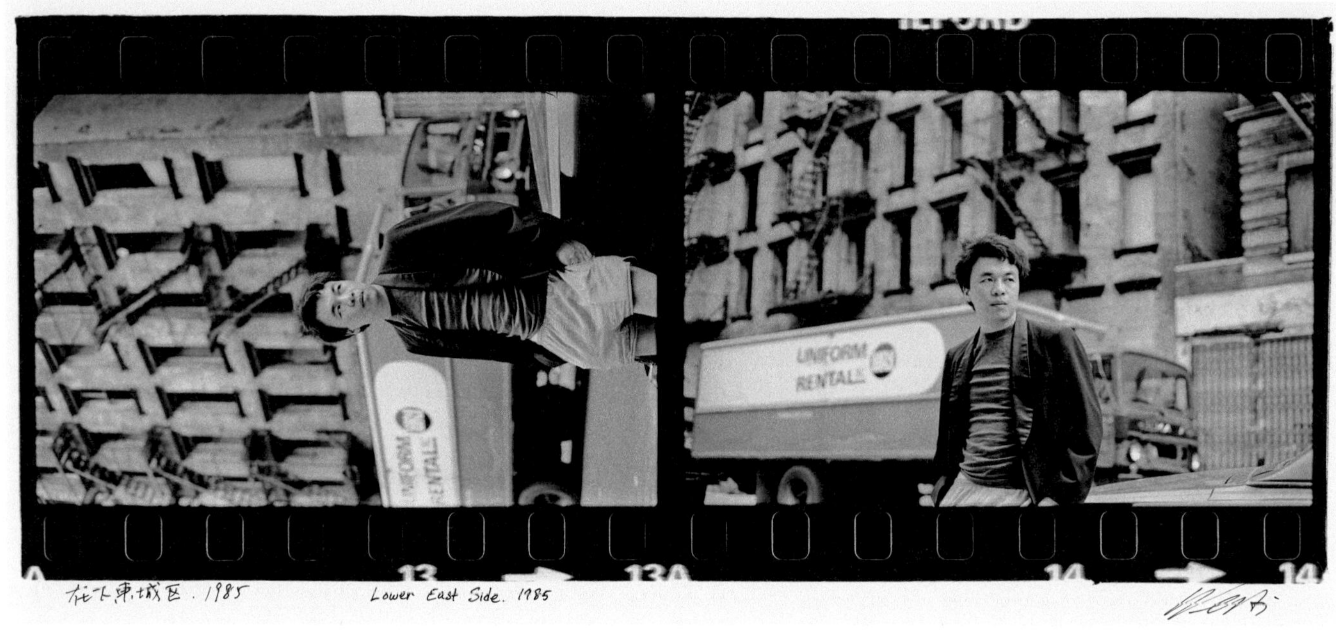

花卉東城區. 1985　　　Lower East Side. 1985

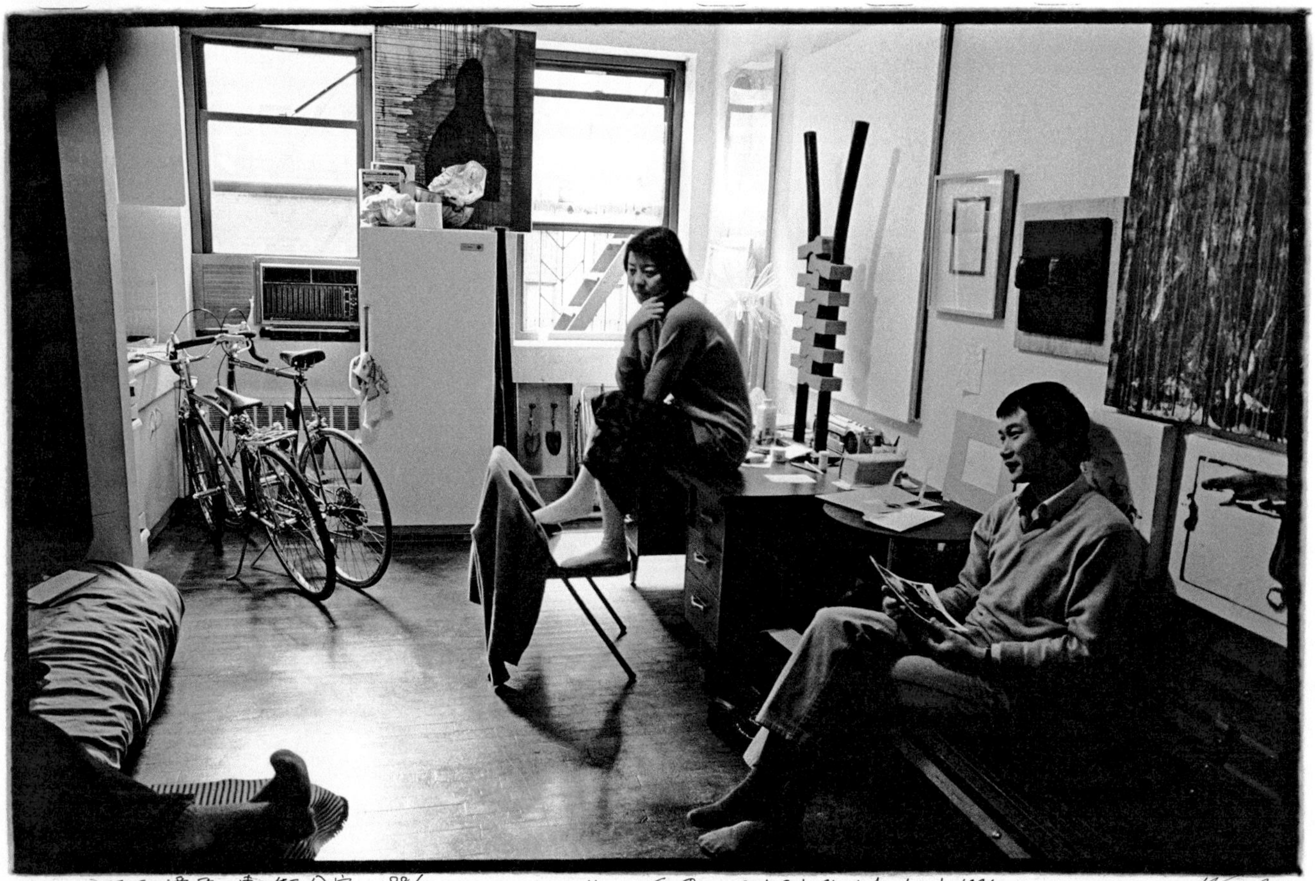

王穎和譚盾. 東三街公寓. 1986.　　　Wang Ying + Tan Dun. East 3rd Street Apartment. 1986

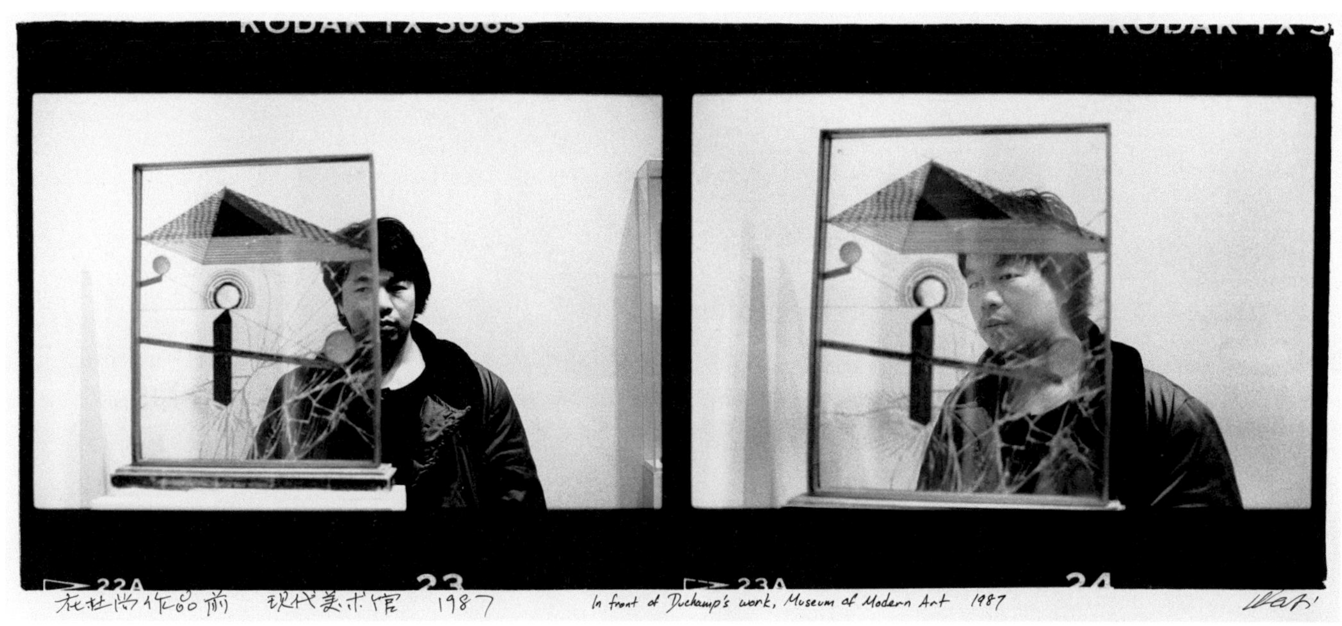

在杜尚作品前　现代美术馆　1987　In front of Duchamp's work, Museum of Modern Art　1987

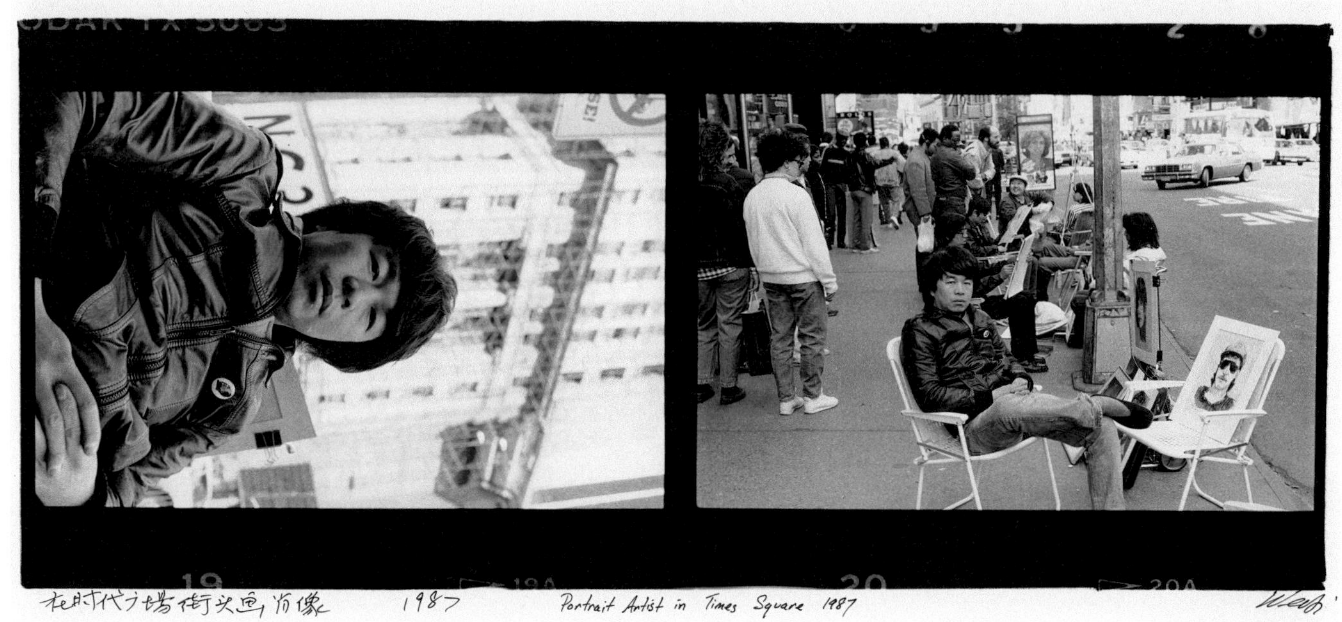

在时代广场街头画肖像　1987　Portrait Artist in Times Square 1987

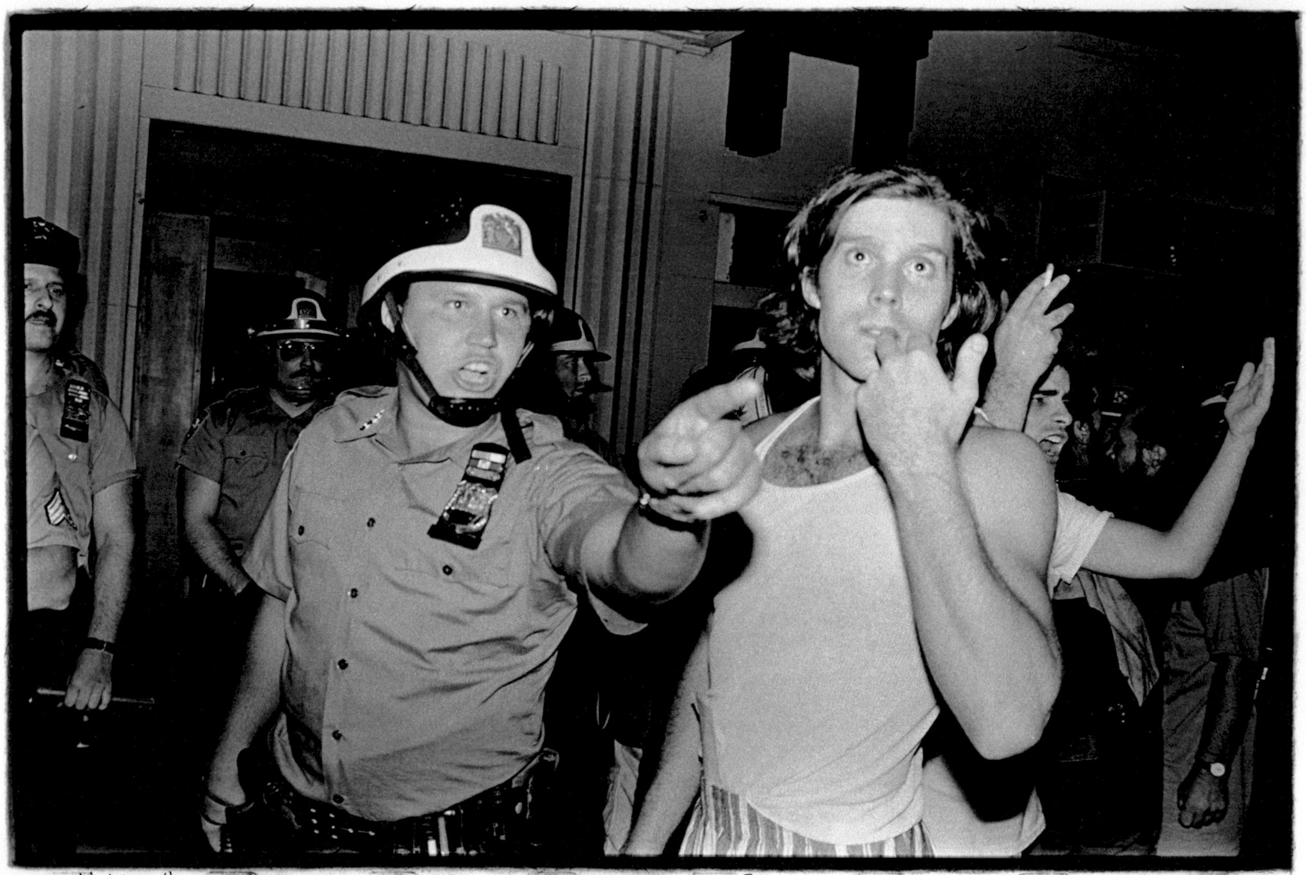

华盛顿广场的抗议活动　　1988　　Washington Square Park protest. 1988

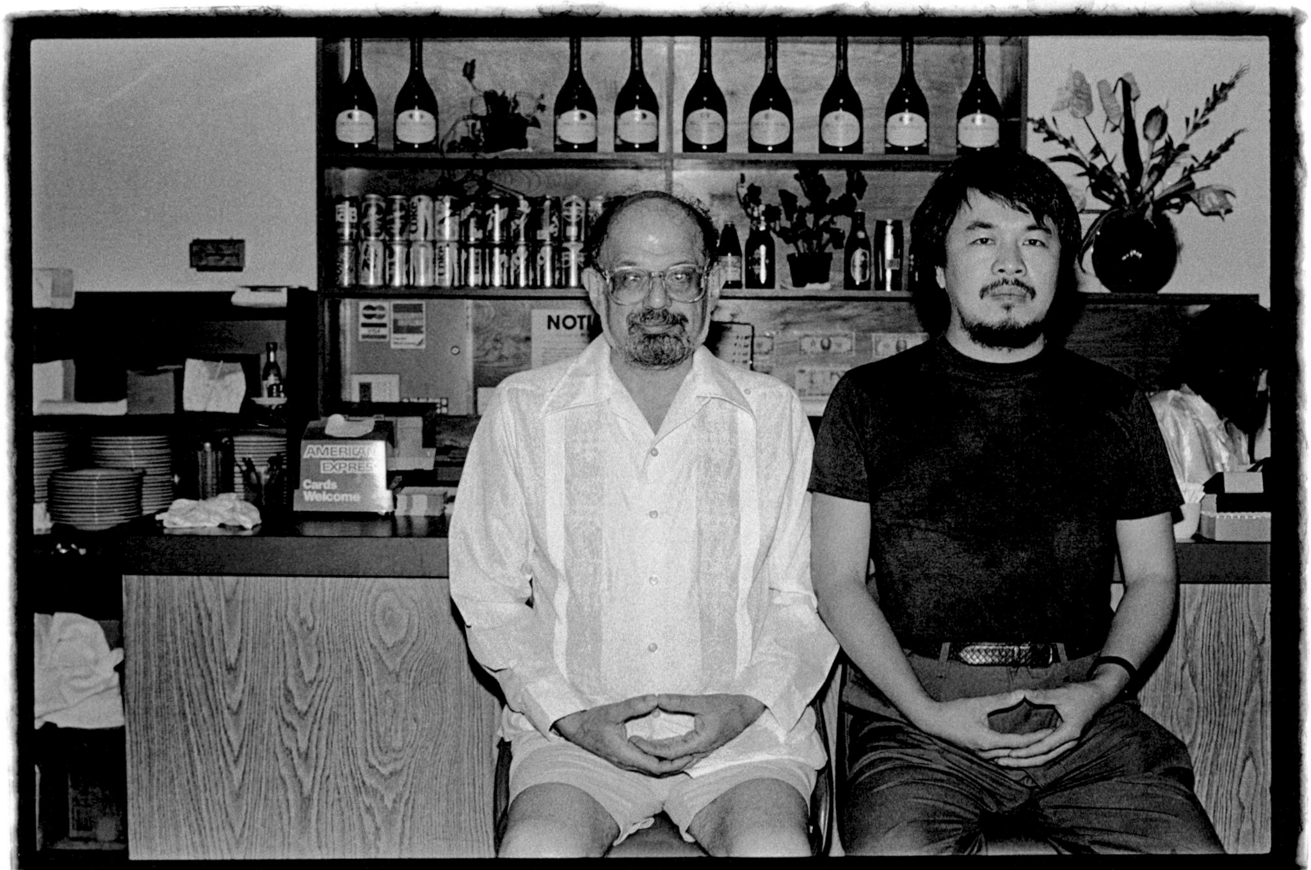

在下東城区的夫餐中.　　Lower East Side Restaurent

228

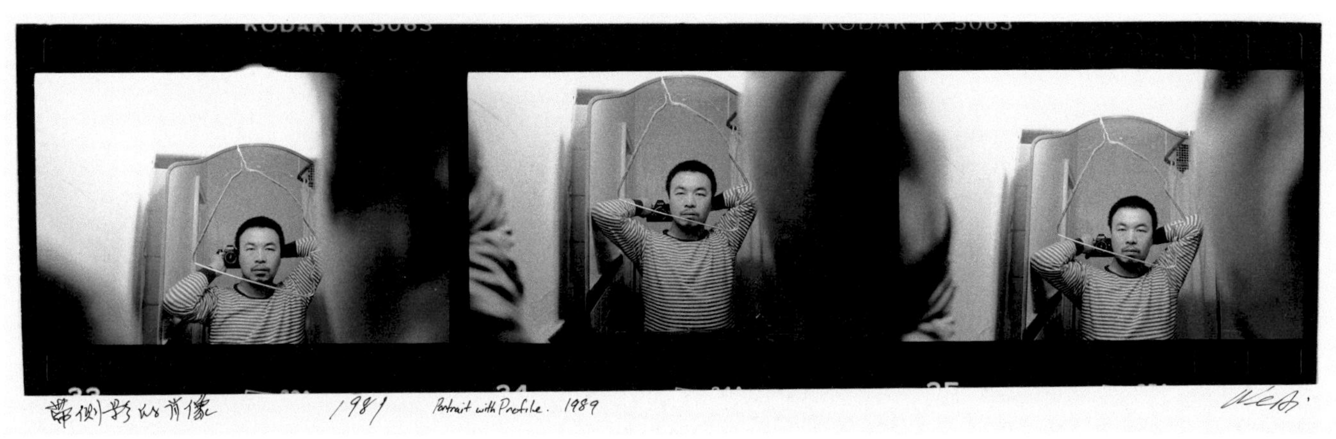

带侧影的肖像 1989 Portrait with Profile. 1989

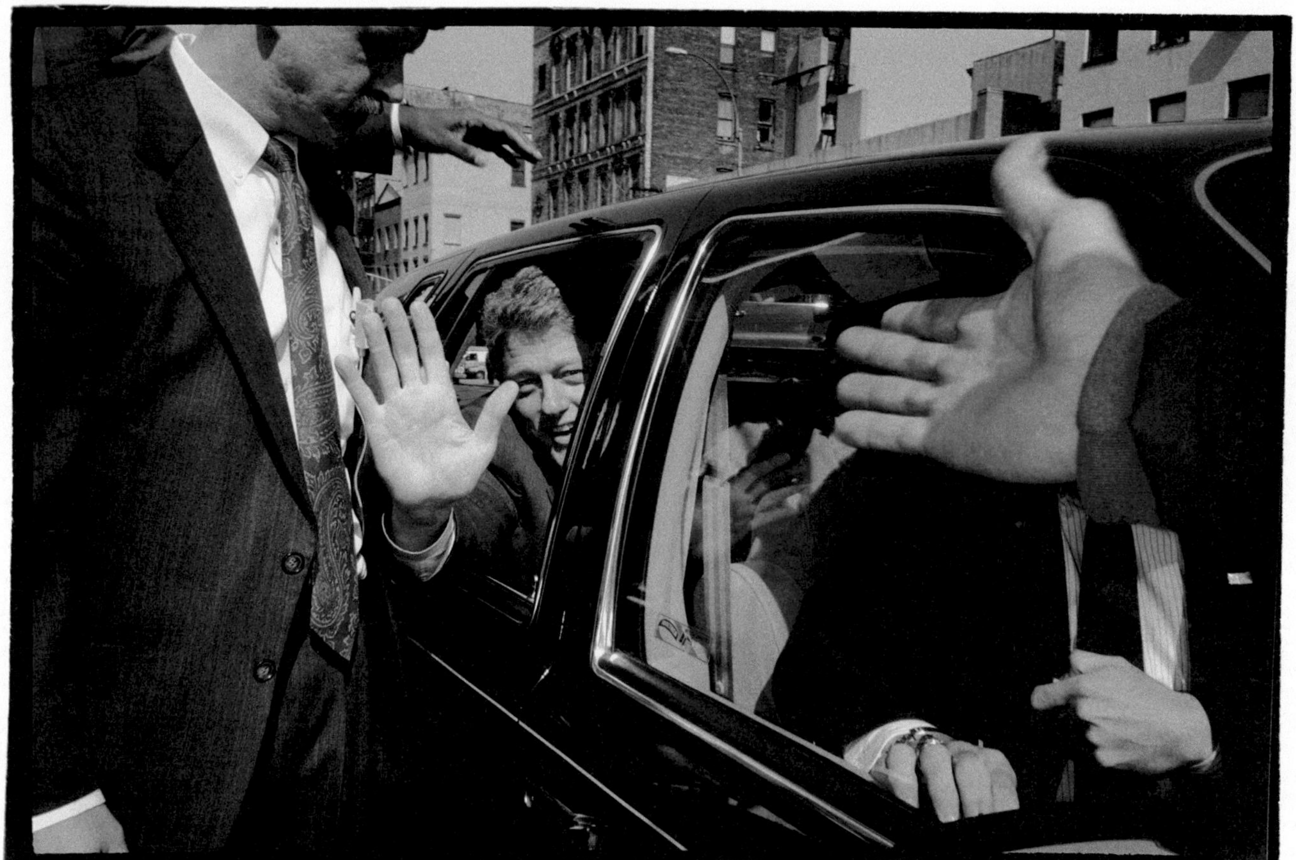

比尔·克林顿竞选的最后时刻 纽约 1992 Bill Clinton at his last campaign stop in New York 1992

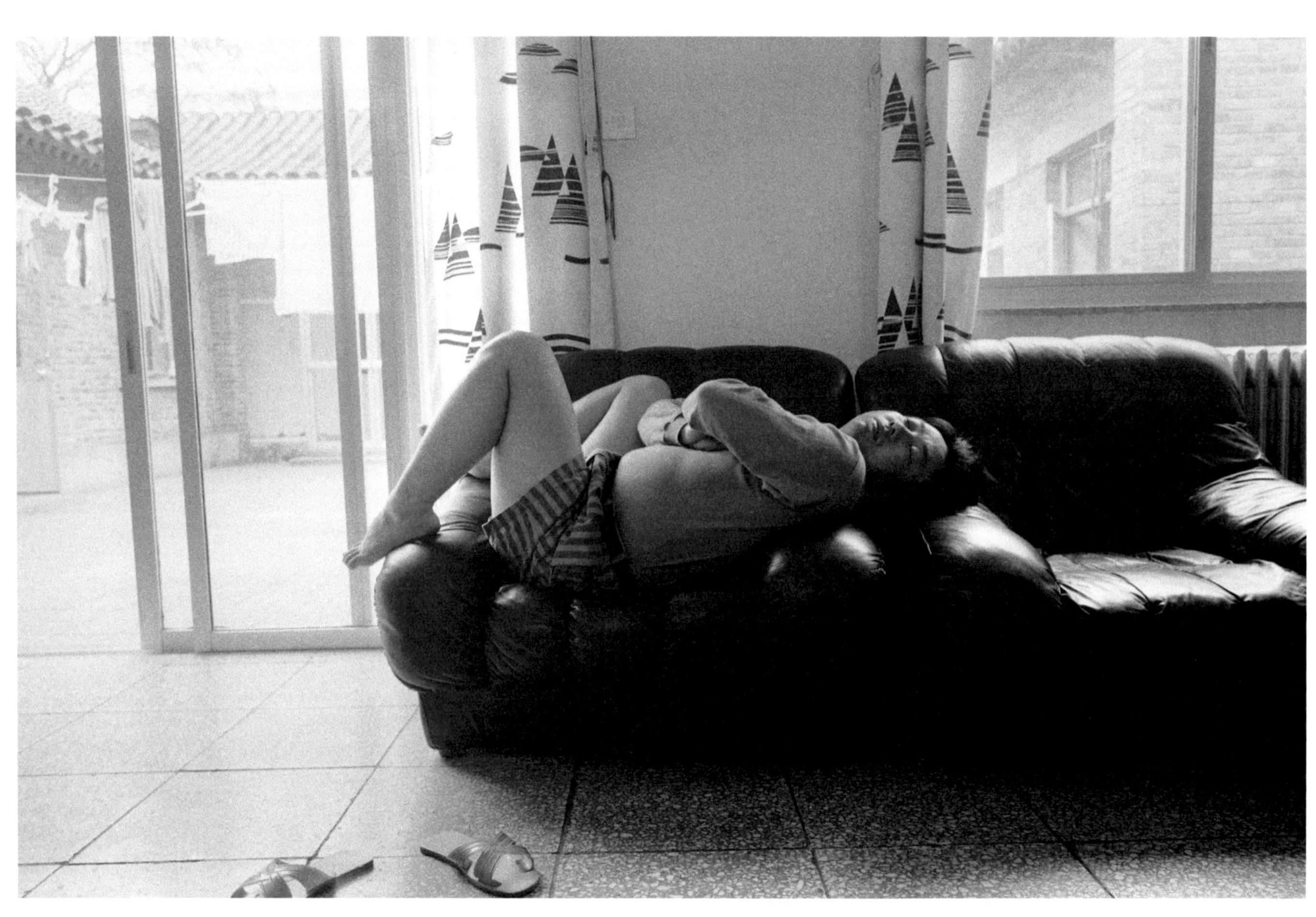

Beijing Photographs,
1993–2003
42 framed photographs,
each: 50 × 50 cm

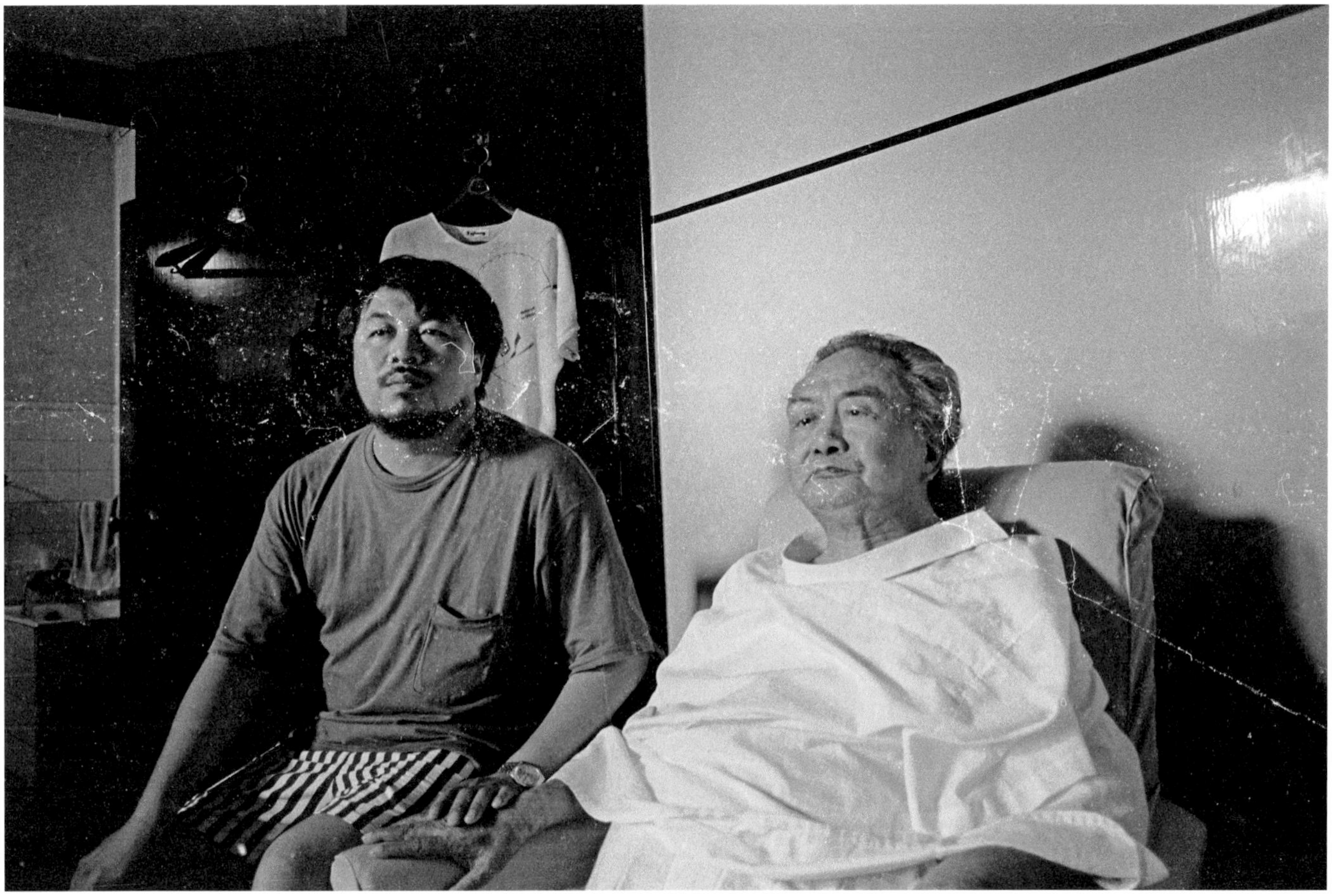

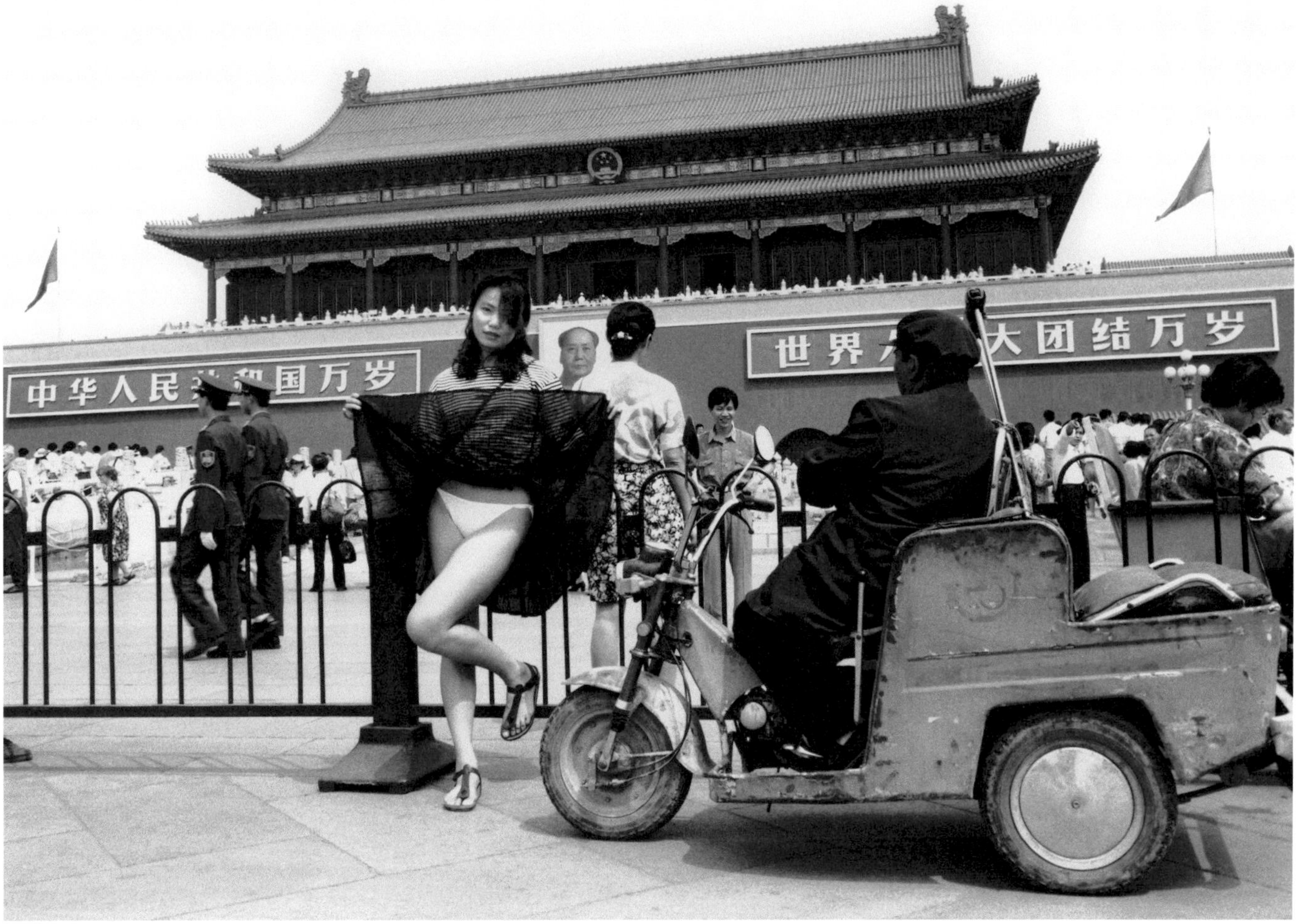

中华人民共和国万岁
世界人民大团结万岁

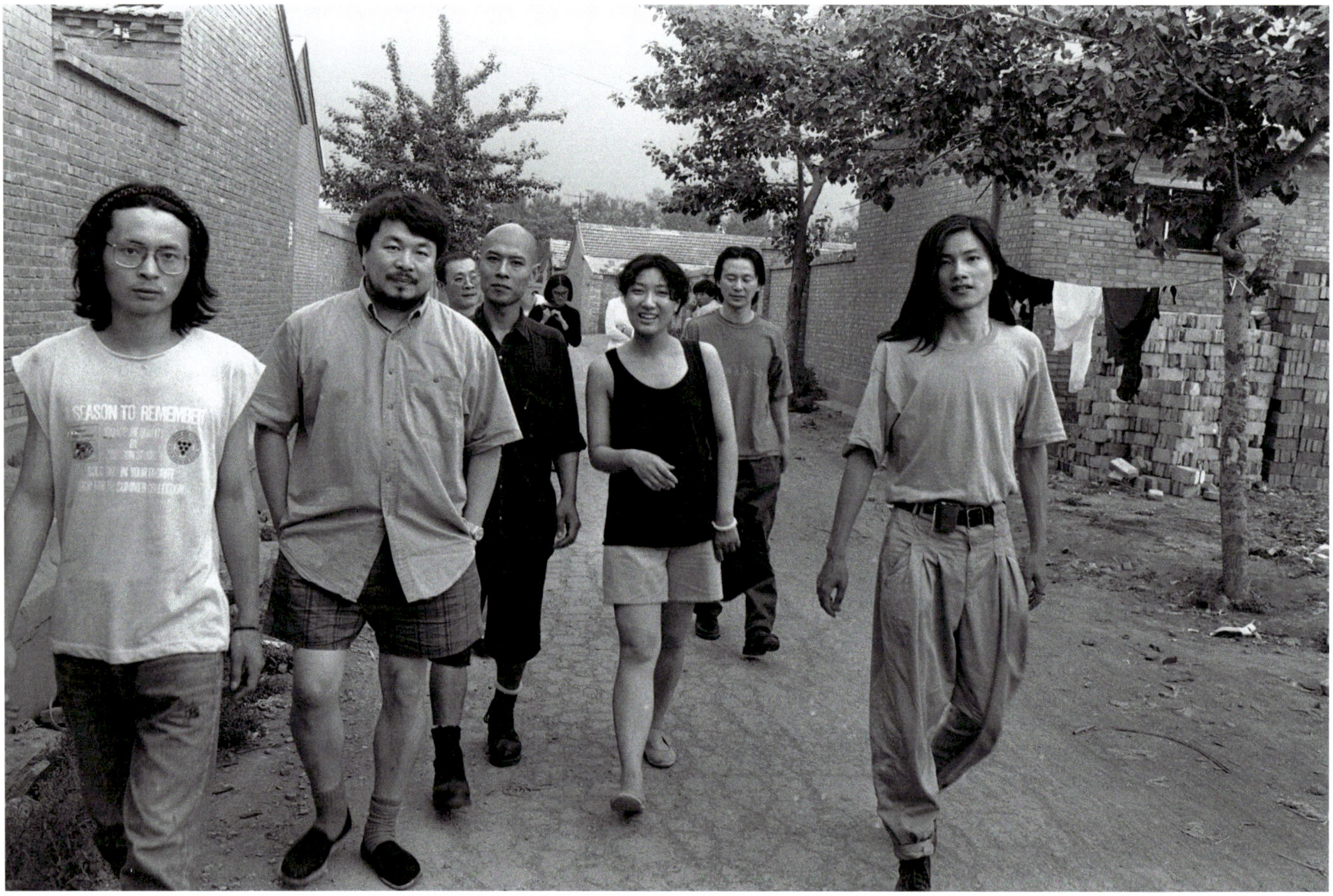
SEASON TO REMEMBER

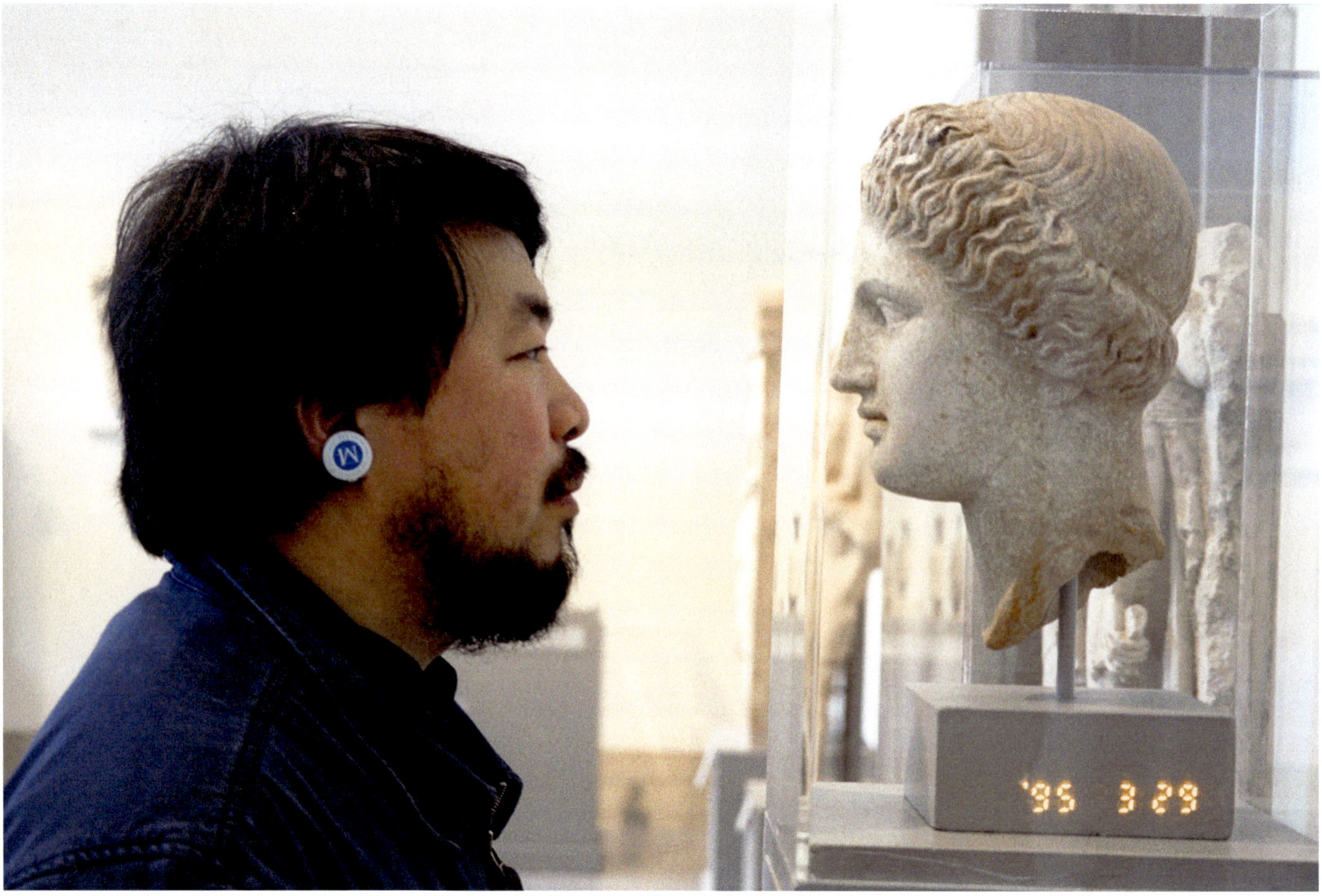
'95 3 29

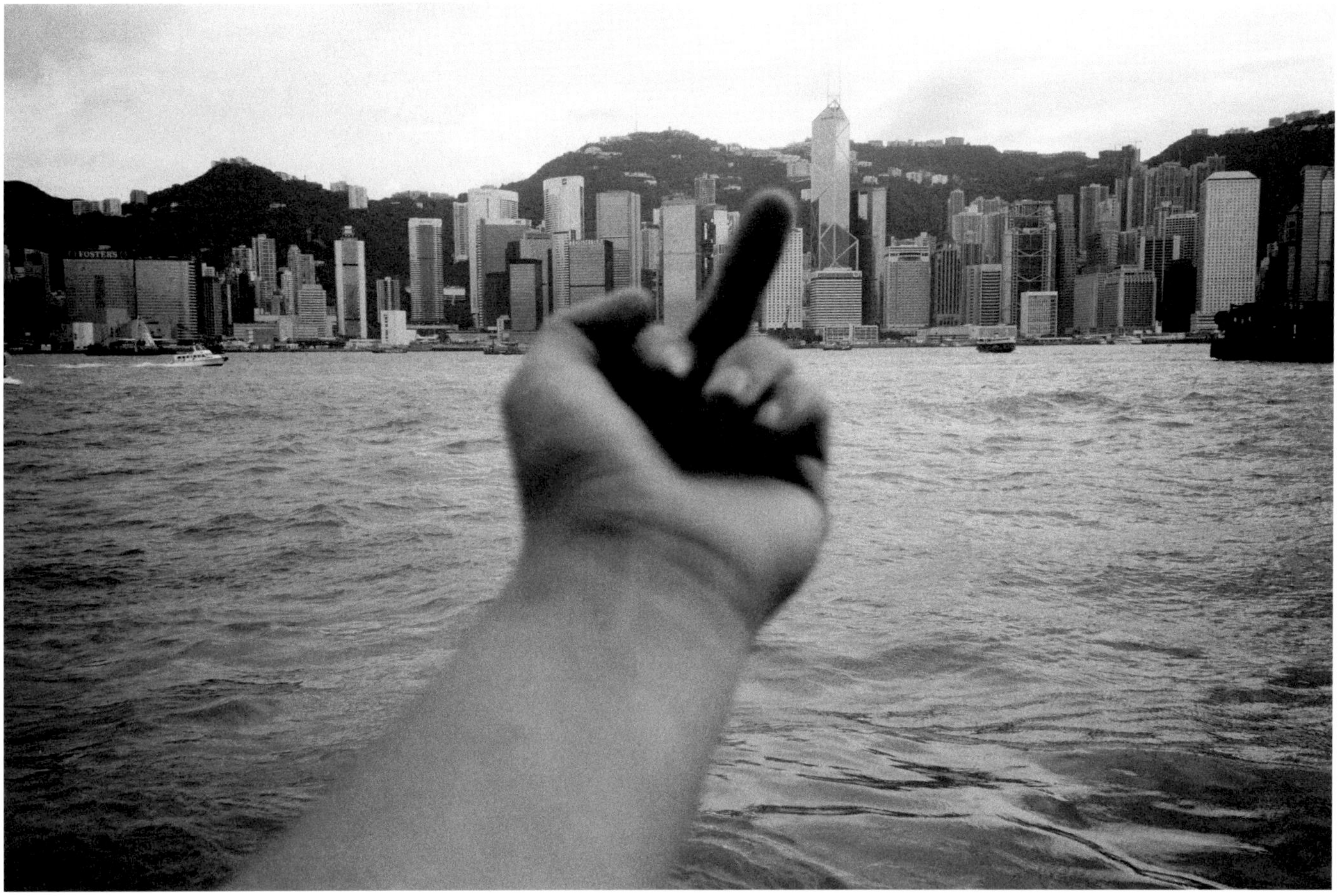

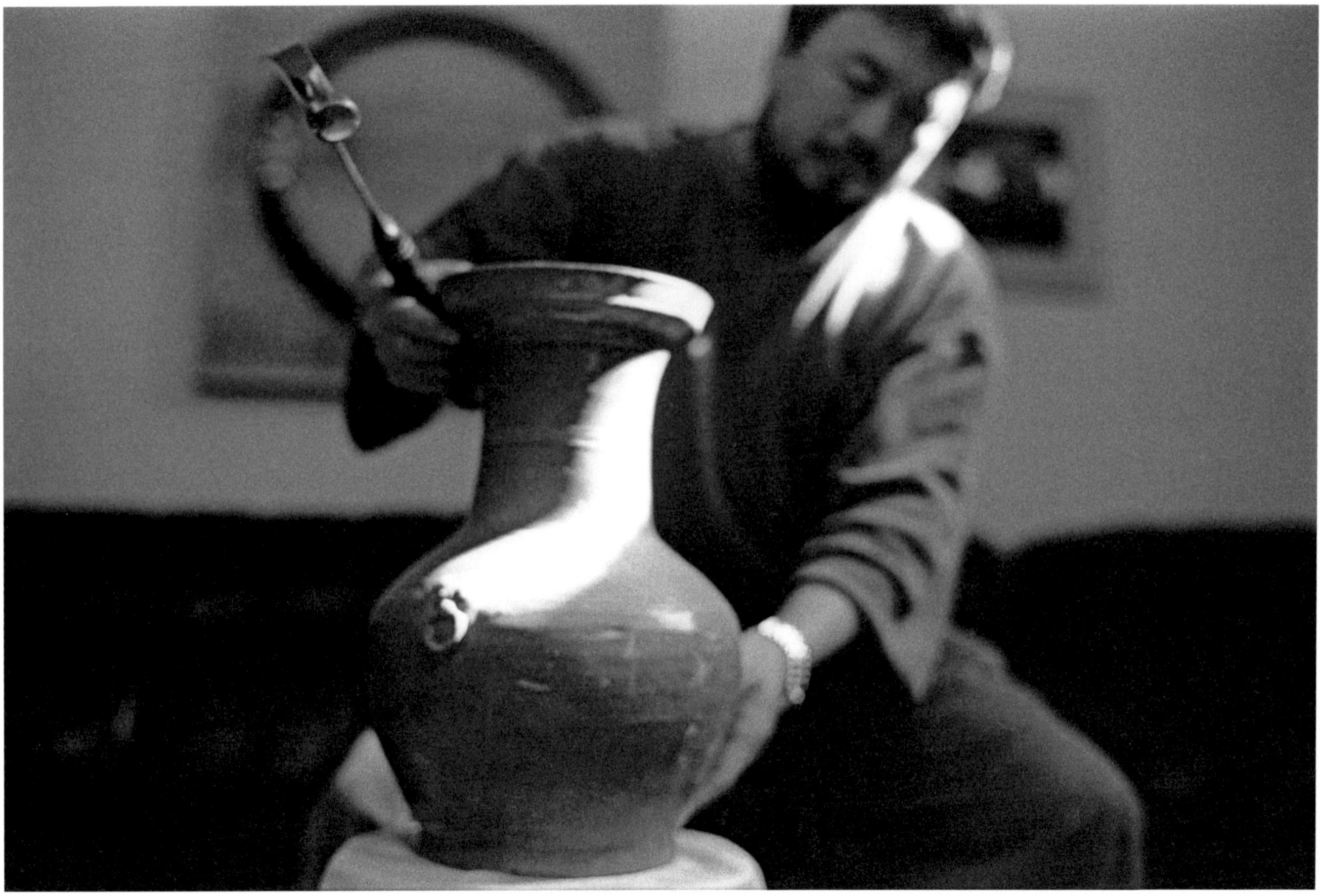

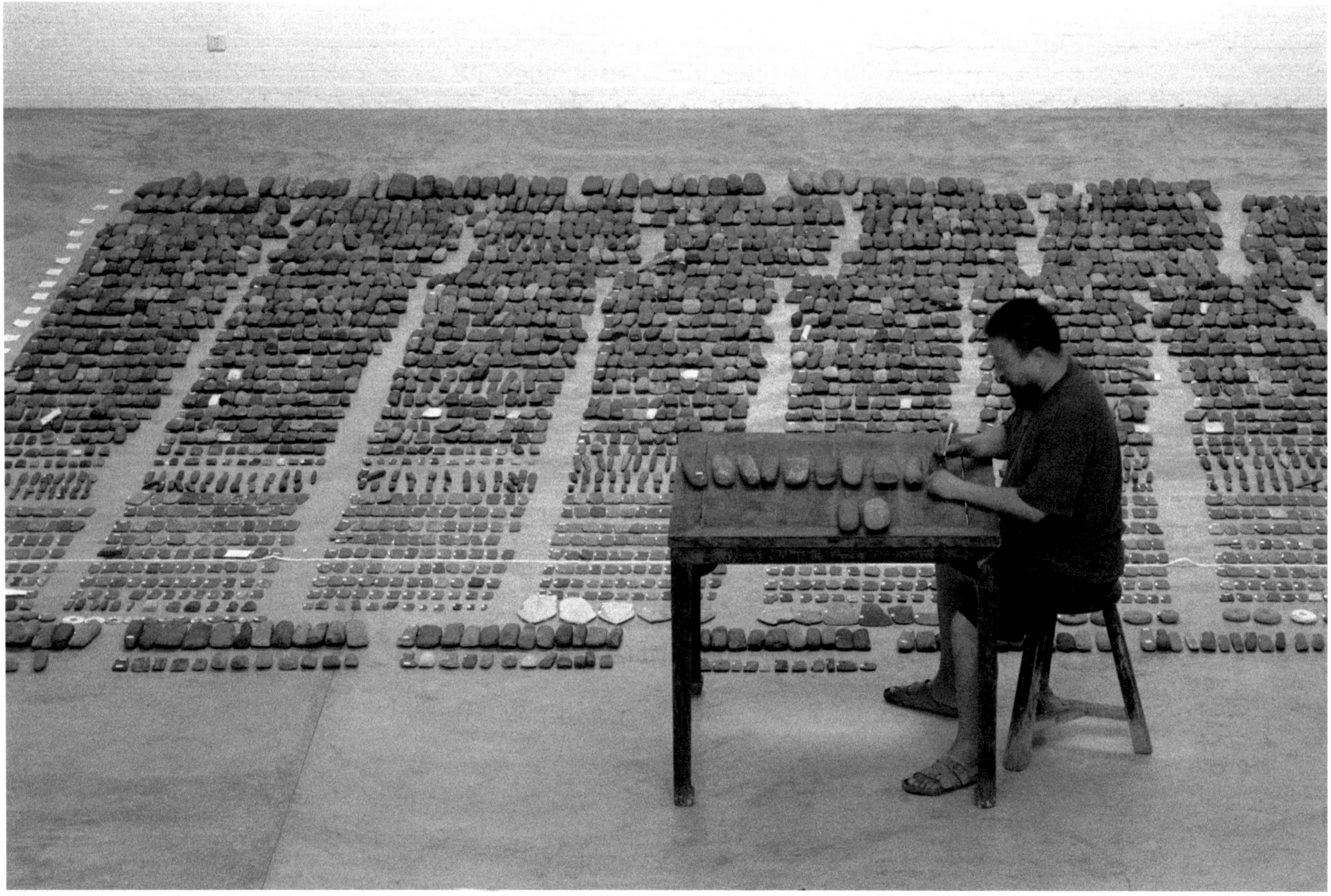

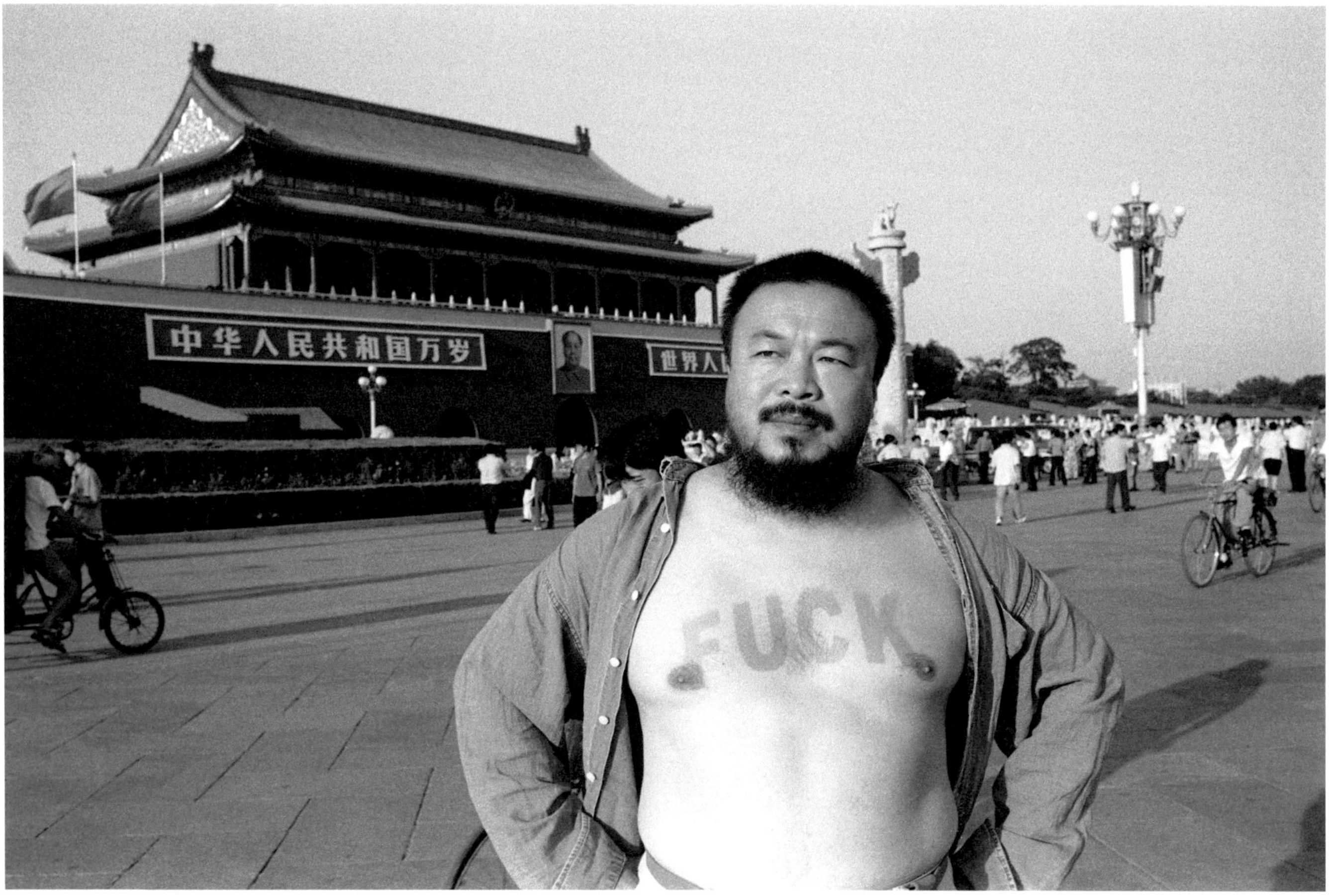

中华人民共和国万岁
世界人...
FUCK

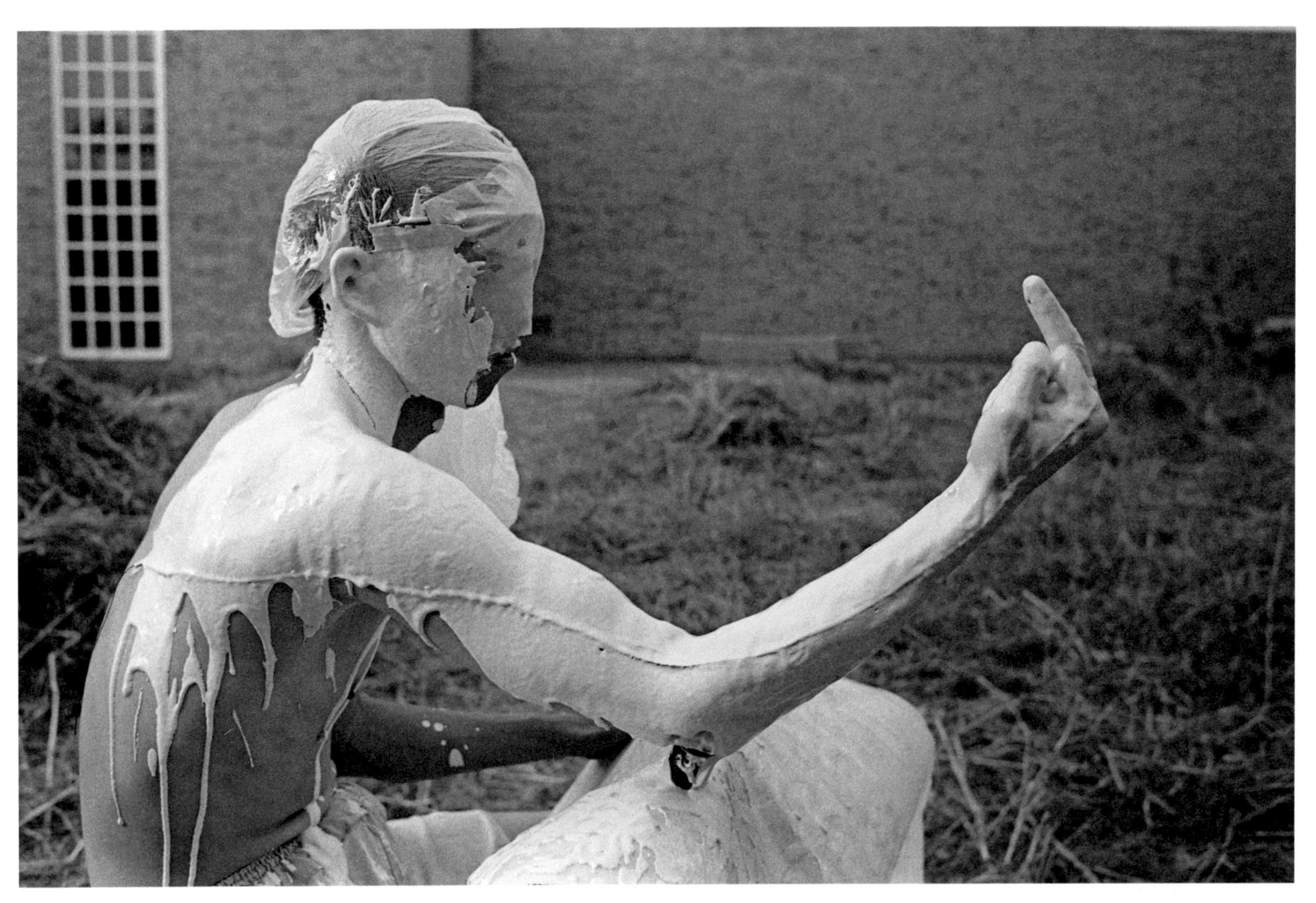

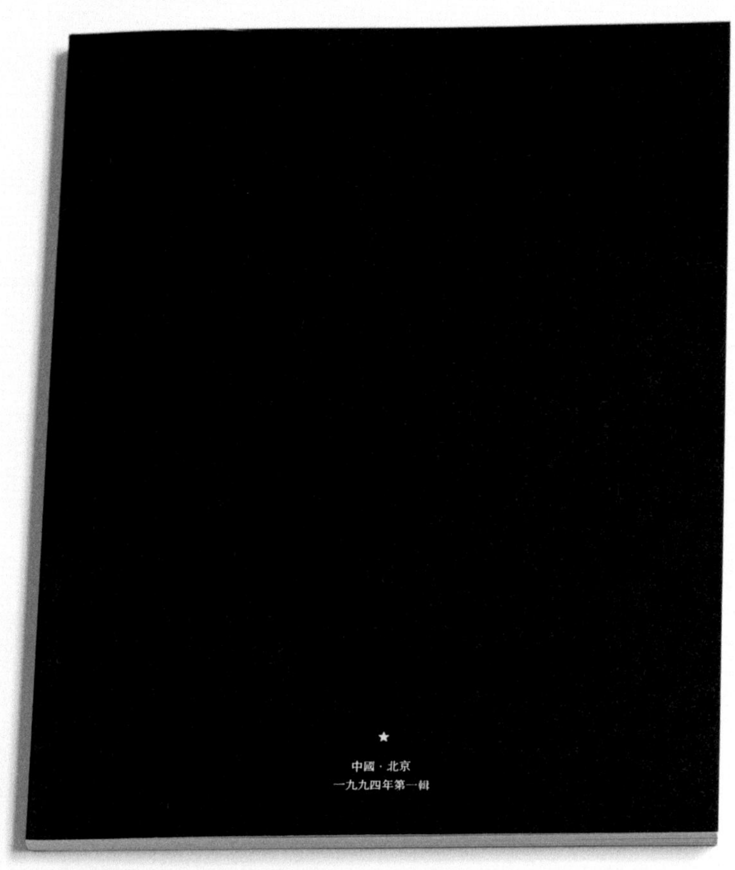
★
中國・北京
一九九四年第一輯

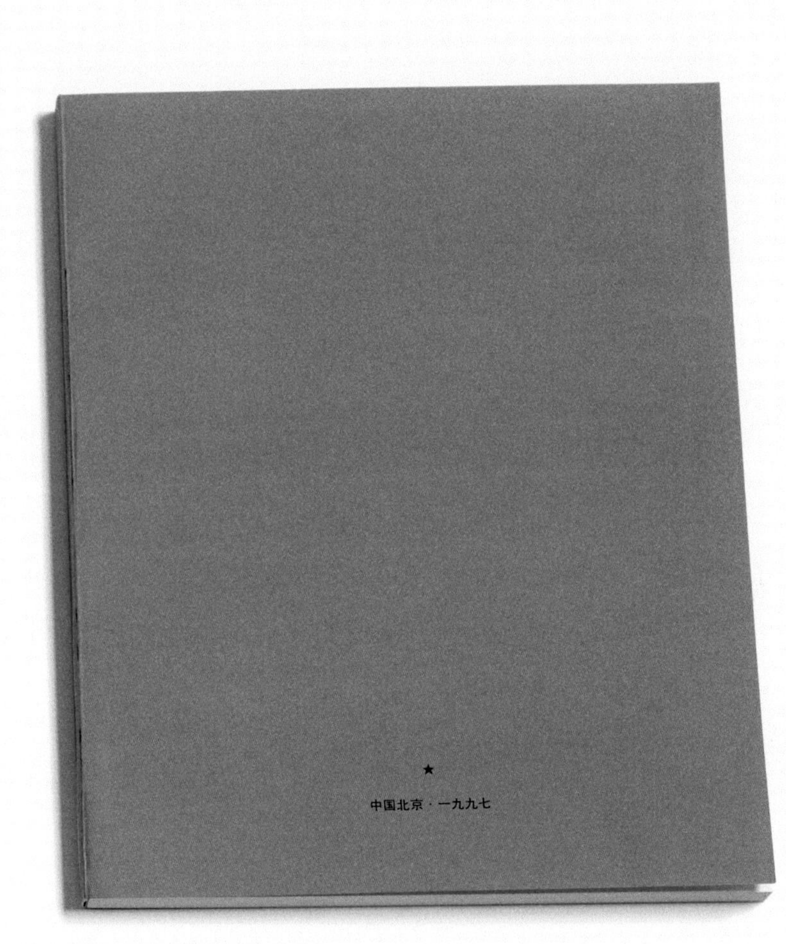
★
中国北京·一九九七

Black Cover Book, 1994
Book
24.8 × 21 × 1.8 cm

White Cover Book, 1995
Book
22.9 × 18.2 × 1 cm

Grey Cover Book, 1997
Book
22.9 × 18.2 × 1 cm

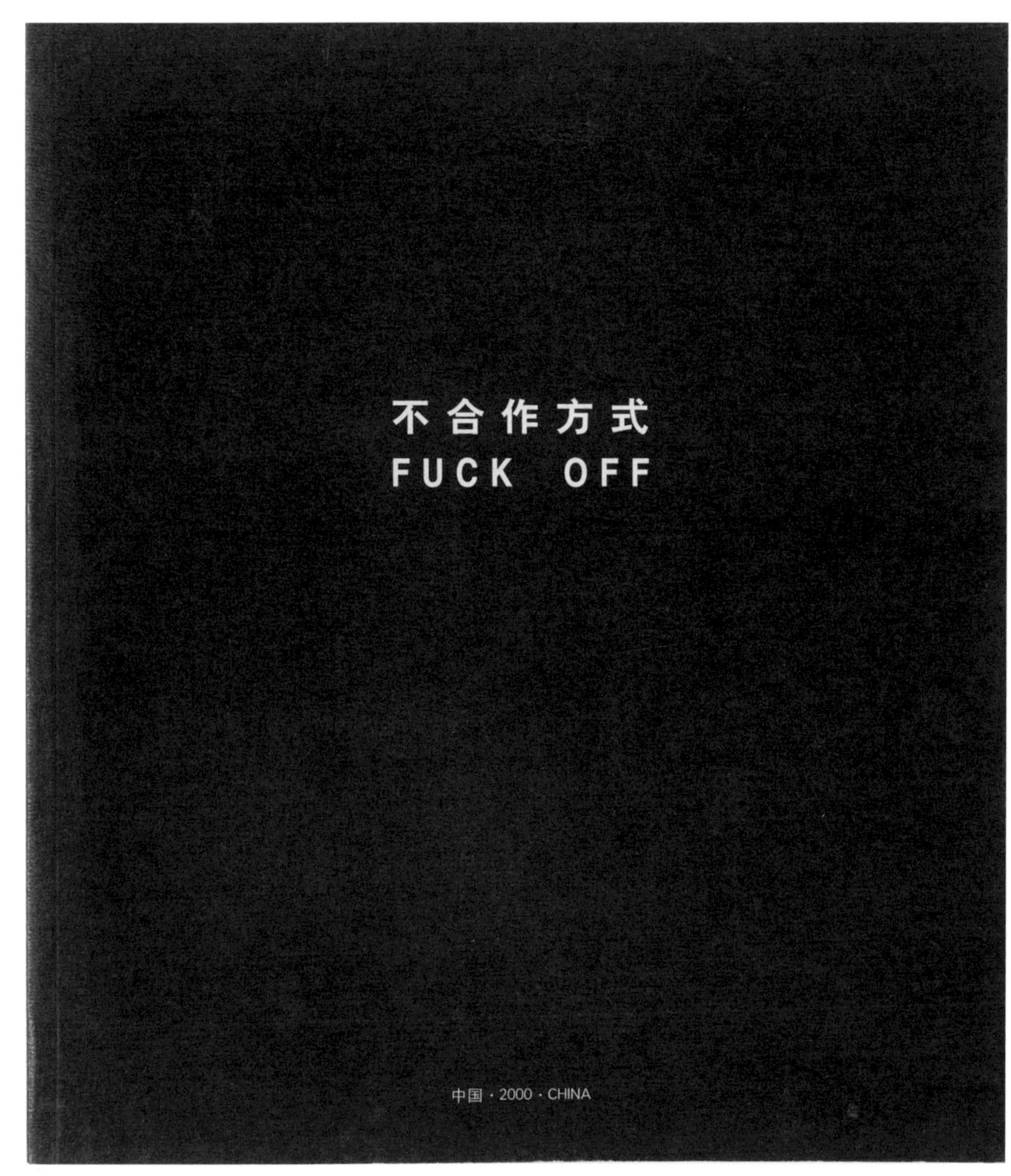

Fuck Off
Exhibition Catalogue, 2000
Book
24.8 × 21 × 1.8 cm

Coca Cola Vase, 2015
Vase, paint
42.5 × 42.5 × 36 cm

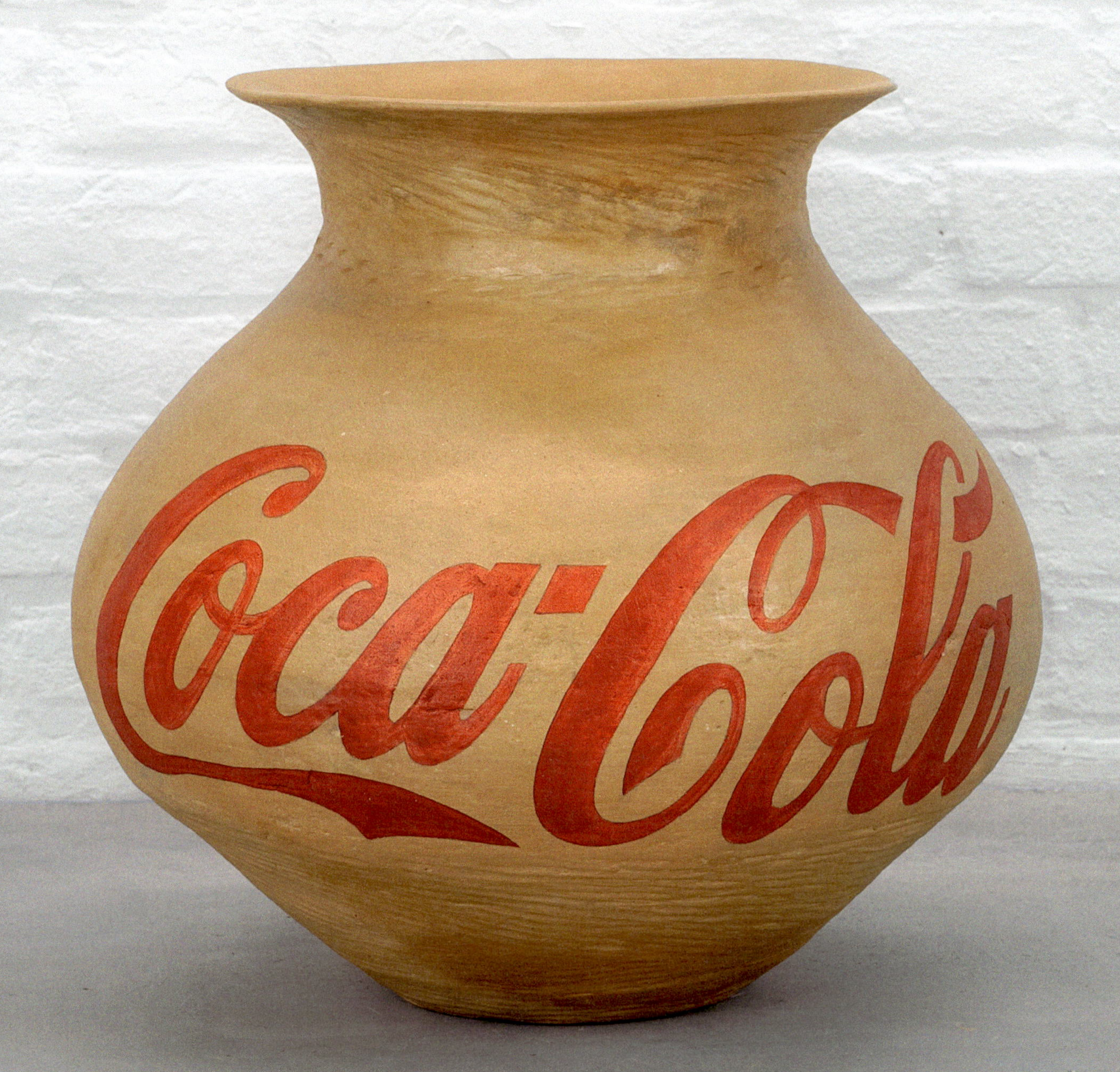
Coca-Cola

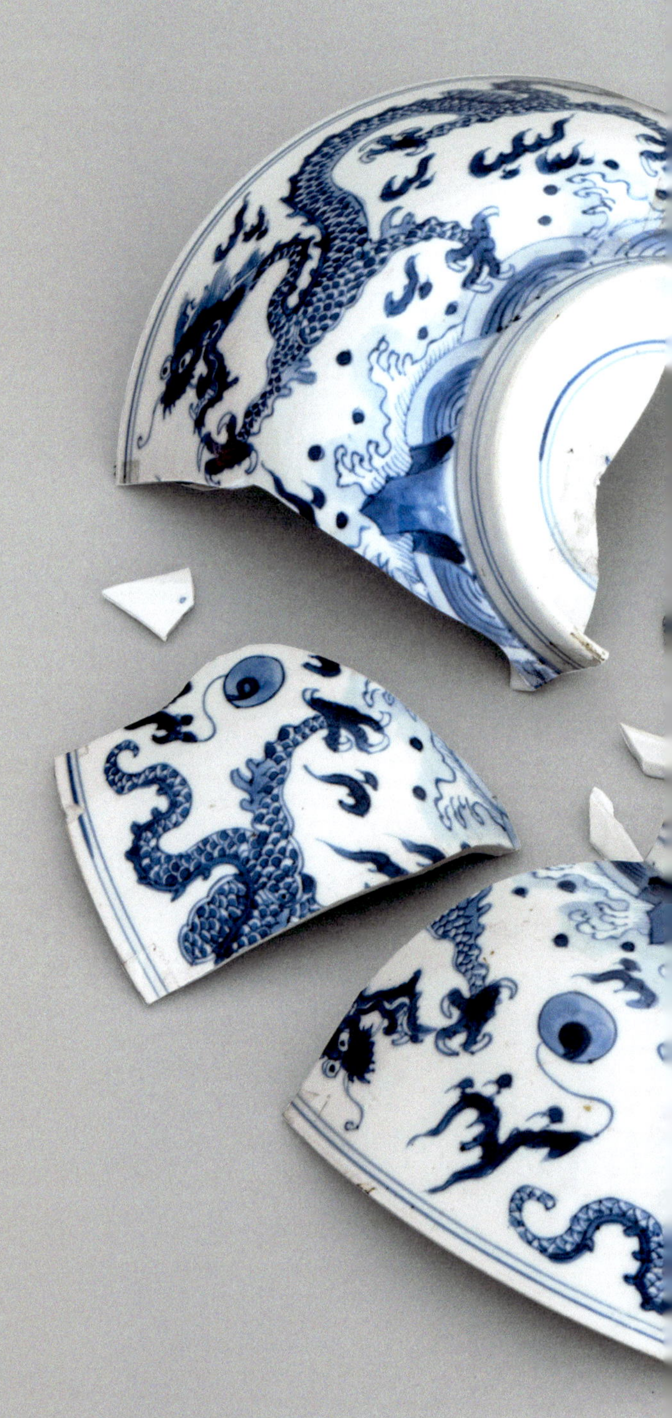

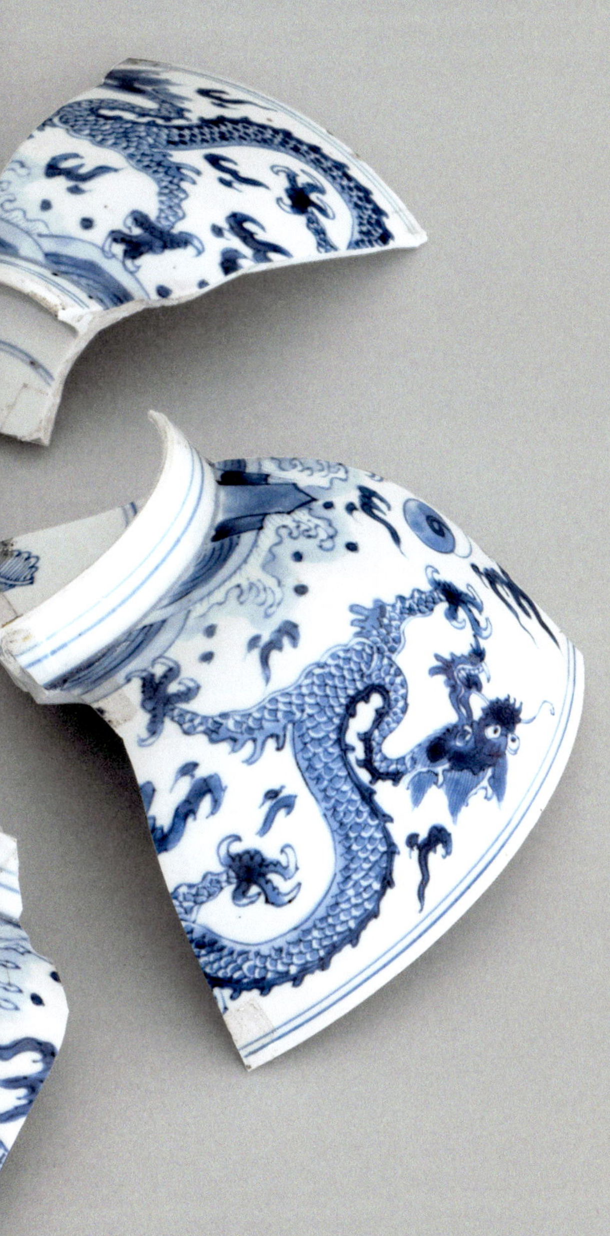

Material Aspects in the Work of Ai Weiwei

Linda Walther

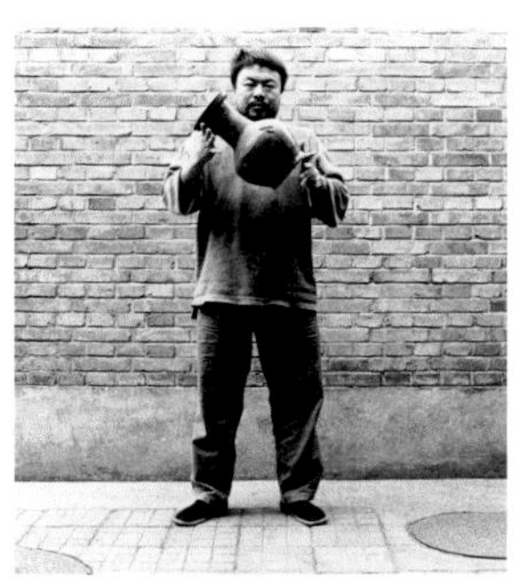
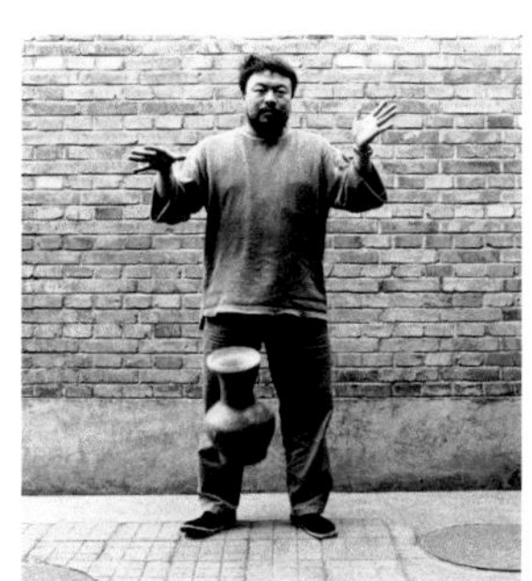
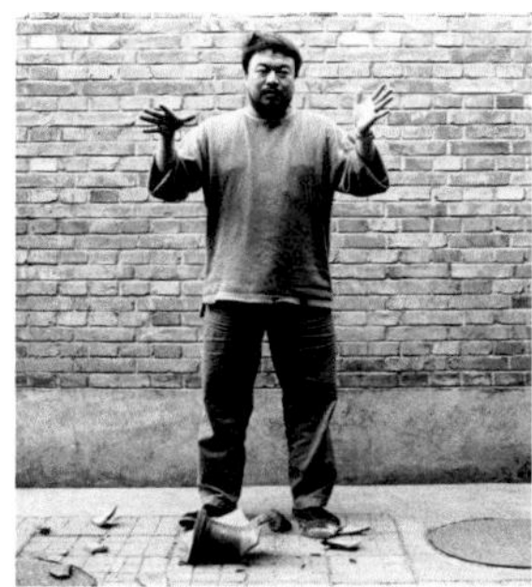

1

1
**Dropping a Han
Dynasty Urn**, 1995,
3 black-and-white
photographs

To approach Ai Weiwei's œuvre means to work through a vast amount of material, material that is as heterogeneous as the artist's works themselves. There are artworks—mainly installations, objects, and photographs—as well as numerous books, texts, and images, news posted daily on social media, countless press releases and media reports, as well as films, and even music. Ai Weiwei's œuvre as a visual artist and political activist encompasses all of this and more. His work thus oscillates between classical artistic and documentary forms of expression, whereby the two levels can never be separated from one another. In view of this, the question as to the artistic material used arises anew since it contains both tangible and intangible elements.

In recent decades, art history has turned more and more to the subject of material. Its specific iconography has been studied, and it has increasingly been perceived and analyzed as a meaningful part of any artwork.[1] Its intrinsic value, its role in the form of a work was emphasized and the material seriously considered as an autonomous, aesthetic category so that works of art "are no longer regarded under the primacy of form [...], but on the contrary, the form [is regarded] as variable in size and result dependent upon material properties and energies."[2] But what does such a re-evaluation and valorization of material mean for the engagement with the work of Ai Weiwei? What is the material of his art, and what functions does it assume?

For the documentary film **Ai Weiwei: Never Sorry**, which was released in 2011, director Alison Klayman accompanied the artist for three years. The portrait shows Ai Weiwei at work, in his studio, in exhibition spaces, on trips, in conversation with journalists, with companions, and with his family, as well as in conflict with the Chinese authorities. Two aspects are impressively reflected in the eighty-seven minutes of film: the destruction of architecture and the omnipresence of cameras.

One sees buildings destroyed during the Cultural Revolution, historical Chinese cities falling victim to rapid modernization, buildings in Sichuan collapsing as a

245

result of the catastrophic earthquake, devastated streets in war zones visited by the artist, and finally Ai Weiwei's studio in Shanghai demolished by the authorities. The problems which the artist places at the center of his work manifest themselves here materially, as do the consequences of his actions. In the material, traces of global, political, social, and cultural conflicts are revealed, which are far from being resolved.

Ai Weiwei and his team are accompanied by cameras. They themselves constantly shoot photographs and films. They document, upload photos to the Internet, and are themselves continuously filmed by fans, by the police, and by permanently installed surveillance cameras. Time and again, the two parties—the artist and the state—fight a duel with their cameras. Both document for their own purposes; the cameras are both instruments of activism and instruments of surveillance. For Ai Weiwei, the resulting images are a life insurance of sorts and an integral part of his art.[3] In the museum space, they materialize as vast wallpapers.

Ai Weiwei's entire œuvre is informed by this balancing act between the material and the immaterial—not only synchronously in the question between activism and artistic practice but also diachronically in his artistic work. At the beginning of his career, during his ten years in New York, he was a "thinking artist,"[4] as he himself says, an artist who was less concerned with the production of objects, who primarily and extensively shot photographs in a documentary fashion. During this time, he captured himself, people around him, and the city in some ten thousand images rich in detail (pp. 224–229). It was only after his return to China in 1993 that Ai Weiwei also began to work more intensely on a material level. Significantly, it is initially book projects (pp. 236–238) that he pursued[5] as well as working with pre-existing materials which he collected, some of which are valuable historical artifacts. Prime examples of this include **Coca Cola Vase** (1993) and **Dropping a Han Dynasty Urn** (1995). In both works, ancient Chinese ceramic vessels are the starting point. For one, the artist painted the well-known, red Coca-Cola logo onto a valuable, antique pot; for the other, he dropped a similar object from his hands, letting it fall to the ground where it shattered in pieces. Both works aim at the viewer's relationship to history, to the past, to memory, and much more at how one deals with this relationship. These altered early testimonies of material culture raise questions. Are old and genuine synonymous with valuable? What does tradition entail, how can it be dealt with, and what relevance do these old objects have? What is maintained when these cultural artifacts are collected and preserved? And what statements are made when they are used as artistic raw material? The breaking and painting of these historical objects provoke a confrontation with the rapid, at times brutal changes of the present. Material things are destroyed, altered, covered, and transformed—and with these changes the identities of the people involved are transformed. These works reveal a critique of the concepts of cultural identity and tradition as formulated by François Jullien: Culture remains alive solely through transformations.[6] Jullien explains that the term "tradition" does not, however, provide for breaks. Yet, it is precisely such breaks that are addressed in these works by exploiting tradition—embodied by historical artifacts—as a resource, as a material, by literally breaking the material. The work **Fragments of Blue-and-White Dragon Bowl** (1996, pp. 242–243) on view in the Düsseldorf exhibition also reflects this artistic strategy. This piece is comprised of the shards of a broken bowl made of the famous blue-and-white porcelain that has been produced in China since the fourteenth century and quickly became one of the country's main exports and a symbol of traditional Chinese craftsmanship.[7]

From the late 1990s to 2008, a further material facet emerged in the work of Ai Weiwei. He designed buildings and was heavily involved in city and landscape planning. Studio, gallery, and residential buildings were built according to his plans. He worked on plans for housing developments and cooperated internationally with renowned architectural firms, such as Herzog & de Meuron for the National Stadium in Beijing (2008). The material design of the present: architecture, with its aesthetic as well as social and socially relevant components, became both a theme and a form of expression. Parallel to this intensive

engagement with the material world,
Ai Weiwei increasingly used the immaterial world, the Internet—social networks
and, since 2006, his own blog, which
has since been shut down—to point out
social injustices and document his activities. Artistic practice and political activism coalesce here in the spirit of Boris
Groys: "For those who devote themselves
to the production of art documentation
rather than artworks, art is identical
to life, because life is essentially a pure
activity that has no end result."[8]
Built architecture—stable, real buildings
made of actual, physical materials, bricks
and reinforced concrete, which cannot
be changed—stands in opposition to the
continuously changing digital world and
its constantly updating, disseminating,
and moving of content. Planning, calculation, the static, and completeness
are on the one hand and spontaneity,
improvisation, the dynamic, and incompleteness are on the other. These two
poles form the opposing cornerstones
on which Ai Weiwei's work stands.

When Sichuan province was hit by a
devastating earthquake in 2008, Ai
Weiwei, his team, and numerous assistants searched, in communication with
other activists, on site and on the Internet
for information about the victims as well
as for the reasons behind the collapse of
thousands of buildings, focusing particularly on collapsed schools following the
question of why schools collapsed while
neighboring, older buildings did not. The
work **Straight** (2008–2012, pp. 63–73)
makes reference to the more than five
thousand schoolchildren who fell victim
to the earthquake and, in particular, to
the poorly constructed school buildings.
Straight takes the destruction of the
material world, of architecture, as its
starting point, includes the investigation
of this in an immaterial, digital space,
and is made-up, quite physically, of
collected material traces, artifacts,
which—like the aforementioned historical
vessels—are reworked and subsequently
presented in an exhibition space. The 164
tons of rebar from school buildings in
Sichuan which were bent when the buildings collapsed—predominantly from a
middle school in Wenchuan, where more
than one thousand children died—were
bent back into shape by hand and packed
into crates, sent around the world on

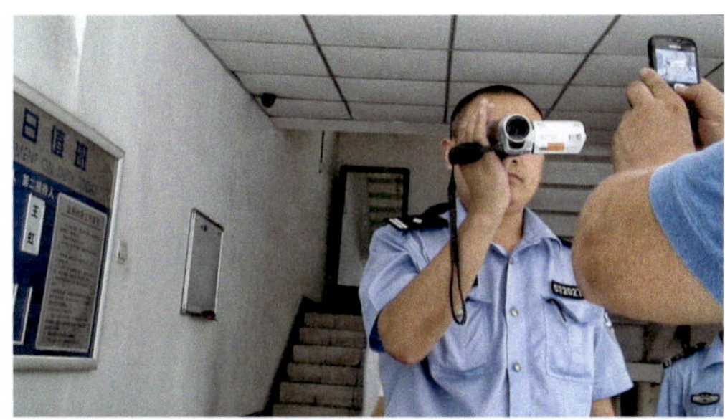

2

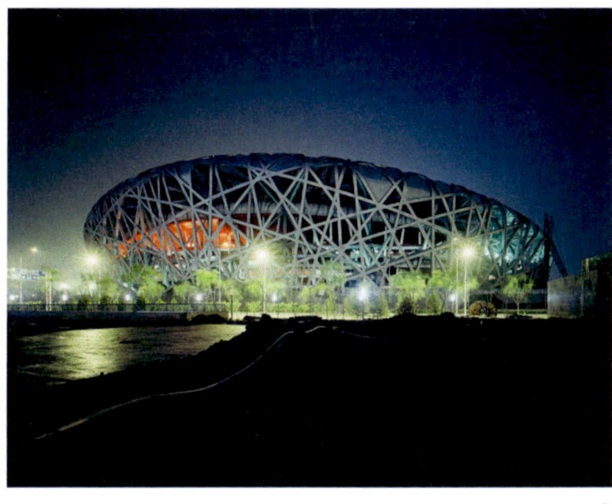

3

2
Disturbing the Peace, 2009,
Film still

3
National Stadium in Beijing,
2005–2008

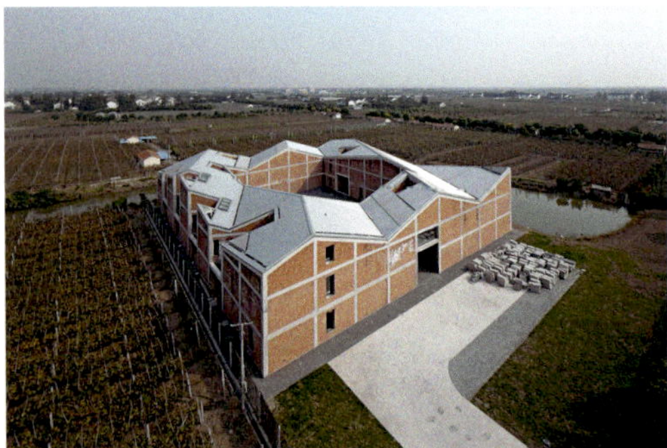

4
Jiading Malu
(**Shanghai Studio**),
2008–2011

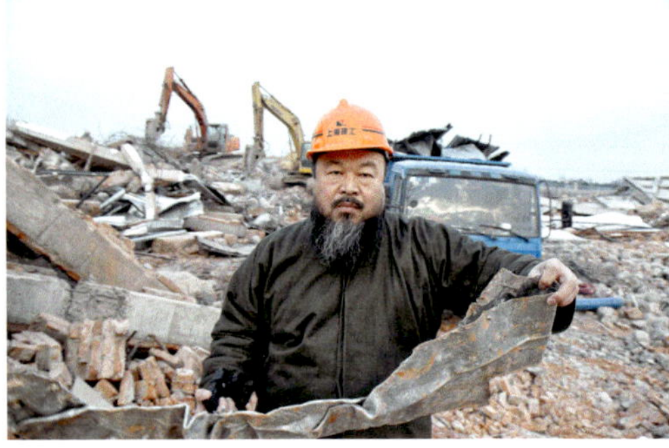

5
Jiading Malu
(**Shanghai Studio**),
2008–2011, Demolition
of the Studio, January 11,
2011

ships, and installed in various exhibition spaces. [9] In the Grabbe Halle of K20, **Straight**—in a new arrangement in which the bars have been left in their crates and have not, as in previous installations, been laid out on the ground—is seen in combination with a large format wallpaper listing the names of the deceased schoolchildren and a video showing the labor of hammering the bars straight. The ensemble of works becomes an installation which acts as a monument for the victims, their relatives, as well as the volunteers following the catastrophe, and against the acts of covering up and forgetting. It focuses on the people suffering from the consequences of corruption and not on those who allegedly helped cause the catastrophe through fraudulent construction of the school buildings. This arrangement of different kinds of materials in K20, which materializes and documents the work, in different ways, of those who collaborated, does not name the accused directly but makes the catastrophic consequences visible. To use François Jullien's terminology, this method could be called a "strategy of obliqueness." [10] He describes this strategy as a Chinese way of pointing out shortcomings and of reprimanding. The person to be criticized is criticized by disregarding them and focusing on something else close to them. This strategy can also be observed in Ai Weiwei's documentary **Human Flow** (2017). He shows fleeing people on the move, in shelters all over the world, in destroyed war zones, and on lifeboats. Here, it is the refugees themselves and those working for aid organizations who are heard; the film likewise focuses on those who suffer and get involved. Possible culprits from the realms of politics, economics, and terrorism do not appear in the over two-hour long film.

The arrangement of works in the Grabbe Halle presents both components of Ai Weiwei's work intimated in Klayman's film: the side determined by material, the starting point which is the architecture that collects, processes, and exhibits artifacts; and the side rooted in the immaterial, which researches, documents, and archives, generates and disseminates images and texts. It becomes clear that one side is not to be had without the other, that both mutually condition and

1
A first comprehensive, systematic study was published by Thomas Raff. See: Thomas Raff, **Die Sprache der Materialien. Anleitung zu einer Ikonologie der Werkstoffe** (Munich 1994). Monika Wagner's research on material in art is particularly noteworthy. She led the DFG research project "Archiv zur Erforschung der Material-ikonographie" (Archive for the Research of Material Iconography), which documents the increasing importance of materiality in twentieth-century art (especially after 1945), and published extensively on the subject; see, among others, Dietmar Rübel, Monika Wagner, and Vera Wolff (eds.), **Materialäs-thetik. Quellentexte zur Kunst, Design und Architek-tur** (Berlin 2005); Monika Wagner (ed.), **Lexikon des künstlerischen Materials. Werkstoffe der modernen Kunst von Abfall bis Zinn** (Munich 2002); Monika Wagner, **Das Material der Kunst. Eine andere Geschichte der Moderne** (Munich 2001); Monika Wagner, "Material," in: Karlheinz Barck, Martin Fontius, Dieter Schlenstedt, Burkhart Steinwachs, and Friedrich Wolfzettel (eds.), **Ästhetische Grundbegriffe** (Stuttgart 2001), vol. 3, pp. 866–82.

2
Thomas Strässle, "Einleitung. Pluralis materialitatis," in: Strässle, Christoph Kleinschmidt, and Johanne Mohs (eds.), **Das Zusam-menspiel der Materialien in den Künsten. Theorien – Praktiken – Perspektiven** (Bielefeld 2013), pp. 7–23, here p. 8 [translated].

3
The photo **Illumination** (2009), which is presented in the Düsseldorf exhibition as large-format wallpaper, depicts Ai Weiwei together with his musician friend Zuoxiao Zuzhou and two police officers in the mirror of a hotel elevator in Chengdu. The artist shot the photo during a nocturnal police attack on him and his team and posted it on the Internet, generating a great deal of

strengthen each other, and that between them there is a flexible network of diverse artistic strategies, various actors, and different materialities. The documentary works from the New York period, thus, cannot do without material—camera, film rolls, photographic paper—just as the material works from the Beijing period cannot do without the documentary aspect. **Dropping a Han Dynasty Urn**, for example, consists of three photographs that document the process of the vessel breaking (holding—letting go—hitting the ground). Both levels increasingly inter-twine within the work so that the material stages the immaterial and the immaterial stages the material.

As a device, the camera is at the center of these entanglements between the material and the immaterial. One such camera can also be seen in the Düsseldorf exhibition: a surveillance camera, such as those usually installed in public spaces. The Chinese government are also said to have installed such cameras around Ai Weiwei's studio house in Beijing in order to record the activities of the artist, his team, his family, and their guests. In the exhibition space, it is presented in relation to works that revolve around the so-called "refugee crisis." The camera has long been a universally understood symbol of ubiquitous and permanent surveillance. Ai Weiwei criticizes these mechanisms of power and control in having **Camera with Plinth** (2015, p. 141) carved from marble. The white stone is one of the oldest and most widely used materials for sculpture; it stands, thus, for permanence and stability, and, in the Western context, it also reflects the dogma of an idealistic aesthetic, making it one of the preferred materials for monuments. The translation of the sur-veillance camera's original material into art-historically relevant stone obviously makes the camera functionless and, at the same time, marks it as a central symbol of our times representative of power. [11] Marble transports the camera into the sphere of art and silently thwarts all questions regarding the material and the immaterial, so that the transgression of this dichotomy is made material in **Camera with Plinth**.

attention. It became an icon
for the use of social media in
political activism.

4
Ai Weiwei, quoted in: "Ai
Weiwei: Life and Work," in:
Hans Werner Holzwarth (ed.),
Ai Weiwei (Cologne 2016),
pp. 560f., here p. 560.

5
Together with the artists Xu
Bing and Zeng Xiaojun, he
published the **Black Cover
Book** (1994), which presents
the Western and Chinese
avant-garde with reproduc-
tions of artworks, texts,
documents, and sketches.
This was followed by the
White Cover Book (1995)
and the **Gray Cover Book**
(1997).

6
For more on Jullien's critique
of the concept of cultural
identity and the associated
continuity in relation to Ai
Weiwei's work, see: François
Jullien, "Ai Weiwei or the
Art of Effective Variation"
in: Susanne Gaensheimer
(ed.), **Ai Weiwei**, **Romuald
Karmakar**, **Santu Mofokeng**,
Dayanita Singh: **German
Pavilion 2013**, **55th International Art Exhibition**,
La Biennale di Venezia, exh.
cat. Venice (Berlin 2013),
pp. 66–73. Here, he proposes
to replace the term "tradition"
with "resource" (p. 66).

7
Specifically, it is comprised
of the shards of a broken
Kangxi period blue-and-white
porcelain bowl. This period
is well known for producing
some of the highest quality
examples of porcelain in Chinese history. The **Fragments**
are the result of a 1996
performative act (similar to
**Dropping a Han Dynasty
Urn**), which was documented
in two photographs and is
titled **Breaking a Blue**-and-
White Dragon Bowl. For
more on the use of classical
Chinese products (ceramics,
porcelain, furniture, etc.) in
the works of Ai Weiwei, see:
James J. Lally, "Chinese
Traditions in the Work of
Ai Weiwei," in: Holzwarth
2016 (see note 4), pp. 542–6.

8
Boris Groys, **Art Power**
(Cambridge, MA 2008),
p. 54.

9
See Ai Weiwei's text on
Straight in: Holzwarth 2016
(see note 4), p. 522.

10
Jullien 2013 (see note 6),
p. 69.

11
Thomas Eller's text "The
Material Rhetoric of Aesthetic
Resistance in the Contem-
porary Art of East and West"
[in: Gereon Sievernich (ed.),
Ai Weiwei: **Evidence**, exh.
cat. Martin-Gropius-Bau,
Berlin (Munich et al. 2014),
pp. 28–39)], with reference
to Jonathan Hay's book
Sensuous Surfaces: **The
Decorative Object in Early
Modern China** (London
2010), explores the complex
question of the translation
of material within a Chinese
context. The point of depar-
ture is the gesture of the
extended middle finger from
the photo series **Study of
Perspective** (1995–2011)—
also on view at K21—which
Ai Weiwei had executed
several times in marble in
2006.

Authors' Biographies

Rembert Hüser has been Professor of Media Studies at Goethe University Frankfurt since 2014. From 2003 to 2013, he was Associate Professor of German and Moving Image and Media Studies at the University of Minnesota, Twin Cities. In 2016, he was Max Kade Professor at Brown University. He is currently Co-Director of the DFG Graduate Program "Configurations of Film" at Goethe University Frankfurt.

Doris Krystof studied art history, history, and languages and literature in Freiburg im Breisgau and Cologne. Following her doctorate in 1993, she was an assistant curator at the Kunstsammlung Nordrhein-Westfalen. From 2000 to 2001, she was a curator at the Kunsthalle Vienna. Since 2002, she has been a curator for contemporary art at the Kunstsammlung Nordrhein-Westfalen, where she has realized numerous exhibitions, predominately for K21, (Akram Zaatari, Marcel Broodthaers, Wael Shawky, Gillian Wearing, Jorge Pardo, Eija-Liisa Ahtila, Martin Kippenberger, amongst others).

Hans Ulrich Obrist is Artistic Director of the Serpentine Galleries in London and Senior Artistic Advisor of The Shed in New York City. Prior to this, he was the Curator of the Musée d'Art moderne de la Ville de Paris. Since his first show **World Soup** (**The Kitchen Show**) in 1991, he has curated more than three hundred exhibitions.

Friederike Sigler studied art history and philosophy in Marburg and Berlin. From 2012 to 2014, she held a scholarship at the DFG Graduate Program "Materiality and Production" at the University of Düsseldorf. Since 2014, she is a researcher and lecturer at the Academy of Fine Arts Dresden. She is the editor of **Work**: **Documents of Contemporary Art** (Whitechapel Gallery/MIT Press, 2017).

Linda Walther studied art history and Romance philology in Bochum and Düsseldorf. At Heinrich Heine University, she was a research assistant at the Institute of Art History and a member of the DFG Graduate Program "Materiality and Production." She completed her doctoral thesis in art history and has been an assistant curator at the Kunstsammlung Nordrhein-Westfalen since 2018.

Falk Wolf is an art historian. He studied at the universities of Bonn, Leicester, and Basel, where he went on to complete a doctoral thesis on media theories in art history as part of the Swiss National Center of Competence in Research "eikones." Since 2016, he has been a curator at K20/K21, Kunstsammlung Nordrhein-Westfalen. Prior to that, he curated exhibitions independently, was an assistant curator for the Museum Ludwig in Cologne, and worked freelance for the Karl Ernst Osthaus-Museum in Hagen.

All exhibited works are illustrated in the
catalog; an overview is provided by the
table of contents on pp. 4 / 5. The works
in chapters I and II are on view at K20
on Grabbeplatz, while the works in chapters III to V can be found at K21 in the
Ständehaus. All works in the exhibition
are in the possession of the artist,
unless otherwise indicated here:

Study of Perspective, 1995–2011:
Courtesy the artist and
neugerriemschneider, Berlin
The edition on exhibition is executed
in 2014.

Straight, 2008–2012:
Courtesy the artist, Lisson Gallery
and neugerriemschneider, Berlin

S.A.C.R.E.D., 2011–2013:
Courtesy the artist and Lisson Gallery

Zodiac, 2018:
Private collection

Photocredits

All images courtesy of Ai Weiwei Studio,
except:

p. 13, fig. 3
© The Israel Museum, Jerusalem,
photo by Eli Posner
p. 27
© Tate, London 2019
pp. 33–45
courtesy of Jeffrey Deitch and the artist,
photo by Joshua White
p. 49, fig. 3
courtesy the Musée cantonal des
Beaux-Arts de Lausanne and the artist,
photo by Etienne Malapert
p. 49, fig. 4
courtesy of Magasin 3 and the artist

p. 52, figs. 5–7
Ken Adlard
pp. 66–67
Sergio Coimbra
pp. 68–73
Achim Kukulies
p. 112
Detail of **Life Cycle**, courtesy of the
Marciano Art Foundation and the artist,
photo by Joshua White
p. 193
fig. 1, Rohit Chawla
p. 196
We would like to credit Hesign with
helping design the Key Visual
p. 198
figs. 5 and 6, Holger Puhl
p. 201
Norbert Miguletz

IMPRINT

This catalog has
been published in
conjunction with the
exhibition Ai Weiwei
Kunstsammlung
Nordrhein-Westfalen,
Düsseldorf
K20 Grabbeplatz and
K21 Ständehaus
May 18–September 1,
2019

Edited by
Susanne Gaensheimer,
Doris Krystof, Falk Wolf

Front Cover
Wo ist die Revolution?,
2019

Catalog

**Introductory texts for
the five chapters**
Doris Krystof,
Falk Wolf

**Editorial Direction,
Museum**
Cordula Frevel
**Editorial Direction,
Prestel**
Markus Eisen
Copyediting
José Enrique Macián
**Translation from
the German**
Gérard Goodrow

Design and Layout
Sascha Lobe,
Simon Brenner,
L2M3 Kommunikations-
design GmbH, Stuttgart

**Production
Management**
Corinna Pickart
Separations
Reproline mediateam
GmbH & Co. KG,
Unterföhring
Printing and Binding
Grafisches Centrum
Cuno GmbH & Co. KG,
Calbe/Saale
Typeface
Parallax
Paper
Arctic Volume White
150 g/m²

Verlagsgruppe
Random House
FSC® N001967

Printed in Germany

Exhibition

Curated by
Susanne Gaensheimer,
Doris Krystof,
Falk Wolf

Curatorial Assistant
Linda Walther

Education
Peter Schüller

Exhibition Managers
Stefanie Jansen,
Dagmar Kurtz

Registrar's Department
Katharina Nettekoven

Conservation
Elena Fernández-Vegue,
Sven Kamp,
Nina Quabeck,
Astrid Roth,
Anne Skaliks,
Susan-Marie Spörl,
Andreas Volkmer

Media Technology
Jens Meller,
Oswin Schmidt

Exhibition Construction
Thomas Hoppe,
Frank Mankel,
Stefan Müller-Stapper,
Ingo Lanninger,
Bernd Schliephake,
Bernd Strauchmann,
Daniel Vetter

Communication and Media
Susanne Fernandes Silva,
Anne Fischer,
Cornelia Heising,
Alissa Krusch,
Marita Rowlands,
Judith Winterhager

Studio Ai Weiwei
Adam Breasley,
Gui Nuo,
Monira Kleineidam,
Darryl Leung,
Li Dongxu,
Lin Meiling,
Max Logsdail,
Ma Yan,
Jennifer Ng,
Eric Gregory Powell,
Fuyuka Sato,
Jennifer Schmachtenberg,
Nadine Stenke,
Kimberly Sung,
Bernhard Uhlig,
Luitgard Wagner
Wang Fen,
Wu Tun,
Xu Ye,
Zeng Yilan

Stiftung Kunstsammlung Nordrhein-Westfalen, Düsseldorf

Board of Directors
Susanne Gaensheimer,
Bianca Knall

Director
Susanne Gaensheimer

Commercial Manager
Bianca Knall

Secretary Assistants to the Directors
Miriam Pohle,
Arpi Sarkissian

Curatorial Department
Anette Kruszynski
Kathrin Beßen,
Dorothee Jansen,
Doris Krystof,
Isabelle Malz,
Susanne Meyer-Büser,
Maria Müller-Schareck,
Agnieszka Skolimowska,
Linda Walther,
Katja Winterpagt,
Falk Wolf

Education
Julia Hagenberg
Regula Erpenbach,
Christine Mittrop,
Annika Plank,
Peter Schüller,
Annkathrin Schwedhelm,
Angela Wenzel

Library
Jeannie Braun,
Andreas Peters,
Marimba Williamson

Exhibition Management
Stefanie Jansen
Dagmar Kurtz,
Charlotte Wagner-de
Souza Silveira

Registrar's Department
Katharina Nettekoven
Johanna Eßer

Conservation
Nina Quabeck
Elena Fernández-Vegue,
Sven Kamp,
Jessica Völkert-Lunk,
Astrid Roth,
Anne Skaliks,
Susan-Marie Spörl,
Andreas Volkmer

**Press and Public
Relations**
Susanne Fernandes Silva

Sales and Publishing
Cordula Frevel
Martin Heyer,
Alexia Krauthäuser,
Roman Majewski,
Uta Rottmann,
Marion Vogt

Visitor Service
Cäcilie Teschner
Nikolaos Kessopoulos,
Berthold Struck,
Philip Trabert

Marketing and Digital
Anne Fischer

Marketing
Cornelia Heising
Marita Rowlands

Digital Communication
Alissa Krusch
Judith Winterhager

Editions
Gabriele Lauser

Administration
Klaus-Peter Allenstein,
Ingo Lanninger,
Frank Mankel,
Stefan Müller-Stapper,
Daniel Vetter

Accounting
Caroline Krump
Susanne Finken,
Kerstin Thielo

**Public Procurement,
Purchasing, Legal**
Christina Rock
Claudia Fischer-Jaworsky

Human Resources
Georgia Coutri,
Monika Fischer

Technical Department
Bernd Schliephake
Andreas Grella,
Thomas Hoppe,
Birger Labinsch,
Jens Meller,
Britta Pfeiffer,
Oswin Schmidt,
Bernd Strauchmann,
Zoltan Ternai

Security
Ramon Karbach
Tobias Becker,
Dietmar Bütau,
Artur Burgner,
Lothar Finken,
Dirk Fittkau,
Andreas Grund,
Philipp Grund,
Wilfried Humberg,
Michael Jaschzyk,
Nicholas Robert Johnson,
Franz Josef Kleschautzky,
Carsten Laaser,
Torsten Machtans,
Tim Martinitz,
Mario Metz,
Dominik Nowak,
Elvis Selim,
Katrin Sondermeier,
Michael Stanaszek,
Jens Wünsche

**ArtPartner Relations
GmbH**
Anne Clever,
Jasmin Kreilos,
Valentina Wolters

**Gesellschaft der
Freunde der
Kunstsammlung
Nordrhein-Westfalen e.V.**
Robert Rademacher
Jutta Müller
Nele Guinand

Stiftung Kunstsammlung
Nordrhein-Westfalen
Grabbeplatz 5
40213 Düsseldorf

K20 Grabbeplatz
K21 Ständehaus

www.kunstsammlung.de

With the generous
support of:

Lisson Gallery
neugerriemschneider, Berlin

Media partner:

Handelsblatt

Supported by:

Ministerium für
Kultur und Wissenschaft
des Landes Nordrhein-Westfalen

Kunstsammlung
Nordrhein-Westfalen